Our Korean Kitchen

'Enthralling, authentic and beautifully written — I haven't been so excited by a cookbook in a very long time.'
Skye Gyngell

Our Korean Kitchen

음식은 나누어 먹을 때 더 맛있다
-
Food is at its most delicious when shared

Jordan Bourke & Rejina Pyo

Photography by Tara Fisher

Introduction 7

The Korean Meal 10

The Korean Pantry 13

Stock 19

Menu Ideas 20

—

01 Rice & Savoury Porridge 23

02 Soups & Stews 55

03 Vegetables, Pickles & Sides 93

04 Pancakes, Fritters & Tofu 133

05 Noodles 155

06 Fish 181

07 Meat 207

08 Dessert 243

—

Suppliers 265

Index 266

Acknowledgements 271

Introduction
소개

Our Korean kitchen is an unusual one, a kitchen found not in Korea, but in London, and with only one true Korean at the helm, my wife Jina, a fashion designer in her own right, but equally passionate about the food of her birthplace. And then alongside her is me, an Irish chef, who somehow found himself besotted with not only the girl from Korea, but also the food and culture of a nation so far away from my own.

While I am still passionate about the classical and Mediterranean food of my upbringing, training and indeed my daily work as a chef, it is fair to say that the allure of Jina's Korean home cooking and the food of her country has been so great that it has, in less than a decade, gained equal footing in my world of food. It has brought us not only together, but on many exciting and extended pilgrimages throughout Korea – Jina retracing her roots, the food of her childhood and a life lived there until her mid-twenties, and I, working in restaurants and learning from chefs and culinary masters of this beautiful and fiery cuisine, the most important of whom being Jina's mother and father.

Years ago, when Jina first introduced me to proper Korean food, I was astonished that I had known so little of it prior to meeting her. I couldn't understand how a food and culture this wonderful could have remained relatively unknown to the rest of the world in comparison with its close neighbouring countries, China and Japan, whose traditional dishes are famous and familiar to us all. Jina too was in astonishment – but for another reason – in her first year of living in London, having longed for a taste of proper Western food, she suddenly realised how lucky she had been growing up in a culture where such affordable, healthy and great-tasting food was available everywhere, from schools and hospitals to street food stalls, corner stores and of course at home.

Good food and cooking is so ingrained in Korean culture and everyday life that even the standard Korean greeting is grounded in food. Korean people don't ask how you are, but, 'bab mogosoyeo?', which translates as, 'have you eaten?' or literally, 'have you eaten rice?'. The idea being that how you are entirely depends on how well nourished you are, so they might as well get straight to the point.

Back in London, with a fridge full of various fermented chilli pastes, homemade kimchi and pickled vegetables, we keep this wonderful country and cuisine alive in our own Korean kitchen, 5,500 miles away from its birthplace. We do this in part out of nostalgia for the food we have eaten there, but mainly we do it because we adore great food, and the food of Korea is quite simply some of the best we have ever encountered, anywhere.

Fortunately, in the years that have passed since Jina first cooked Korean food for me, it has exploded on to the world stage, with food trucks and restaurants popping up all over the place and Korean produce becoming increasingly easy to find. The word is out, and it could not be more positive. People are enthralled by the robust, complex and subtle flavours of this country's food and what was for many years the 'secret' Asian cuisine is now fast becoming the most popular Asian food of all.

This book is somewhat of a shared journey through the most loved and authentic recipes of Korea, dishes that have in some cases been cooked by Korean families in one form or another for centuries, and yet here we are in London cooking a version of those same recipes. While we have made these dishes our own, we were very keen to keep as close as possible to the traditional and authentic ingredients and methods of Korean cooking.
This is particularly important now, as up to this point there has been relatively little written about the food and cooking of Korea, so we feel an extra onus has been placed upon us to get it right.
We want to honour the truly exceptional food of Jina's home country, her family and indeed the many great chefs and masters of Korean food from whom we have had the great privilege of learning. You can of course tweak the recipes if you like, swapping one vegetable for another, or lowering the quantity of chilli paste to suit your palate, but at the very least we wanted you to have as authentic and traditional a starting point as possible.

What is fascinating about Korean cuisine is the sheer quantity, literally hundreds, of national dishes, each one being unique to the country, and within that there are numerous regional varieties. This is even more impressive when you consider Korea's difficult past. Although hard to imagine when you visit the historic but ultra-modern and sophisticated city of Seoul today, over its history Korea has regularly been levelled, rebuilt and then obliterated once again by its expansionist neighbours, China and Japan. Even as recently as the 1950s Korea remained a war-torn and poverty-stricken land, as the communist north and the capitalist south fought for control in the civil war.

The result of which is the present day North and South Korea – two countries which now share little more than a border and a similar name – the south having leapfrogged in a matter of only a few decades from a decimated post-war country to one of the wealthiest nations in the world, with a capital city so cosmopolitan and fast-paced it would make New York look parochial.

Despite all this historical jostling and extended periods of occupation, Korean cuisine remains distinct from its neighbours with a range of differing cooking techniques. The most noticeable of which are the preservation and fermentation techniques they employ, giving their food a unique combination of flavours. Perhaps because of their past, Koreans are incredibly passionate about their national dishes, and have very strong views on how certain foods should taste and be presented. Even the slightest departure from the norm can cause ructions with heated debates ensuing – each person declaring their way of cooking said dish to be 'the best'.

However, if you then ask to be guided through their version of a recipe, it all becomes rather vague, 'a little bit of this, a little bit of that'. This is largely because Koreans are natural and instinctive cooks, using recipes passed down from generation to generation. They cook intuitively, according to a clear set of flavour profiles that they have been brought up with. Asking them to provide you with precise measurements is pointless – you just have to watch and learn, slowly building up your palate to match theirs.

Of course, not everyone has a brilliant Korean cook on standby to watch and learn from. In light of this, we hope that this book will be a good alternative, guiding you through the traditions and staples of authentic Korean home cooking.

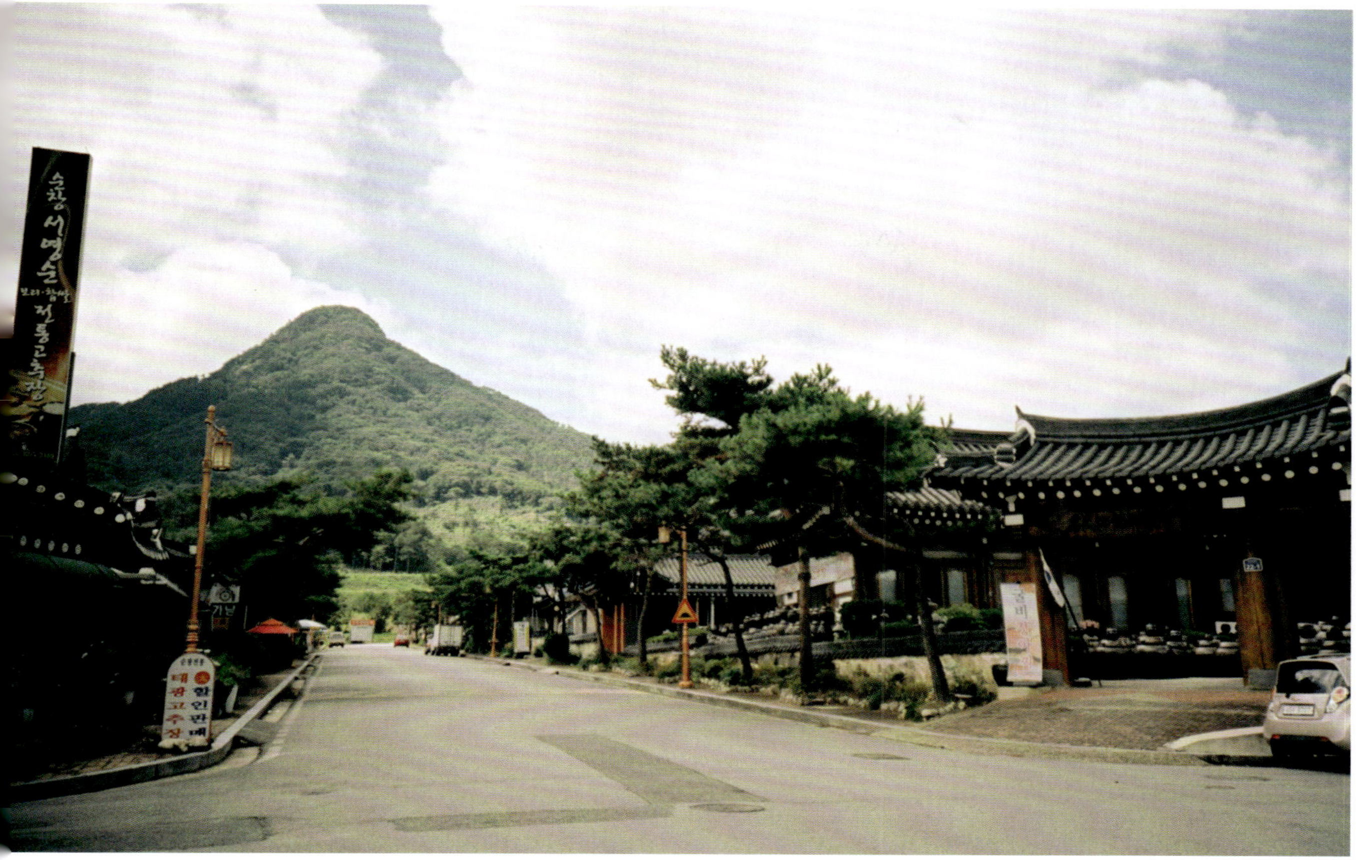

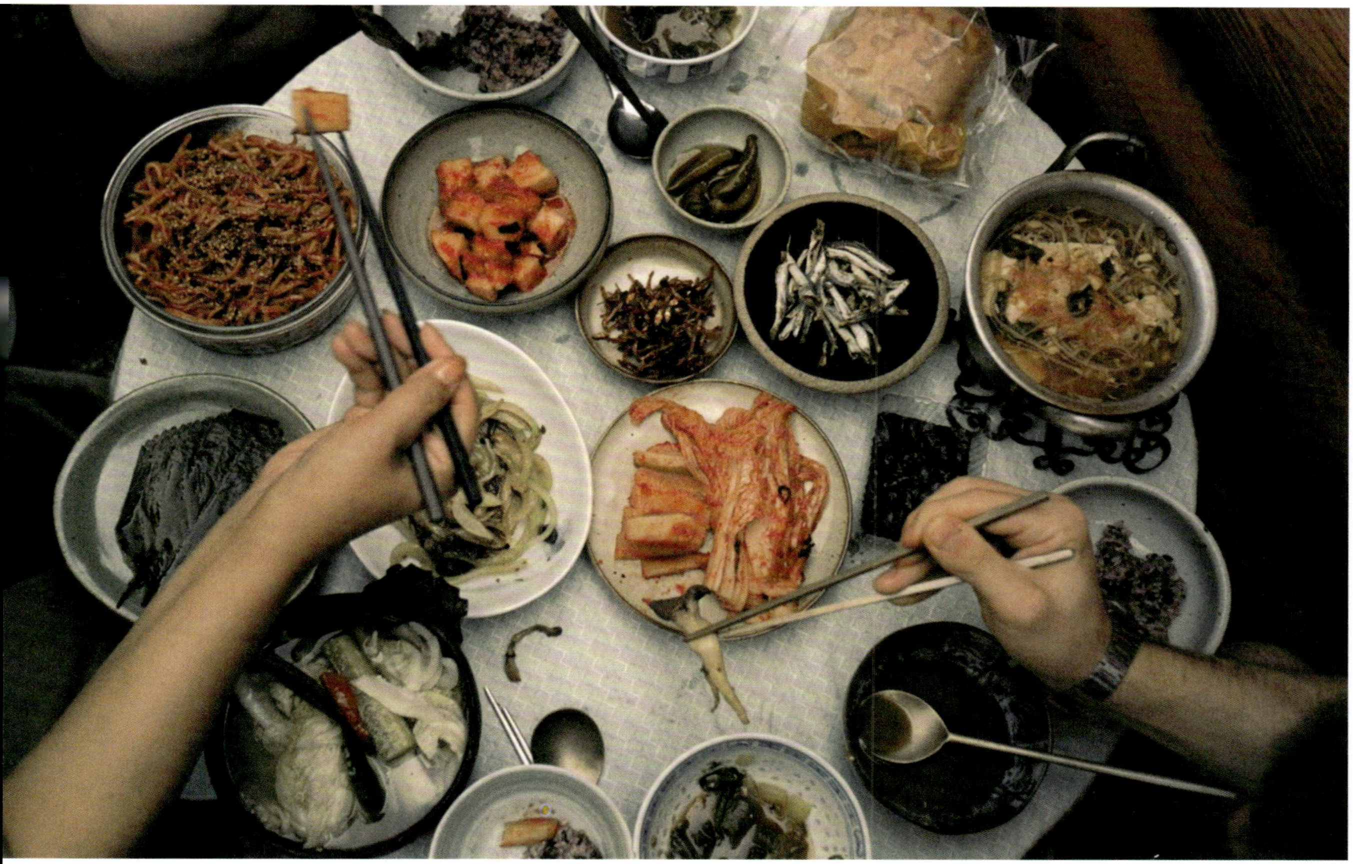

The Korean Meal
한국의 식사

For anyone new to Korean food, one of the most enjoyable aspects of the meal, aside from eating it of course, is the presentation of the dishes. Unlike the Western world, Korean meals are not separated by courses. Instead, everything comes to the table at the same time. This can be a most impressive sight, particularly in traditional restaurants, as the number of side dishes (known as banchan) can seem endless, and that's before an individual bowl of rice and soup is served for each guest. Whatever main dish is to accompany the meal is then served in a large communal platter in the centre of the table, for everyone to share. The overall effect is one of a banquet, with practically every inch of the table taken up with small plates of food.

This method of presentation is known as 'bap-sang', which literally means 'rice' (bap) 'table' (sang), where each person's bowl of rice is considered the main dish with the multitude of other dishes there to accompany it. If the main dish was noodles, then it becomes 'myeon-sang', 'myeon' meaning noodle. Historically, the social status of a household would dictate the number of side dishes that could be served at any given meal, which would generally be an odd number. So three or five side dishes would be considered acceptable in working-class households, with the number of side dishes increasing according to social rank – nine dishes reserved for nobility and finally twelve side dishes, known as 'surasang', which could only ever be served to the king.

Key among any Korean table of food however, is a balance of flavours and textures, being mindful to always offer contrasting dishes, both hot and cold. So alongside a particularly spicy dish you might also serve a more subtly flavoured soup.

For every hot stew there might also be some room-temperature side dishes and so on – each dish prepared to complement the other.

Of course at home, such grand and lavish affairs are not expected, particularly these days. However, as a lot of the side dishes served in Korea can be prepared in advance and keep very well, as with kimchi, or other preserved vegetables, even a rushed lunch will often include a bowl of rice, two or three side dishes and then perhaps soup or some other dish which might have been prepared for the previous night's dinner.

For Westerners dining in Korea for the first time, there may be some surprise to see a table of friends or family all diving into a central shared dish, with enough double dipping to send a germaphobe foreigner running for the hills! This concept of sharing comes from Korea's Confucian heritage, which places considerable significance on a sense of community and fellowship, and so with food they believe that sharing from the same dish can forge closer relationships between friends and family.

Spoons and chopsticks are the main utensils used for eating in Korea. The spoon is considered the primary utensil, as Korean cuisine is made up of so many stews, soups and mixed rice dishes, which require one. Chopsticks are generally reserved for side and main dishes, and for this reason it is also considered impolite to lift your rice bowl off the table, like they do in Japan where they eat rice with chopsticks, as your spoon should be more than adequate. Although, if you really are struggling, you are permitted to lower your head down towards your bowl.

As with most Asian countries, Korea also uses chopsticks, which are unique to their country – in this case they are flat and metal, rather than round and wooden. They do require an extra degree of dexterity, but once you get used to them they are very practical, especially when dealing with something like slippery noodles. Chopsticks can also do things that a fork and knife can't, for example it is common in Korea to wrap crispy seaweed or kimchi around rice, creating a little parcel, which would be almost impossible to do one handed with a fork.

A NOTE ON RICE COOKERS

The one piece of equipment that is used in every Korean kitchen, from a student flat to a high-end restaurant, is an electric rice cooker, and while you can of course cook rice in a pot, we find ours indispensable.

Initially, I was very sceptical of Jina's rice cooker, having cooked rice on the hob for my entire life I couldn't see the need for one. But then I met 'Cuckoo', one of the most famous brands of Korean rice cookers. Not only does it have multiple rice settings that cook the different types of rice to perfection, it also works as a pressure cooker. And as if that was not enough, it also talks to you, keeping you abreast of how your rice is doing.

Fortunately for those of us outside Korea, there are no other essential pieces of Korean cooking equipment that you will be lost without. Stone and earthenware bowls called 'dolsot' and 'dduk-baegi' are commonly used for both cooking and serving food as it keeps food piping hot. While they are certainly a nice addition to your kitchen cupboard if you are cooking a lot of Korean food, they are not essential by any means.

A NOTE ON SPICE LEVELS

While we have kept the recipes in this book, including the levels of heat, authentic to what you might find in Korea, we of course appreciate that not everyone will be able to tolerate the same level of heat as a Korean person, so do feel free to adjust the quantity of gochujang chilli paste and gochugaru red pepper powder used in the recipes. However, please remember these two ingredients are not as hot as some of the chilli pastes, powders and sauces that you might find in other Asian countries – they have a rounder, more full-bodied flavour that a lot of people tolerate very well. If you are concerned, start by adding half the stated quantity and then build up from there. Of course the beauty of Korean food is that for every spicy dish there is an equally delicious yet altogether more subtly flavoured counterpart, so there really is something for everyone.

The Korean Pantry
한국의 식재료들

The following pages run through the most common ingredients used in Korean cooking. Most of them have an extremely long shelf life, which means you can buy all the key ingredients necessary in one go. They can then sit in your cupboard until the next time you need them, so you don't have to worry about going to an Asian supermarket every time you want to cook.

There are a growing number of Asian stores these days, making it relatively easy to find all the ingredients used in this book. However, there are also a huge amount of online stores selling everything that you will need (page 265). Websites such as Amazon will also sell most of these ingredients, so you can just order everything you need and have it delivered to you.

RICE, NOODLES & RICE CAKES

01. Short-grain white rice
ssal 쌀

Much like the Japanese short-grain sushi rice, the Korean grain becomes soft and sticky when cooked, not at all like other varieties from south-east Asia and India. Brown short-grain rice (hyeon-mi) can also be used in place of white rice. It is less sticky and more chewy so lots of Koreans mix them.

02. Glutinous rice
chap ssal 찹쌀

Known as either glutinous or sweet rice, yet it contains neither gluten or any kind of sweetener. Glutinous/sweet rice has an especially sticky consistency and mildly sweet flavour when cooked, in comparison to other varieties of rice, which resulted in its name. Glutinous rice is used in Baby Chicken Soup (page 64) to stuff the cavity, and is also in a variety of porridge dishes (pages 42), where the rice is ground down, providing a silky smooth and wonderfully rich texture to the porridge. The rice flour is also used in Korean desserts such as Sweet Rice Cakes (page 256).

03. Sweet potato glass noodles
dang-myeon 당면

These sweet potato glass or cellophane noodles are unique to Korea, and while other brands of glass noodles could be used in their place, it is worth seeking these out for their wonderful texture and ability to absorb all the flavours of the dish in which they are cooked. They can be soaked in cold water prior to cooking to reduce the cooking time, but it is not essential. They are the main ingredient in the Beef & Vegetables with Sesame Glass Noodles dish (page 166) – this dish would not be the same without them. The noodles are also added to soups and stews to provide texture.

04. Udon noodles
udong 우동

Rather confusingly, this thick and bouncy wheat flour noodle comes from Japan, but is used in some Chinese-influenced Korean dishes, like the Black Bean Noodles (page 176) and Spicy Seafood Noodle Soup (page 178). They have a very springy texture and can be bought ready-made in single portion, vacuum-packed bags in Asian supermarkets making them extremely quick to cook.

05. Naeng-myeon noodles
냉면

These long and thin noodles are made from the flour and starch of various ingredients including buckwheat and sweet potato. They are exclusively used for the dish of the same name, meaning 'cold noodles' (page 160) and can be found in Korean markets.

06. Soba/buckwheat noodles
memil-gooksu 메밀 국수

Korean buckwheat noodles are much the same as Japanese soba, a thin noodle, which can be made entirely from buckwheat flour, or more commonly mixed with varying quantities of wheat flour. Despite the name, buckwheat is wheat and gluten free. Try them in the Spicy Chilled Buckwheat Noodle Salad (page 172).

07. Wheat noodles
so-myeon 소면

These very thin noodles are made from wheat flour and are used in the Chilled Kimchi Spiced Noodles (page 158) and also the Noodles in Chilled Soybean Soup (page 162).

08. Rice cakes
ddeok 떡

These uniquely Korean soft rice cakes made from steamed and shaped glutinous rice are essential for the Crispy Chilli and Crispy Soy Rice Cakes (pages 50 and 51). Their squidgy consistency is quite unusual at first, but soon becomes addictive.

SPICES & PASTES

09. Soybean paste
doen-jang 된장

This fermented soybean paste, is similar to Japanese miso, however it has a deeper more concentrated flavour profile. Used in many soup and stew bases such as in the Tofu & Soybean Paste Soup (page 82), it is rich in flavonoids, minerals and vitamins and is considered an essential component in Korean cuisine.

10. Chilli paste
gochujang 고추장

Like doen-jang, gochujang is also made from fermented soybeans, but with the addition of glutinous rice flour, salt and plenty of dried powdered red chilli, giving it its characteristic spicy kick. The paste is aged in the sun over a period of months or years, resulting in a pungent, and deeply flavoured savoury paste that is used extensively in Korean cooking. Its flavour is quite unlike any other chilli paste and so it really is worth getting your hands on it for Korean cooking. Gochujang chilli paste keeps extremely well in the fridge.

11. Red pepper (chilli) powder
gochugaru 고추가루

This powdered sun-dried red chilli is used to make gochujang, and is also the key spice ingredient for kimchi, and many sauces too. The flavour profile is smoky, slightly sweet and well rounded, and while it is of course spicy, it is not as hot as an Indian chilli powder for example. There is no direct substitute – you could use another chilli powder but the result would not be authentically Korean in flavour. The powder keeps very well in an airtight container stored in a dark environment, so it is worth buying when you find yourself in an Asian supermarket.

12. Dried chilli threads
sil gochu 실고추

Made from the same sun-dried chilli as gochugaru red pepper powder, the chilli is very thinly sliced into thread-like pieces. These chilli threads are often used to garnish dishes and add flavour, however, they are by no means as essential as gochugaru.

OTHER COMMON INGREDIENTS

13. Roasted sesame seed oil
cham girum 참기름

Like most good Asian sesame seed oils, Korean roasted sesame oil is leagues ahead of anything you will find in a Western supermarket – you simply could not even compare the two ingredients – the former having a much more intense and pure nutty flavour. As with all of these storecupboard ingredients, it keeps for months on end, so it is well worth buying. Roasted sesame seeds are also heavily used in Korean cooking, and you can buy ready toasted, good-quality Korean sesame seeds in Asian supermarkets.

14. Roasted crispy seaweed
kim 김

These sheets of roasted crispy seaweed are sold in little packs already cut up or as larger, full sheets. The seaweed is brushed with sesame seed oil and sprinkled with a little salt and pan-fried or roasted until deliciously crispy. Roasted crispy seaweed is usually used cut into thin strips to add flavour and texture to dishes, or small sheets are wrapped around rice to create bite-size crispy seaweed parcels. They are also great as a snack, like a packet of crisps, only healthier. Once opened, they loose their crispiness rather quickly, so only open what you need and if you have any left over store them in an airtight container.

15. Dried kelp
dashima 다시마 *and miyok* 미역

There are two main types of dried kelp used in Korean cooking: 'dashima' – the flat dried sheets (*15a*) and more commonly known by its Japanese name 'dashi kombu', and 'mee-yeok' – the rougher more stringy variety (*15b*), also more commonly known as wakame. The former is used to make stocks (page 19) and as a flavour enhancer for all kinds of stews and broths. However, it is not eaten and is always removed before serving. 'Mee-yeok' on the other hand is eaten, and is used in the very popular Seaweed & Beef Soup (page 68).

16. Korean jujube red dates
daechu 대추

This dried date is widely used for its medicinal properties as well as its flavour and could not really be compared to a Western date, their only similarity being that they are both sweet. It is famously used in the Baby Chicken Soup (page 64), as well as a wide variety of sweet treats and teas. It is not an essential storecupboard ingredient, but it does add a unique flavour profile if you are looking to create very authentic Korean dishes.

17. Chinese or Napa Cabbage
baechu 배추

This oblong, white and pale green cabbage is the key ingredient in traditional Korean cabbage kimchi. It is quite different to round white cabbage and is easy to find in good markets and large supermarkets.

18. Daikon radish
mu 무

Daikon radish is not in fact the Korean variety of radish, which is oval in shape with a pale green and white skin. However, it is far easier to find so we have used it in this book as the flavour and texture is practically the same. If you do happen to come across the Korean variety, use the same quantity as the daikon.

19. Asian/Korean pear
bae 배

Asian pears are large, light brown and round, very juicy and with a crispy texture that is lovely in salads or to add a little sweetness, such as in the Sesame, Soy & Chilli Beef Tartare (page 210). The pears are most often used to tenderise meat, as in the Sesame & Soy-marinated Beef (page 212). They are about twice the size of a regular Western pear, so if substituting, you will need about two Western pears for every one Asian pear.

20. Dried squid
ojingeo-chae 오징어채

Dried, shredded squid is seasoned and served as a side dish (page 124) and it keeps very well in the fridge.

21. Dried anchovies
mareun myeolchi 마른멸치

Dried anchovies come in three different sizes and are sold in packs, which are usually kept in the freezer section of Asian supermarkets. In this book, we only use the large and small size. The large anchovies (*21a*) are used to flavour stocks and stews. The very small anchovies (*21b*) are fried and seasoned and eaten as the most delicious crispy side dish and are a great source of calcium too. Keep them stored in your freezer where they will keep for months, if not years, on end.

22. Salted baby shrimp
saeujeot 새우젓

This is an optional storecupboard ingredient. It is mainly used when making cabbage kimchi to add a more pronounced fish flavour. If you are not sure, you can leave it out.

23. Persian (pickling) cucumbers
oh-ee 오이

Persian cucumbers are essential for making the Whole Pickled Cucumbers (page 110). The pickling variety, with their rough and slightly bumpy skin, are best for pickling, but either will do.

24. Pickled yellow radish
danmuji 단무지

Rice & Seaweed Rolls (page 34) are always filled with long strips of yellow pickled radish. Black Bean Noodles (page 176) are also always served with it. It has a very distinctive slightly sweet-sour taste that takes us back to Korea with the first taste. It is not absolutely essential to use it with these recipes, but it keeps well so we buy it and keep it refrigerated until we need to use it again, which could be months later.

SOY SAUCE
ganjang 간장

In Korea, two types of soy sauce are used: a regular variety, very similar to Japanese soy sauce and those you would find in Western shops, and a second, much saltier variety known as 'gook gan jang', which is used to season vegetables, soups and stews. This kind of soy sauce is unique to Korea, and can be difficult to get your hands on, so in this book we have used regular soy sauce in all of our recipes. If you do happen to have Korean 'gook gan jang', then feel free to use it, but you will need to decrease the quantity according to taste. As a general rule, try to seek out naturally brewed soy sauce made without additives or sweeteners.

Stock
육수

Having your own freshly made stock at hand really transforms the flavour of dishes, so it is well worth making a big batch of this and keeping a few portions in your freezer. You can double the recipe if you wish.

Beef stock
sogogi yook-su 소고기 육수

Makes roughly 1.4 litres
1 tbsp vegetable oil
1 leek, roughly chopped
2 garlic cloves, crushed
½ onion, chopped
500g beef rump, sliced into thin strips
2 tbsp soy sauce
1 tbsp roasted sesame seed oil
1 x 12cm piece of dried kelp (dashima, page 16)

In a large, heavy-based pan, heat the vegetable oil over a medium heat. When hot, add the leek, garlic and onion, sauté for 3 minutes, making sure not to burn the garlic. Add the beef, turn up the heat a little and fry for a further 3 minutes until lightly coloured. Add the soy sauce, sesame seed oil and kelp and fry for a further minute, then pour in 2 litres of water. Turn the heat up, cover and bring to a rolling boil. Reduce the heat and simmer for 40 minutes, removing any scum from the surface. Strain the stock through a sieve, into a jug, reserving the meat to add to any fried rice dish such as the Kimchi Fried Rice (page 31).

Leave the stock to cool completely then skim off any surface oil. Store in sealed containers in the fridge for up to 3 days or for a few months in the freezer.

Fish stock
myeolchi yook-su 멸치 육수

Korean fish stock differs from its Western counterpart as dried anchovies and kelp are used as the main ingredients. These give the stock a subtle taste that makes it a good base to almost any soup, stew or broth, as it is not overpoweringly fishy.

Makes roughly 1.3 litres
12 large dried anchovies, about 5cm in length (page 17)
4 x 10cm pieces of dried kelp (dashima, page 16)
½ onion, peeled and roughly chopped

Pull the heads off the dried anchovies, then gently tease open the underside of the belly and remove the little black pouches (the guts).

Put all the stock ingredients into a large pan along with 1.5 litres of water and bring to the boil. Maintain a rolling boil for 10–15 minutes until the stock has reduced by about 200ml. Strain the stock through a fine sieve, into a jug, and discard the kelp and anchovies.

Leave the stock to cool completely then skim off any surface oil. Store in sealed containers in the fridge for up to 3 days or for a few months in the freezer.

Menu Ideas
메뉴 아이디어

The wonderful thing about Korean food is that most of the base flavourings (roasted sesame seed oil, soy sauce and gochujang chilli paste) have long shelf lives, so once you have them on hand you will always be able to throw together a reasonably quick meal. Of course, as with any cuisine, there are slow-cooked dishes that take a little longer to prepare, but you will find the majority of Korean dishes are actually quite straightforward and quick to make, especially once you have become familiar with the ingredients. Here are a selection of dishes for some mealtime inspiration.

Quick & Easy

We always have some shop-bought kimchi on standby in case we run out of our homemade batch, just so that we are never left wanting. Here are a few more quick and easy dishes to try out.

Kimchi Fried Rice *(page 31)*
Pan-fried Mackerel *(page 194)*
Kimchi Pancake *(page 138)*
Tofu & Soybean Paste Soup *(page 82)*
Instant Chicken Ramen *(page 173)*
Crispy Chilli Rice Cakes *(page 50)*
Pan-fried King Prawns *(page 196)*
Stir-fried Spicy Squid *(page 192)*

Light Lunches

It is not for no reason that Korea is consistently ranked in the top ten healthiest nations of the world. The diet there is impeccable, with vegetables and wholesome grains appearing in just about every meal. There are also numerous light dishes that are in no way lacking in flavour. Here are some of our favourites.

Chilled Cucumber Soup *(page 88)*
Bean Sprout Soup *(page 70)*
Raw Fish, Vegetable & Rice Salad *(page 32)*
Steamed Eggs with Spring Onion & Chilli *(page 128)*
Clear Clam Broth *(page 61)*
Tofu with Soy Dressing *(page 147)*
Raw Tuna with Chilli Sauce *(page 186)*
Seafood Salad with Wasabi Dressing *(page 204)*
Chilled Kimchi Spiced Noodles *(page 158)*

Weeknight Meals

These dishes are ideal for a weeknight dinner, when you need to rustle something up reasonably quickly. We always make more than we need so we can have the leftovers for lunch the next day.

Warming Chicken and Potato Stew *(page 76)*
Black Bean Noodles *(page 176)*
Braised Rice Cakes with Cabbage & Fishcakes *(page 48)*
Chicken & Sesame Oil Porridge *(page 42)*
Kimchi Stew *(page 86)*
Beef & Vegetables with Sesame Glass Noodles *(page 166)*
Braised Halibut in Seasoned Soy *(page 197)*
Chicken, Rice Cake & Vegetable Hotpot *(page 230)*

FEASTS

Without a doubt one of the best and most traditional ways to enjoy a Korean meal, or any meal for that matter, is with family and friends all diving into a selection of dishes, with contrasting flavours, textures and levels of spice. When you think of a Western meal, the idea of a table full of different dishes can seem quite daunting, as most dishes cannot be prepared that far in advance. However, when it comes to Korean food, many of the sides can be prepared ahead of time and because most of them are made up of fermented or pickled food, they will not only last for a single meal but for many more meals thereafter.

Barbecue-style Eating

All of the suggested dishes can be prepared in advance (or in the case of the kimchi you could always use a store-bought version if you are pushed for time). The Sesame & Soy-marinated Beef *(page 212)* or Grilled Beef Short Ribs *(page 224)* are ideal, as you can marinate them the day before, and then they are ready to be thrown on the barbecue as and when needed. Serve the following dishes with freshly cooked rice.

Classic Cabbage Kimchi *(page 98)*
Radish Water Kimchi *(page 106)*
Quick Pickled Onions *(page 123)*
Soy-seasoned Mushrooms *(page 118)*
Sesame and Soy-marinated Beef *(page 212)*
Grilled Beef Short Ribs *(page 224)*
Tofu & Soybean Paste Soup *(page 82)*
Persimmon with Maple Syrup & Lime *(page 253)*

Dinner Parties

As with the barbecue menu, this dinner party feast, while involved, can mostly be prepared in advance, including the kimchi, soup, potatoes and noodles. Simply reheat them at the last moment. The bibimbap toppings can also be made in advance, ready to serve on freshly cooked rice when your guests arrive. For ease, we often prepare one very large bibimbap as a central serving dish as it looks spectacular and is always a crowd-pleaser.

Almost-instant Cucumber Kimchi *(page 104)*
One other kimchi of your choosing
  (see chapter Vegetables, pickles & sides, page 93)
Tofu & Soybean Paste Soup *(page 82)*
Honey and Soy-glazed Potatoes *(page 127)*
Beef & Vegetables with Sesame Glass Noodles *(page 166)*
Seafood & Spring Onion Pancake *(page 136)*
Fried Minced Meat Patties with Sesame Seeds *(page 237)*
Mixed Rice with Vegetables & Beef *(page 28)*
Shaved Ice with Sweet Red Beans,
  Ice Cream & Rice Cakes *(page 248)*

Rice & Savoury Porridge

밥 & 죽

01

26. **Short-grain Rice**
밥

26. **Five-grain Rice**
오곡밥

28. **Mixed Rice with Vegetables & Beef**
비빔밥

30. **Jeonju Bibimbap**
전주 비빔밥

31. **Kimchi Fried Rice**
김치볶음밥

32. **Raw Fish, Vegetable & Rice Salad**
회덮밥

34. **Rice & Seaweed Rolls**
김밥

39. *The Grain of Life*

40. **Pine Nut & Rice Porridge**
잣죽

42. **Chicken & Sesame Oil Porridge**
닭죽

43. **Black Sesame Seed Porridge**
흑임자죽

44. **Pumpkin Rice Porridge**
호박죽

48. **Braised Rice Cakes with Cabbage & Fishcakes**
떡볶이

50. **Crispy Chilli Rice Cakes**
기름 떡볶이

51. **Crispy Soy Rice Cakes**
기름 간장 떡볶이

Serves 6

Short-grain Rice & Five-grain Rice
bap & ogokbap

밥 & 오곡밥

<u>Short-grain Rice</u>
400g short-grain white rice

<u>Five-grain Rice</u>
75g aduki beans, soaked overnight
70g black beans, soaked overnight
180g short-grain white rice
180g glutinous rice
85g millet
½ tsp sea salt

Five-grain rice *is traditionally eaten on the first full moon of the year, and sharing the dish is believed to bring you good fortune for the coming year. The Korean way of cooking the beans is to have them dense and almost chewy as opposed to boiling them until completely soft. Five-grain rice is hearty and filling and it's best enjoyed in small portions with a soup or stew.*

Here we have included the two basic rice dishes, plain short-grain and five-grain rice. Of course you can use any rice you like, but if you want to experience the authentic flavour and texture of true Korean rice dishes then we would really encourage you to try short-grain rice. Brown short-grain rice can be used anywhere white short-grain rice is used and Koreans often mix the two together for added texture.

For the Short-grain Rice: Rinse and drain the rice 3 times in cold water, then place it in a bowl, cover with cold water and leave to soak for 30 minutes.

Drain the rice through a sieve and place it in a large heavy-based pan with a tightly fitting lid. Pour in 500ml of water, place the lid on top and bring it to a boil over a high heat. As soon as it boils, reduce the heat to medium and leave it to simmer (with the lid on) for 7 minutes until most of the water has been absorbed. Working quickly so as not to let all the steam escape, remove the lid and stir the rice, making sure the bottom and sides are not catching. Cover with the lid again, reduce the heat to very low and cook for another 3 minutes. Turn the heat off completely and leave to steam for another 10 minutes, resisting the temptation to peak at the rice. Finally, remove the lid, and while it's still hot, use a wooden spoon to fluff up the rice.

For the Five-grain Rice: If you have a rice cooker you can add everything in and cook according to the instructions below. Otherwise, drain the soaked beans, place in a large pan and cover with water. Bring to the boil, skim off any scum then reduce the heat to a rolling simmer for 1 hour until the beans are almost fully cooked. They should be tender with a little bite. Make sure to top up the water as it evaporates so that the beans are always covered.

Drain the water from the beans, then add both rice grains and the millet to the pan. Add in 750ml of water and the salt. Bring to the boil for 1 minute with the lid on, then reduce the heat and simmer gently for 5 minutes. Gently stir the mixture from time to time to ensure none of the grains stick to the bottom of the pan. Continue to simmer gently over a low heat for a further 10 minutes, or until the beans are tender and the liquid has been fully absorbed by the rice and millet. Turn off the heat and leave to steam with the lid on for 10 minutes. Use a wooden spoon to fluff up the rice and grains. Serve immediately.

Serves 4

Mixed Rice with Vegetables & Beef
bibimbap

400g short-grain white rice

Marinated beef
300g beef sirloin, very thinly sliced
2½ tbsp soy sauce
2 tsp roasted sesame seed oil
3 garlic cloves, crushed
3 spring onions, very finely chopped
½ tsp ground black pepper

Toppings
150g carrots, cut into very thin strips
300g courgette, quartered lengthways and thinly sliced
150g cucumber, halved lengthways, deseeded and thinly sliced
150g daikon radish, peeled and cut into thin strips
150g bean sprouts
200g shiitake mushrooms, sliced
300g spinach
4 eggs
roasted sesame seed oil, to season
soy sauce, to season
sunflower or vegetable oil, to fry
toasted sesame seeds, to serve
few leaves of salad cress, to serve

Gochujang sauce
3 tbsp gochujang chilli paste (page 14)
1 tbsp soy sauce
1 tbsp roasted sesame seed oil
2 garlic cloves, crushed
1 tbsp sugar or maple syrup

It is hard not to fall in love with bibimbap. The bed of pearly white rice adorned with a ring of colourful vegetables and beef, and a bright yellow egg, the shining star in the centre. It is almost hypnotic. Like a lot of Korean dishes, individual ingredients are plated up beautifully so you can fully appreciate each one, and then, with gleeful abandon, you madly mix everything together. The possibilities for toppings are endless, so feel free to use your favourite ingredients – spinach and onion also work very well.

In a bowl, combine together all the sauce ingredients and set aside. In another bowl, mix together the ingredients for the beef marinade, add the sliced beef, cover and set aside for 30–60 minutes.

Cook the rice according to the packet instructions or as per the recipe on page 26. Keep warm. Meanwhile, fill a large pan with water and bring it to a rolling boil. One by one, blanch the carrots, courgette, cucumber and radish for 1 minute and the bean sprouts for 2½ minutes. Use a slotted spoon or sieve to remove them from the water and drain fully. Season each vegetable with ½ a teaspoon of roasted sesame seed oil and soy sauce, keeping the vegetables separate at all times.

Heat 1 tablespoon of sunflower oil in a pan. Add in the mushrooms and stir-fry over a high heat for 4–5 minutes until softened. Remove from the pan and season with ½ a teaspoon of roasted sesame seed oil and soy sauce.

In the same pan, add in the spinach and sprinkle over 2 teaspoons of water. Fry over a high heat for a few minutes, stirring all the time, until the spinach has wilted. Remove the spinach, squeeze out any excess water and season as before with the ½ teaspoon of roasted sesame seed oil and soy sauce. In Korea, these vegetables are served at room temperature so don't worry about keeping them warm.

In the same pan, add the marinated beef. Stir-fry over a high heat for 3–5 minutes, until the sauce has reduced and the meat is cooked through. In a clean frying pan, fry the eggs to your liking.

Serve the hot rice in 4 individual bowls. Place 1 egg onto the centre of the rice, then arrange the vegetables and meat around it. Sprinkle over some sesame seeds and salad cress and serve with the gochujang sauce. Start with a couple of spoonfuls of the sauce and mix everything together well. Add more gochujang sauce to taste.

Serves 4

Jeonju Bibimbap
Jeonju bibimbap

<u>Rice</u>
400g short-grain white rice
460ml beef stock

<u>Additional toppings</u>
30g dried bracken, covered in cold water and soaked overnight
30g dried bellflower root, cut into very thin strips and soaked overnight
2 tsp roasted sesame seed oil
2 garlic cloves, crushed
2 tbsp soy sauce
2 spring onions, very finely chopped
freshly ground black pepper, to season
1 tsp toasted sesame seeds

<u>Optional</u>
If using a dolsot stone bowl:
½ tsp roasted sesame seed oil, to coat
4 egg yolks

I had the great honour of learning from Kim Yeon Im, the 78-year-old owner and head chef of Kajok Hwe-gwan (가족 회관), a restaurant in the city of Jeonju, which is known as the capital of food in Korea. Kim – who has been given the title of 'master of bibimbap' and has cooked for all of the Korean presidents over the past 40 years – explained how Jeonju bibimbap is an extremely elaborate dish, with more than 30 different possibilities for toppings. In many ways, it is still similar to the bibimbap on page 28, however, it differs slightly: the rice is cooked in a beef stock, the eggs are raw and there is the addition of bracken and bellflower roots. These two ingredients, which can be found in good Korean supermarkets, are specific to this dish – they have an earthy flavour and need to be soaked overnight.

Here, we have served it in a hot stone bowl called a 'dolsot', which gives the bottom layer of rice a wonderful crunchiness and cooks the raw egg yolk. You can find these bowls in all good Korean stores. You can also serve this in regular bowls – just use fried eggs in place of the raw egg yolks.

Follow the recipe for Mixed Rice with Vegetables & Beef on page 28, with the exception of the rice and eggs, and with additions as below:

For the rice, cook according to the packet instructions, or as per the instructions on page 26, using 460ml of beef stock instead of water. Once cooked, keep warm. Cook the beef and vegetables as on page 28 and keep to one side. Drain the bracken and bellflower root.

Bring a saucepan of water to the boil. Add the drained bracken and cook for 15–25 minutes until they are soft and cooked through. (The time will depend on the age of the bracken, so test a piece after 15 minutes.) Once cooked, use a slotted spoon to remove the bracken and allow to drain.

In a frying pan, add the sesame oil and put the pan over a medium-high heat. Add in the drained bracken and half the garlic and stir-fry for 2–3 minutes over a medium heat, making sure you don't burn the garlic. Add 1 tablespoon of soy sauce and half the spring onions and continue to stir-fry for a further 3 minutes. Season with black pepper and mix in half the sesame seeds, then remove. Stir-fry the bellflower root as per the bracken, seasoning in the same way.

Jenonju Bibimbap
continued

If you are using the dolsot stone bowls, brush the inner surface with just enough sesame oil to coat. Place directly onto a medium flame for 10 minutes until extremely hot. Carefully transfer to a wooden base (or a wooden board), add the rice, crack the egg yolks onto the centre (or put the fried egg on top) then arrange the vegetables and meat around it. Serve immediately with the gochujang sauce, thoroughly combining everything together to cook the egg yolk with the heat from the stone bowl.

Serves 4

Kimchi Fried Rice
kimchi bokkeum-bap

1 tbsp vegetable or sunflower oil
320g kimchi, chopped into bite-size pieces
50ml kimchi juice
2 tbsp gochujang chilli paste (page 14)
4 tsp soy sauce
600g cooked short-grain white rice
3 tsp roasted sesame seed oil
4 eggs
5 spring onions, finely chopped
2 tsp toasted sesame seeds
1 sheet of roasted crispy seaweed, shredded

The simplicity of this dish belies its wonderfully deep and tangy flavours. Jina pretty much won me over the first time she cooked it for me. The flavours were so complex and addictive I could have sworn she had been slaving for hours, when in fact she had whipped it up in minutes. Since then this has been a go-to dish. Perfect for when you have no time on your hands but still want a really flavour-packed meal.

For anyone who is wary of kimchi, and its rather pungent odour, this is the dish for you. The frying radically alters the flavour of the kimchi, mellowing it and rounding out all those hard-edged flavours that assault your nostrils every time you open the fridge. We dare you not to love this dish.

Heat the vegetable oil in a large pan over a high heat. When hot, add the kimchi and stir-fry for 3 minutes, keeping it moving the whole time, until it begins to caramelise. In a bowl, mix the kimchi juice, gochujang and soy sauce, then add them into the pan along with the cooked rice. Mix everything together until well combined. Reduce the heat to medium-low and fry for another 3 minutes until the rice has absorbed all the flavours, then stir in the sesame oil and remove from the heat.

In the meantime, in a separate pan, fry the eggs to your liking.

To serve, mix most of the spring onions into the rice, then plate up with a fried egg on top and the remaining spring onions, sesame seeds and shredded seaweed scattered over the top. Serve immediately.

Rice & Savoury Porridge

Serves 2

Raw Fish, Vegetable & Rice Salad
hoedeopbab

200g sushi-grade skinless fish fillets of your choice (such as salmon or tuna), ice-cold
1 sheet of roasted crispy seaweed (optional), shredded
300g cooked short-grain white or brown rice, at room temperature
1 little gem lettuce head, leaves separated
3 leaves of red leaf lettuce, leaves separated
50g rocket
100g cucumber, halved lengthways, deseeded and cut into thin slices
100g carrots, halved lengthways and cut into thin slices
3 spring onions, finely sliced
1 tbsp roasted sesame seed oil
small handful of salad cress or pea shoots
2 tsp black or white sesame seeds

<u>Sauce</u>
3 tbsp soy sauce
1½ tbsp gochujang chilli paste (page 14)
1½ tbsp rice wine vinegar
2 small garlic cloves, crushed
1 tbsp honey or maple syrup
1 red chilli, deseeded and finely sliced

This is a bit like a spicy sushi bowl, with the added bonus of it being far easier to prepare. The only absolute with this dish is incredibly fresh fish. Go to your local fishmongers and let them know you are eating the fish raw. This salad is served cold and is best enjoyed in the summer. If you prefer your food spicy, add an extra teaspoon of gochujang chilli paste to the sauce.

In a bowl, combine all the ingredients for the sauce, cover and put in the fridge for at least 1 hour or until well chilled.

Cut the fish into 1.5cm cubes, cover and place in the fridge.

To serve, divide the cooked rice between 2 bowls and arrange the lettuce, rocket, cucumber, carrots and spring onions on top along with the fresh fish. Drizzle over the sesame oil, then scatter over the seaweed, salad cress and sesame seeds. Serve with the sauce alongside rather than pouring it over the top, as you want to be able to see the beautifully fresh fish. When ready to eat, mix in a few spoons of the sauce to taste (you may not need all of it) and mix thoroughly.

Makes 5 rolls

Rice & Seaweed Rolls
kim-bap

Seasoned rice
400g short-grain white rice
½ tsp salt
1 tbsp roasted sesame seed oil

Marinated beef
1½ tsp soy sauce
1½ tsp honey
1 spring onion, finely chopped
1 garlic clove, finely chopped
1½ tsp roasted sesame seed oil
180g beef sirloin, cut into long ½cm thin strips
salt and freshly ground black pepper

Fillings
2 eggs
3 tsp vegetable oil
300g spinach leaves
1½ tsp roasted sesame seed oil, plus extra to grease
1 tsp toasted sesame seeds
70g carrot, cut into julienned strips
5 sheets of roasted crispy seaweed
70g cucumber, halved lengthways, deseeded and cut into thin strips
180g pickled yellow radish, cut into thin strips (optional) (available in Asian supermarkets)
soy sauce, to serve
pickled garlic (page 108) or pickled ginger, to serve (optional)
salt and freshly ground black pepper

For us, kim-bap awakens so many great memories of road trips and picnics in Korea, where it is one of the most popular dishes for a lunch on the go. Most people describe kim-bap as Korean sushi, although it is quite different; fish is rarely used, the rolls are sliced thinner and they have a much deeper, richer flavour mainly due to the addition of roasted sesame seed oil. You can choose to dip them in soy sauce and wasabi, if you like, but most Koreans serve them without.

Wash the rice thoroughly in cold water until the water runs clear. Place it in a saucepan with a lid and add in 600ml of water. Leave to soak in the pot for 30 minutes, then set over a high heat and bring to the boil. Immediately reduce to the lowest heat and simmer gently, covered, for 20–25 minutes until most of the water has been absorbed. (Resist the temptation to remove the lid otherwise you will release too much steam.) Remove from the heat, keeping the lid in place, and set aside for 15 minutes to steam.

Remove the rice from the saucepan and spread it out in a thin layer on a large wooden board. Season with the salt and the sesame oil. Fan it to help it cool down as quickly as possible while turning it with a flat wooden spoon or spatula.

In a bowl, mix together the ingredients for the beef marinade, add the beef and set aside while you prepare the other fillings.

Break the eggs into a bowl, add in a good pinch of salt and lightly whisk together. In a non-stick pan, add 2 teaspoons of vegetable oil and place over a medium heat. When hot, add the eggs and cook them, undisturbed, for 2 minutes then carefully flip over and cook for a further 2 minutes, or until fully cooked. Transfer the egg to a chopping board and cut into 1cm wide strips.

Next, rinse the spinach. Place a large pan over a high heat and add the spinach along with any water clinging to the leaves. Cook for a few minutes until completely wilted. Drain in a colander and gently press out any remaining water. Spread out onto a plate and season with the sesame seed oil, seeds and salt and pepper. Set aside.

In the same pan, add the remaining 1 teaspoon of vegetable oil and place it over a high heat. Add the carrot and stir-fry for 1 minute. Remove and place in a bowl and set aside. Add the beef and its marinade and fry for 2–3 minutes until the beef is cooked through and the marinade is sticky.

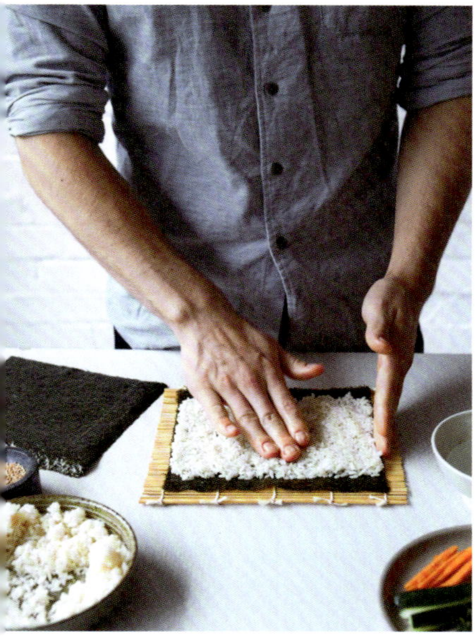
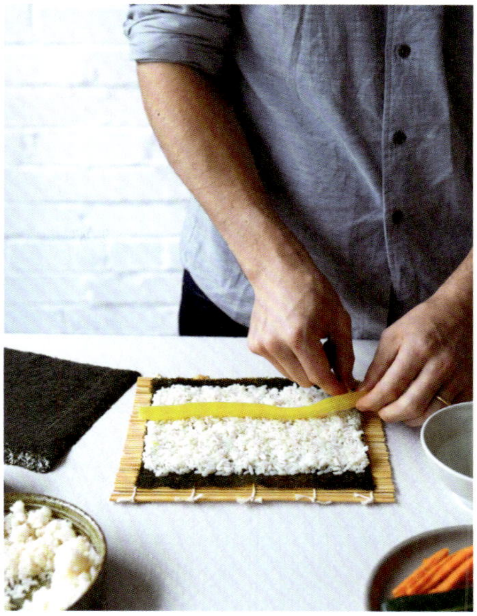
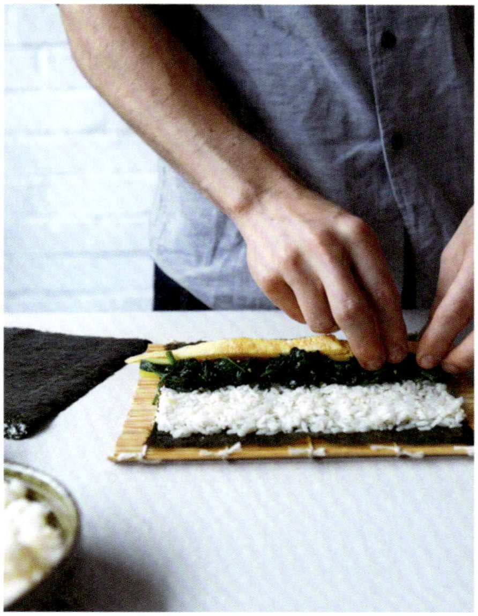
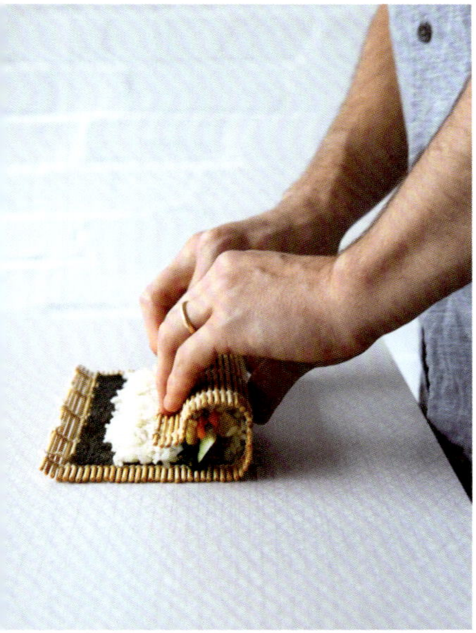
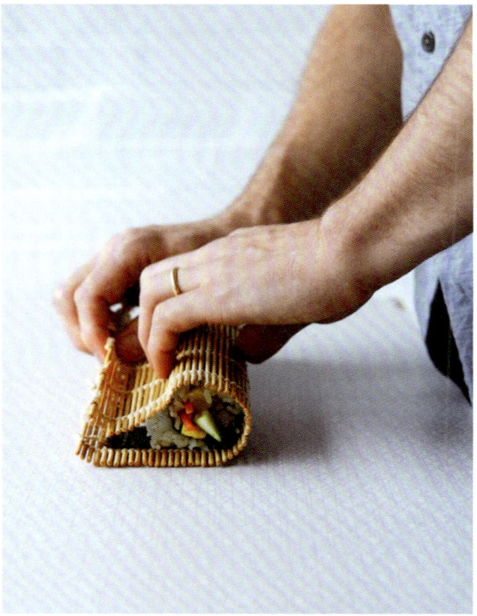
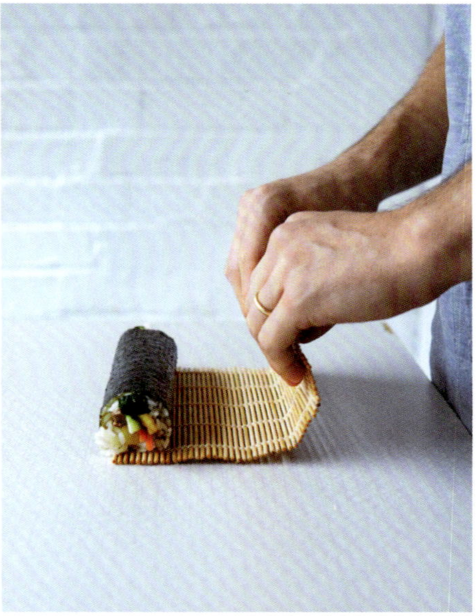
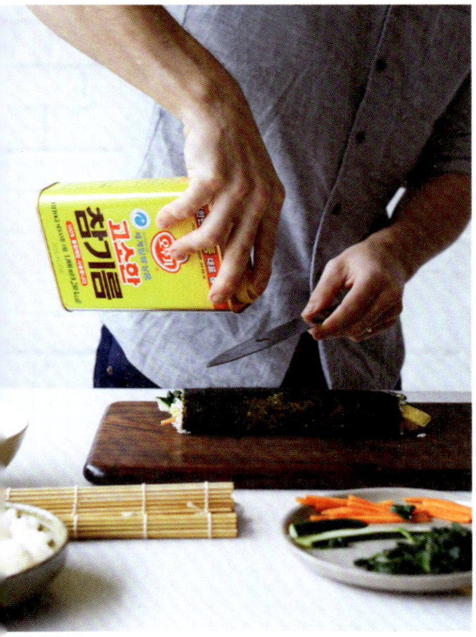
고소한
참기름
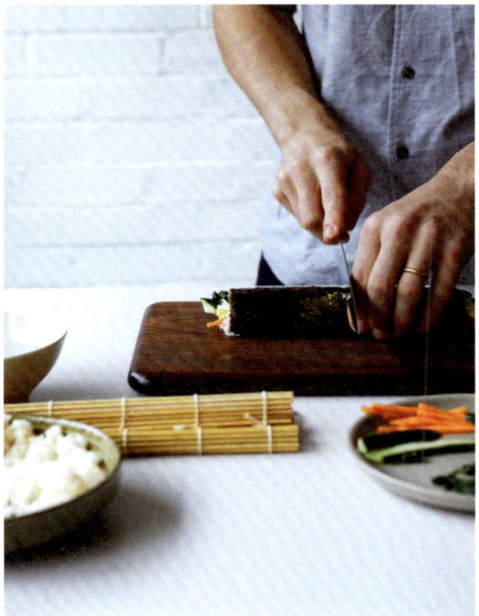
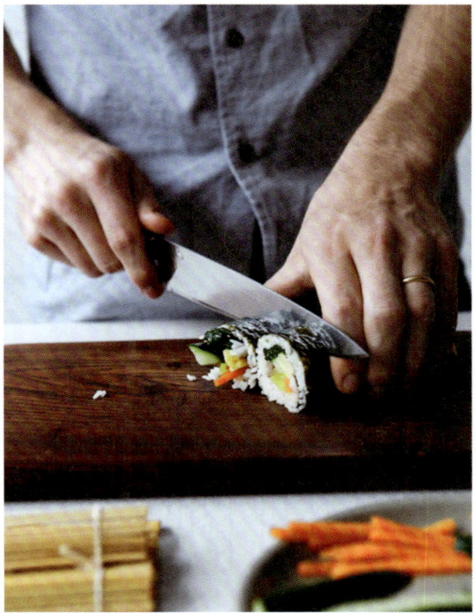

Rice & Seaweed Rolls
continued

To assemble, wrap a bamboo mat in cling film, squeezing out any trapped air – this helps prevent the rice from sticking. Lay the mat out lengthways in front of you. Take 1 sheet of seaweed and place it, shiny-side down, onto the bamboo mat. Wet your hands and take a fifth of the seasoned rice. Starting at the end closest to you, spread and pat the rice across the seaweed leaving a ½ cm border running along the edge closest to you and a 2cm border along the edge furthest from you. If the rice starts to stick to your hands, wet them again.

Place a few strips of each ingredient – beef, egg, spinach, carrot, cucumber and radish – horizontally onto the centre of the rice. Moisten the edge of seaweed sheet furthest from you with a drop of water, then, holding onto the bamboo mat, roll the edge of the seaweed sheet closest to you over the filling in the centre, tucking in the nori firmly so that the filling is enclosed. When it looks like you are about to roll the mat into the roll, pull the mat back and continue to roll, applying even pressure and tightening as you roll, using the mat to shape it into a cylinder. Repeat with the remaining seaweed sheets and filling. Once fully rolled, take off the mat and grease a sharp knife with a little sesame oil, then cut the roll into 2cm slices. Clean and moisten the knife as you go with more sesame seed oil to prevent it sticking. Serve straightaway with some soy sauce and the pickled garlic if you like or keep it for a packed lunch the next day.

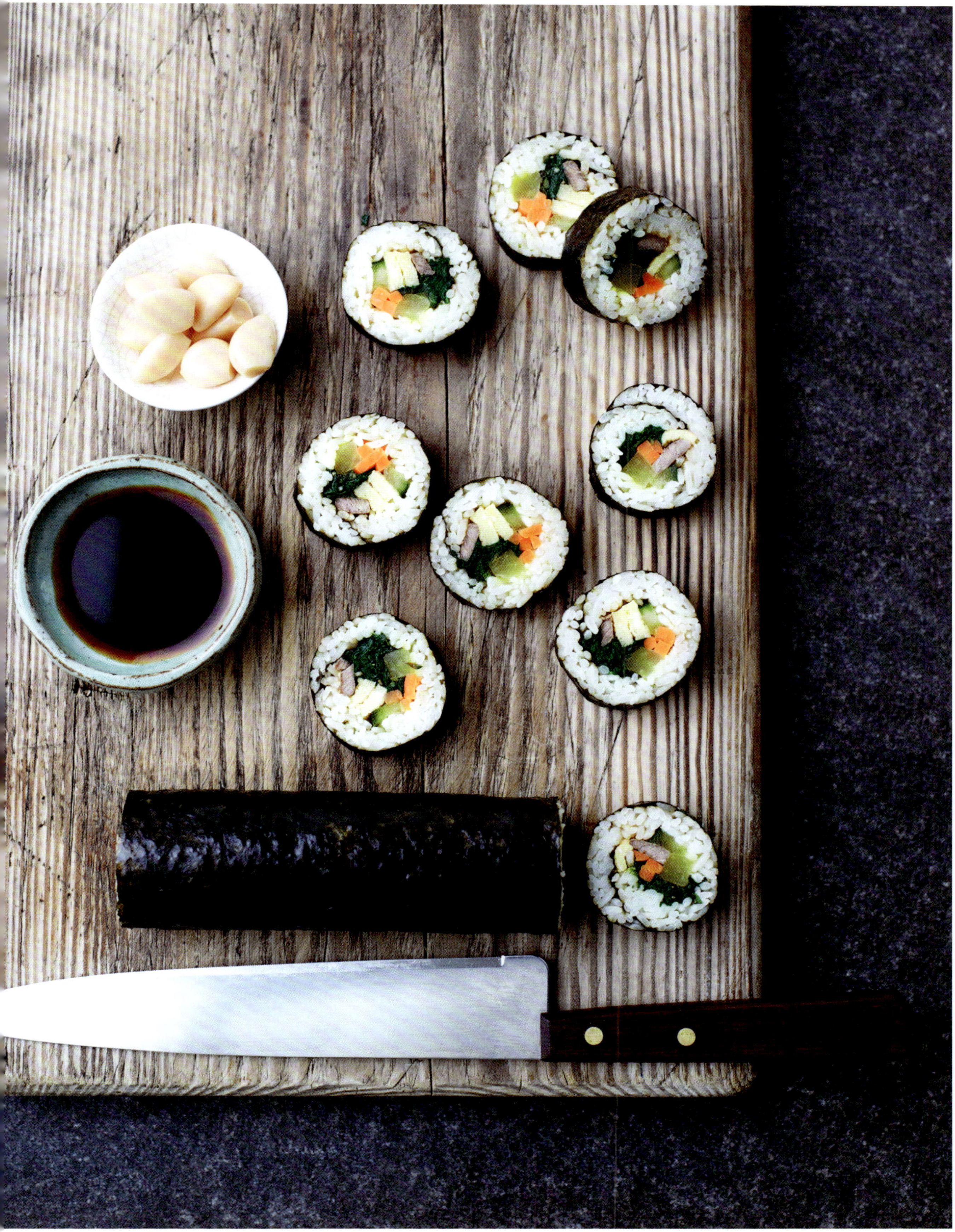

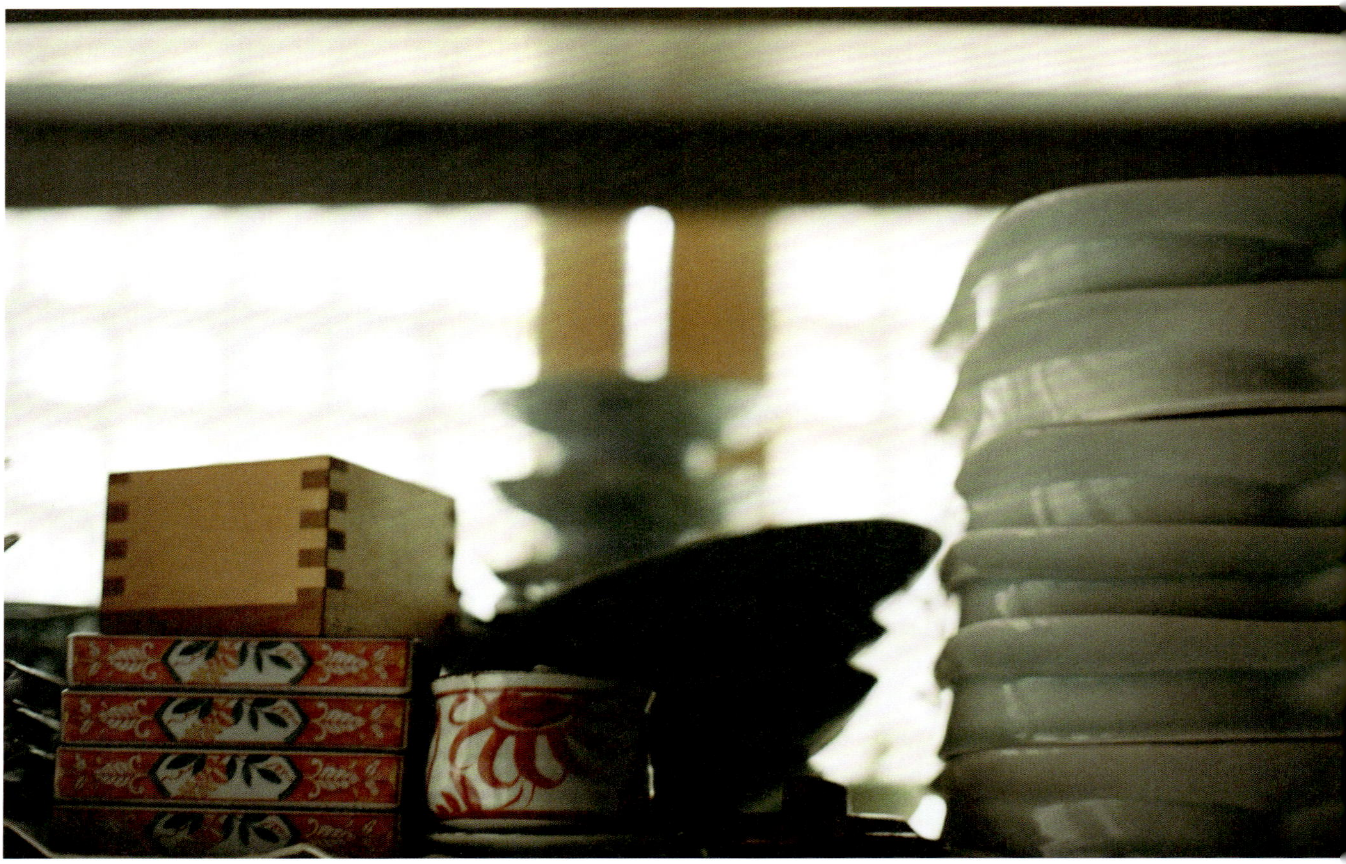

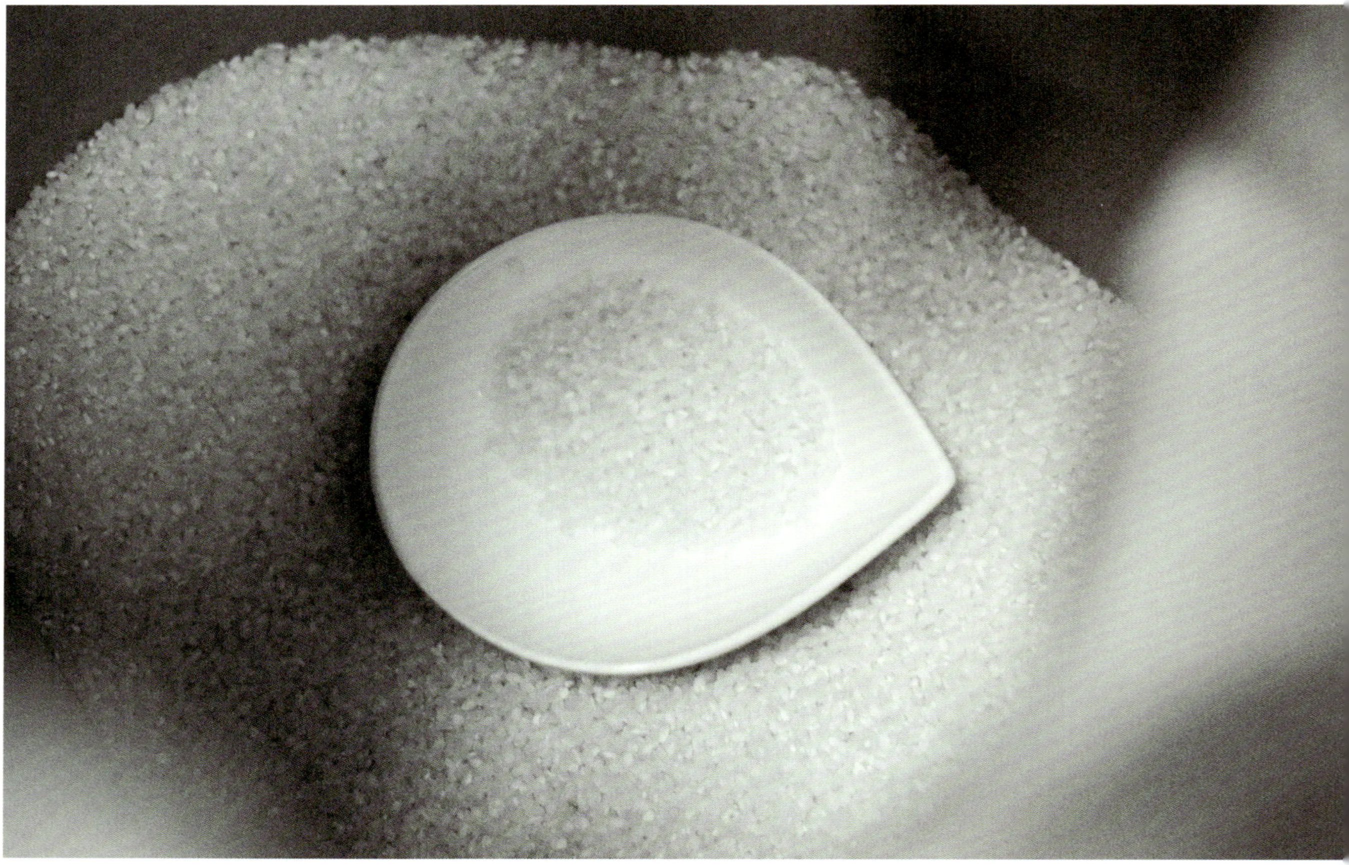

The Grain of Life

Rice has been the foundation of all Korean meals for centuries, to such an extent that the Korean word for cooked rice 'bap' is synonymous with the word for meal and they are used interchangeably in everyday language. Even the common greeting refers to the grain – rather than asking how someone is, you would ask 'have you eaten rice?' This is not a literal question as such, but a way to ask if someone is well, as rice is believed to be vital for energy and stamina and an integral part of a healthy Korean diet.

The rice itself is a medium short-grain, which becomes sticky when cooked. When served with a meal, Koreans prefer it plain, to balance out the punchier flavours of the main and side dishes. It is also often mixed with barley, millet, soybeans and a range of other grains to add texture, flavour and nutrition to the cooked dish. Rice is not only served as an accompaniment to a meal, but is also the main ingredient of hundreds of stand-alone dishes, from snacks to desserts. It is even used to make tea, soft drinks, wines and spirits – the most famous of which is 'makgeoli', a fermented, milky coloured rice wine – which we love.

Cooking perfect rice is considered quite a skill; making sure to get the ratio just right so it is neither too wet nor too dry. In the Korean tradition, rice was cooked in a steamer or in a stone bowl (dolsot), directly on a flame, nowadays however, an electric rice cooker is the preferred option.

Serves 2

Pine Nut & Rice Porridge
jatjuk

200g short-grain white or brown rice, soaked in water for at least 2 hours or overnight
100g pine nuts, plus extra to garnish
½ tsp sea salt
1 tsp honey, to taste
½ tsp black sesame seeds

Once reserved for only the Korean elite, this subtle and soothing porridge is perfect as a winter breakfast, or thinned out with a little more water it makes a delicious soup. Seek out very fresh, preferably organic pine nuts, as the vast majority of supermarket packs are already slightly stale – the quality of the pine nuts will make all the difference.

Drain the rice, then add it to a food processor with the pine nuts and blitz for 2 minutes, scraping down the sides at intervals until everythig is very finely ground down. Then slowly add in 400ml of cold water. Strain everything through a very fine sieve, or a sieve lined with cheesecloth or muslin, into a bowl, squeezing the pulp to extract as much liquid as possible. Discard the pulp and pour the strained liquid into a saucepan and place over a low heat. Stir the mixture continuously for 2–3 minutes until it is noticeably thicker. Let it come to a gentle boil as you stir for another 2 minutes, adding in a little more water if it becomes too thick, or just until the porridge is at your desired consistency. Season with the salt and honey, adding in a little more of either to taste.

Serve immediately in bowls with a few pine nuts and sesame seeds scattered over the top.

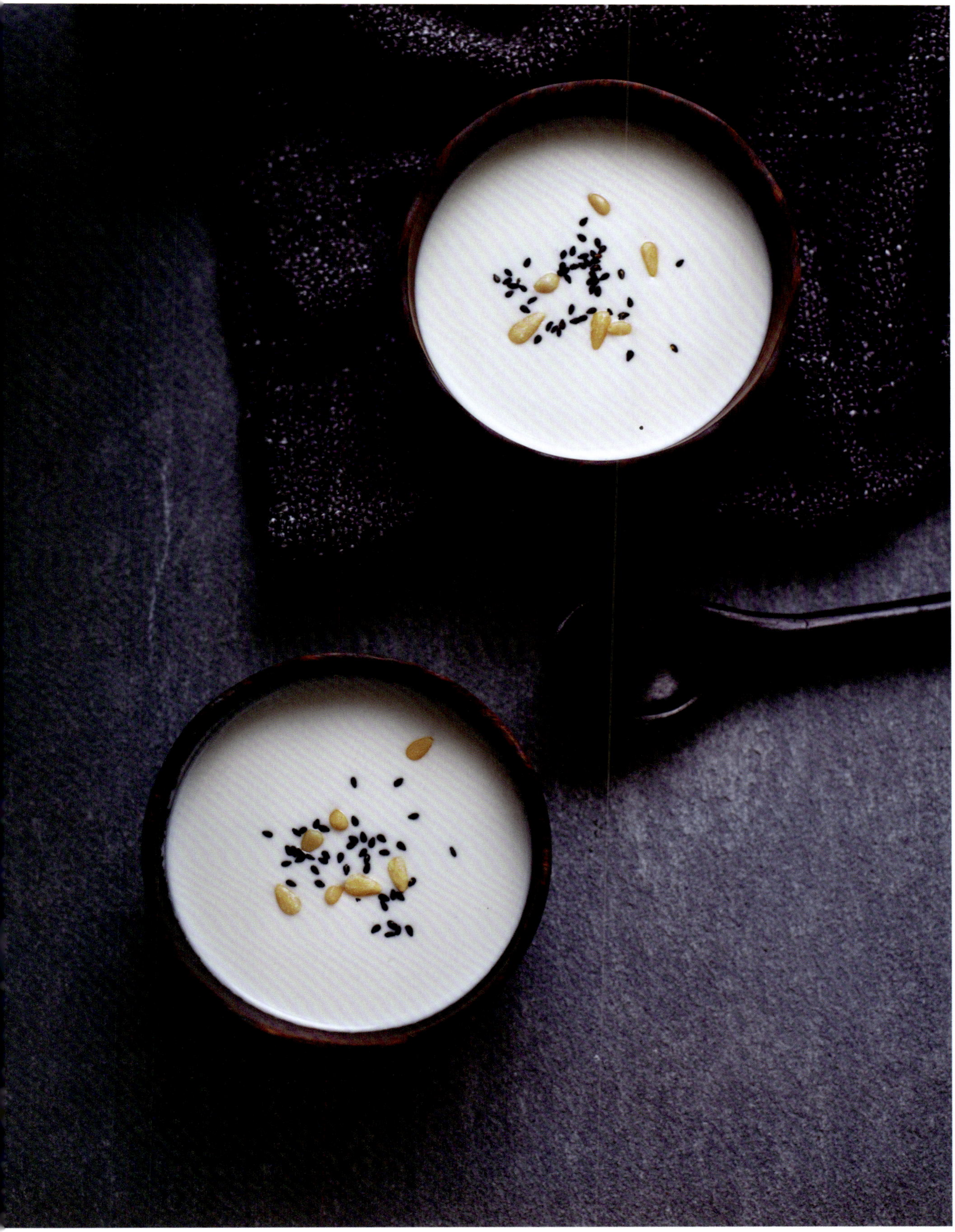

Serves 6

Chicken & Sesame Oil Porridge
dakjuk

150g glutinous rice or short-grain white rice
1 x whole free-range chicken (about 1kg)
8 garlic cloves, peeled
1 small carrot, chopped into small cubes
½ courgette, chopped into very small cubes
1½ tsp sea salt
1 tsp roasted sesame seed oil
1 tsp soy sauce
¼ tsp freshly ground black pepper
3 spring onions, finely chopped

Traditionally, this thick and soothing chicken and rice porridge was prepared for people who were ill or in need of simple sustenance. These days it is equally popular with those in the peak of health, such is the allure of its gentle and warming goodness. The key to this dish is boiling up the whole chicken to create a deeply flavoured broth, so don't skip this step in favour of stock cubes as they won't do it justice.

Put the rice in a bowl and cover with water. Soak for 1½ hours.

Place the chicken in a large pan and cover with just enough cold water to barely submerge it. Add the garlic and bring to the boil, then reduce the heat and simmer (remove any scum that forms on the surface with a spoon) for 45 minutes or until the chicken is cooked through (test with a knife inserted into the thickest part). Remove the chicken from the pan and measure out 1 litre of the stock, keeping the cloves of garlic aside. Pour the remaining stock through a sieve, into a bowl, and freeze for later use once cool. Once the chicken is cool enough to handle, tear the meat away from the bones and roughly slice the chicken into strips. Discard the skin and bones.

Drain the rice and put it into a pan with the stock, cooked chicken, carrot, courgette and salt. Bring to the boil, then reduce the heat and simmer for 20–25 minutes until the rice is completely cooked. The mixture should be thick and porridge-like. Stir in the sesame seed oil, soy sauce and pepper, then taste and adjust the seasoning if necessary.

Serve in bowls with the spring onions sprinkled over the top.

Serves 4

Black Sesame Seed Porridge
heukimjajuk

흑 임 자 죽

100g black sesame seeds
200g short-grain white rice, soaked in water for 2 hours or overnight
2½ tbsp honey
1½ tsp sea salt
1 tsp toasted white sesame seeds, to garnish

Pictured overleaf

Here, the aromatic black sesame seeds make this porridge both visually beautiful as well as delicious. It is important to use good-quality fresh black sesame seeds though, as they are a major component to the success of this dish.

Put the black sesame seeds in a dry frying pan over a medium heat and fry them for 2 minutes, stirring all the time. Once they become aromatic remove them from the heat and leave to cool.

Drain the rice and add it to a food processor together with the cooled black sesame seeds. Blitz for 2–3 minutes until they are ground down to a fine powder. Slowly pour in 800ml of water until combined. Pass the mixture through a very fine sieve or a sieve lined with cheesecloth or muslin, into a bowl, squeezing the pulp to extract as much liquid as possible. Discard the pulp.

Pour the strained liquid into a medium-size pan and place over a medium heat, stirring quickly and constantly to prevent lumps from forming for 2–5 minutes. The mixture will become noticeably thicker and porridge-like. Let it come to a gentle boil as you stir, then reduce the heat to low and add the honey and salt. Remove from the heat immediately and serve with the white sesame seeds on top.

Rice & Savoury Porridge

Serves 4

Pumpkin Rice Porridge
hobakjuk

- 800g pumpkin or onion squash or butternut squash
- 200g short-grain white or brown rice, soaked in water for at least 2 hours or overnight
- 2½ tbsp honey
- 1 tsp sea salt
- 2 tsp pine nuts, to serve

Although this dish is called pumpkin porridge in Korea, the vegetable they use is in fact closer to an acorn or onion squash. You can use pumpkin – the delica variety is ideal – and onion or butternut squash work well too.

Rinse the pumpkin, then halve and deseed it. Place it in a large pan and pour in enough water to just cover it. Bring to the boil, then simmer for 25–30 minutes or until a knife easily glides into the flesh. Drain in a colander and stand it in the pan to cool (the residual heat will dry out the pumpkin). Once cool enough to handle, peel off the skin and use a knife to scrape off as much of the flesh as possible. Add this to a food processor and blitz until smooth. Transfer to a bowl and set aside.

Drain the rice and add it to the food processor (there is no need to rinse the food processor). Blitz for 4–5 minutes or until you have a fine powder. Slowly pour in 800ml of water, blitzing until combined. Strain the liquid through a very fine sieve, or a sieve lined with cheesecloth or muslin, into a bowl, squeezing the pulp to extract as much liquid as possible. Discard the pulp. Pour the reserved rice liquid into the puréed pumpkin flesh, whisking until smooth.

Put the mixture into a pan and place over a medium heat, stirring quickly and constantly to prevent lumps from forming. Keep stirring for 3–5 minutes until the mixture becomes noticeably thicker and porridge-like. Let it come to a gentle boil then reduce the heat to low and stir in the honey and salt. Taste and adjust the seasoning if necessary.

Remove from the heat immediately and serve. Do not keep on boiling the porridge after adding in the salt and honey as it becomes thinner in consistency, and you want it to remain thick. Serve sprinkled with a few pine nuts.

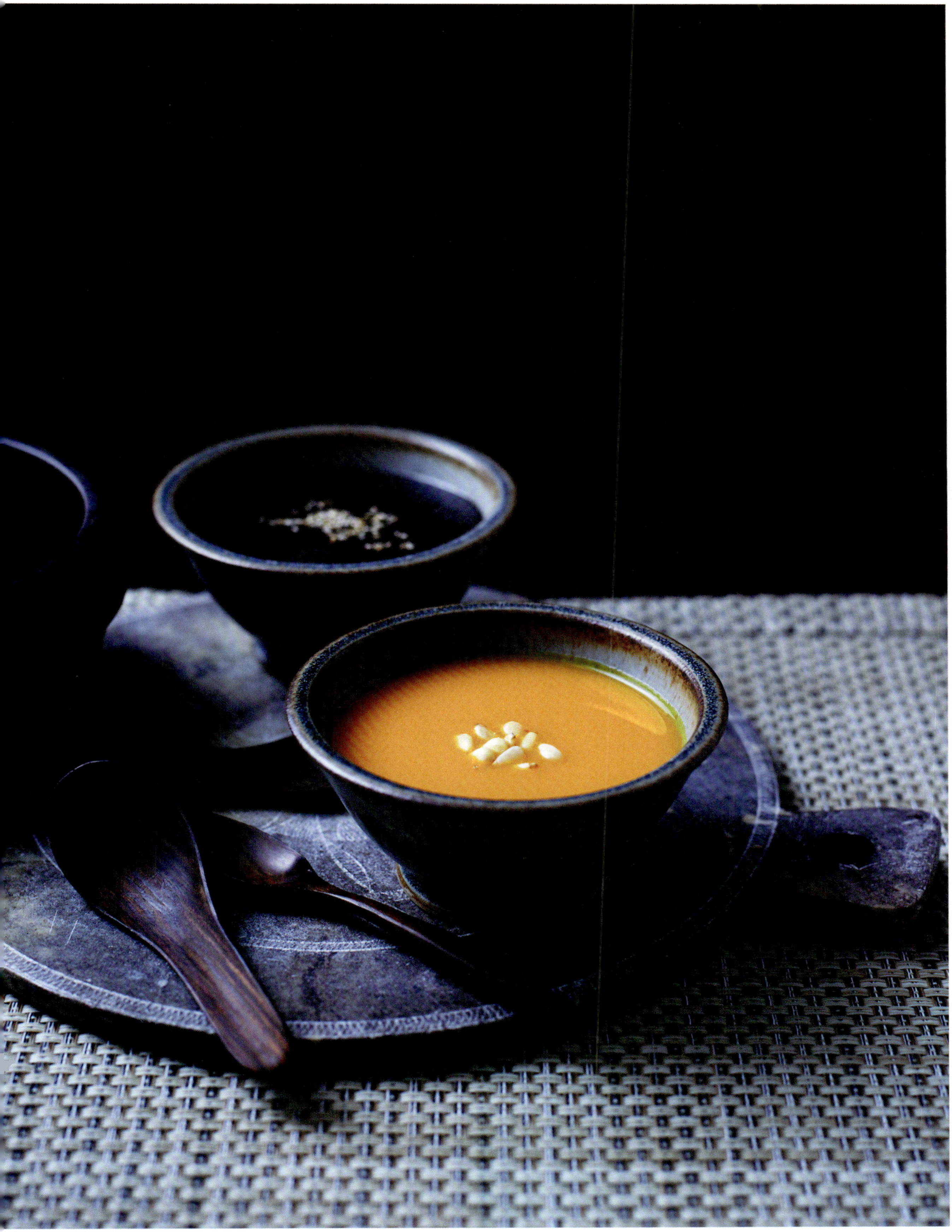

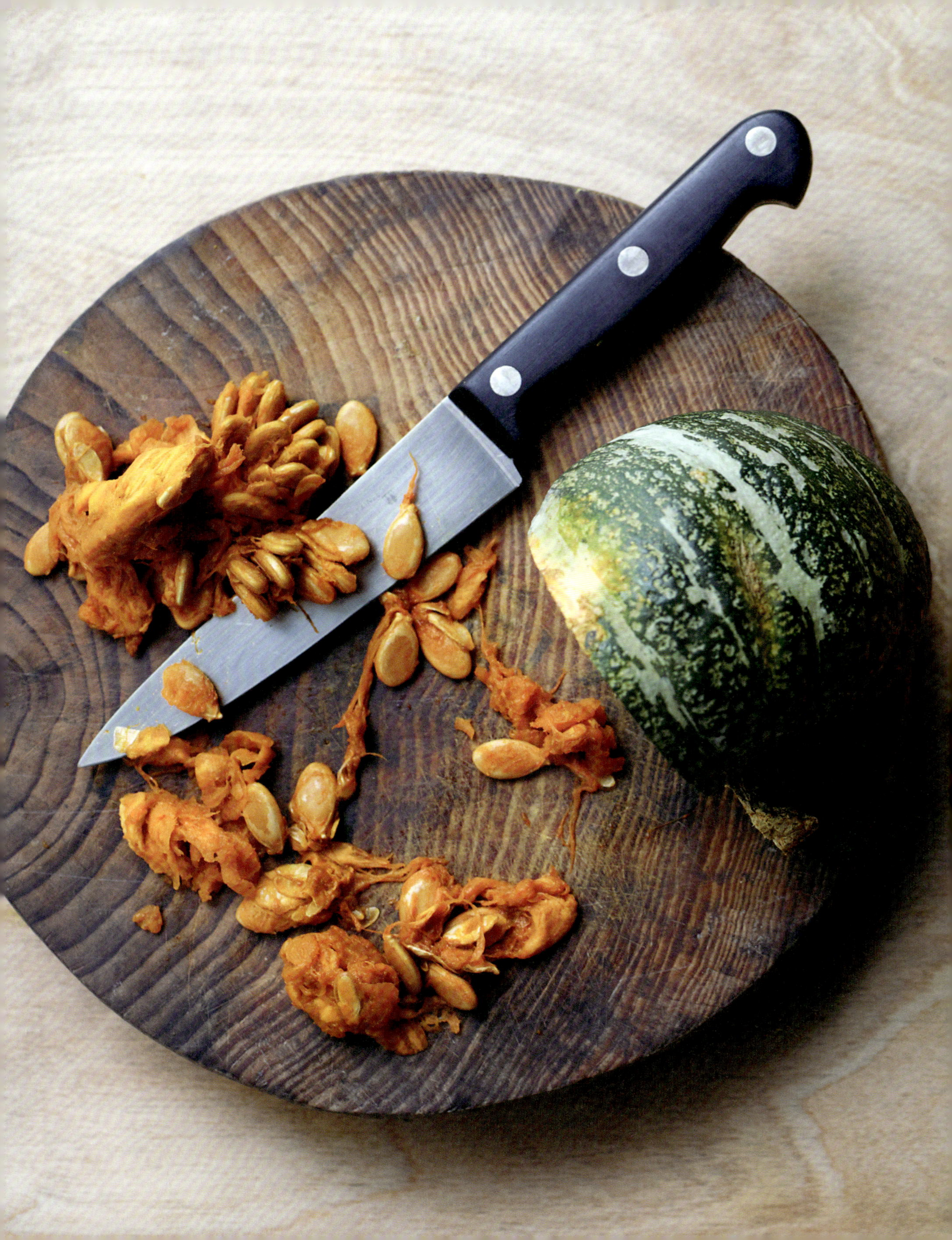

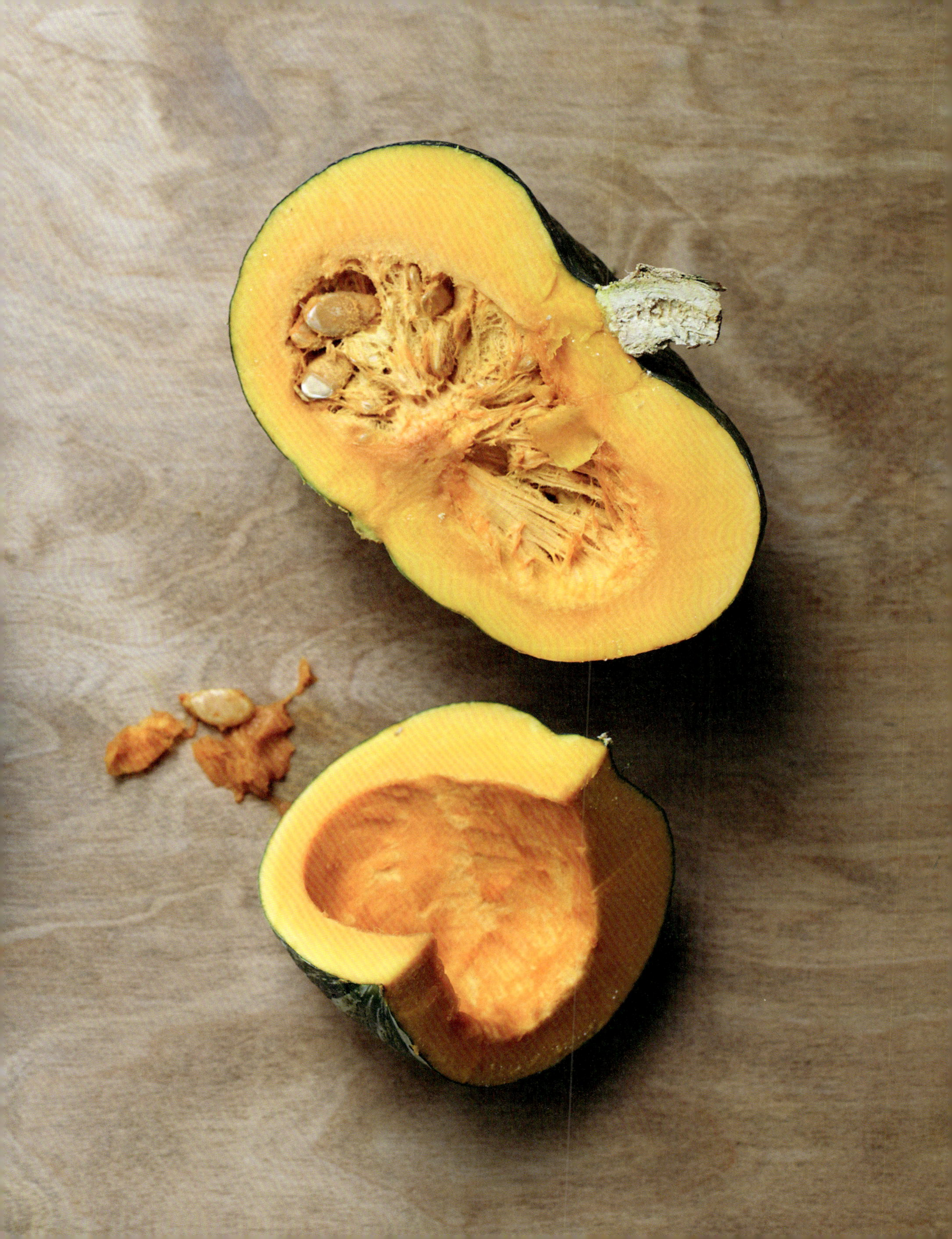

Serves 4

Braised Rice Cakes with Cabbage & Fishcakes
ddeokbokki

3½ tbsp gochujang chilli paste (page 14)
1 tbsp gochugaru red pepper powder (page 14)
2 tbsp honey
2 tsp soy sauce
2 garlic cloves, crushed
4 spring onions, 3 cut into lengths and 1 finely chopped
450g rice cakes (page 14)
200g fishcakes, cut into bite-size pieces (optional)
100g cabbage, chopped
2 hard-boiled eggs, peeled and cut in half
1 tsp toasted sesame seeds, to garnish
sea salt and freshly ground black pepper

Stock (optional)
6 large dried anchovies (page 17)
1 x 8cm piece of dried kelp (dashima, page 16)

Or use 650ml instant dashi or fish stock

Jina adores ddok-boki, especially when consumed standing at a street side stall with a throng of hungry Koreans peering over the enormous vats of steaming rice cakes. The idea of flattened fish and rice cakes swimming around together might not appeal to you at first but give it a try and we promise that you will become an avid fan.

Korean rice cakes are truly unique and perhaps not what you might expect. Squidgy and soft in texture, they are sold either fresh in long cylinders, ready to cut up, or frozen and pre-cut. If you are using frozen rice cakes, submerge them in a bowl of cold water until defrosted, and then continue as per the recipe. This is an easy dish to prepare, and the spice levels can be reduced if you prefer, simply use less gochujang chilli paste and gochugaru red pepper powder. Using homemade stock definitely improves the taste, and all of the ingredients are easy to find in an Asian supermarket but you can also use shop-bought stock.

If making your own stock, pull the heads off the dried anchovies, then gently tease open the underside of the belly and remove the little black pouches (the guts). Put them into a large pan along with the kelp and 800ml of water and bring to the boil. Keep a rolling boil for 5 minutes until the stock has reduced to about 650ml. Strain the stock into a bowl and discard the flavouring ingredients.

Pour the stock into a large pan and add the gochujang paste, gochugaru powder, honey, soy sauce, garlic and the spring onion lengths. Stir to fully combine. Adjust the seasoning to taste.

Add the rice cakes, fish cakes and cabbage, bring to the boil then reduce the heat. Simmer for 6–8 minutes over a medium-low heat until the rice cakes are soft and the sauce has reduced and appears glossy. Serve immediately with the eggs and sprinkle over the remaining chopped spring onion and sesame seeds. Mashing the eggs into the sauce is also advised!

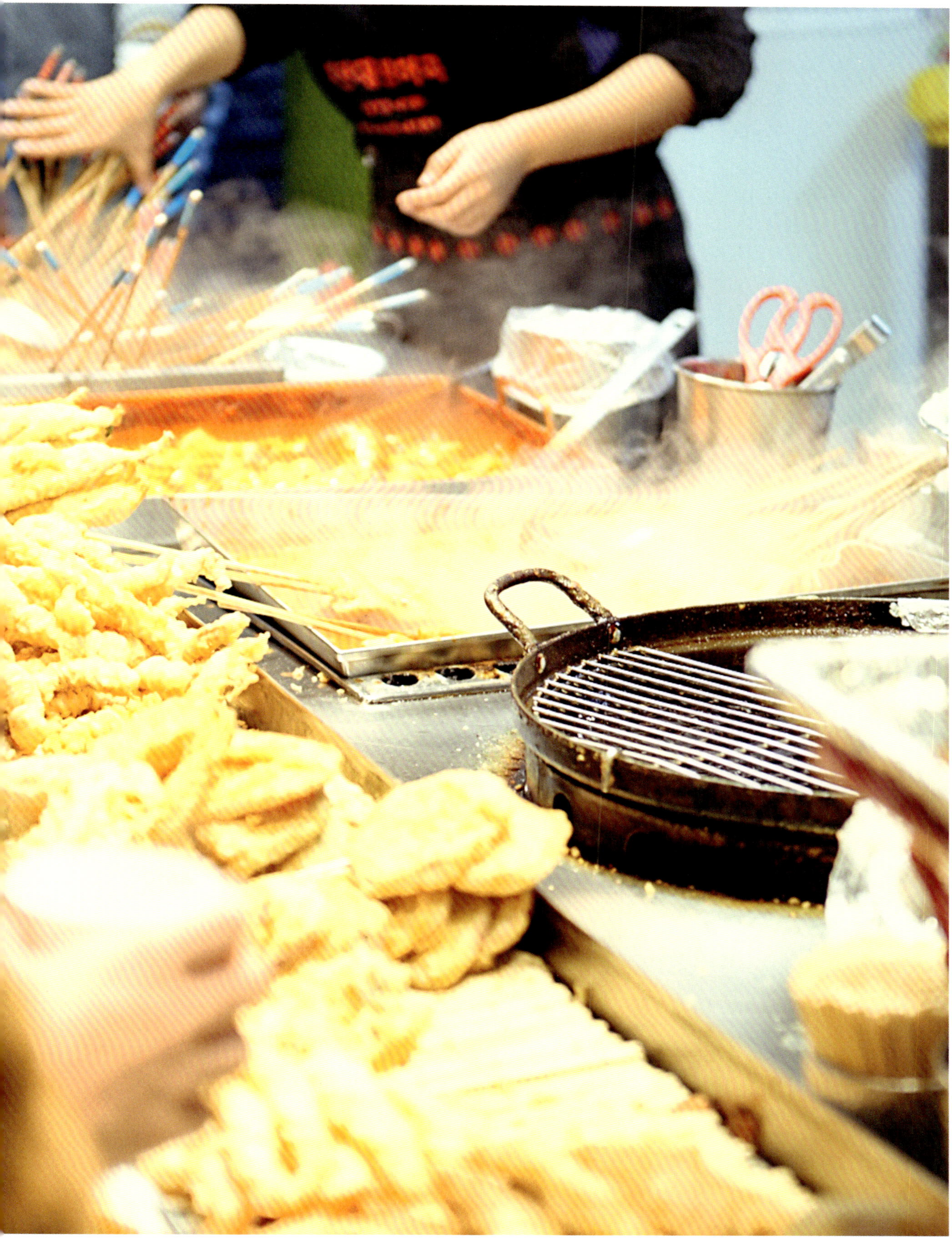

Serves 2–3

Crispy Chilli Rice Cakes
ki-rum ddeokbokki

400g rice cakes (page 14)
3 tbsp vegetable oil, plus extra to drizzle
4 spring onions, finely chopped, to serve
1 tsp black sesame seeds, to garnish

<u>Sauce</u>
2 tbsp gochugaru red pepper powder (page 14)
1 tsp gochujang chilli paste (Page 14)
1 tbsp soy sauce
2 tsp maple syrup or honey
2 tsp roasted sesame seed oil

Pictured overleaf

Crispy on the outside and gloriously chewy on the inside, these lip-smacking, subtly-spiced rice cakes are seriously addictive.

In a large bowl combine the gochugaru, gochujang, soy sauce, maple syrup and sesame seed oil.

Bring a large pan of water to the boil. Add in the rice cakes and return to the boil for 2–3 minutes or until the rice cakes float to the surface of the water. Drain and transfer the rice cakes to a large flat tray. Spread the rice cakes out into a single layer, separating them from one another to prevent them sticking. Drizzle over a little vegetable oil and turn to coat them.

In a large frying pan, heat the vegetable oil over a high heat. When hot, add the rice cakes, in batches, and fry for 3–4 minutes, turning every now and again until crispy. Use a slotted spoon to remove the rice cakes from the pan and add them to the sauce. Thoroughly toss everything together until evenly coated. Plate up with the spring onions and black sesame seeds sprinkled over the top.

Serves 2–3

Crispy Soy Rice Cakes
ki-rum ganjang ddeokbokki

2 tbsp soy sauce
1 tbsp maple syrup or honey
1 tbsp roasted sesame seed oil
1 tbsp mirin
400g rice cakes (page 14)
3 tbsp vegetable oil, plus extra to drizzle
4 spring onions, finely chopped, to serve
1 tsp black sesame seeds, to garnish

Pictured overleaf

These non-spicy, crispy rice cakes are just as delicious as their more fiery cousins, and are really good with some crunchy Classic Cabbage Kimchi (page 98).

In a large bowl, combine the soy sauce, maple syrup, sesame seed oil and mirin.

Bring a large pan of water to the boil. Add in the rice cakes and return to the boil for 2–3 minutes or until the rice cakes float to the surface of the water. Drain and transfer the rice cakes to a large flat tray. Spread the rice cakes out into a single layer, separating them from one another to prevent them sticking. Drizzle over a little vegetable oil and turn to coat them.

In a large frying pan, heat the vegetable oil over a high heat. When hot, add the rice cakes, in batches, and fry for 3–4 minutes, turning every now and again until crispy. Use a slotted spoon to remove the rice cakes from the pan and add them to the soy sauce mixture. Thoroughly toss everything together until evenly coated. Plate up with the spring onions and black sesame seeds sprinkled over.

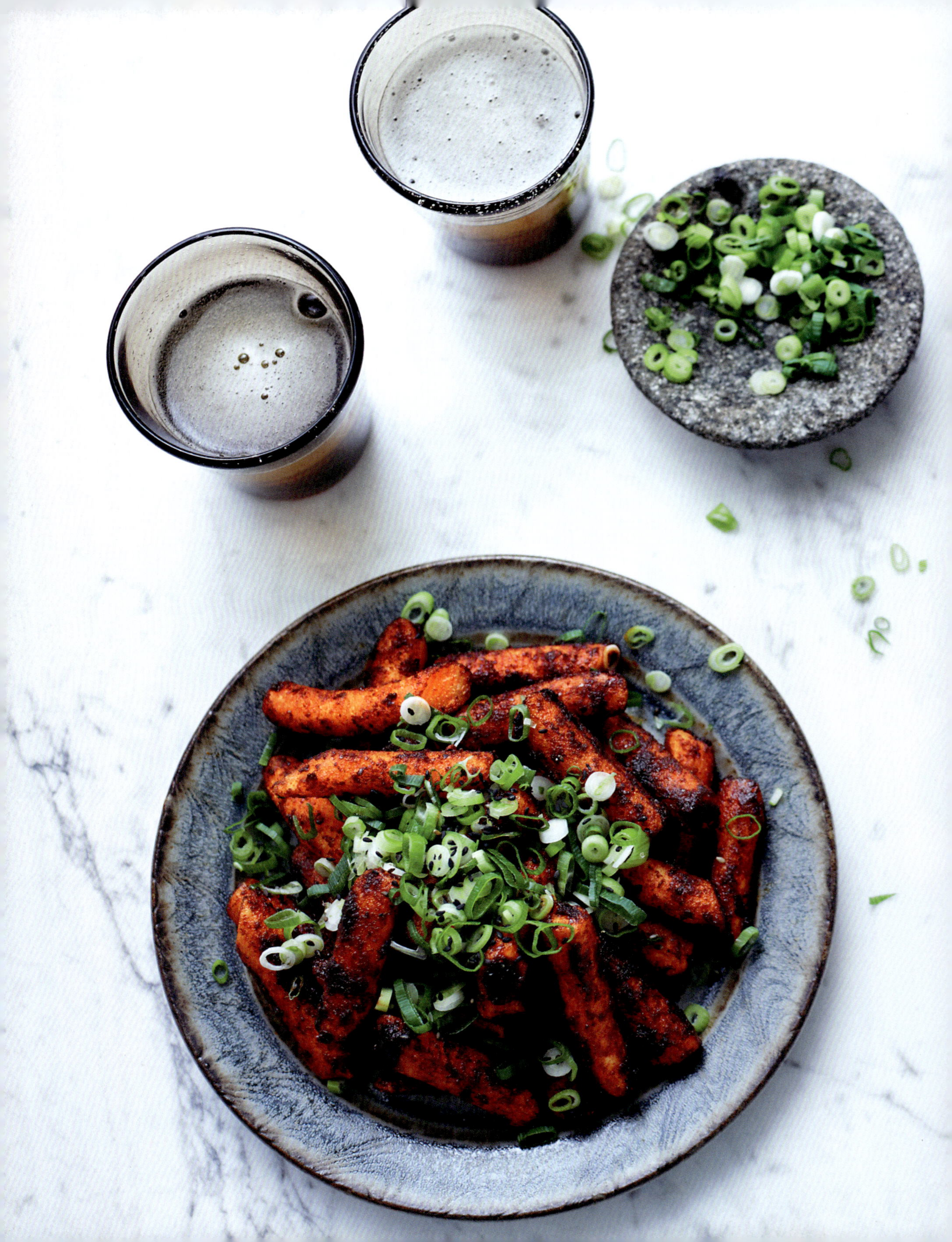

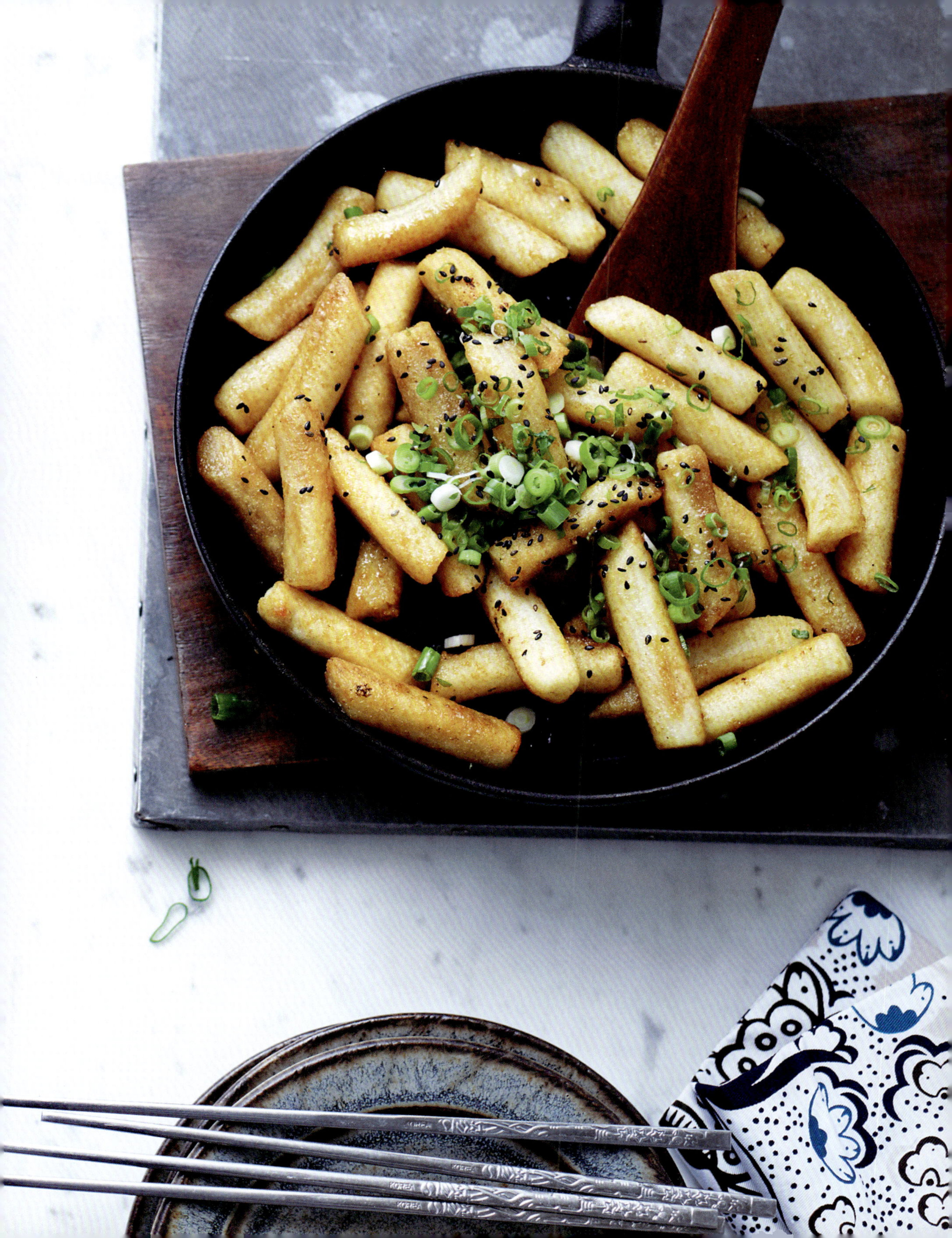

Soups & Stews

국, 찌개 & 탕

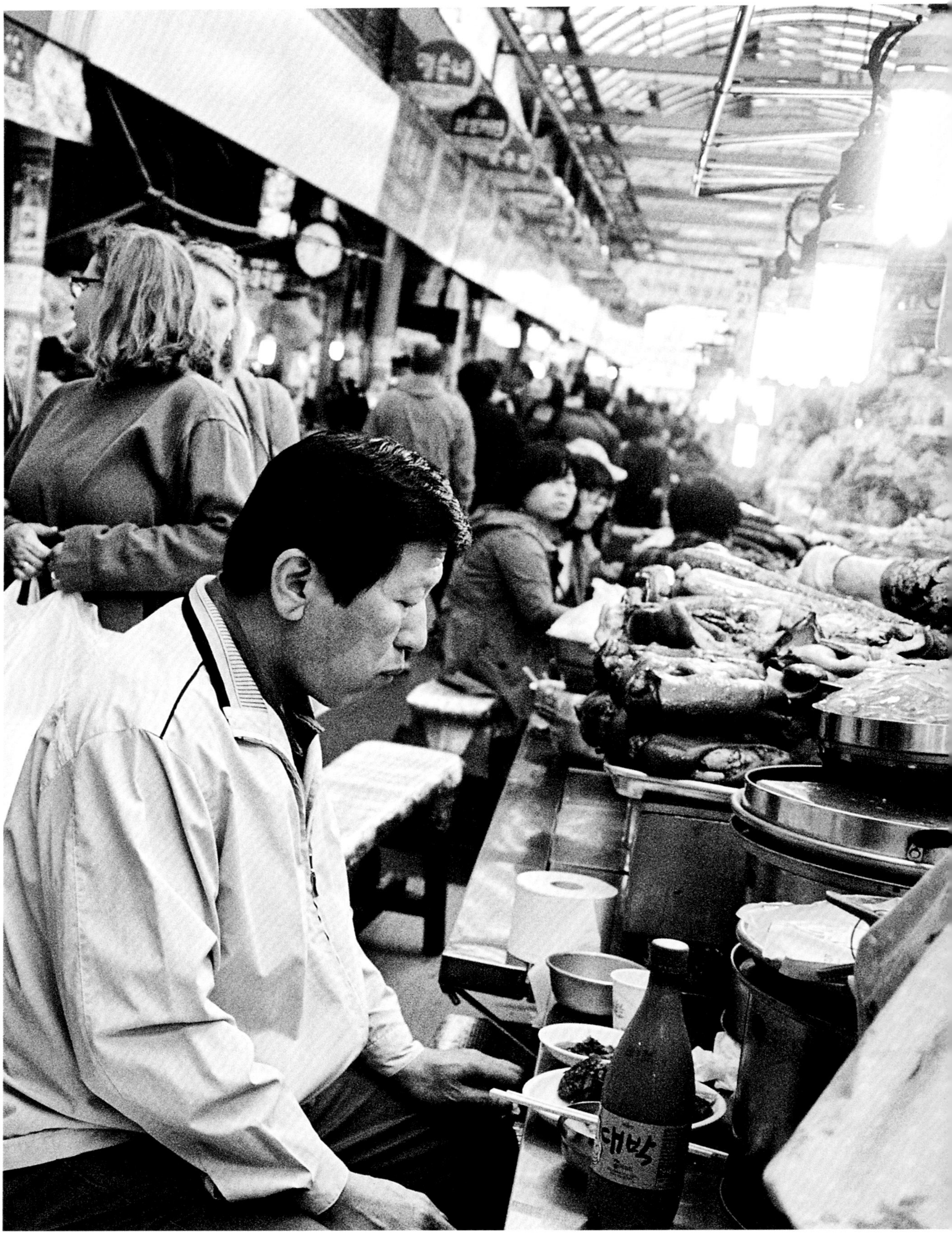
대박

02

58. **Fishcake Soup**
    어묵국

61. **Clear Clam Broth**
    조개탕

62. **Chicken Dumpling Soup**
    떡만두국

64. **Baby Chicken Soup**
    삼계탕

68. **Seaweed & Beef Soup**
    미역국

69. **Beef Rib Soup**
    갈비탕

70. **Bean Sprout Soup**
    콩나물국

72. **Spicy Beef & Vegetable Stew**
    육개장

76. **Warming Chicken & Potato Stew**
    닭도리탕

78. **Marinated Beef & Vegetable Stew**
    불고기 전골

81. *Tofu*

82. **Tofu & Soybean Paste Soup**
    된장찌개

85. **Seafood & Silken Tofu Stew**
    순두부찌개

86. **Kimchi Stew**
    김치찌개

88. **Chilled Cucumber Soup**
    오이 냉국

90. **Chilled Tofu, Cucumber & Kimchi Broth**
    묵사발

Soups & Stews 57

Serves 4

Fishcake Soup
aw-muk guk

<u>Broth</u>
12 large dried anchovies (page 17)
200g daikon radish, peeled and cut into slices
¼ onion, chopped
1 x 13cm piece of dried kelp (dashima, page 16)
1 red chilli, halved lengthways and seeds removed (optional)
2 spring onions, finely chopped
1 tbsp soy sauce
4 flat fishcakes
24 fish balls
sea salt

<u>Dipping sauce</u>
2 tbsp soy sauce
1 tsp wasabi paste
½ tsp toasted sesame seeds

One of our favourite memories of this dish was from a bar owned by a friend of Jina's where it is served as ahn-joo, which is essentially food that accompanies alcoholic drinks in a bid to keep you sober for longer. We're not quite sure how well that theory works though, as Jina's friend still managed to have us paralytic by the end of the night, despite plying us with food! Korean fishcakes are made by blitzing together a variety of fish with garlic, seasoning, egg and flour and then shaping the mixture into balls or flat sheets. When buying, look out for brands with a high content of fish as they are usually the best quality.

In a bowl, combine the dipping sauce ingredients and set aside.

Make the broth. Tear the heads off the dried anchovies, then use a small, sharp knife to gently tease open the underside of the belly and remove the little black pouches. Place them in a pan over a high heat and stir-fry for 2 minutes. Add them to a large pan along with 2 litres of water, cover with a lid and bring to a rolling boil for 10 minutes.

Use a slotted spoon to remove the anchovies from the broth and discard. Add the radish, onion, kelp and chilli, if using, to the broth. Cover and simmer for 10 minutes.

Strain the broth through a sieve, into a bowl, and discard the flavouring ingredients but reserve the radish. Return the radish to the same pan with the strained stock, the spring onions and soy sauce.

Prepare the flat fishcakes. Soak them in a bowl of just-boiled water for about 15 seconds, just until soft and pliable. Fold them twice, lengthways, as you would an A4 letter – you should have 3 layers. Take 1 folded fishcake and thread it onto a wooden skewer (see photo opposite). Repeat with the remaining fishcakes. For the fish balls, simply thread 3 balls onto each skewer. Add the fish skewers to the pan and bring to the boil, then immediately turn off the heat, otherwise the fishcakes will loose their shape and fall apart. Taste and season with a little salt if necessary. Serve immediately with a couple of fish skewers in each bowl and the dipping sauce on the side.

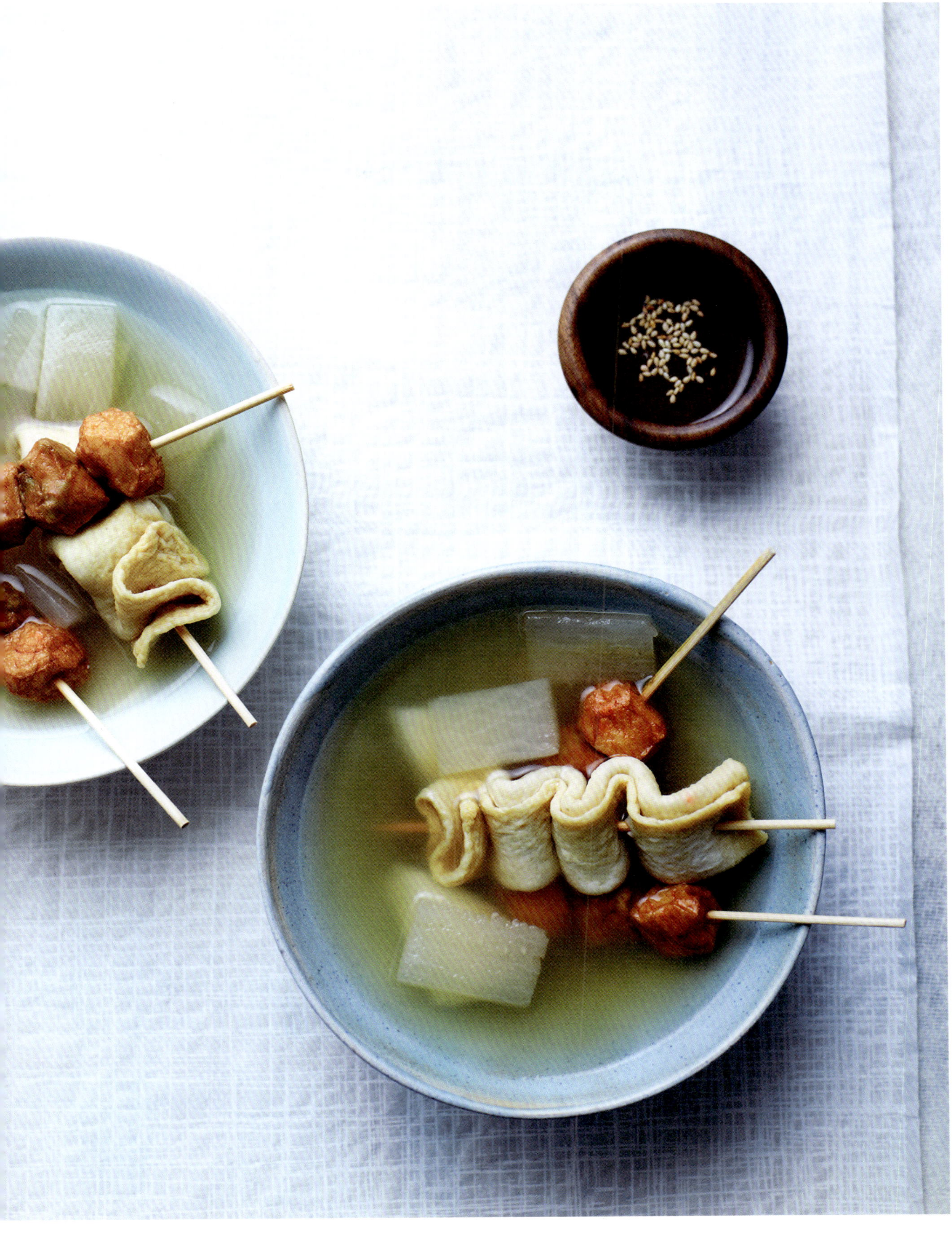

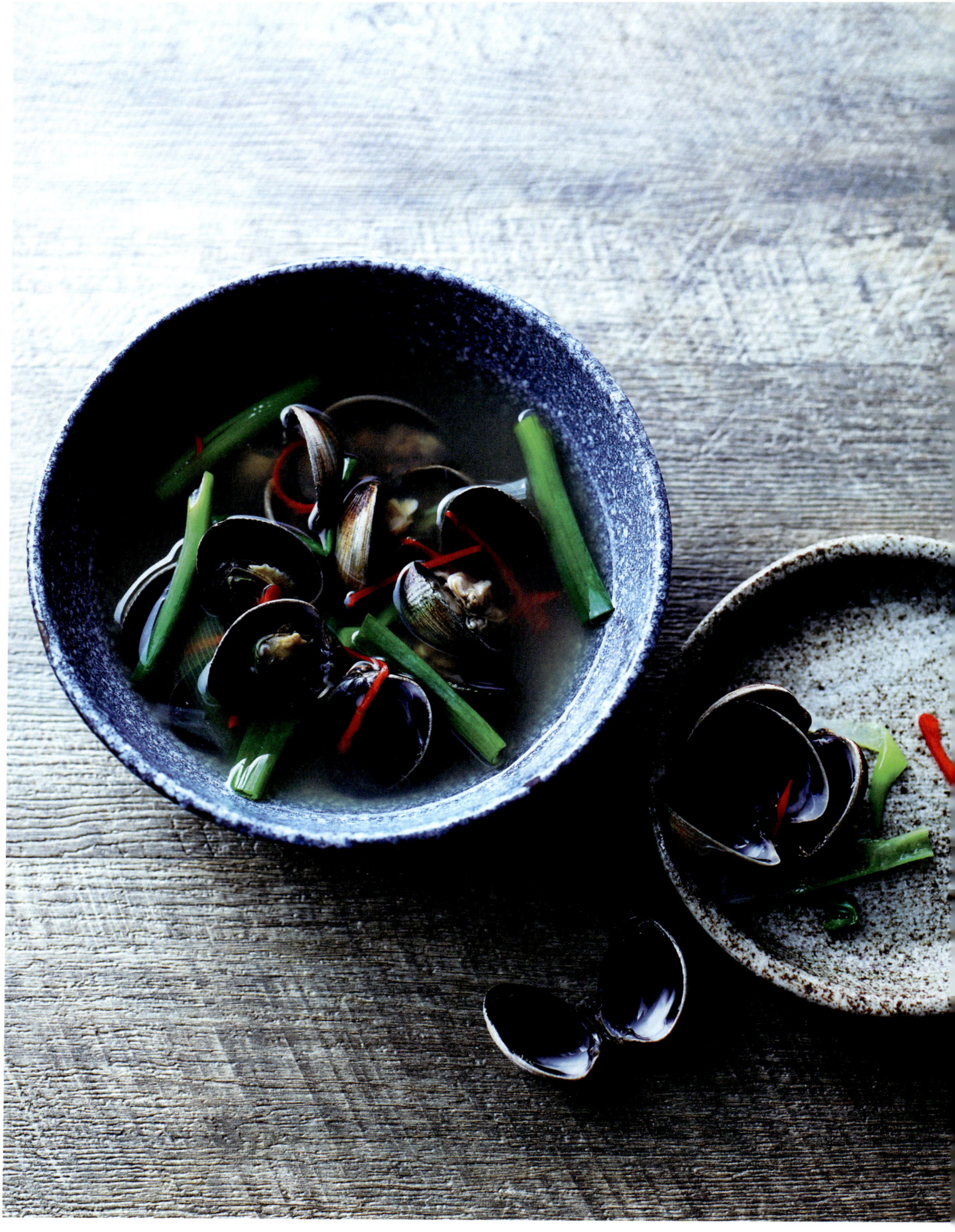

Serves 4

Clear Clam Broth
jogae-tang

조개탕

300g clams
2 spring onions, halved lengthways and cut into lengths
2 garlic cloves, crushed
2 tsp doen-jang soybean paste or miso paste (page 14)
1 red chilli, halved lengthways, seeds removed and thinly sliced into strips
sea salt
cooked rice, to serve

This is a gentle, soothing soup – and it takes no time at all to make. The doen-jang soybean paste gives it a great depth of flavour, but you can leave it out if you want a really clean-tasting soup.

Scrub the clams under cold running water to remove any dirt and sand. Discard any that remain open when given a firm tap.

Place the clams in a pan with 1.2 litres of water, cover and bring to the boil. Remove any scum that appears at the surface of the water, then reduce the heat and simmer for 5 minutes, or until the clams open. Add in the spring onions, garlic, soybean paste and the chilli. Taste and season with salt, bearing in mind the saltiness of the clams and soybean paste. When ready to serve, return to the boil briefly, remove from the heat and serve immediately with some rice on the side.

Chicken Dumpling Soup
ddeok mandu guk

Serves 6–8

- 2 litres homemade or good-quality shop-bought chicken stock
- 2 garlic cloves, crushed
- 2 tbsp soy sauce
- 1 tbsp roasted sesame seed oil
- ¼ tsp salt
- 24 dumplings, homemade (page 232, using chicken instead of pork) or shop-bought
- 200g fresh or frozen rice cake slices (optional) (page 14)
- 3 spring onions, diagonally sliced
- 2 eggs, lightly beaten
- 1 tsp toasted sesame seeds, to serve
- 1 piece of roasted crispy seaweed, shredded (optional), to serve

Korean dumplings differ to most other Asian dumplings in that they include cabbage and tofu, as well as meat. Kimchi and glass noodles (dang-myeon) are also common additions. You can of course use store-bought frozen dumplings, but if you have the time, homemade dumplings are really worth making.

This dish is always eaten on the first day of the Korean lunar New Year. It is made with a clear beef stock, but we also like it as it is done here with chicken stock flavoured with garlic and soy sauce. You could of course use beef stock if you wish. Traditionally flat rice cakes are used but the cylindrical shapes also work well.

In a large pan, bring the stock, garlic, soy sauce, sesame seed oil and salt to the boil. If you are using stock that has already been salted, reduce the salt and soy sauce to taste.

Add the dumplings, rice cakes, if using, and spring onions, bring back to a rolling boil, then reduce the heat a little and simmer for 8–10 minutes until the dumplings are cooked through and begin to float on the surface of the broth and the rice cakes are soft. Pour in the beaten egg and stir until cooked through.

Taste the broth and adjust the seasoning if necessary. Spoon about 4 dumplings into each bowl, cover with the broth and sprinkle over some sesame seeds and shredded crispy seaweed, if using. Serve immediately.

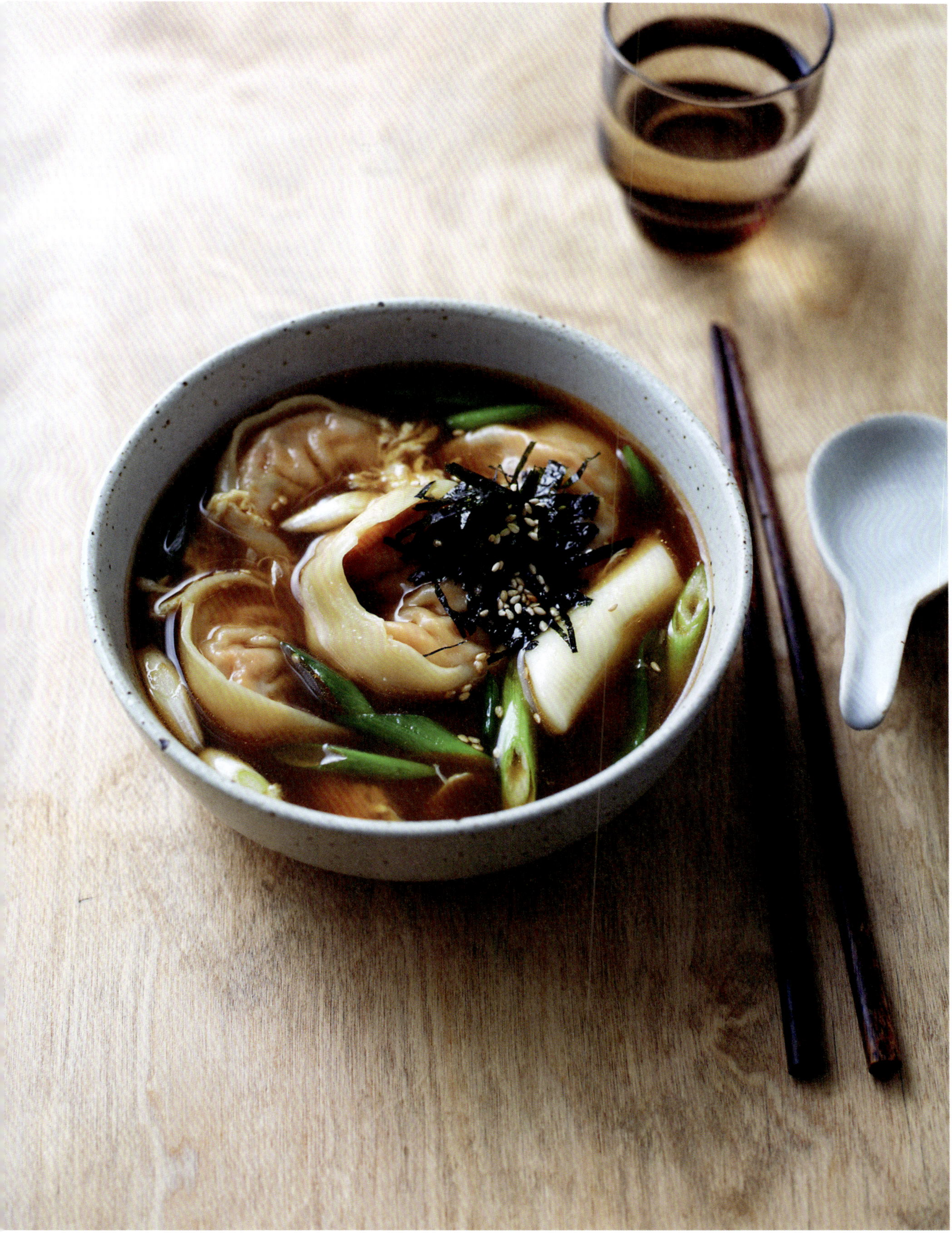

Baby Chicken Soup
samgyetang

Serves 2 as a starter, or 1 as a main course

2 tsp sea salt, plus extra to season
1 tsp freshly ground black pepper
1 x 450g baby chicken or poussin
80g glutinous rice or short-grain white rice, soaked in water for at least 2 hours or overnight
8 garlic cloves, peeled
1 ginseng root (optional)
3 Korean jujube red dates (optional)
3 spring onions, finely sliced
radish kimchi (page 102), or shop-bought, to serve (optional)

Warm and soothing, this simple chicken soup seems the perfect option for a winter meal. However, in Korea it is traditionally eaten during the hottest period of the summer months. Koreans adore eating certain foods for their perceived health benefits, and they will inform you with the greatest zeal the merits of eating said food. In this case, it is believed that nutrients lost through sweat are replaced by those present in the soup. Whether you fall in line with this theory or not is irrelevant really, as the dish is so good you will want to eat it regardless.

Traditionally, this soup is cooked with ginseng and Korean jujube red dates (page 16). Both ingredients add another layer of flavour and are widely available in Asian supermarkets but the soup is equally delicious without them.

In a small dish, combine 1 teaspoon of the salt and the pepper and set the mixture aside.

Season the chicken with a little sea salt. Drain the rice from the soaking water and stuff it into the cavity of the chicken along with 3 of the garlic cloves and the ginseng root, if using. You might not get all the rice into the cavity – set any remaining rice aside. Use a sharp knife to make 2 small incisions on either side of the cavity opening, then cross each leg over and insert it into the incision on the opposite side – this will keep the rice secure inside the cavity. Alternatively, tie the legs together with kitchen string.

Place the chicken in a heavy-based, 20cm wide pan with the remaining garlic cloves and any remaining rice. Cover with about 1.6 litres of water (or just enough to cover), pop the lid on and bring to the boil. Add the dates, if using, reduce the heat to low and simmer for about 1 hour until the soup has a light milky appearance and the chicken is cooked through. Season the broth with the remaining teaspoon of salt to taste.

Transfer the chicken and garlic to a large serving bowl and pour in most of the liquid, to almost cover the bird. Heap the sliced spring onions on top and serve immediately with the salt and pepper mix on the side. To eat, tear the chicken off the bone and eat it by the spoon with the rice and broth, very lightly dipping pieces of the chicken into the salt and pepper mix to taste. Radish kimchi is a very common accompaniment in Korea, and works really well with this otherwise mild dish.

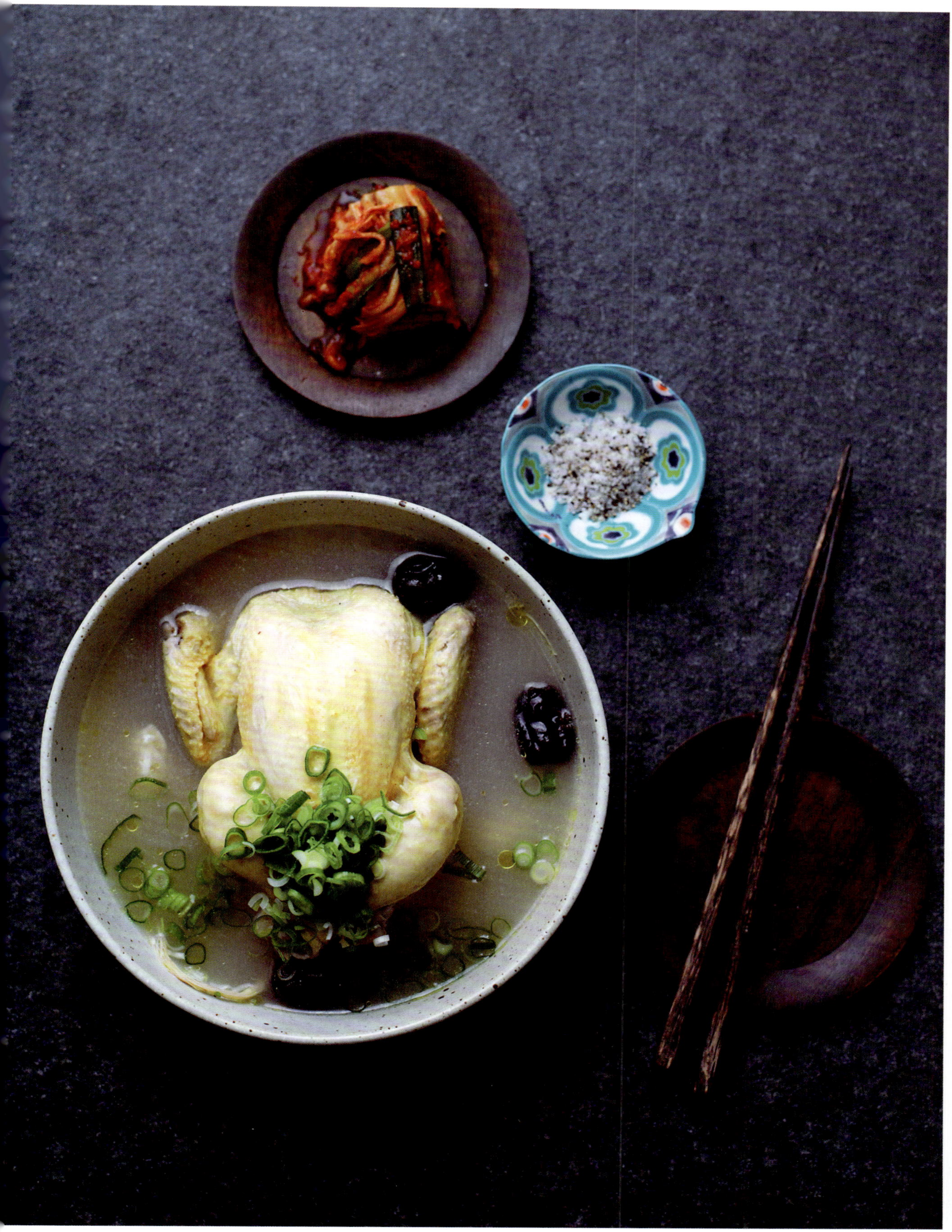

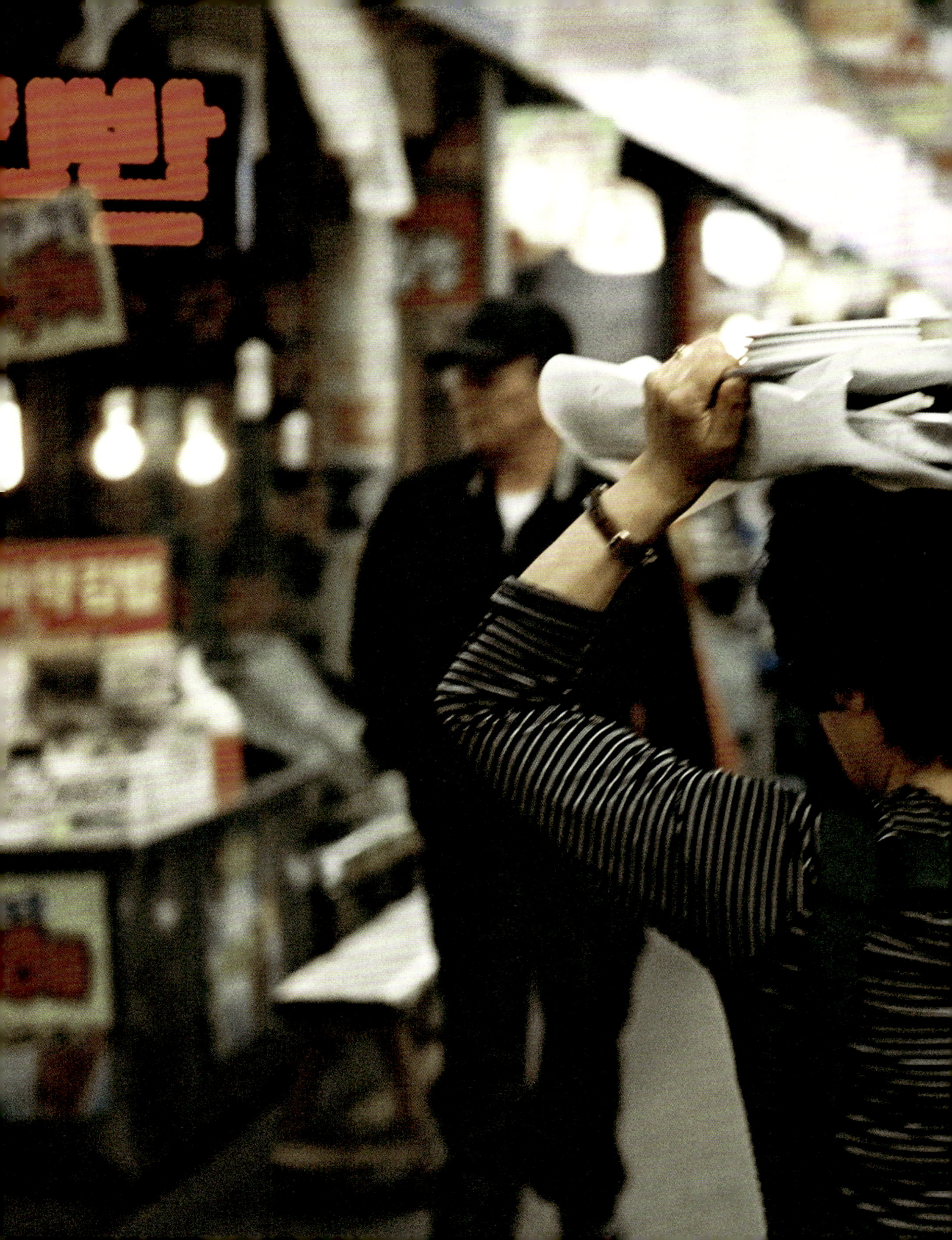

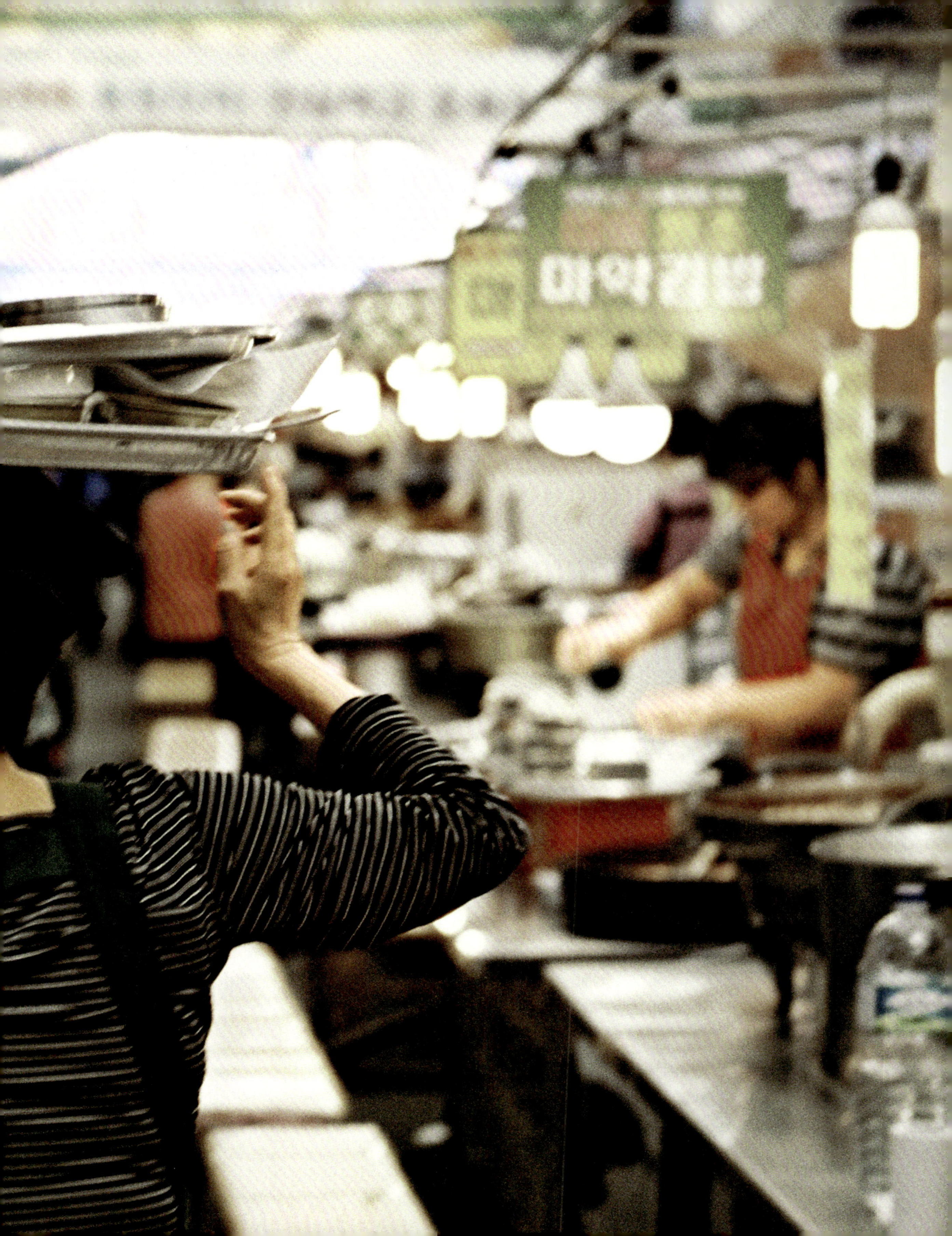

Serves 4

Seaweed & Beef Soup
miyok-guk

10g wakame dried kelp (page 16)
1 tbsp vegetable oil
100g beef sirloin, thinly sliced
3 garlic cloves, crushed
4 spring onions, finely chopped
1½ tbsp soy sauce
1½ tbsp roasted sesame seed oil
1.4 litres homemade (page 19) or shop-bought beef stock
sea salt and freshly ground black pepper

This soup is traditionally served for birthdays in Korea and it might come as a shock that this dish is a favourite among Korean children. We are fairly certain that if you told a Western child they were having seaweed and beef soup for their birthday they would become hysterical! This soup is delicious and comforting so it's easy to understand its unwavering popularity. However, it also explains the Korean mindset and attitude towards food and why they consistently rank highly in studies of the healthiest countries in the world.

In a bowl, soak the dried kelp in plenty of tepid water for 10 minutes to rehydrate it.

Add the oil to a large heavy-based pan and place it over a medium-high heat. Add the beef and cook until it begins to brown. Stir in the garlic, most of the spring onions, leaving a little for the garnish, and fry for another minute being careful not to burn the garlic.

Drain the kelp and chop it into bite-size pieces, then add it to the pan together with the soy sauce, sesame seed oil and stock. Bring everything to the boil, reduce the heat and simmer for 10 minutes. Season with salt and pepper to taste. Serve in bowls with the remaining spring onions scattered over the top.

Serves 4

Beef Rib Soup
kalbi tang

800g beef short ribs
350g daikon radish, peeled and cut into bite-size slices
1 onion, quartered
2.5cm piece of ginger
6 garlic cloves, crushed
80g sweet potato glass noodles (page 13) or rice noodles
1 tsp sea salt
¼ tsp freshly ground black pepper
2 spring onions, finely chopped

<u>Optional:</u>
<u>For a slightly richer broth</u>
3 tbsp soy sauce
1 tsp roasted sesame seed oil
1 tsp toasted sesame seeds
1 tsp gochugaru red pepper powder (page 14)

This slow-cooked beef rib soup is the kind of dish you would hanker for after a long windswept walk in the depths of winter. Warm and comforting it brings you back to life. It does take a few hours to cook, but most of this time it is just simmering away on the stove, so you can carry on with something else. We have included a plain broth and a slightly richer version, so you can make whichever one you prefer. The latter is our personal favourite.

Ask your butcher to cut the ribs through the bone into 5cm chunks or buy them pre-cut in the freezer section of Korean supermarkets and ask for the galbi jjim cut of meat.

Soak the ribs in cold water for 1–2 hours to draw out any blood and impurities, refreshing the water every now and again. Fill a large pan of water and bring to the boil, add the ribs and bring back to a rolling boil, then use a pair of tongs to remove the ribs and then refresh them in cold water. Discard the boiling water and rinse out the pan.

Place the ribs back in the same pan and cover them with fresh water. Bring them to the boil, then reduce the heat and simmer for 2 hours, uncovered. Top up periodically with just enough water to submerge the ribs.

Add the radish to the pan together with the onion, ginger and garlic. Continue to simmer for a further hour, using a spoon to remove any scum that rises to the surface, and topping up with extra water as needed. Remove the ginger and onion, then add the noodles and simmer for 10 minutes or until the noodles are soft. (There is no need to top up with water at this point.) If you are having the plain version, season with the salt, pepper and spring onions, combine and serve immediately.

Alternatively, if making the richer broth, don't add the salt and pepper and instead season with the soy sauce, sesame seed oil, sesame seeds, gochugaru powder and the spring onions. Stir to combine and serve immediately.

Serves 4

Bean Sprout Soup
kongnamul guk

1 litre chicken, fish or vegetable stock
5 x 7cm pieces of dried kelp (dashima, page 16)
1 onion, quartered
3 garlic cloves, crushed
350g bean sprouts
1½ tbsp soy sauce
2 spring onions, finely chopped
1 tsp roasted sesame seed oil
1 tsp toasted sesame seeds, to serve
1 red chilli, seeds removed and finely sliced on the diagonal, to serve (optional)
cooked rice, to serve

This is a very simple, delicate soup, which probably explains why Koreans most often eat it following a particularly heavy night out, when they themselves are feeling a little delicate! If your stock is already salted, reduce the quantity of soy sauce to taste. Koreans rarely eat soup on its own so pair it with rice, Classic Cabbage Kimchi (page 98) and Seasoned Lotus Root (page 112).

In a large pan, pour in the stock and add the kelp, onion and garlic. Put the lid on and bring to the boil for 15 minutes. Use a slotted spoon to remove the kelp and onion then add the bean sprouts, soy sauce, spring onions and sesame seed oil. Stir and simmer for a further 10 minutes, until the sprouts are tender.

Serve in bowls with the sesame seeds and, if using, chilli scattered over the top with some rice on the side.

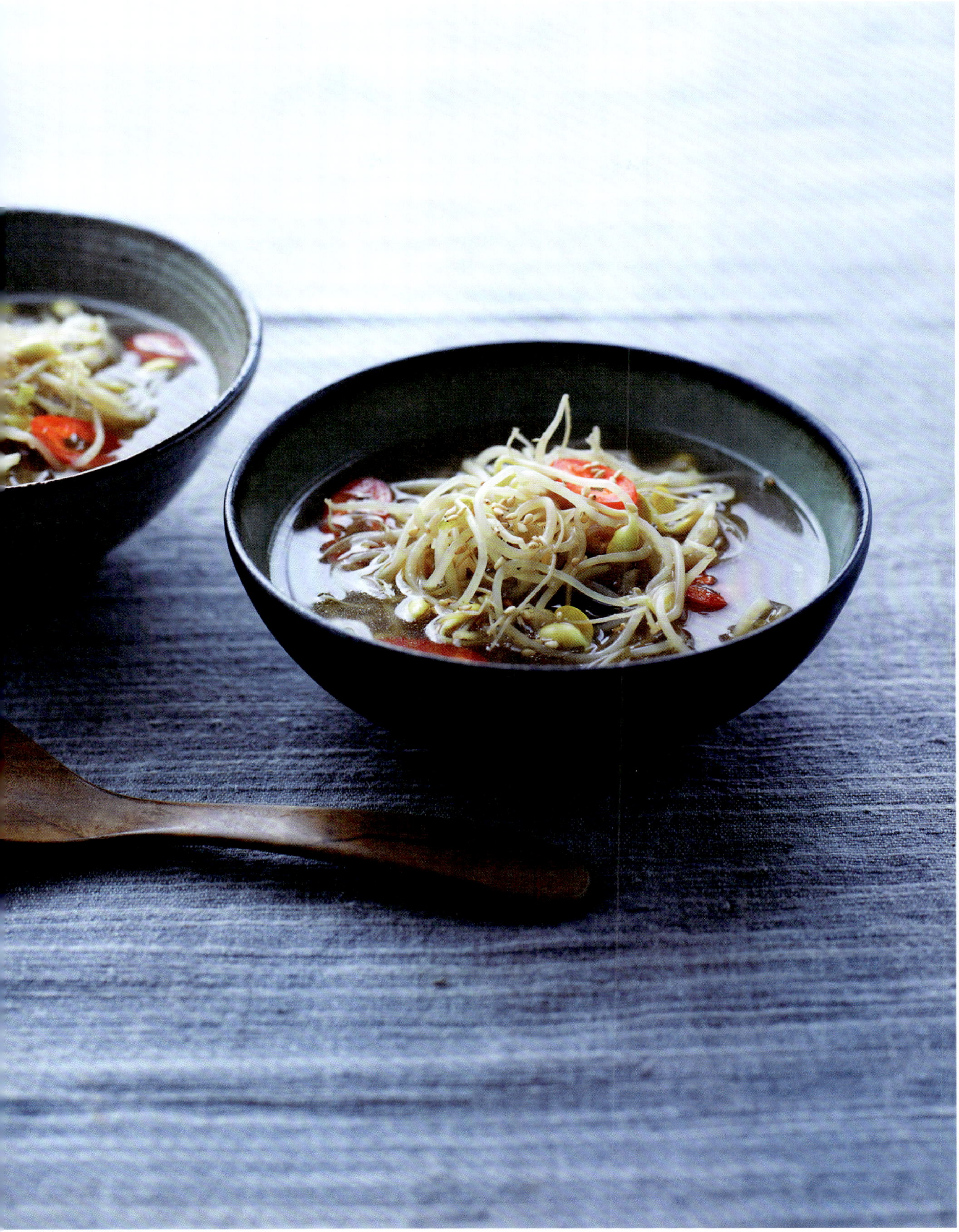

Serves 4

Spicy Beef & Vegetable Stew
yuk gaejang

400g beef brisket
1 onion, quartered
10 garlic cloves, 6 left whole and 4 crushed
1 tbsp vegetable oil
150g shiitake mushrooms, sliced
1 leek, halved and thinly sliced
2 tbsp soy sauce
2 tbsp roasted sesame seed oil
3 tbsp gochugaru red pepper powder (page 14)
1½ tsp sea salt
10 spring onions, halved lengthways then cut into 6cm long strips
cooked rice, to serve (optional)

Like many Korean soups and stews, they take some time to cook, but it is relatively hands off. We like to cook this dish on a weekend morning, as we can get on with other things while it simmers away, and by lunchtime it is ready to go. This is a medium spicy stew, so you can adjust the spice level to your taste by adding or taking away a teaspoon or two of the gochugaru red pepper powder.

Place the brisket in a medium pan and cover with 3 litres of water. Bring to the boil, reduce the heat a little, add the onion and 6 whole garlic cloves and simmer for 2 hours with the lid off, using a spoon to remove any scum that rises to the surface. Top up with water while cooking to ensure that the meat is submerged.

Transfer the brisket to a plate and set aside to cool. Strain the stock through a fine sieve, into a bowl or jug, and discard the flavouring ingredients. When the brisket is cool enough to handle, slice or tear the meat into thin bite-size strips, discarding any fat.

In the same pan, heat the vegetable oil over a medium heat, add the mushrooms and leek and sauté for 5 minutes. Add the beef along with the soy sauce, crushed garlic, sesame seed oil and gochugaru powder. Turn up the heat and fry for 1–2 minutes until aromatic. Pour 1.3 litres of the strained stock back into the pan and freeze the rest for future use. Add the salt and bring to the boil, then reduce the heat a little and add the spring onions. Simmer for 3 minutes, until all the flavours have come together.

Serve up in bowls with rice alongside if you like.

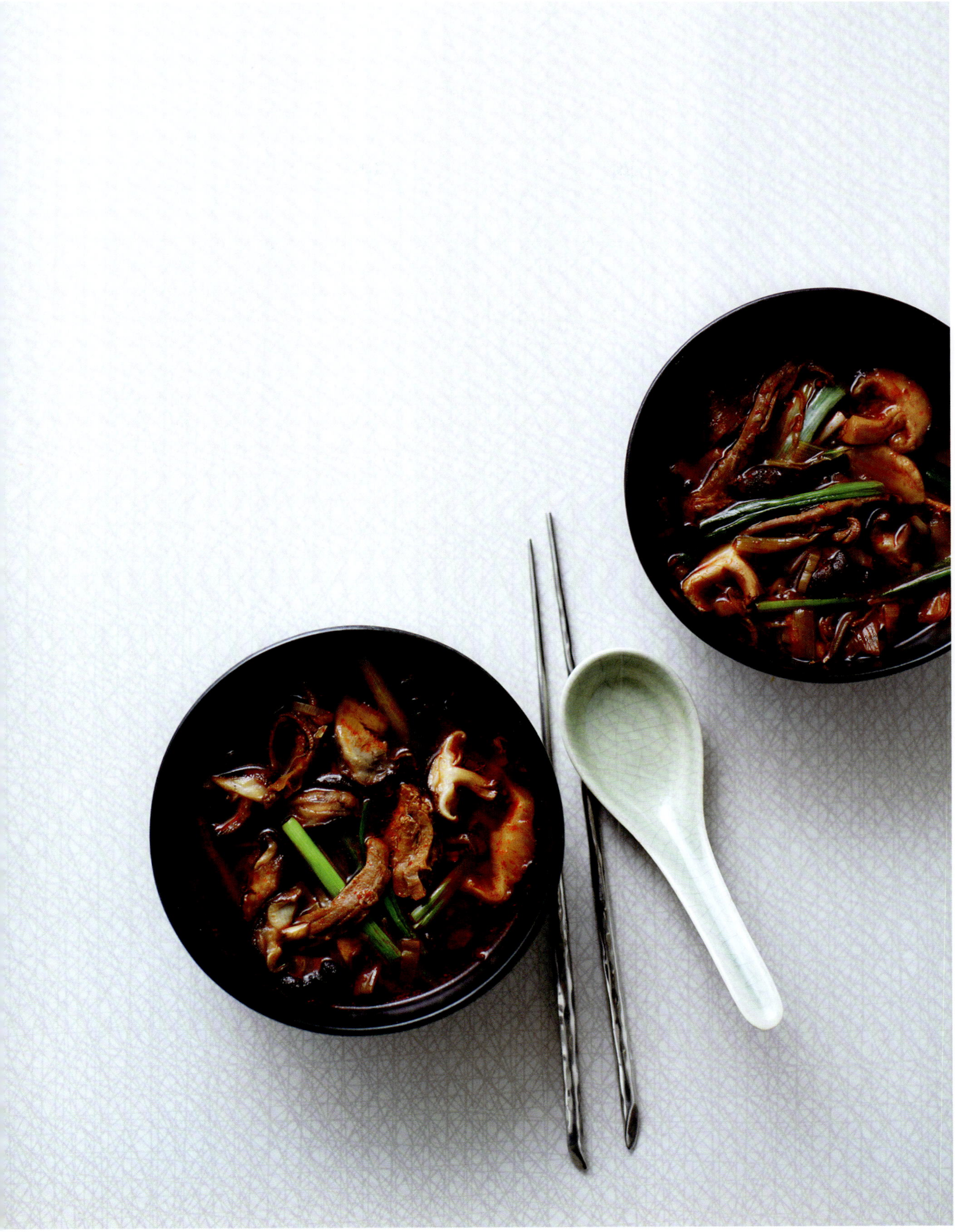

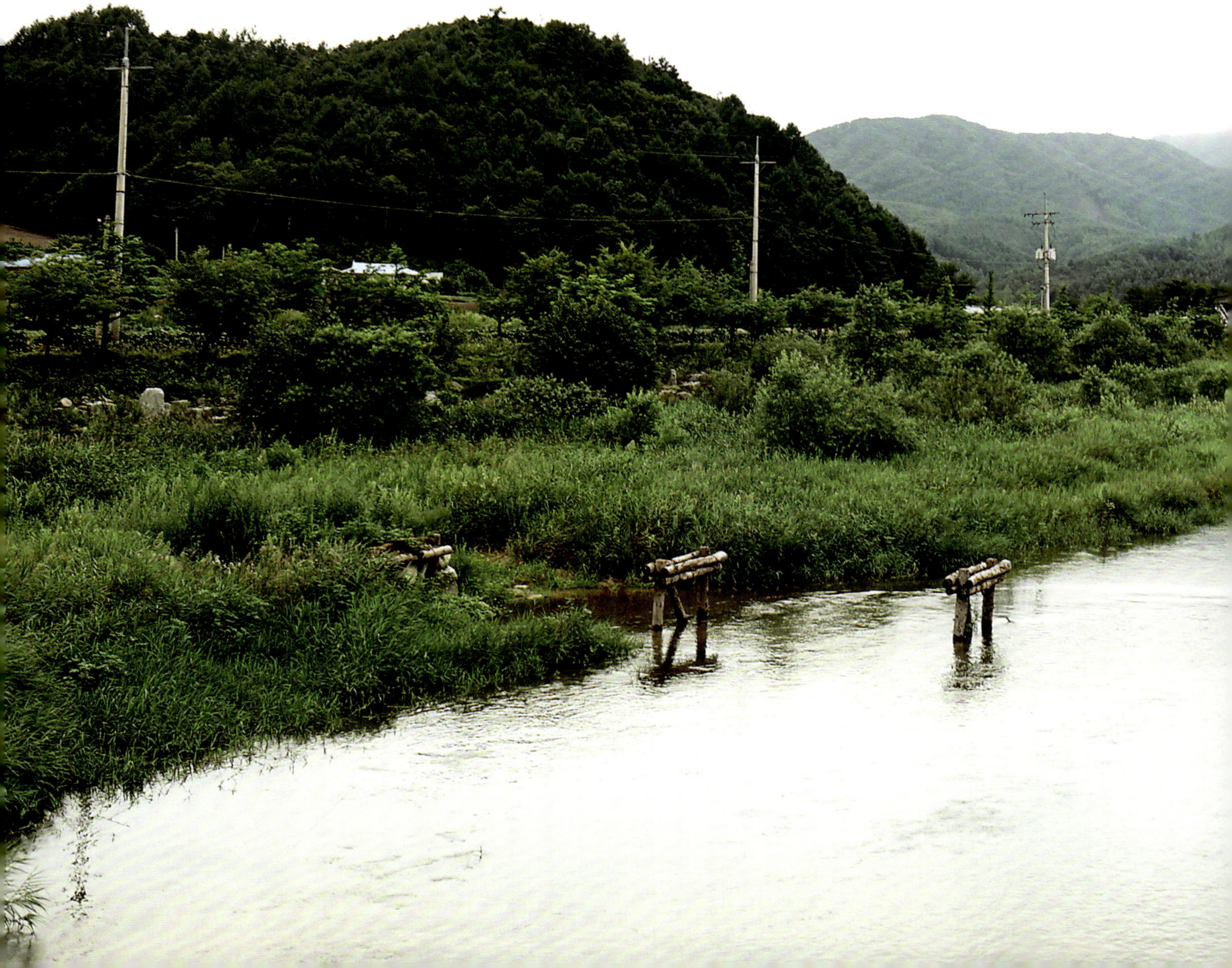

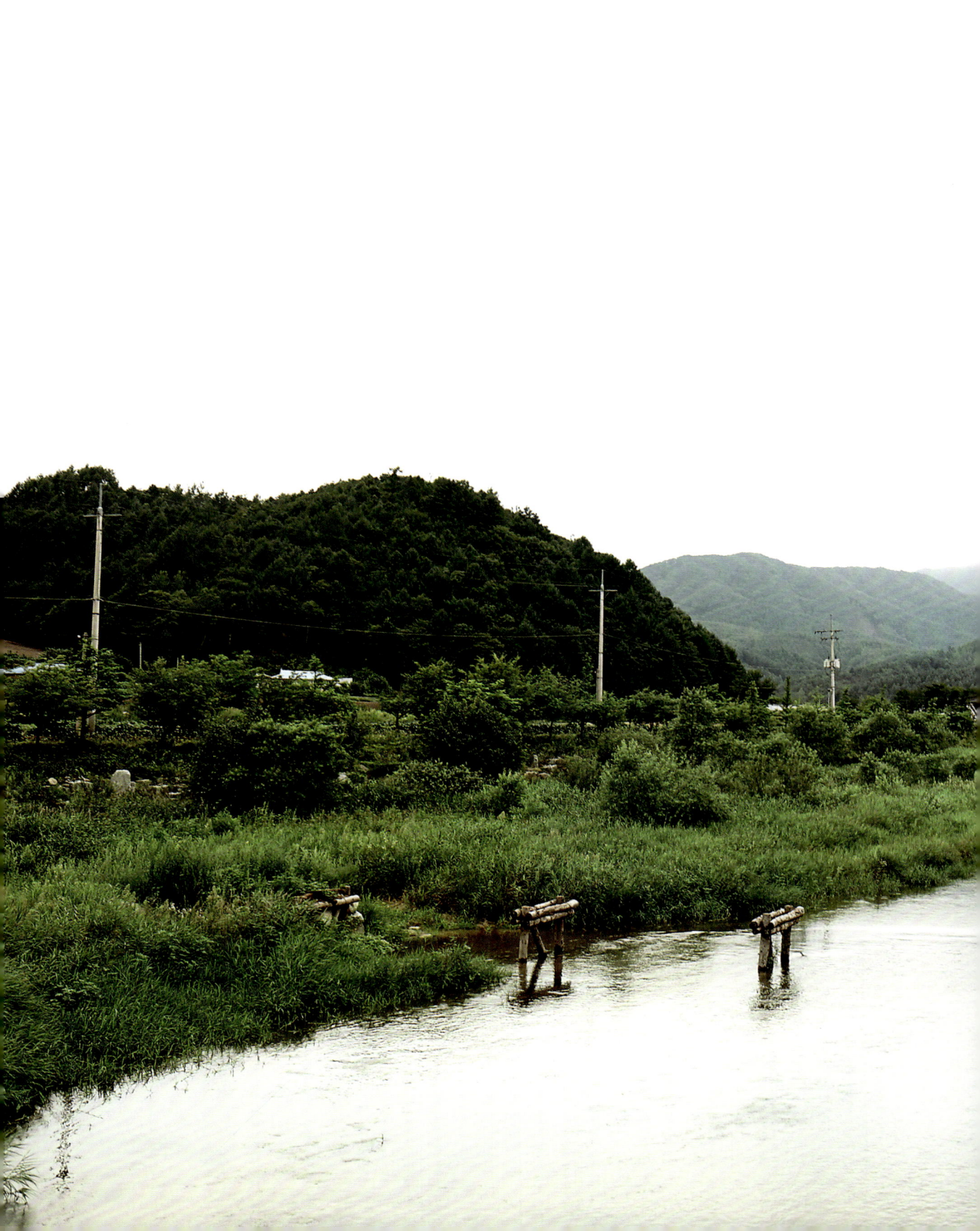

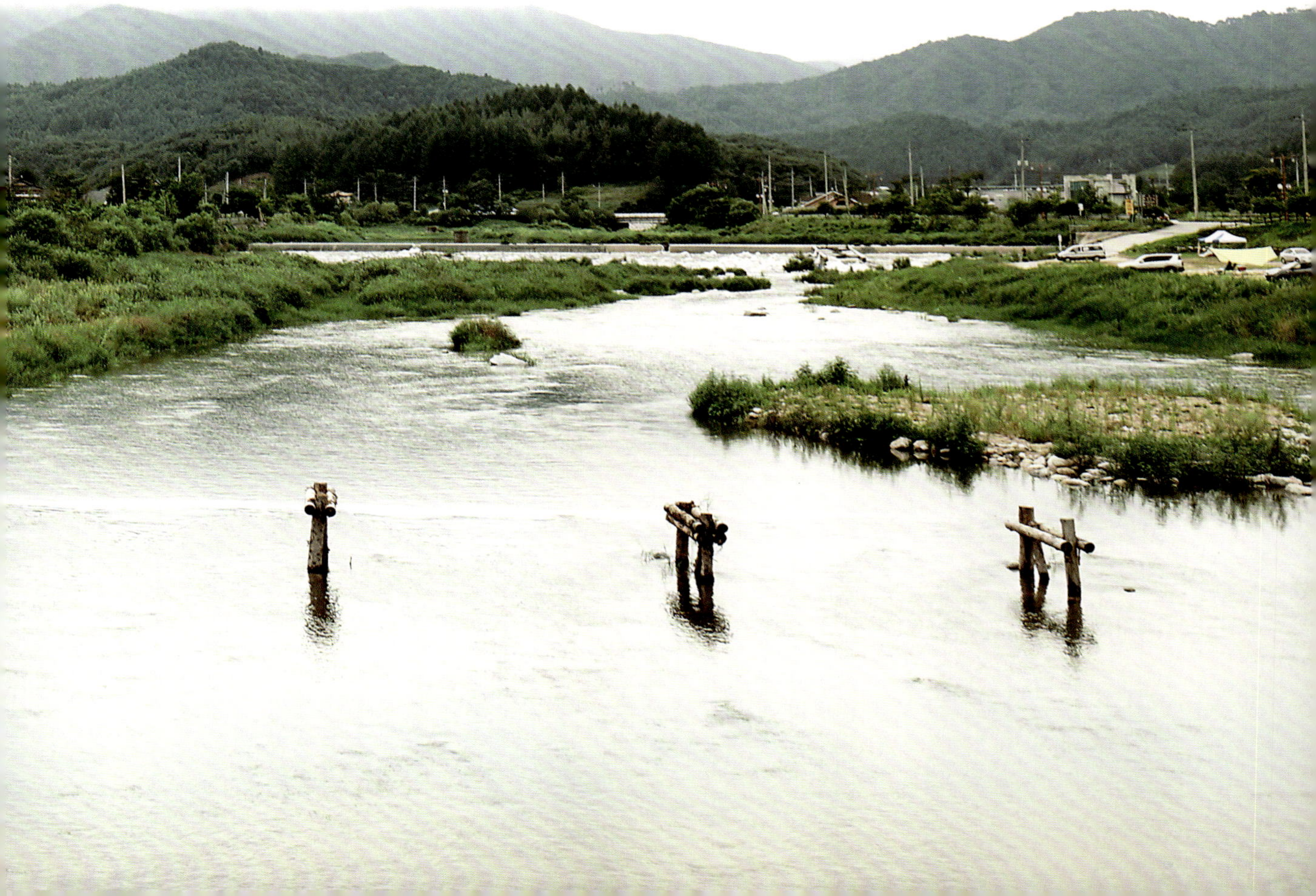

Serves 6

Warming Chicken & Potato Stew
dak doritang

1 tsp vegetable oil
800g chicken thighs and drumsticks
2½ tbsp gochujang chilli paste (page 14)
3 tbsp gochugaru red pepper powder (page 14)
2½ tbsp soy sauce
6 garlic cloves, crushed
1 tbsp honey
3 medium-size potatoes, peeled and cut into chunks
2 small onions, cut into wedges
1 carrot, peeled and cut into chunks
1 green chilli, deseeded and finely chopped
1 red chilli, deseeded and finely chopped
1 tbsp roasted sesame seed oil
2 spring onions, thinly sliced
2 tsp toasted sesame seeds

This was Jina's favourite childhood dish to cosy up with after school. The warmth of the spices and sesame oil, together with the comforting potatoes, are perfect on a cold winter evening. It's a one-pot dish and really easy to make, so it is a good recipe to add to your weekday dinner repertoire. As Jina's native Korean spice level tolerance as a child was likely higher than the average Western child, you may want to reduce the quantity of chilli paste and powder to taste.

Heat the vegetable oil in a large heavy-based pan over a high heat. When hot, add the chicken and brown on all sides for 4–5 minutes. Carefully pour off any excess oil.

In a bowl, combine the gochujang paste, gochugaru powder, soy sauce, garlic and honey. Add this to the pan along with 400ml of water. Stir to combine and pop the lid on. Bring to the boil, then reduce the heat and simmer gently for 5 minutes.

Add the potatoes, onions, carrot and most of the chillies. Bring to the boil again, then reduce the heat and simmer for 20–25 minutes until a sharp knife glides into the potato and carrot without any resistance. Stir in the sesame seed oil and cook for a further minute.

Serve in bowls with the remaining chilli, spring onions and toasted sesame seeds scattered over the top.

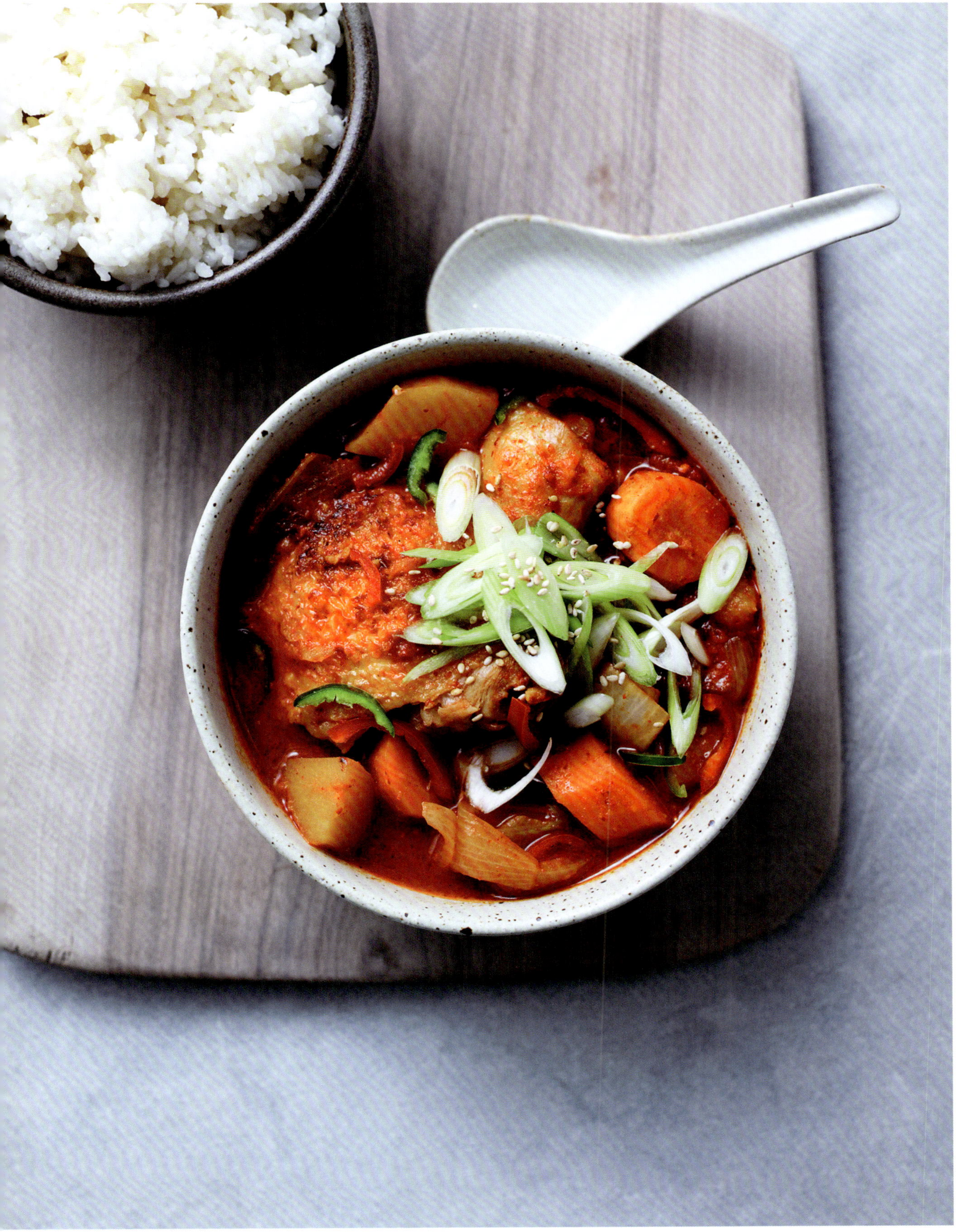

Serves 6

Marinated Beef & Vegetable Stew
bulgogi jeongol

1 quantity Sesame & Soy-marinated Beef (page 212)
100g sweet potato glass noodles (page 13) or rice noodles (optional)
1 litre homemade (page 19) or shop-bought beef stock
1 tbsp gochujang chilli paste (page 14)
1 tbsp soy sauce
1 tbsp roasted sesame seed oil
2 garlic cloves, crushed
½ onion, finely sliced
½ red pepper, sliced into strips
½ courgette, halved lengthways and sliced into thin strips
1 large carrot, halved lengthways and sliced into thin strips
50g enoki or shiitake mushrooms
4 spring onions, thinly sliced
1 tsp toasted sesame seeds

The garlic, sesame and soy make this stew almost addictive – and it is the perfect way to use up any vegetables hanging around your fridge. Whenever we make the Sesame and Soy-marinated Beef, we like to double the quantity so we can enjoy this dish the following day. In Korean restaurants, the large pan of vegetables, meat and stock are brought to the table raw and cooked in front of you on a mobile gas stove, which you can also do at home, and it makes a great focal point at a dinner party table. Koreans also love to use up any remaining sauce by adding in rice and frying it with egg and crispy seaweed. It's so good!

Prepare the bulgogi recipe as per page 212 then cover and refrigerate for at least 30 minutes.

If using the sweet potato noodles, soak them in a bowl of water for 15 minutes.

Put the beef stock, gochujang paste, soy sauce, sesame seed oil and garlic into a pan and bring everything to the boil.

Meanwhile, arrange the onion, red pepper, courgette, carrot, mushrooms and most of the spring onions in a pile around the edge of a large high-sided frying pan or pot with a lid, and place the raw marinated bulgogi in the centre. If using noodles, drain them and tuck them in beside the beef in the centre.

When the beef stock has come up to a rolling boil, place the pan of vegetables over a high heat and carefully pour the stock into the pan. Cover and bring to the boil, then reduce the heat and simmer for 10–15 minutes, stirring from time to time until the noodles, vegetables and meat are cooked through.

Just before serving, mix everything together in the pan and sprinkle over the sesame seeds and remaining spring onions.

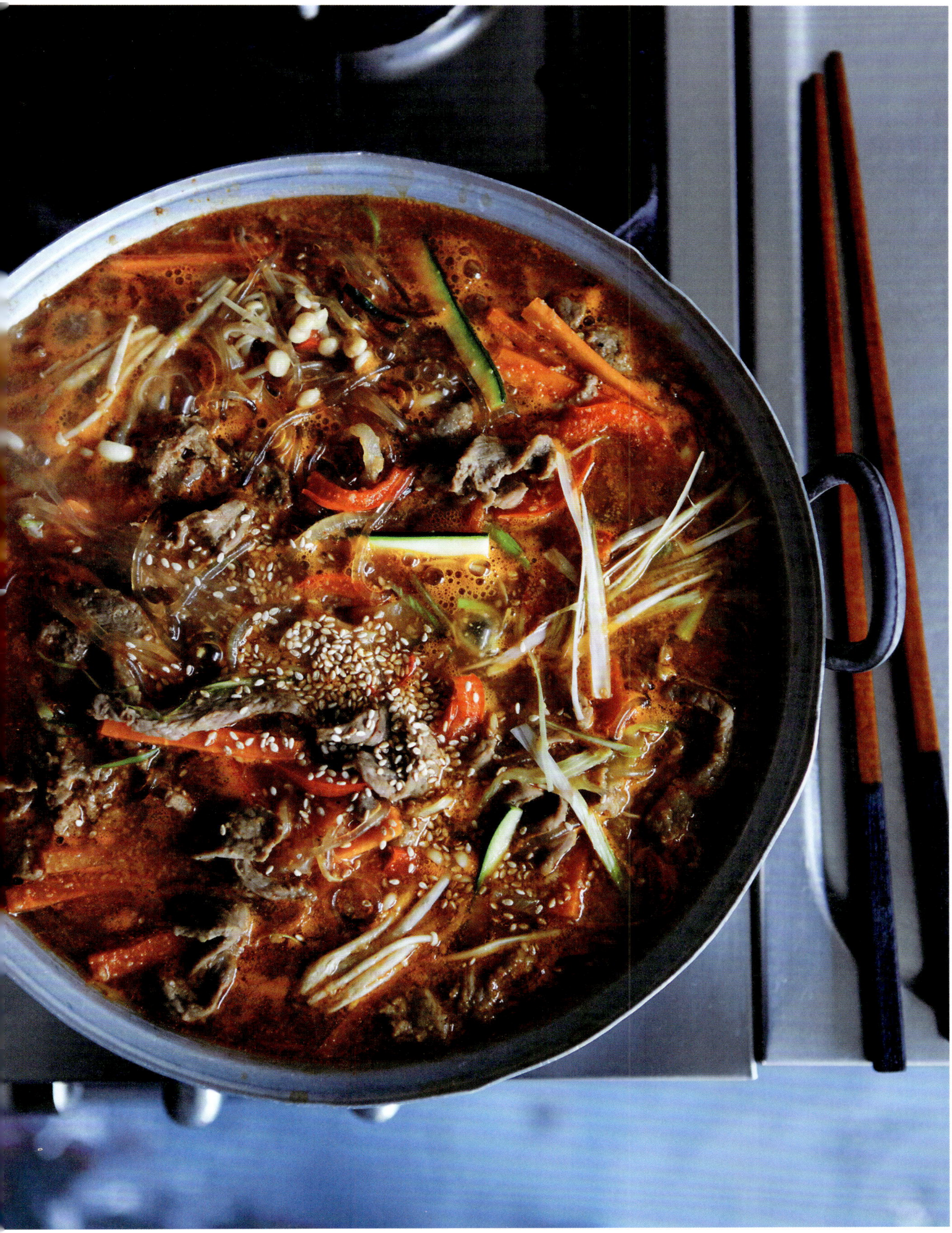

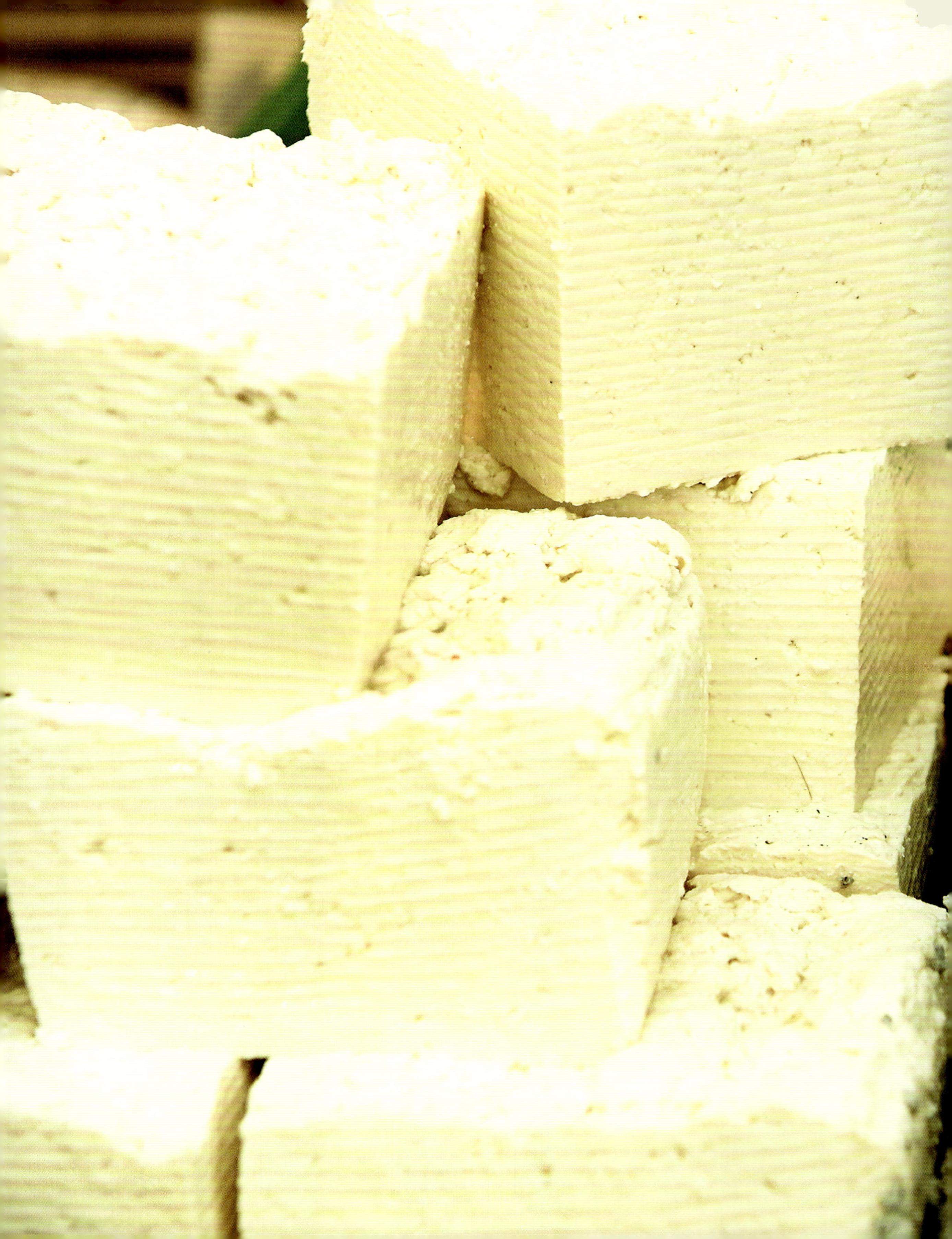

Tofu

Tofu, also known as soybean curd, is an extremely popular ingredient right across Asia, its high level of protein and affordable price making it an attractive alternative to meat for centuries. Believed to have been introduced to Korea by the Chinese, somewhere between the eighth and tenth century AD, its use in cooking became integral to a number of the country's national dishes in the centuries that followed. Two of which are the Tofu & Soybean Paste Soup (page 82) and Seafood & Silken Tofu Stew (page 85).

Tofu is made with dry yellow soybeans, which have been soaked in water until slightly softened, then ground down, mixed with water and boiled. The liquid is then strained off, leaving the pulp and a soy milk of sorts, to which a coagulant is added resulting in the milk separating into curds and whey. These fresh soft curds are transferred to moulds and submerged in water to set. In Korea, you can still buy wonderfully fresh artisan tofu from local family producers who cut off blocks to size.

They even deliver it to residential areas, announcing their arival with a ring of their bell like a Korean tofu version of an ice cream truck! In Western countries, tofu is most often sold as firm tofu in 400g plastic tubs. You can also buy silken tofu, which is made from the unpressed curds and has a somewhat gelatinous texture that is sublime in deeply seasoned soups and stews.

As a rule of thumb when it comes to firm tofu, allow at least 20–30 minutes to drain the tofu fully. When packaged to sell, it is submerged in water to keep it fresh, but when it comes to cooking, its subtle flavour and texture is greatly improved by pressing out the water contained within it. Simply drain the tofu, then wrap it in a clean tea towel and place a weighted object on top. Not so heavy that it will distort its shape, but heavy enough to keep an even pressure on it. A couple of books on top of a chopping board usually does the trick.

Tofu & Soybean Paste Soup
doen-jang jjigae

Serves 4

1 tbsp vegetable oil
100g beef sirloin, cut into thin strips
100g enoki mushrooms, base removed (or shiitake mushrooms, sliced)
1 small onion, sliced
3 garlic cloves, crushed
2 tsp soy sauce
1 tbsp roasted sesame seed oil
4½ tbsp doen-jang soybean paste (page 14)
300g firm tofu, drained and cut into 2cm cubes
1 red chilli, deseeded and sliced
1 small courgette, halved lengthways and sliced into half-moon shapes
2 spring onions, finely sliced

Stock
5 large dried anchovies (page 17) or 800ml of shop-bought fish stock

Doen-jang is a fermented soybean paste, similar to Japanese miso, but with a much richer, deeper flavour. It is really delicious and brings this dish to life. This soup is simple and quick to make, so we often turn to it when we are lacking the motivation to think of anything to cook. Feel free to vary the vegetables to whatever you have at home, but the tofu is integral to this dish. For a vegetarian version, leave out the meat and dried anchovies and use vegetable stock instead.

If you are using the dried anchovies, remove their heads, then gently tease open the underside of the belly and remove the guts (little black pouches). Add the anchovies to a pan along with 800ml of water, place the lid on, and bring to the boil for 3 minutes. Remove from the heat and strain the stock, into a bowl, discarding the dried anchovies. Keep the strained stock to one side.

Add the vegetable oil to a pan and place over a medium-high heat. When hot, add the beef, mushrooms and onion and fry for 2–3 minutes until the meat begins to colour. Add the garlic, soy sauce, sesame seed oil, doen-jang paste, tofu and most of the sliced chilli. Pour over the stock, put the lid on the pan and bring to the boil for 6 minutes, then reduce the heat a little, add in the courgette and simmer for a further 4 minutes.

Remove from the heat and serve in bowls with the remaining chilli and the spring onions scattered over the top. A bowl of plain rice is a lovely accompaniment.

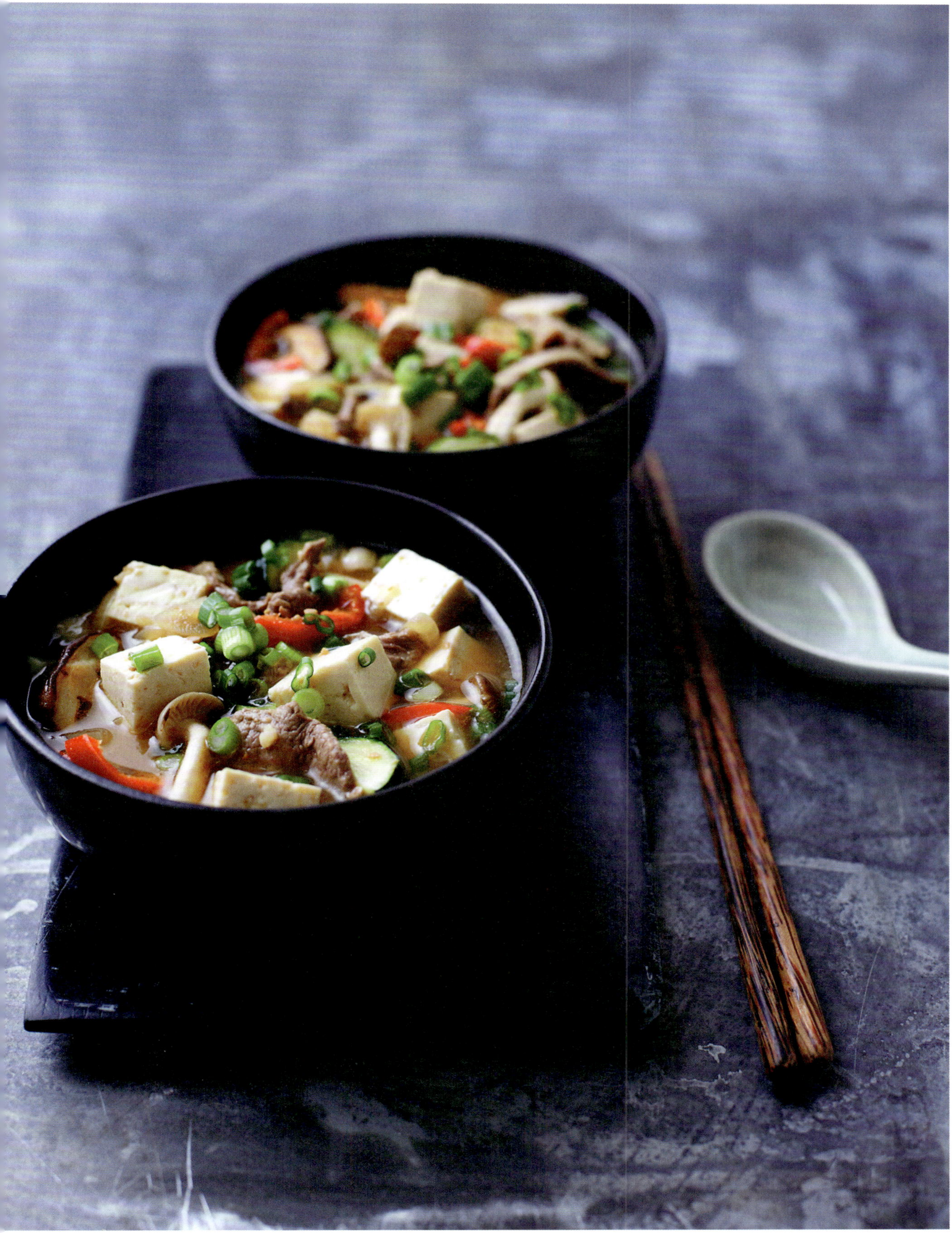

금강침구
금강침구
2269-7437
보은커텐상사
동대문
광장시장 맛집
마약김밥
010-9250-2717
마약김밥
할머니집
순대
2266-0559
2265-4539
우리옷

Serves 4

Seafood & Silken Tofu Stew
sundubu jjigae

1 tbsp gochugaru red pepper powder (page 14)
2 garlic cloves, crushed
1 tbsp soy sauce
1 tbsp roasted sesame seed oil
2 spring onions, 1 very finely chopped, 1 finely sliced
300g silken tofu
350ml homemade (page 19) or shop-bought beef stock
100g clams (discard any that remain open when given a sharp tap)
100g raw prawns
1 red chilli, deseeded and thinly sliced
2 eggs (optional)
sea salt and freshly ground black pepper, to taste
cooked rice, to serve

This stew is made with very soft tofu that has a luscious, almost creamy consistency. In Korean restaurants, there are whole eggs at your table ready to crack into your bowl of molten stew on arrival. You can do this at home too, just make sure to serve the stew while it is still boiling hot to ensure the eggs cook.

In a bowl, combine the gochugaru powder, garlic, soy sauce, sesame seed oil and the finely chopped spring onion.

In a pan, add the tofu, stock and clams, then place over a high heat and bring to the boil. Reduce the heat a little, break up the silken tofu into chunks and add the prawns, gochugaru-soy sauce mixture along with the chilli. Simmer for 3–4 minutes, taste and adjust the seasoning if necessary with a little more salt or pepper. Just before removing from the heat, stir in the sliced spring onion. If using eggs, crack them in at this point as well, stirring quickly to distribute. Serve immediately, with rice on the side.

Soups & Stews

Serves 4

Kimchi Stew
kimchi jjigae

김치찌개

2 tbsp roasted sesame seed oil

200g pork belly, cut into bite-size strips

300g cabbage kimchi (page 98), or shop-bought, chopped into bite-size pieces

1 tbsp gochujang chilli paste (page 14)

2 garlic cloves, crushed

2½ cm piece of ginger, finely grated

2 tsp honey

4 tbsp kimchi juice

800ml beef stock or water

½ courgette, halved lengthways and sliced into half-moon shapes

200g firm tofu, drained and cut into bite-size cubes

2 spring onions, finely chopped

cooked rice, to serve (optional)

This extremely popular hearty and flavoursome kimchi stew is perfect for slightly more mature kimchi, as the sourness cuts through the deep, earthy and caramelised flavours of the fried chilli paste and pork. This is also a good dish to try for anyone new to the strong flavours of kimchi, as it mellows considerably during the cooking process. In Korea, tinned tuna is commonly used in place of the pork in this dish. You can even make it vegetarian by using tofu and vegetable stock.

Heat the sesame seed oil in a large heavy-based pan over a medium heat, add the pork and kimchi and sauté for 8–10 minutes, until they start to caramelise. Add in the gochujang paste, garlic, ginger and honey and fry for a further 2 minutes, stirring regularly to avoid burning. Add in the kimchi juice and stock or water, if using, and bring to the boil, reduce the heat a little and simmer for 20 minutes.

Add the courgette, tofu and most of the spring onions and simmer for another 5 minutes, or just until the courgette is cooked but retains a little bite. Serve in bowls immediately with the remaining spring onions scattered over the top and, if you wish, some rice on the side.

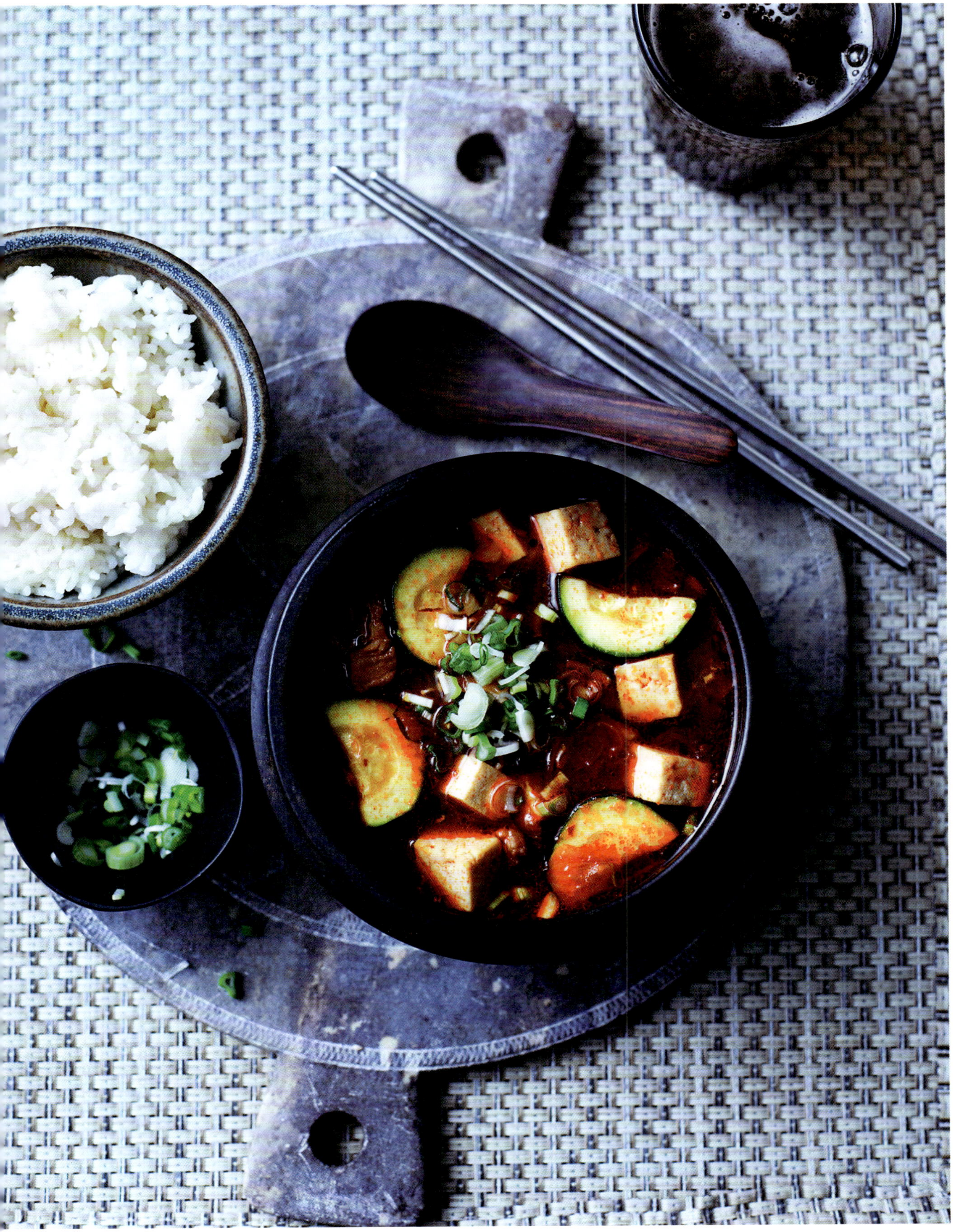

Serves 4 as a starter

Chilled Cucumber Soup
oh-ee neng-guk

5g wakame dried kelp (page 16)
120g cucumber, halved and thinly sliced
2½ tbsp rice wine vinegar
4 tsp honey or agave syrup
1 garlic clove, crushed
½ small onion, very finely sliced
1 spring onion, very finely sliced
½ tsp fine sea salt
1 red chilli, deseeded and finely sliced (optional)
1 tsp toasted sesame seeds, to serve
ice cubes, to serve

This soup is absolutely our favourite thing to eat on a hot summer's day – cool and refreshing, and so full of flavour, we could eat it all day long. It is also a perfect example of the subtleties and contrasts of Korean food and cooking. Although the cuisine is often described as predominantly spicy, in fact, dishes like this one or the Baby Chicken Soup (page 64), Buckwheat Noodles in Chilled Broth (page 160), Mung Bean Pancakes (page 142) and many others provide beautiful depth of flavour without any spice at all.

In a bowl, soak the kelp in cold water for 15 minutes.

Drain the kelp and cut it into bite-size strips. Place it in a medium-size mixing bowl with all of the remaining ingredients (apart from the sesame seeds and ice). Cover with 600ml of cold water. Gently combine then cover and refrigerate until very well chilled.

Serve in bowls with a few ice cubes and the sesame seeds scattered over the top.

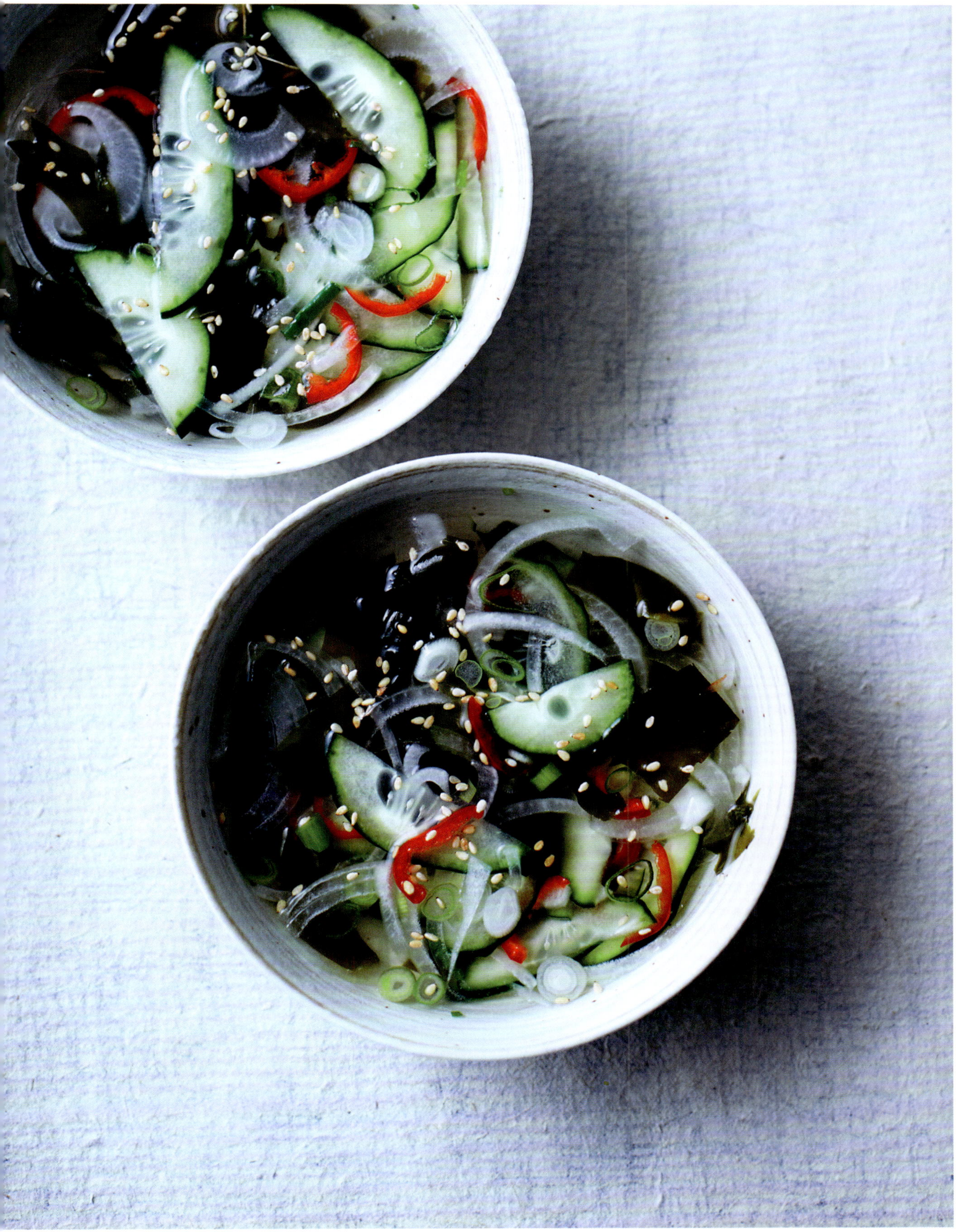

Serves 4

Chilled Tofu, Cucumber & Kimchi Broth
muk sabal

목사발

400g firm tofu (or acorn jelly), drained and cut into 1cm wide x 5cm long strips
200g kimchi (page 98) or shop-bought, cut into bite-size strips
120g cucumber, halved lengthways and cut on the diagonal into thin slices
4 sheets roasted crispy seaweed (page 16), cut into thin strips
2 tsp toasted sesame seeds

<u>Sauce</u>
1½ tbsp soy sauce
1½ tbsp honey
2½ tsp roasted sesame seed oil
4 tsp rice wine vinegar
½ tsp wasabi paste
1 spring onion, very finely sliced
1 garlic clove, crushed

<u>Stock</u>
6 large dried anchovies (page 17)
2 x 7cm pieces dried kelp (dashima, page 16)
¼ onion, roughly chopped
½ red chilli, halved and deseeded

Traditionally, acorn jelly is used in this Korean dish. It can be found freshly made in some good Korean stores, but we also make this with tofu and find it to be just as delicious. One of our favourite places to eat this dish is in a lovely little restaurant called Chang Sarang in Seoul, which is well worth a visit if you ever find yourself in Korea.

In a small bowl, combine all the sauce ingredients and set aside.

For the stock, pull the heads off the dried anchovies, then gently tease open the underside of the belly and remove the guts (little black pouches). Put all the stock ingredients into a pan, cover with 800ml of water and bring to the boil. Remove the lid, reduce the heat and simmer for 5 minutes until the stock has reduced by about a quarter. Strain the stock through a fine sieve, into a bowl, and leave to cool completely. Cover and refrigerate until well chilled.

Divide the chilled broth and tofu strips between 4 bowls, with the kimchi and cucumber piled on top in mounds. Place the seaweed on top, scatter over the sesame seeds and drizzle over all the sauce between the 4 bowls. Serve immediately, mixing everything together until well combined.

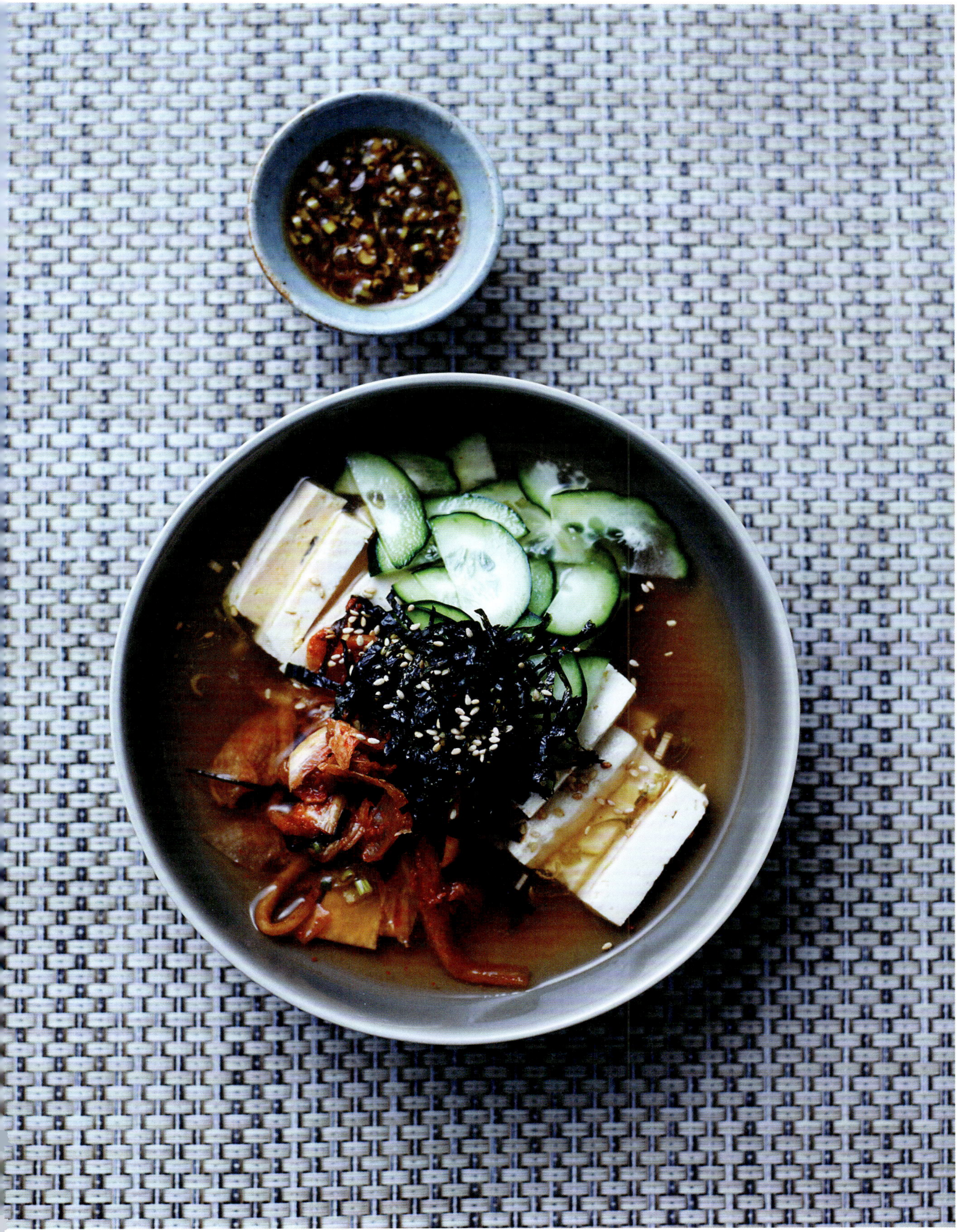

Vegetables, Pickles & Sides

야채, 김치 & 반찬

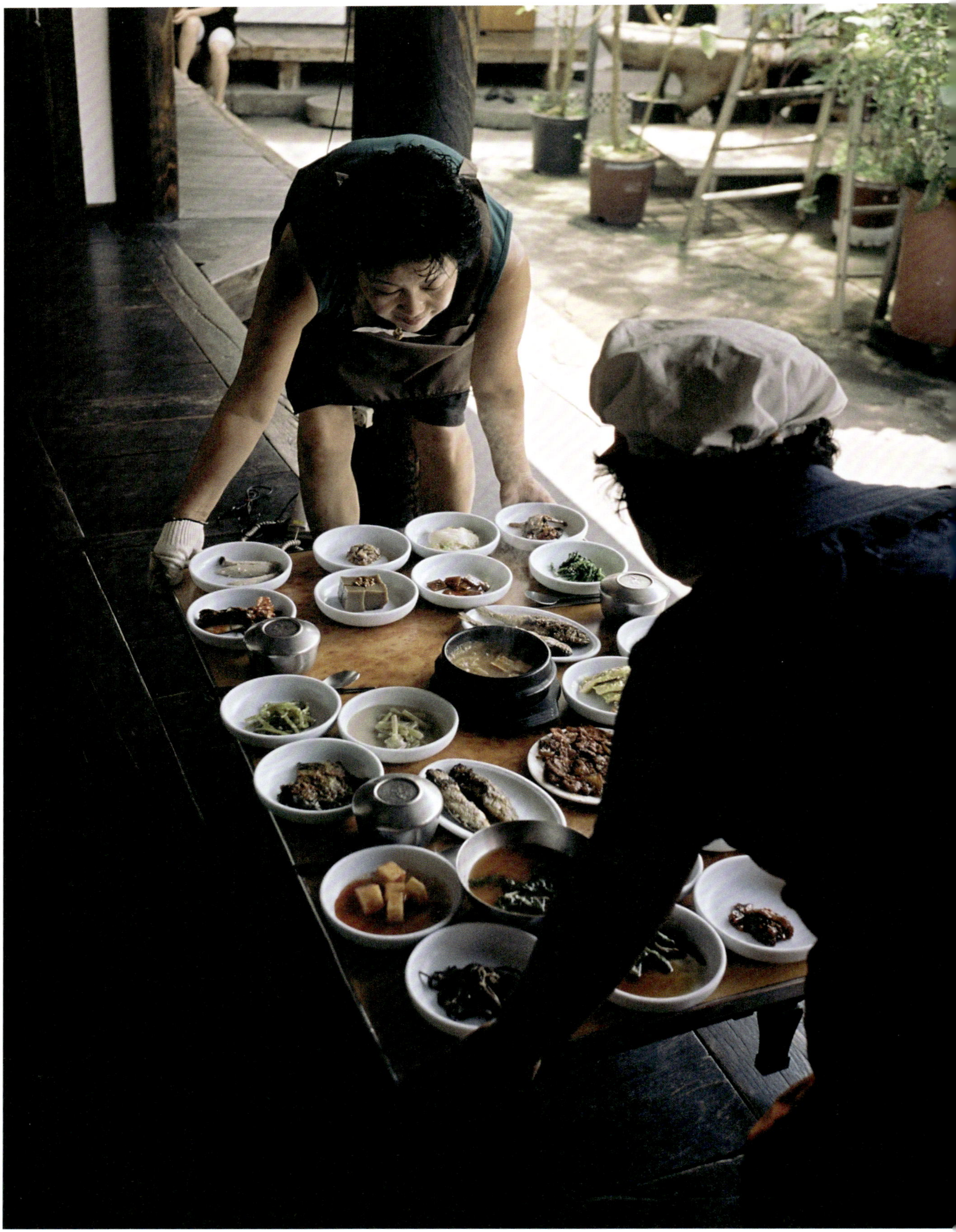

03

96. *Kimchi*

98. **Classic Cabbage Kimchi**
배추김치

102. **Radish Kimchi**
무김치-깍두기

104. **Almost-instant Cucumber Kimchi**
오이김치

106. **Radish Water Kimchi**
동치미

108. **Pickled Garlic**
마늘장아찌

110. **Whole Pickled Cucumbers**
오이지

112. **Seasoned Lotus Root**
연근 조림

116. **Pickled Perilla Leaves**
깻잎절임

118. **Soy-seasoned Mushrooms**
버섯나물

120. **Seasoned Courgettes**
호박나물

123. **Quick Pickled Onions**
양파절임

123. **Garlic & Sesame Bean Sprouts**
숙주나물

124. **Dried Seasoned Anchovies**
오징어채

124. **Mum's Spicy Dried Squid**
멸치 볶음

127. **Soy Sauce & Garlic-steamed Aubergine**
가지나물

127. **Honey & Soy-glazed Potatoes**
감자조림

128. **Steamed Eggs with Spring Onion & Chilli**
계란찜

Vegetables, Pickles & Sides

Kimchi

Kimchi assaults the senses before you've even figured out whether or not you would like to try it, its wonderfully robust smell wafting up to say a big 'hello'. In fact its taste is far less explosive, with an incredibly complex mix of spice, hits of garlic and a sour undertone. For the uninitiated, don't be put off by the initial pungent smell, as it can only really be appreciated whe tasted alongside a meal.

This national dish of Korea is essentially a pickle. The fermentation process leaves the vegetables soft to the touch, but with a characteristic and very pleasing crunch in the mouth. In Korea the ingredients and flavour profile of kimchi changes depending on where in the country it is made. Kimchi from the northern provinces tends to be somewhat less salty and a little more watery and they usually do not use fermented prawns or anchovies in the recipe. Whereas southern kimchi will more often than not use this fermented seafood as a way of adding salt, and also to give it a more robust flavour. Seasons will also dictate the type of kimchi made, as traditionally Koreans would only have had access to whatever was in season. So radishes and cucumbers would be the vegetables of choice in the summer, while cabbage would be the norm in autumn and winter, when it is made in bulk and buried in the ground in earthenware pots to last the year.

Kimchi's place on the table is very much as a side dish, there to offer spice and a sourness to cut through heavier dishes and to refresh the palate, as and when needed. Koreans boast more than 150 different types of kimchi, but the two most popular are made from Chinese cabbage (page 98) and radish (page 102). You will now find this fiery pickle being used in a whole range of Western dishes, from mayonnaise to burgers, and it's not hard to see why – the more you eat, the more addictive it becomes. And as if all that were not enough, it also packs an impressive nutritional punch, high in vitamins and healthy gut bacteria.

Kimchi can be kept in an airtight jar in the fridge for at least five or six months, with its flavour gradually becoming progressively sour over time. We know people who have kept their kimchi perfectly well for up to a year, but ours never lasts that long. Koreans tend to use mature kimchi in cooked dishes, such as Kimchi Stew (page 86) or Kimchi Pancake (page 138). Whichever way you choose to enjoy kimchi, it is truly magnificent.

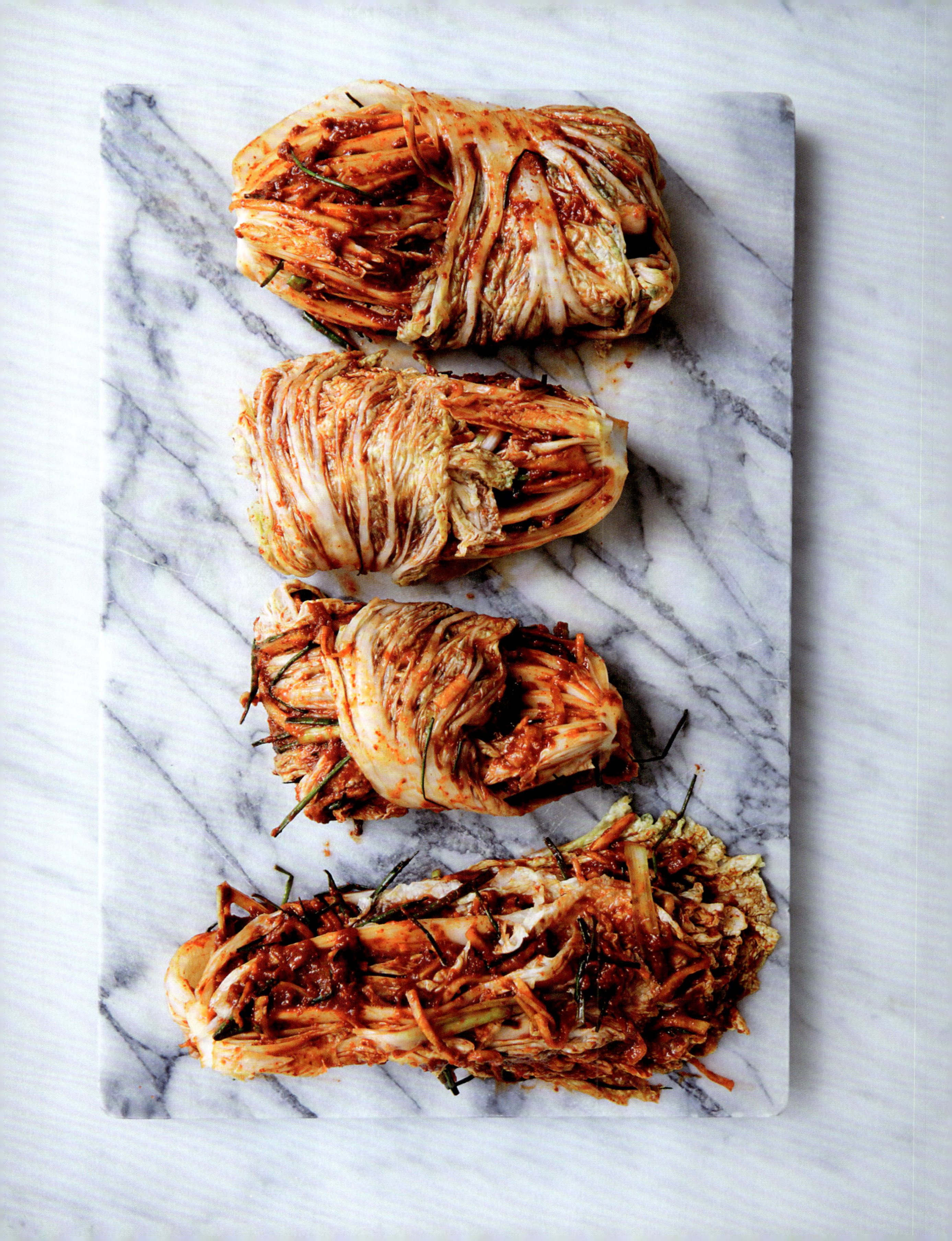

Makes approximately 2kg

Classic Cabbage Kimchi
baechu kimchi

1 large Chinese cabbage (about 1kg)
50g table salt
70g sea salt
450g daikon radish, cut into fine julienne strips
30g chives, cut into 4cm lengths
4 spring onions, halved lengthways and cut into 4cm lengths

Flour paste
1½ tbsp glutinous rice flour or plain flour

Paste
8 garlic cloves
20g ginger
100g onion
1 tbsp salted baby shrimp (saeujeot) (optional)
70g gochugaru red pepper powder (page 14)
100ml fish sauce
2 tsp soy sauce
1 tbsp unrefined sugar or coconut palm sugar
2 tbsp rice vinegar

Kimchi is Korea's national dish and you will never be served a meal without it, so this classic cabbage kimchi is a good place to start. Making your own kimchi does take a bit of time, but once done it sits in the fridge for months and the taste is better than shop-bought brands. The salted baby shrimp is optional – it gives the kimchi a slightly more pronounced fish flavour that is popular with Koreans, but if you are unsure, just leave it out. This will need at least two days in the fridge to ferment before you can begin eating it. When using kimchi, take out only what you need and never return any unused kimchi to the jar – just store it, covered, separately so as not to contaminate the main jar.

Start by preparing the cabbage. Cut about 10cm deep across the base of the cabbage, then gently split the entire cabbage in half lengthways and rinse well under running water, rinsing well in between the leaves.

In a large flat bowl or container, combine 1 litre of water with the table salt. Sprinkle the sea salt over each leaf of the halved cabbage, focusing your attention on the thicker root end and working up to the thinner leaf. Place the cabbage cut-side down in the bowl of salted water. Leave to soak for 2 hours, then turn over and soak for a further 2 hours until the leaves are limp and bend easily without breaking.

Drain the cabbage and rinse it carefully under running water at least twice. Taste the cabbage leaf – it should be very salty, however if it is too strong, rinse it again and then drain it completely.

Meanwhile, make the flour paste. Mix the flour with 2 tablespoons of water, using a fork or whisk to ensure there are no lumps. Once you have a smooth paste, gradually pour in 230ml of water, stirring to combine. Place the mixture in a saucepan, bring to the boil, stirring all the time, then reduce the heat to low and simmer gently for 5 minutes until thick and gelatinous. Remove from the heat and leave to cool completely.

In a food processor, combine all the paste ingredients and the cooled flour mixture until you have a smooth paste. Transfer to a large bowl together with the daikon, chives and spring onions and mix well until thoroughly combined. Carefully spoon (or use your hands) the mixture onto the drained cabbage halves, making sure to cover every leaf with the mixture. Taking the outer leaf of each cabbage half, wrap it around the cabbage to keep the mixture secure.

Put the cabbage into a sterilised jar or other airtight container, leaving about 3cm between the cabbage and the lid. Seal tightly. Keep the jar at room temperature for 2 days, by which stage it should have begun to ferment and smell a little sour. Use a spoon to press the kimchi down, submerging it in its own juices. Seal the container again and refrigerate. Most people find they like the kimchi best after a few weeks in the fridge, others like it after a month or 2 when it has a bit more of a sour kick to it. Try it out at intervals and see when you like it best.

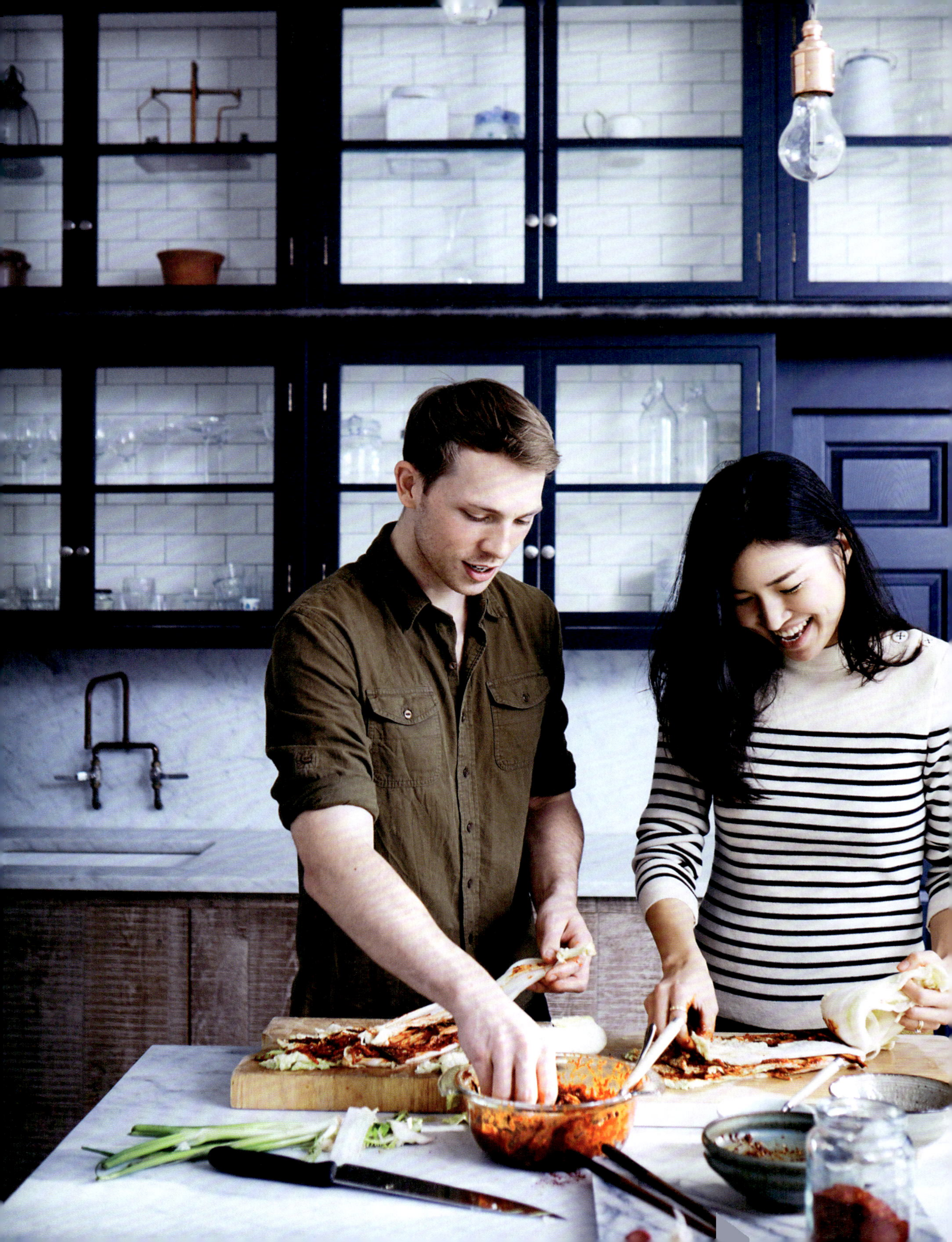

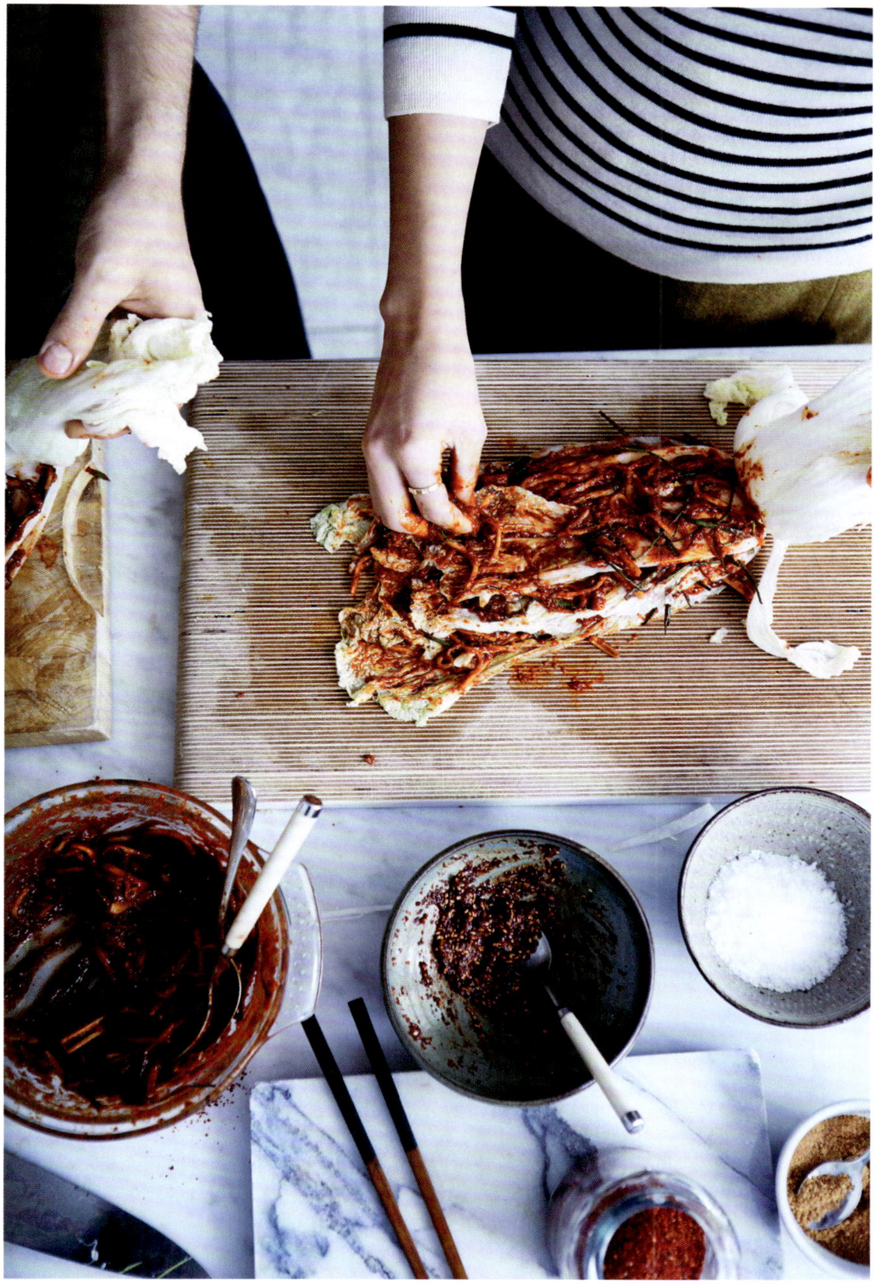

Radish Kimchi
moo kimchi

Makes enough to fill a 1-litre kilner jar

1½ kg Korean or daikon radish, peeled
1½ tbsp sea salt
1½ tbsp unrefined sugar or coconut palm sugar
7 garlic cloves, crushed
5cm piece of ginger, very finely grated
2½ tbsp fish sauce
6 tbsp gochugaru red pepper powder (page 14)
4 spring onions, chopped into 4cm lengths

This cubed radish kimchi is phenomenally popular in Korea, second only to the kingpin cabbage. It is very easy to make and can be eaten immediately, giving a vibrant and fresh flavour, or fermented for a few days or weeks, giving it a chance to develop stronger sour notes. At the Korean table, radish kimchi is usually served with Baby Chicken Soup (page 64) but is equally tasty with almost any mild-flavoured dish, so that its punchy flavours can come to the fore. Ideally, use Korean radish – available from Asian supermarkets – these are shorter and more rounded in shape. You can make this dish with daikon radish too.

Rinse the radish, then cut it into 2cm cubes and put the cubes into a large bowl. Add the salt and sugar and combine until the radish is evenly coated. Leave to marinate for 1 hour, then drain the liquid into a small bowl and set both the radish and liquid aside.

Add the garlic, ginger, fish sauce and gochugaru powder to the radish and thoroughly combine. Finally, add the spring onions and gently combine. Very tightly pack the radish into a glass jar. Add 2 tablespoons of the reserved radish liquid and discard the rest. Press down firmly and seal with the lid.

It can be eaten on the day it is made or for a stronger flavour, leave it to stand for about a day, at room temperature, letting the fermentation process begin. Once a few bubbles appear in the liquid (the time will vary depending on the temperature of your room) put the jar in the fridge. If there are a great deal of bubbles, carefully open the jar to release some of the gas then reseal it and refrigerate immediately. The flavour profile of the kimchi will evolve with age, becoming more sour. Taste it at intervals so you know what your ideal ripeness is. For us, anywhere between 2–3 weeks onwards is ideal – still fresh, but mature enough for all the flavours to have got to know each other very well.

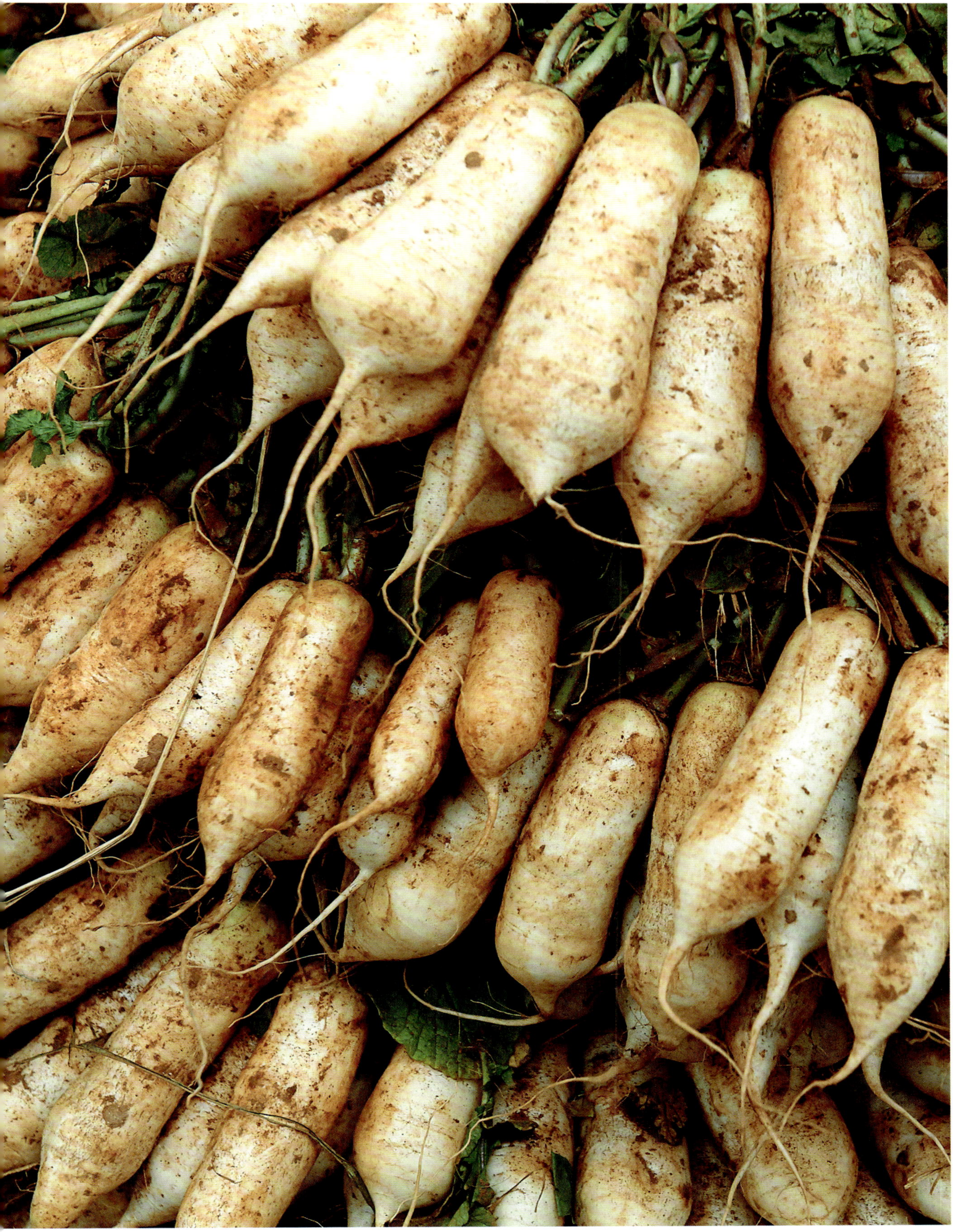

Serves 4–6 as a side dish

Almost-instant Cucumber Kimchi
oh-ee kimchi

오이김치

- 3 Persian (pickling) cucumbers (page 17) or 1 regular cucumber
- 1 tsp fine sea salt
- 1 garlic clove, crushed
- 2 tsp gochugaru red pepper powder (or a little less if you prefer) (page 14)
- 2 tsp unrefined sugar or coconut palm sugar
- 2½ tsp rice wine vinegar
- 2 tsp roasted sesame seed oil
- 2 tsp toasted sesame seeds

This is for those days when you open the fridge and realise that you are out of kimchi! All is not lost however, as this almost instant cucumber kimchi can be made in no time, omitting the fermentation process. The shorter, squatter Persian cucumber – sometimes labelled as pickling or baby cucumber – is ideal for this recipe, being less watery with a more pronounced flavour. Persian cucumbers are easily available in good supermarkets and fruit and veg markets. If you can't find it, you can use normal cucumber, but it will be a little more watery.

Wash the cucumbers and pat them dry. Halve them lengthways and then slice them into very thin half-moon shapes. Put the slices in a bowl with the salt and combine together. Set aside for 30 minutes.

Combine the remaining ingredients, apart from the sesame seeds, in a bowl. Drain the cucumbers of any liquid then add them to the bowl. Gently, but thoroughly, combine. Cover and refrigerate for at least half an hour or until chilled.

Serve sprinkled with the sesame seeds. It will keep for up to a week in the fridge if stored in an airtight container.

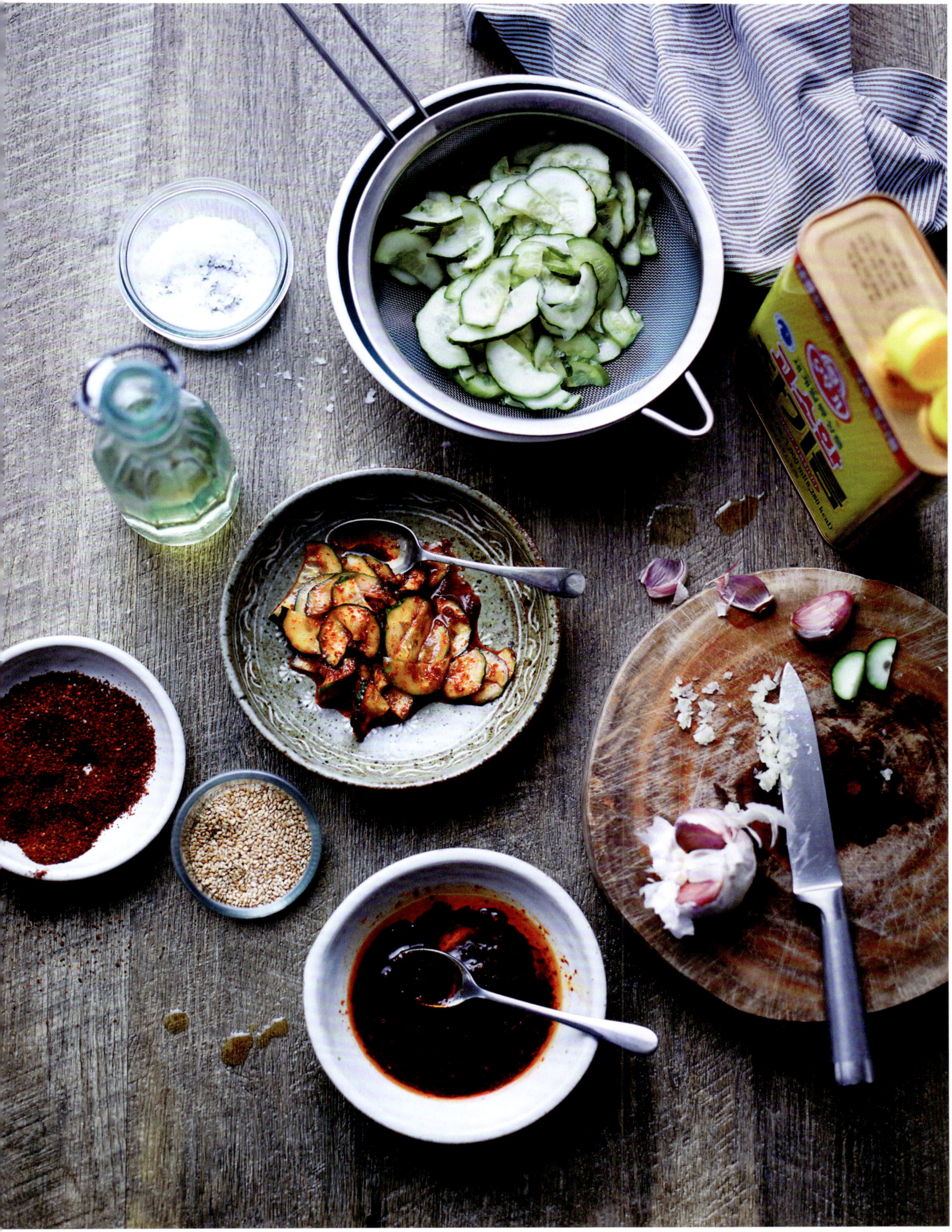

Makes 15 servings as a side

Radish Water Kimchi
dongchimi

1kg daikon radish, peeled, halved lengthways and cut into ½ cm thick slices
2 tbsp sea salt
2 garlic cloves, crushed
2½ cm piece of ginger, finely chopped
1 green chilli, halved lengthways and deseeded
1 red chilli, halved lengthways and deseeded
½ small white onion, peeled and cut into 1cm thin wedges
1 tbsp honey
1 spring onion, halved lengthways

You would be forgiven for thinking that all Korean food was red hot spicy. In fact, the beauty of this country's cuisine is in the careful balancing act of flavours within the most famous Korean dishes. For every chilli-paste-laden stew, there is an equally satisfying and subtly flavoured soup. This yin and yang approach extends to kimchi too. Beautifully crisp, clean and refreshing, this radish water kimchi doesn't have a hint of spice in sight. The chillies added here play the part of subtly flavouring the water and don't add any heat. In fact, this cooling kimchi is the ideal antidote to other fiery Korean dishes.

Place the radish in a 2-litre large resealable container and cover with the salt, mixing well to ensure the radish is well-coated. Cover and leave at room temperature overnight.

The following day, thoroughly rinse and drain the radish and the container to remove the salt. Return the radish to the empty container with the garlic, ginger, chillies, onion, honey and spring onion. Cover with 600–700ml of water and gently stir everything to combine. Cover and leave at room temperature for 2 days, then keep refrigerated for up to 2 weeks. The liquid can also be used as the base for chilled noodle broths, including Buckwheat Noodles in Chilled Broth (page 160).

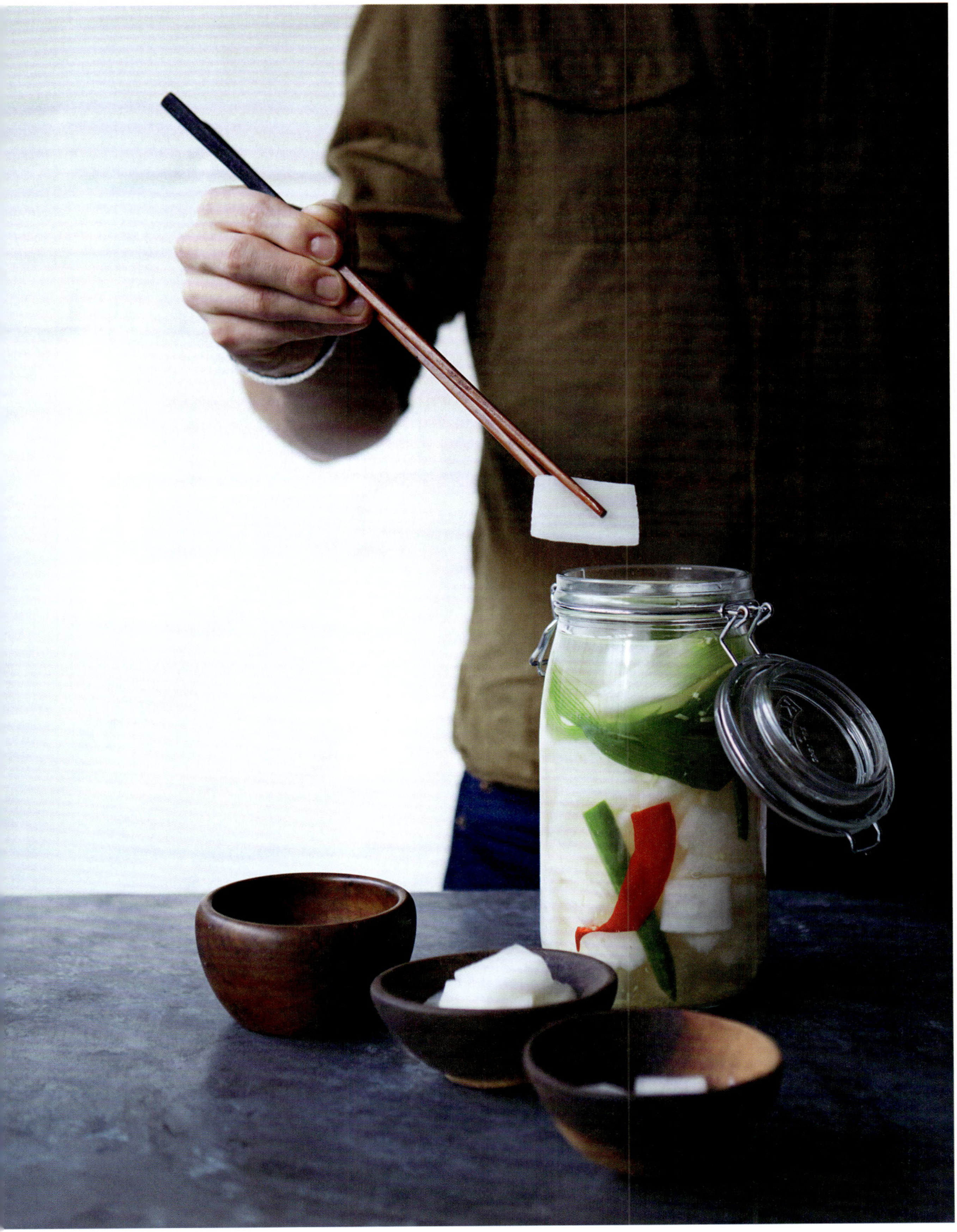

Makes 4 bulbs

Pickled Garlic
maneul chang-achi

마늘장아찌

4 whole garlic bulbs, peeled and root end removed
220ml rice wine vinegar
120ml soy sauce
4 tbsp honey

Pickling garlic dulls the potent flavour, making it a great side dish. You can also crush it and add it to fried rice or chilli-based sauces. It takes a good 4 weeks to pickle it, but once done it lasts almost indefinitely refrigerated. It is worth noting that when raw garlic is mixed with vinegar there is a reaction caused by compounds present in the garlic resulting in it turning a rather alarming shade of blue. You can avoid this by blanching it first, but if you don't mind the colour (it is harmless) you can skip this step.

Fill a medium pan with water and bring it to the boil. Add the garlic, cover and blanch for 1 minute. Drain and immediately plunge the garlic into cold water, repeating the process until it is completely cold. Drain again, then place the garlic in a resealable glass jar or container just large enough to hold all the garlic. Pour over the vinegar and if necessary, top with just enough water to completely submerge the garlic, leaving about ½ cm at the top. Seal the jar and store it at room temperature for 2 weeks.

Strain the vinegar from the garlic, reserving about 100ml. Combine the reserved vinegar with the soy sauce, honey and 2 tablespoons of water and mix well. Pour this mixture into the jar of garlic. The garlic should be completely covered by the mixture, if not, top with just enough water to completely submerge the garlic. Store at room temperature for a further 2 weeks, then store in the fridge.

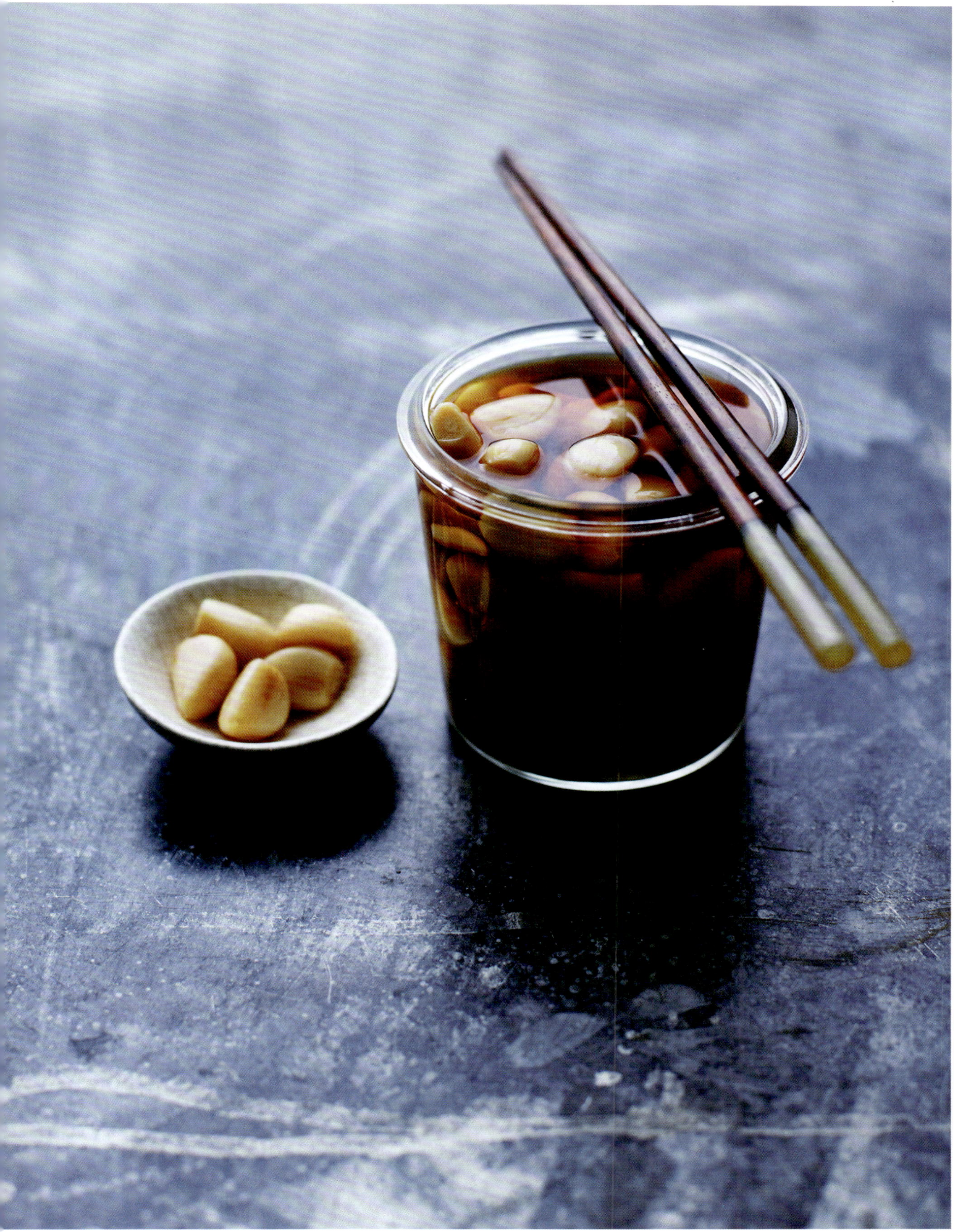

Makes 4–5 pickled cucumbers

Whole Pickled Cucumbers
oh-ee ji

오이지

- 4–5 (500g) Persian (pickling) cucumbers (page 17), ends sliced and discarded
- 4 tbsp sea salt
- 1 spring onion, root end cut off and discarded
- 2 garlic cloves, peeled and halved
- 150g honey
- 190ml rice wine vinegar

These small pickled cucumbers pack in a lot of flavour, but the best part is the satisfying crunch that is achieved by covering the cucumbers with boiling pickling liquid. Small pickling cucumbers are ideal for this dish, their slightly rough, bumpy skin provide great texture.

Rinse the cucumbers under cold running water. Place the salt in a large bowl, add the cucumbers and roll them in the salt to coat them. Set aside for 2 hours.

Drain the cucumbers of any liquid. In a heatproof glass jar or resealable container (large enough to fit the cucumbers), add the salt, cucumbers, spring onion and garlic.

In a medium saucepan, add the honey, rice wine vinegar and 220ml of water and bring to the boil over a high heat for 1 minute. Immediately pour this boiling mixture over the cucumbers (this helps to achieve the crunchy texture unique to this dish). The cucumbers should be completely submerged, leaving a centimetre or so at the top. Set the jar aside until completely cool. Cover tightly and leave at room temperature for 3 days, then refrigerate and use as needed. It will keep well for a good few months in the fridge.

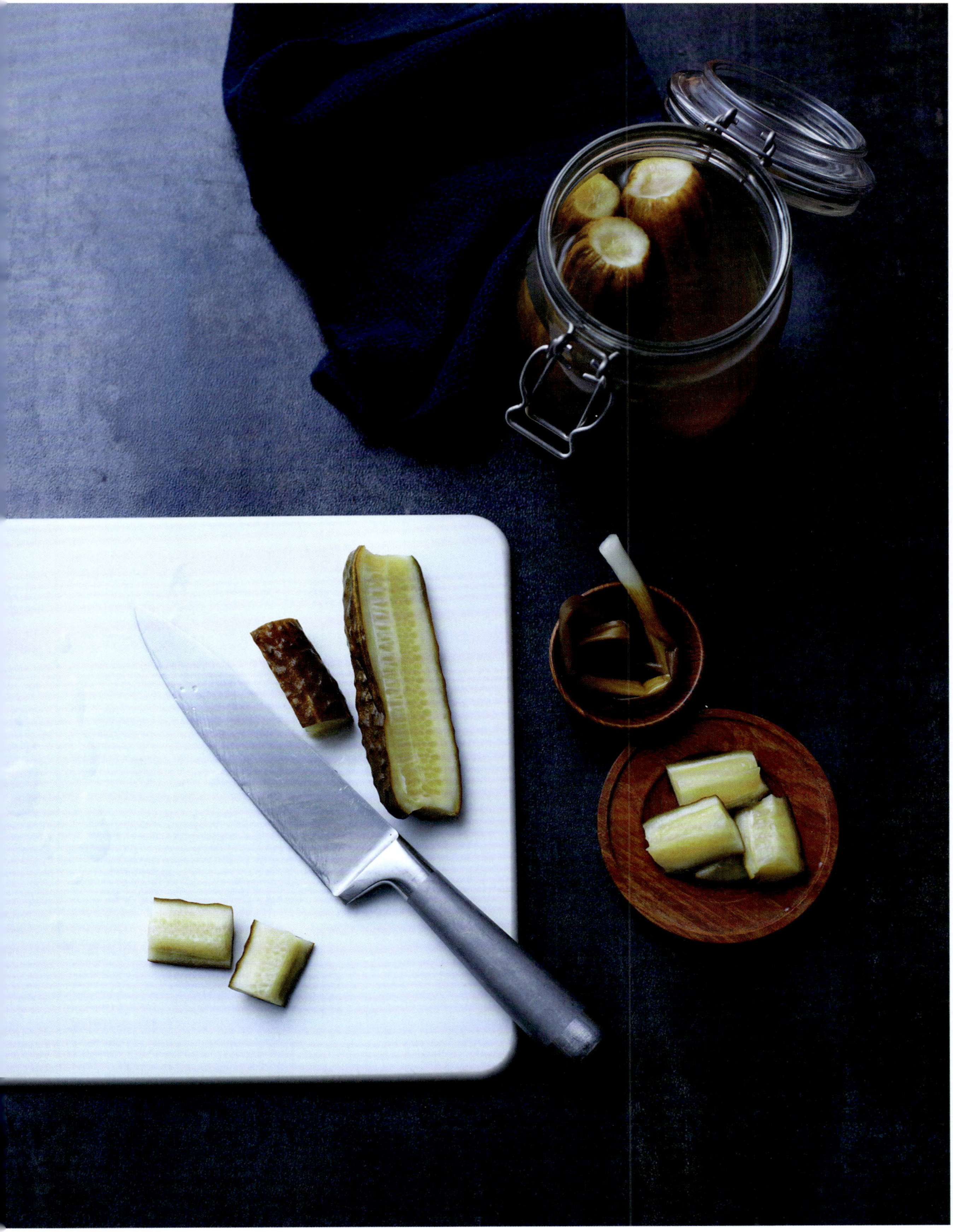

Serves 4 as a side dish

Seasoned Lotus Root
yeongeun jorim

연근 조림

300g lotus root, peeled and sliced into 1cm thin rounds
3½ tbsp soy sauce
2 tbsp honey
1½ tbsp roasted sesame seed oil
1 tsp toasted sesame seeds

One of the great things about Korean side dishes is the myriad of textures. Here, the lotus root is simmered in soy sauce until nothing more then an unctuous syrup remains giving the lotus root a dense texture, with a bit of bite. When buying lotus root, look out for ones with a thick and even texture and smooth skin.

Rinse the lotus root slices under running water. Fill a large pan with water and add the lotus root, then bring to the boil. Reduce the heat to medium and simmer for 15 minutes. Remove from the heat and drain off the water, returning the lotus root to the pan.

Add the soy sauce, honey, sesame seed oil and 500ml of water to the lotus root. Put the pan back on the heat, with the lid on, and bring to the boil. Reduce the heat and simmer for 45 minutes. Remove the lid and simmer for a further 15–20 minutes or until the liquid has reduced to 1–2 tablespoons. The lotus roots should be glistening and a rich caramel in colour. Remove from the heat and leave to cool.

Serve on a small side dish with the sesame seeds sprinkled over the top. Kept refrigerated in an airtight container, they will last perfectly for months.

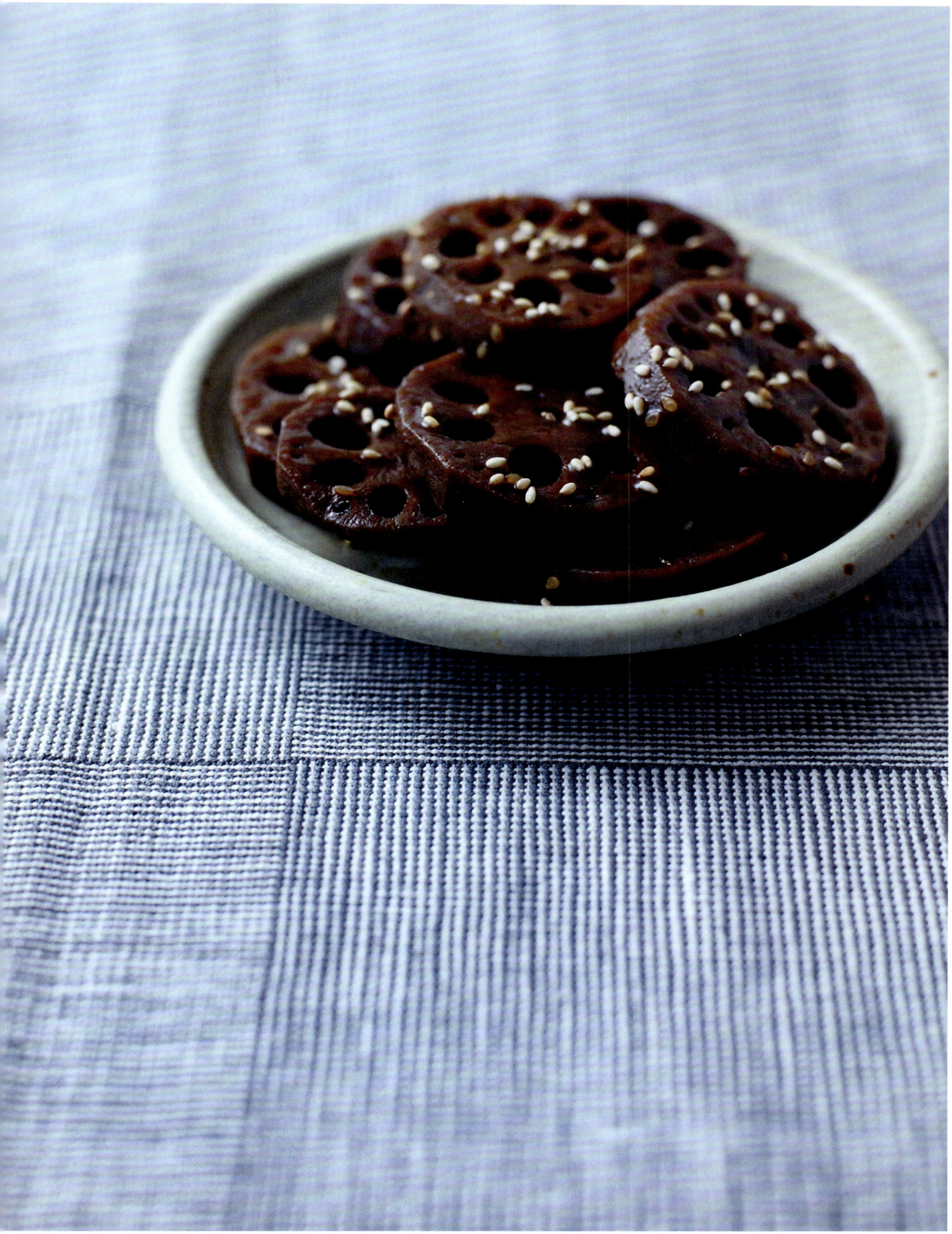

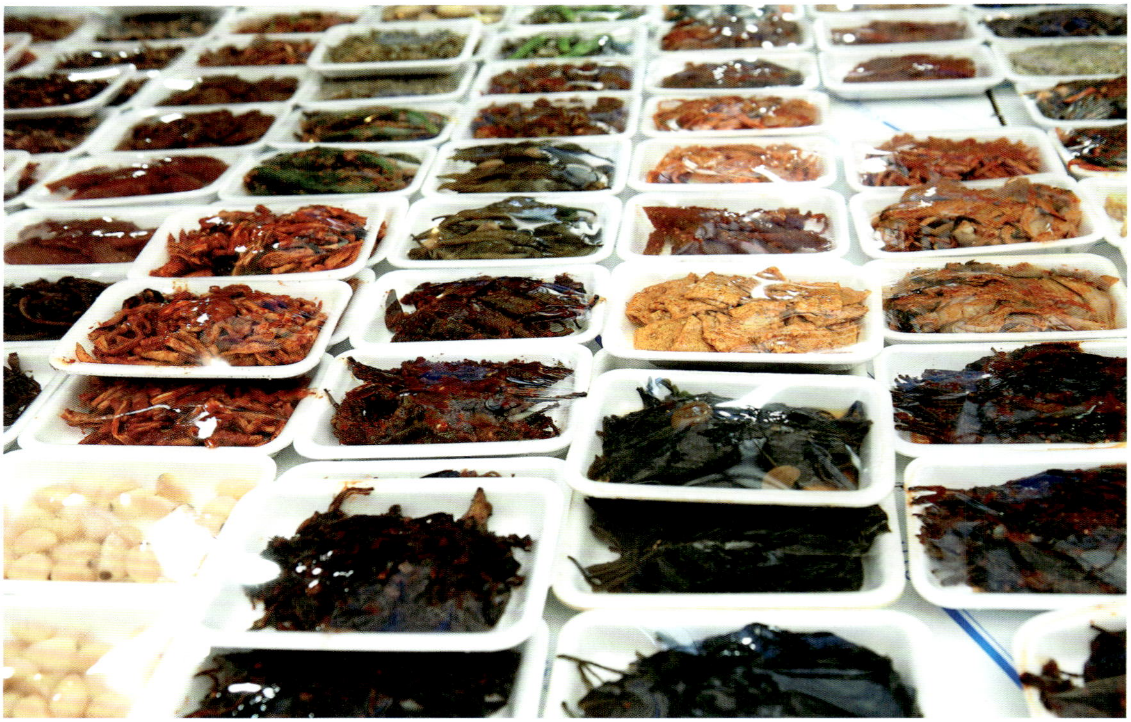

위하여 구입
NA
세일 꿀 연시
종이
세흥인쇄
SE HEUNG PRINTING CO.,LTD.
TEL.053/591-7222~6. FAX.053/591-7221
(신)

Makes 30 leaves

Pickled Perilla Leaves
kaenip jorim

30 large perilla leaves
100ml soy sauce
3 spring onions, finely chopped
3 garlic cloves, finely sliced
1 green chilli, halved, deseeded and sliced
2½ cm piece of ginger, very finely chopped
1 tbsp gochugaru red pepper powder (page 14)
1 tbsp honey
2 tbsp roasted sesame seed oil
1 tsp toasted sesame seeds

Perilla leaf is a very popular Korean ingredient, delicious eaten raw in salads, chopped up in stews or pickled, as in this recipe. Also known as 'sesame leaf', it in fact tastes nothing like sesame, and has a more pronounced citrus flavour. Perilla leaves can be found in Asian and Korean supermarkets and shouldn't be confused for the similar looking Japanese shiso leaf, which has a somewhat different flavour. The photograph on the right shows freshly-made leaves but over time they will become softer and darker in colour.

Wash the leaves and pat them dry. Pour a little of the soy sauce into a shallow bowl. Place a single leaf flat in the bowl and drizzle a little more of the soy sauce on top. Continue like this, stacking each leaf on top, until all the leaves are covered in the soy sauce. Pour any remaining soy sauce over the leaves. Set aside and leave at room temperature for an hour.

Drain the soy sauce from the leaves, gently squeezing out any residual sauce and set the leaves to one side. Add the drained soy sauce to a pan, add in the spring onions, garlic, chilli, ginger, gochugaru powder, honey and 100ml of water. Cover and bring to the boil, reduce the heat and simmer gently for 20 minutes. Remove from the heat, strain the soy sauce through a sieve and discard the flavouring ingredients. Leave the sauce to cool then stir in the sesame seed oil.

Put the leaves into a resealable container then pour over the sauce and cover. Serve a few leaves as a side dish with a few sesame seeds sprinkled over the top. They are particularly nice wrapped around rice, creating little parcels.

Kept covered and refrigerated, they will last for a few months.

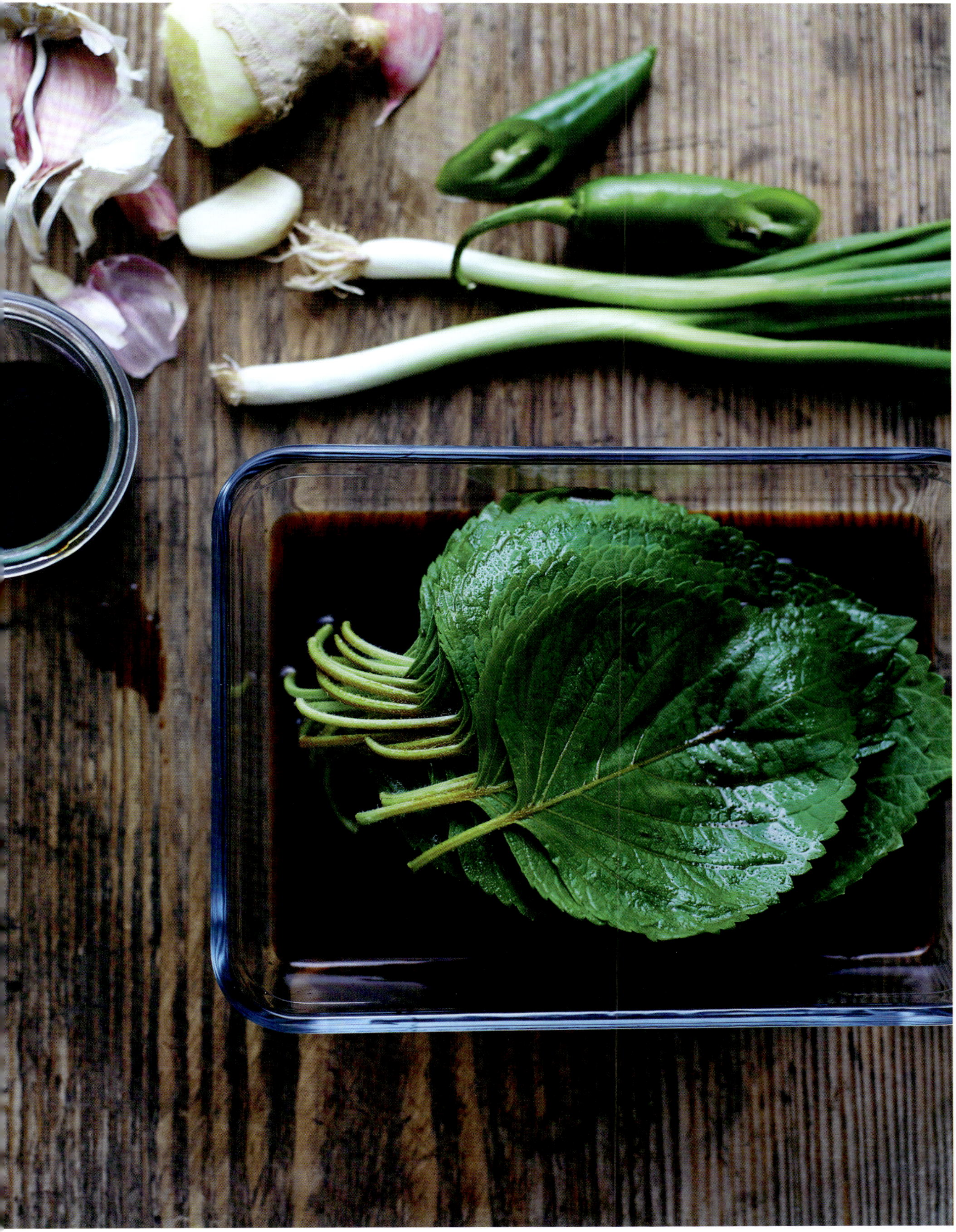

Serves 4 as a side dish

Soy-seasoned Mushrooms
bo-seot namool

1½ tbsp sunflower oil
250g wild mushrooms of your choice (such as shiitake, oyster, enoki, girolle), sliced into ½ cm strips
2 tsp soy sauce
2 garlic cloves, crushed
2 tsp roasted sesame seed oil
1 tsp toasted sesame seeds

Any selection of wild mushrooms would be lovely here, but shiitake mushrooms are a good start. The key here is to cook the mushrooms over a very high heat for a short amount of time, keeping everything on the move to avoid burning.

Heat the oil in a wide pan over a high heat. Once hot, add the mushrooms and stir-fry for 30 seconds, then add the soy sauce and garlic and stir-fry for a further minute. Add the sesame seed oil and stir-fry for another minute, tossing to keep everything moving all the time so as not to burn the garlic.

Transfer to a bowl, mix in the sesame seeds and set aside to cool a little, giving the flavours time to get acquainted before serving. This dish is equally nice cold.

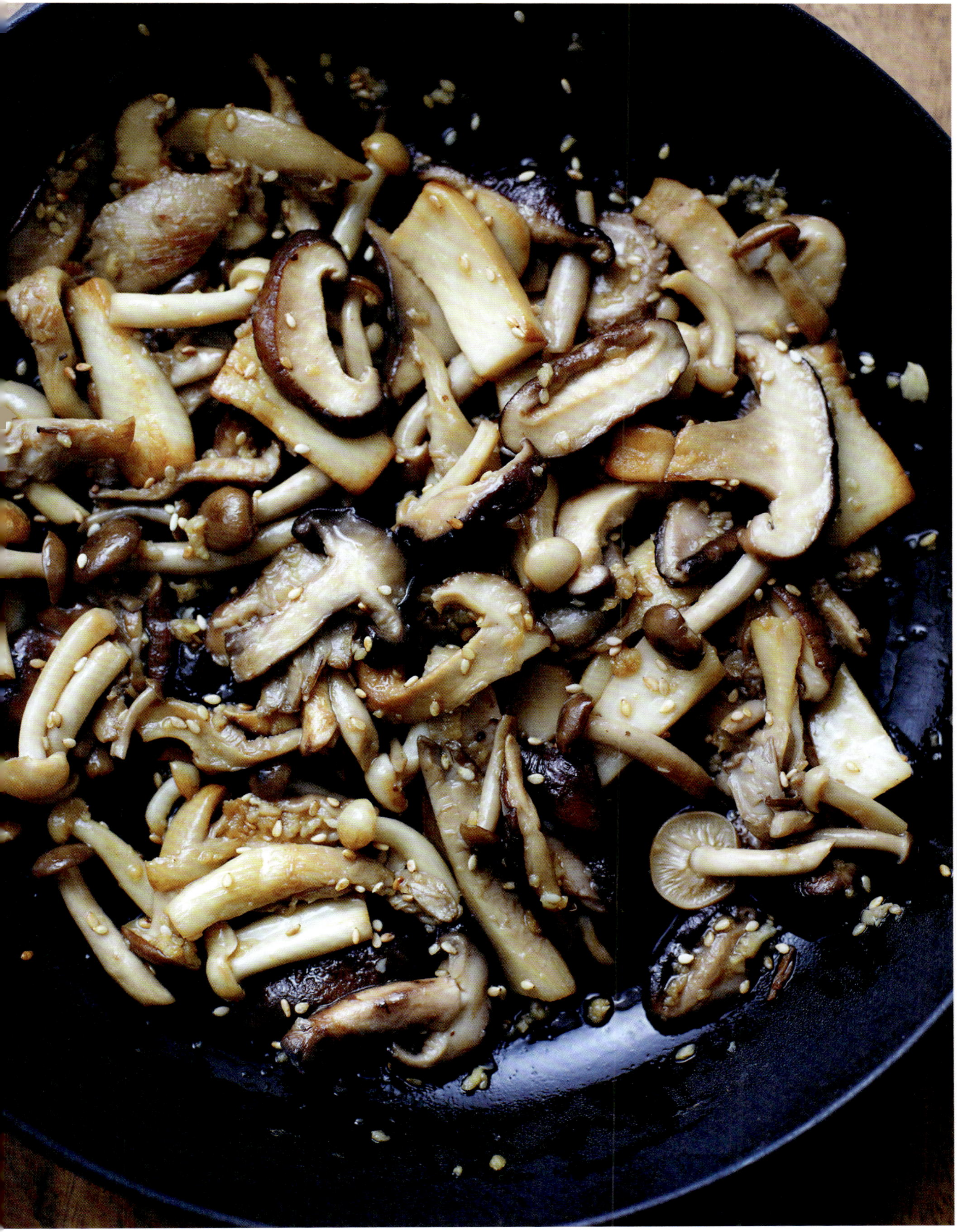

Serves 6 as a side dish

Seasoned Courgettes
hobak namool

2 courgettes
1 tbsp vegetable or sunflower oil
2 tsp roasted sesame seed oil
1–2 garlic cloves, crushed
1 spring onion, finely chopped
1 tsp toasted sesame seeds
pinch of sea salt, to taste

Either Western or Asian courgettes can be used in this dish, the latter being fatter and their skin being a much paler green. You can cook most vegetables in this way and mixed with rice it creates a kind of instant bibimbap.

Slice the courgettes in half lengthways, then cut on the diagonal into thin half-moon shapes.

Heat the oil in a pan over a high heat. Add in the courgettes and stir-fry them for 1 minute. Add the sesame seed oil and garlic and stir-fry for a further minute. Finally, add the spring onion and sesame seeds then season with a pinch or 2 of salt, to taste. Remove from the heat and leave to cool a little before serving.

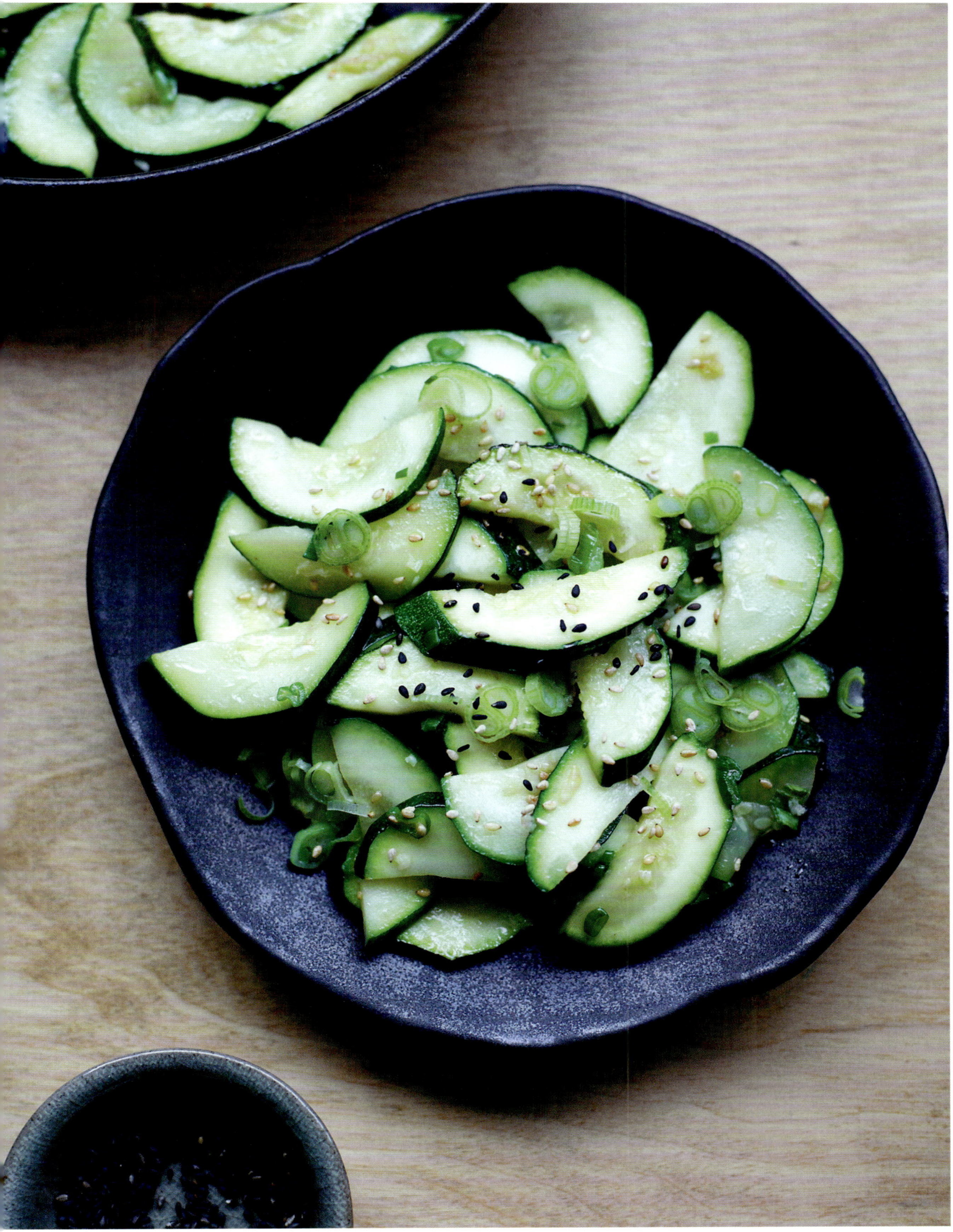

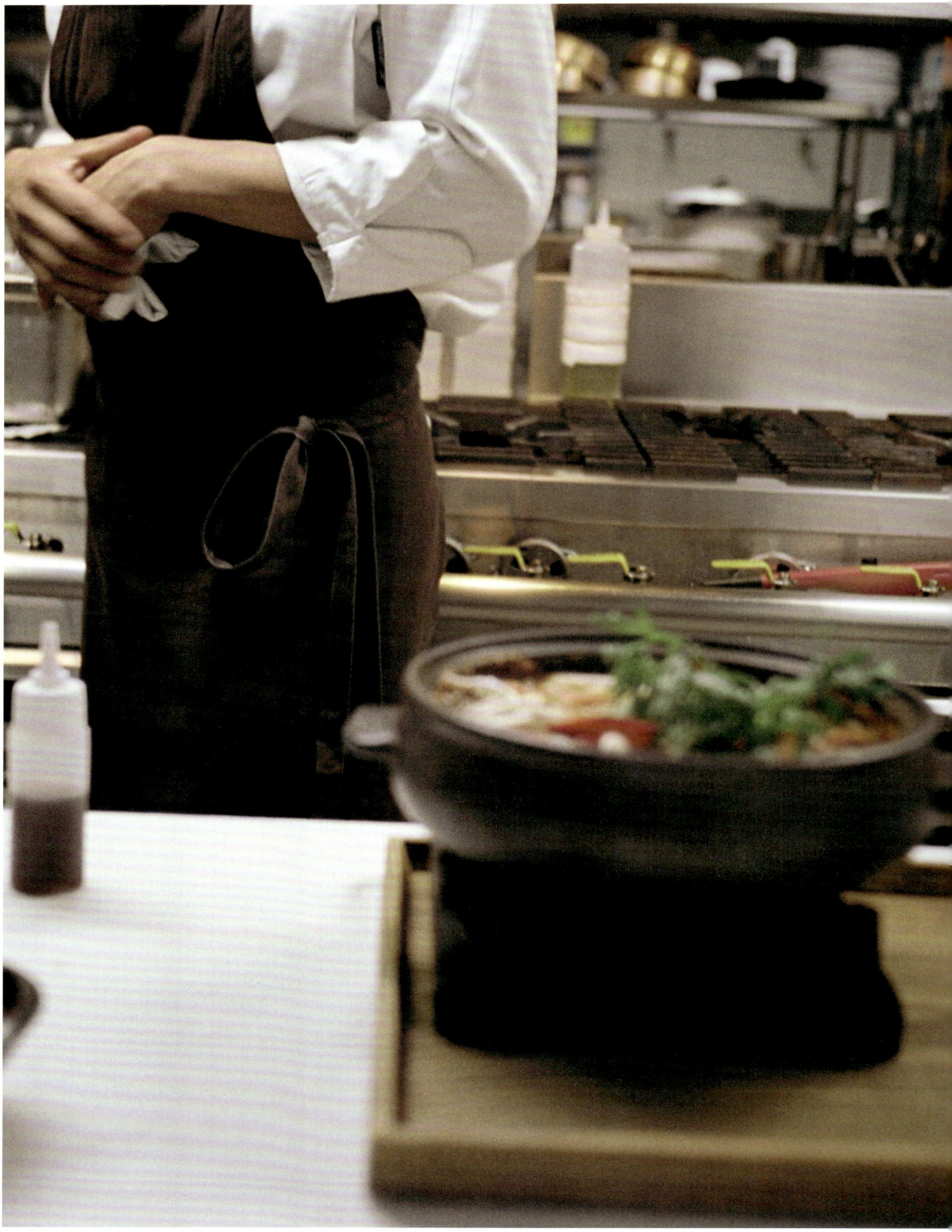

Serves 4 as a side dish

Quick Pickled Onions
yangpa jorim

1 white onion, halved and very thinly sliced
1 tbsp rice wine vinegar
1 tbsp mirin
1 tbsp soy sauce
1 tsp honey

This is an incredibly quick and easy pickled onion dish, which is always served with Korean barbecues and is a must with the Grilled Beef Short Ribs (page 224).

In a bowl, combine the sliced onion and the remaining ingredients, mixing well until evenly coated. Cover and refrigerate for at least 1 hour or until ready to serve. It will keep for up to a week, covered, in the fridge.

Serves 6 as a side dish

Garlic & Sesame Bean Sprouts
sook-ju namool

300g bean sprouts
2 tsp sea salt, plus extra to season
2 spring onions, finely chopped
3 garlic cloves, crushed
2 tsp roasted sesame seed oil
2 tsp toasted sesame seeds
½ tsp gochugaru red pepper powder (optional) (page 14)

This dish is very quick and easy to prepare. It is usually served with rice dishes, adding a lovely crunch, but you can have it with whatever you like.

Put the bean sprouts in a pan with the salt and add water to barely cover them. Place the lid on and bring to the boil, then reduce the heat to medium and simmer for 8 minutes. Drain in a colander.

Transfer the hot bean sprouts into a bowl with the remaining ingredients along with a pinch of salt to season. Mix thoroughly, taste and adjust the seasoning if necessary. This can be served hot, but it is usually served at room temperature, and will keep for a couple of days in the fridge. Make sure to let it come back up to room temperature prior to serving if it has been refrigerated.

Dried Seasoned Anchovies & Mum's Spicy Dried Squid
myeolchi bokkeum & ojingeo chae

Dried Seasoned Anchovies

Serves 4–6 as a side dish

1 tbsp mirin
2 tbsp maple syrup
2 tsp soy sauce
3 garlic cloves, crushed
80g small dried anchovies (page 17)
2 tbsp sunflower oil
2 tsp toasted sesame seeds
1½ tsp roasted sesame seed oil

These tiny, crisp, stir-fried anchovies are seriously good, and quick to make. The smallest are about 1cm in length and don't require any preparation at all, making them a convienient choice for this recipe.

In a bowl, combine the mirin, maple syrup, soy sauce and garlic.

Put a large frying pan over a medium-high heat and add the anchovies. Stir-fry for 4 minutes, tossing to keep them moving. Add the sunflower oil and fry for a further 4 minutes until the anchovies are golden and crisp.

Reduce the heat to low, add the mirin and soy sauce mixture then stir-fry for 2–3 minutes, stirring all the time until the anchovies are completely coated and almost dry.

Remove from the heat and stir in the sesame seeds and oil. Leave to cool. Store in an airtight container in the fridge where it will keep for at least 2 months. Serve cold or at room temperature as a side dish.

Mum's Spicy Dried Squid

Serves 8 as a side dish

3 tbsp gochujang chilli paste (page 14)
2 garlic cloves, crushed
2 tbsp honey or rice syrup
4 tsp roasted sesame seed oil
2 tsp soy sauce
2 tsp sunflower oil
2cm piece of ginger, finely grated
¼ tsp ground cinnamon
230g dried squid, cut into bite-size lengths
½ tsp toasted sesame seeds

Jina's mother makes a stellar version of this glossy, chewy and spicy dried squid, which she posts over to us from Seoul – like a Korean version of receiving a slice of tinfoil-wrapped Christmas cake from Granny in Ireland! To the uninitiated, this may not sound very appetising but it is worth trying and we are certain you'll be hooked in no time.

In a large mixing bowl, combine all the ingredients apart from the dried squid and sesame seeds. Add the squid and use your hands to thoroughly mix everything together for several minutes until each and every piece of squid is evenly coated. (You can wear plastic gloves if you like.)

Transfer the mixture to an airtight container, sprinkle over the sesame seeds, seal the box and refrigerate until needed. If kept in an airtight container in the fridge, this will last for at least a few months.

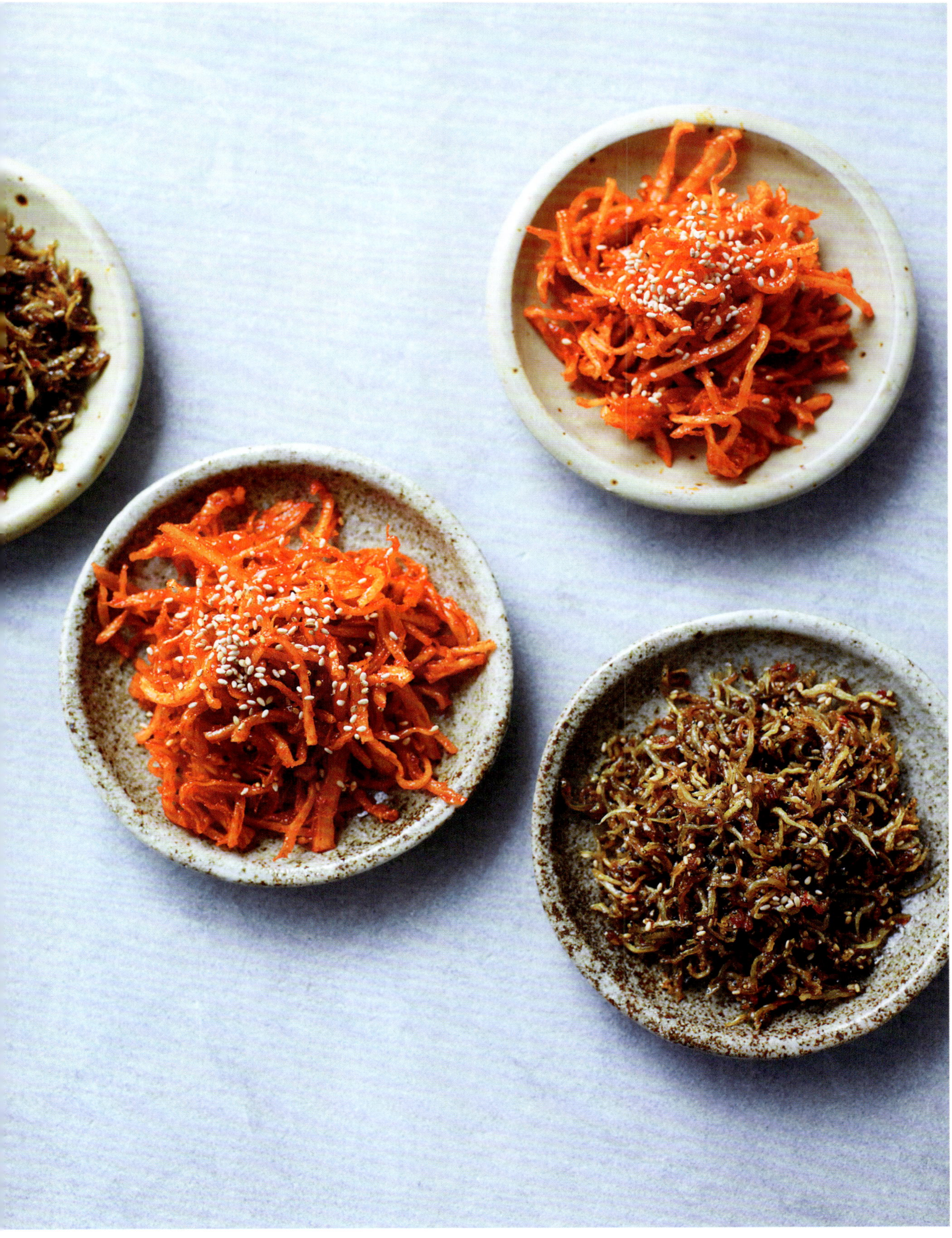

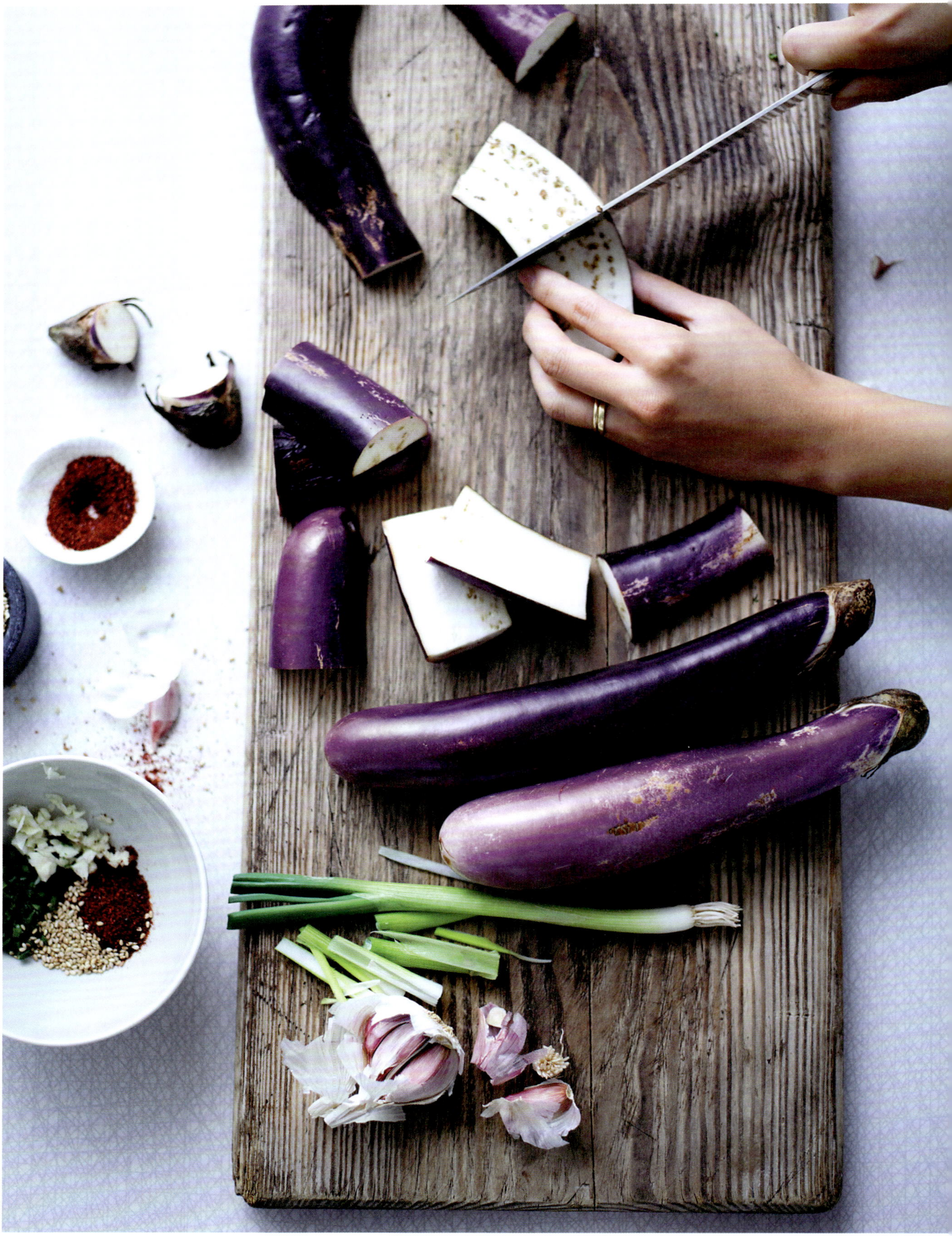

Serves 4 as a side dish

Soy Sauce & Garlic-steamed Aubergine
ka-jee namool

가지나물

- 4 Asian aubergines (available from Asian supermarkets), cut in half lengthways and sliced into 7cm pieces
- 2 tbsp soy sauce
- 2 garlic cloves, crushed
- 2 spring onions, finely chopped
- 1 tbsp roasted sesame seed oil
- 1 tsp gochugaru red pepper powder (optional) (page 14)
- 2 tsp toasted sesame seeds

We often eat this very simply with plain rice, as there is so much flavour packed into the aubergine, you don't need much else. Asian aubergines have skin that is thinner than Western aubergines, making them ideal for this dish. You can use Western aubergines, but make sure to steam them very well until the skin and flesh are completely tender.

If you have a steamer, steam the aubergines for 10 minutes over a high heat. If not, pour 400ml of water into a large saucepan that is large enough to hold a sieve or colander inside it. Put the aubergines into the sieve and cover with a lid. Bring the water to the boil over a high heat and simmer for 10–15 minutes until the aubergines are soft. Remove from the heat. Transfer to a bowl and leave to cool completely.

Once cooled, pour off any liquid that has collected in the bowl and use a clean tea towel or kitchen paper to gently squeeze any excess liquid from the aubergines. Finally, cut or tear each piece of aubergine into thin strips. Place the strips in a bowl with the rest of the ingredients and stir well to combine. Leave to marinade for at least 30 minutes, or until ready to serve.

Serves 4 as a side dish

Honey & Soy-glazed Potatoes
kamja jorim

감자조림

- 500g baby new potatoes
- 1 tbsp roasted sesame seed oil
- 1 tsp toasted sesame seeds

Sauce
- 80ml soy sauce
- 4 tbsp unrefined sugar or coconut palm sugar
- 1 tbsp mirin
- ½ cm slice of ginger, finely grated
- 1 garlic clove, crushed
- 5 tbsp honey
- 1 tbsp vegetable oil

These sweet and salty potatoes are one of our favourite side dishes – they are even good as a snack.

Place the sauce ingredients into a saucepan with 480ml of water and bring to the boil. Add the potatoes, cover with a lid and return to the boil for 1 minute. Take off the lid, lower the heat and simmer until almost all of the liquid has evaporated, leaving about 2 tablespoons. Stir in the sesame seed oil and remove from the heat, then leave to cool.

Serve at room temperature with the sesame seeds scattered over the top.

Vegetables, Pickles & Sides

Serves 2–4 as a side dish

Steamed Eggs with Spring Onion & Chilli
geran jjim

계란찜

100ml fish or chicken stock (or water)
½ tsp sea salt
4 large eggs
1 spring onion, finely chopped
1 red chilli, deseeded and thinly sliced
½ tsp toasted black and white sesame seeds

We were taught this recipe by Kim Yeon Im. She is the 78-year-old owner and head chef of Kajok Hwe-gwan (가족 회관), a restaurant in the city of Jeonju. Kim is an exceptionally kind and generous woman and our time spent cooking with her was one of those unforgettable experiences. Traditionally, this recipe is made in a stone bowl called a 'dduk-baegi', which is the ideal shape and is placed directly onto the stove to cook. They are easy to find in good Korean markets. However, it can also be made in any small saucepan.

In a medium-size mixing bowl, add the stock, salt and 100ml of water. Crack in the eggs and gently whisk the mixture together, then pass it through a sieve into a small, heatproof bowl.

Take a pan with a lid that is large enough to fit the bowl of eggs and fill with water, up to about 5cm, then bring to the boil. Once boiling, fold a couple sheets of kitchen paper in half and place them on the base of the pan. Place the bowl on top of the paper so that it is not sitting directly on the bottom of the pan. Cover the bowl with a plate and then place the pan lid firmly on top. Reduce the heat to medium and simmer for 10 minutes then reduce the heat to low and continue to steam for a further 5 minutes.

Turn off the heat and use a tea towel to carefully remove the bowl. Scatter over the spring onion, chilli and sesame seeds and serve immediately.

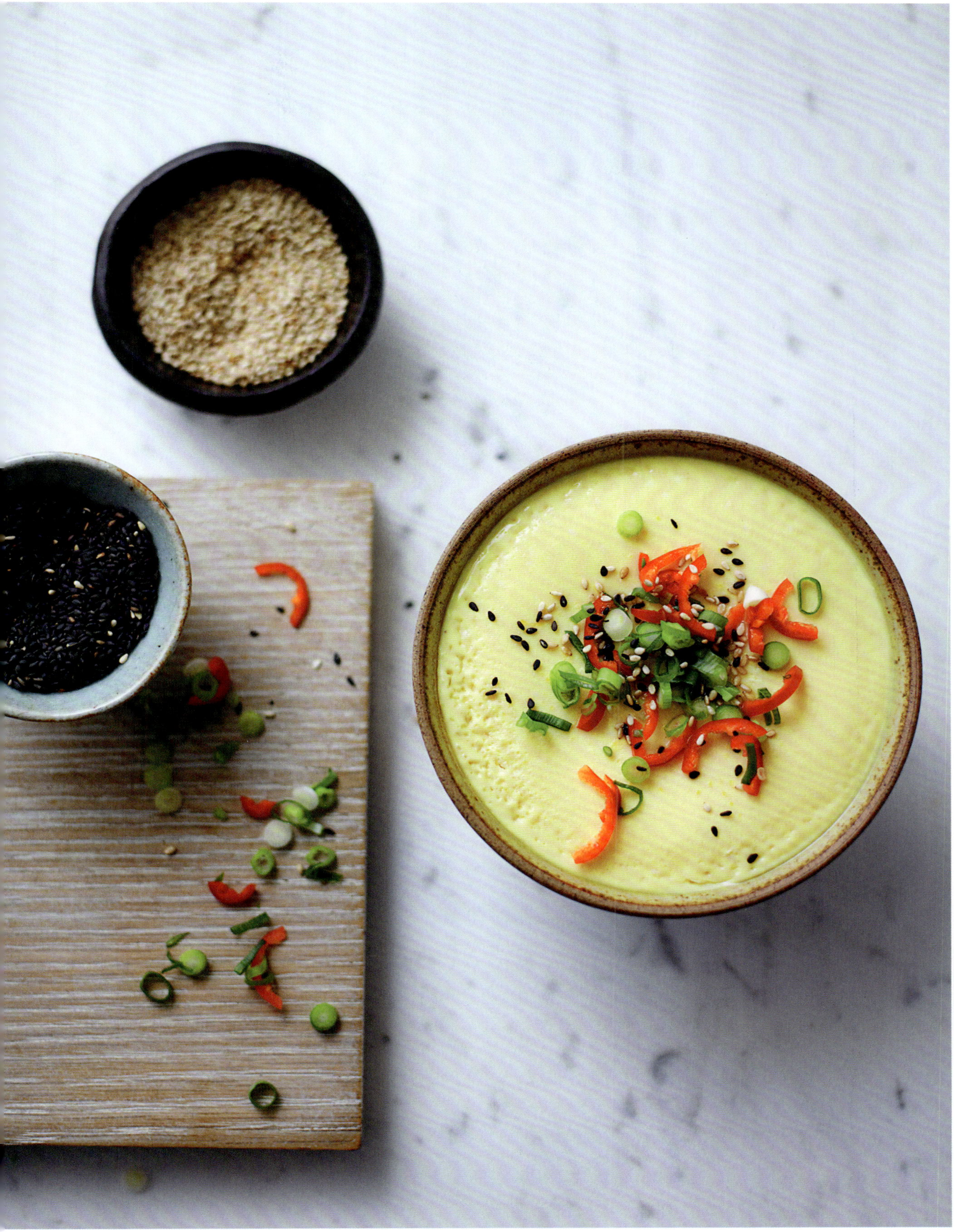

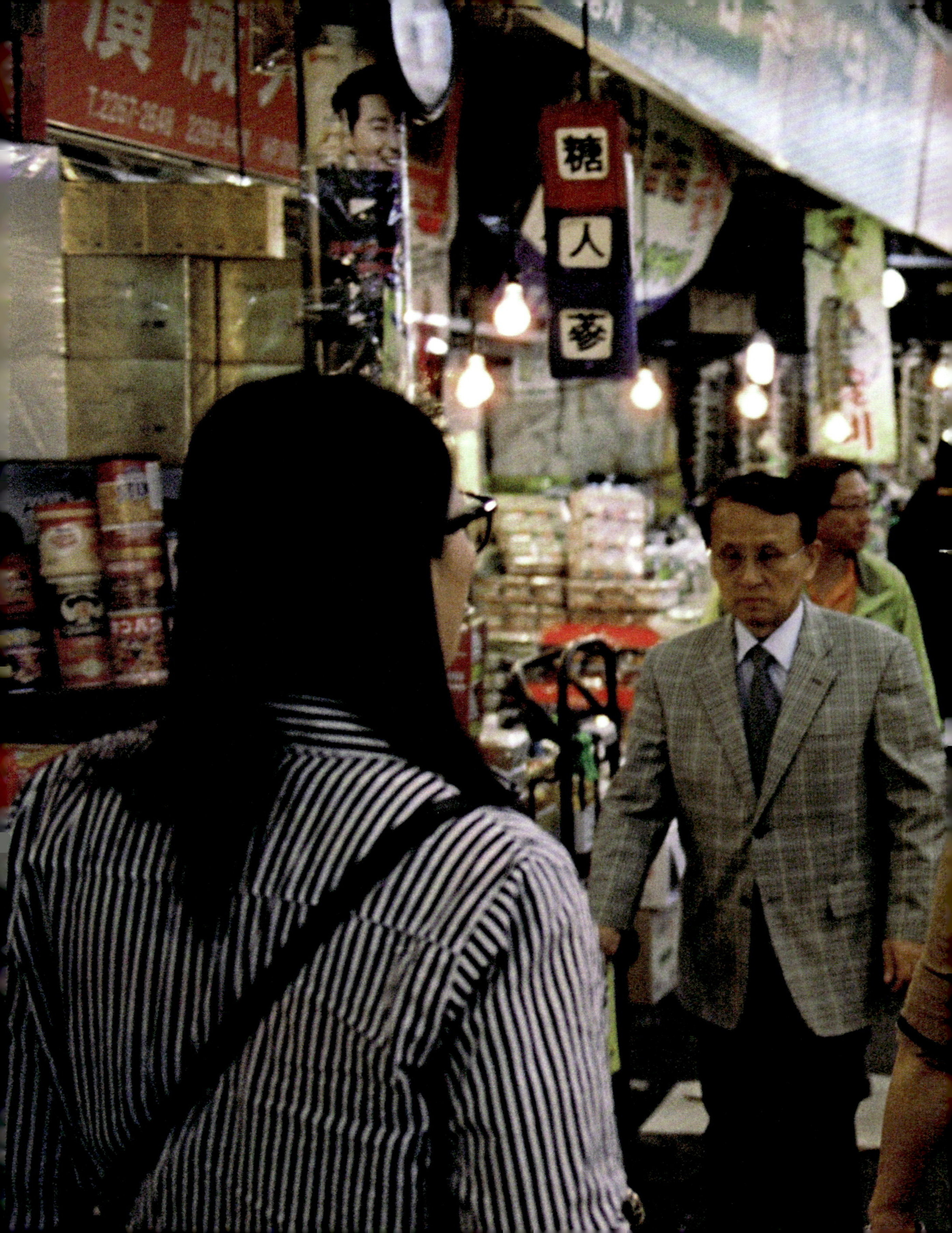
糖人蔘

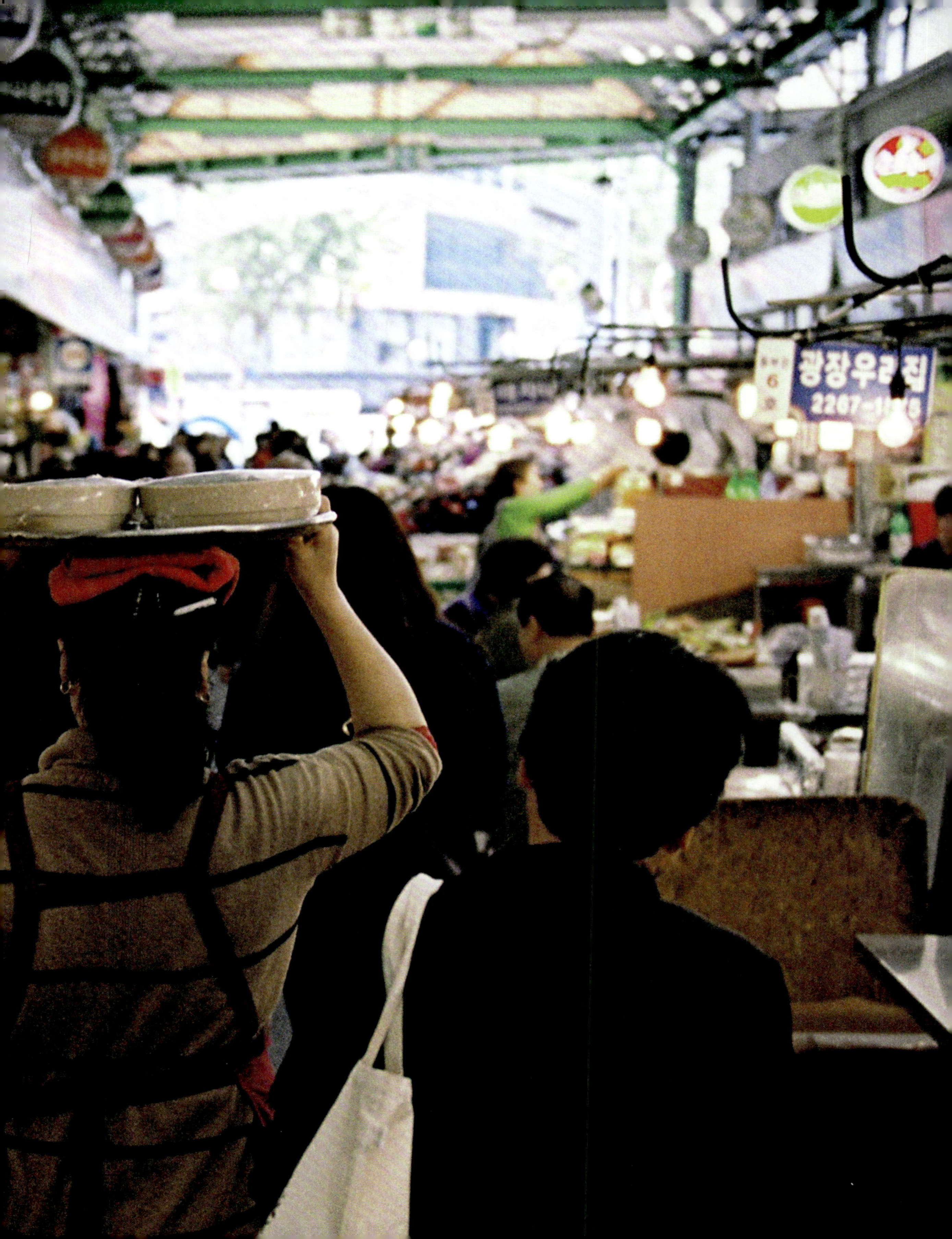

Pancakes, Fritters & Tofu

전, 튀김 & 두부

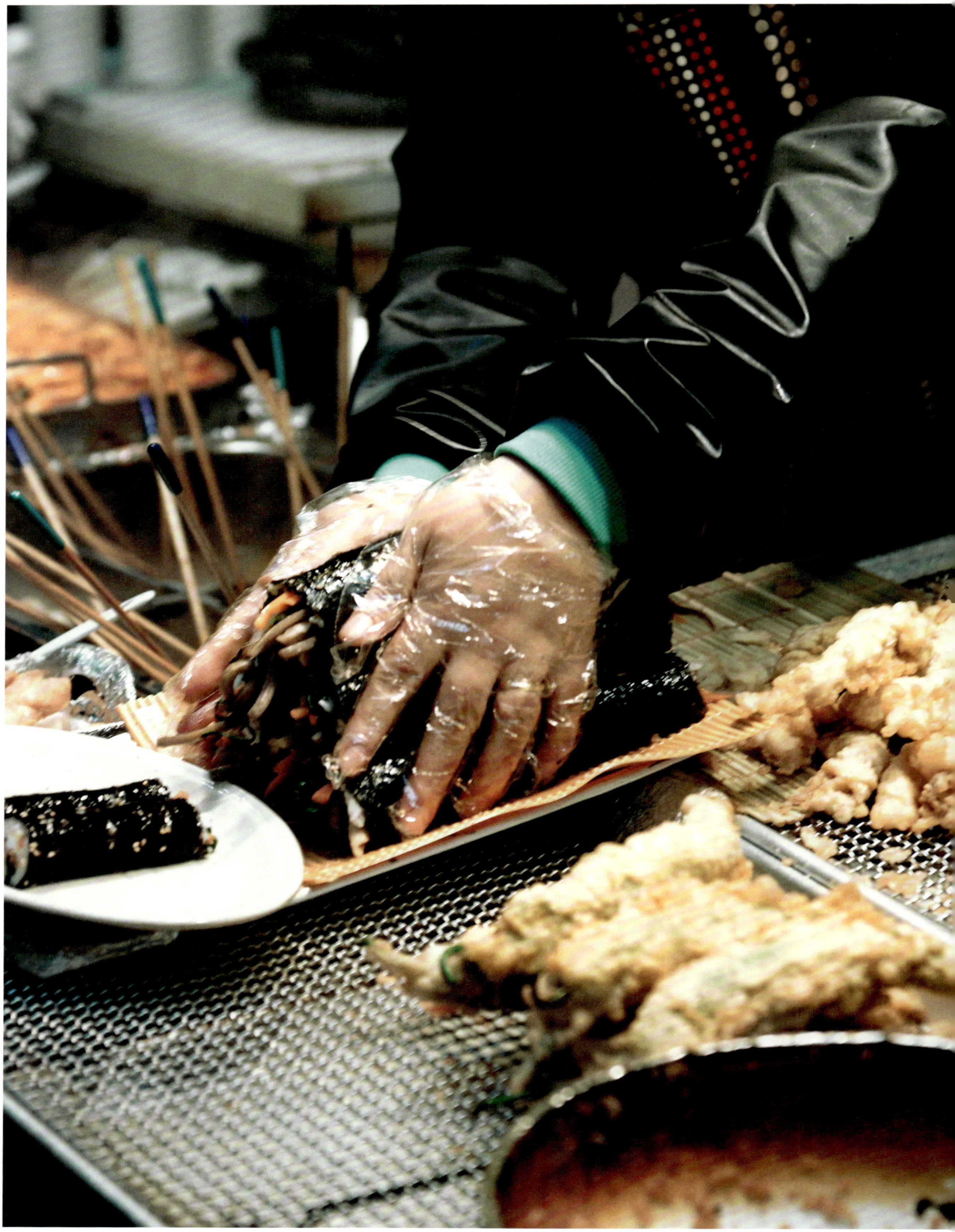

04

136. Seafood & Spring
Onion Pancake
해물파전

138. Kimchi Pancake
김치전

142. Mung Bean Pancakes
빈대떡

144. Stuffed Chilli Fritters
고추전

146. Battered Cod &
Courgette
생선전 호박전

147. Tofu with Soy Dressing
양념 두부

150. Prawn & Sweet Potato
Tempura
튀김

152. Tofu & Fried Kimchi
두부김치

Serves 2

Seafood & Spring Onion Pancake
haemul pa-jeon

200g mixed squid rings and prawns
4 garlic cloves, crushed
1 tsp toasted sesame seeds
2 tsp roasted sesame seed oil
100g plain flour (or white spelt flour)
3 level tbsp glutinous rice flour (or cornflour)
2 eggs, beaten
2 tbsp sunflower oil
6 spring onions, sliced lengthways
½ green chilli, deseeded and sliced
½ red chilli, deseeded and sliced
sea salt and freshly ground black pepper

Dipping sauce
2 tbsp soy sauce
1 tsp rice wine vinegar
½ tsp roasted sesame oil
1 small garlic clove, crushed
¼ tsp toasted sesame seeds

This dense, savoury pancake makes a fantastic starter or sharing dish with everyone diving in with their chopsticks, mopping up some of the soy dipping sauce along the way. Extremely popular as a snack in Korea, you can make this dish your own with whatever selection of seafood you like. A plain spring onion version of this pancake, without any seafood, is also a very popular Korean dish, so feel free to leave out the fish if you prefer – just double the quantity of spring onions.

In a bowl, combine all the dipping sauce ingredients together and set aside.

Wash the seafood and drain. Place it in a bowl with half the crushed garlic, the sesame seeds, sesame oil and a pinch of salt and pepper. Set aside.

In a separate bowl, combine the flours with a ¼ teaspoon of salt, then add half the beaten egg, the remaining garlic and slowly whisk in 150ml of ice-cold water. (Do not add in all the water at once, as you may not need the full amount.) The batter should be the consistency of thick pouring cream. If you are not using fish, add the garlic, salt, sesame seeds and sesame seed oil straight into the batter.

Place a 22cm non-stick frying pan over a medium heat, add the sunflower oil and when hot ladle in 2 thirds of the batter. Use the back of a spoon to coat the base of the pan with the batter. Place the spring onion strips onto the pancake, with the green ends lying in both directions, then scatter over the chillies and seafood. Add the remaining beaten egg to the remaining batter and whisk to combine, then drizzle it over the spring onions and seafood so that they do not come loose when flipping the pancake. Fry over a medium heat for 3–4 minutes until the bottom is set then carefully invert the pancake onto a plate and slide it back into the pan and fry for a further 3–4 minutes, or until the fish is cooked through and the pancake is golden and crispy.

Serve up the pancake by cutting it into bite-size pieces. Serve immediately with the dipping sauce.

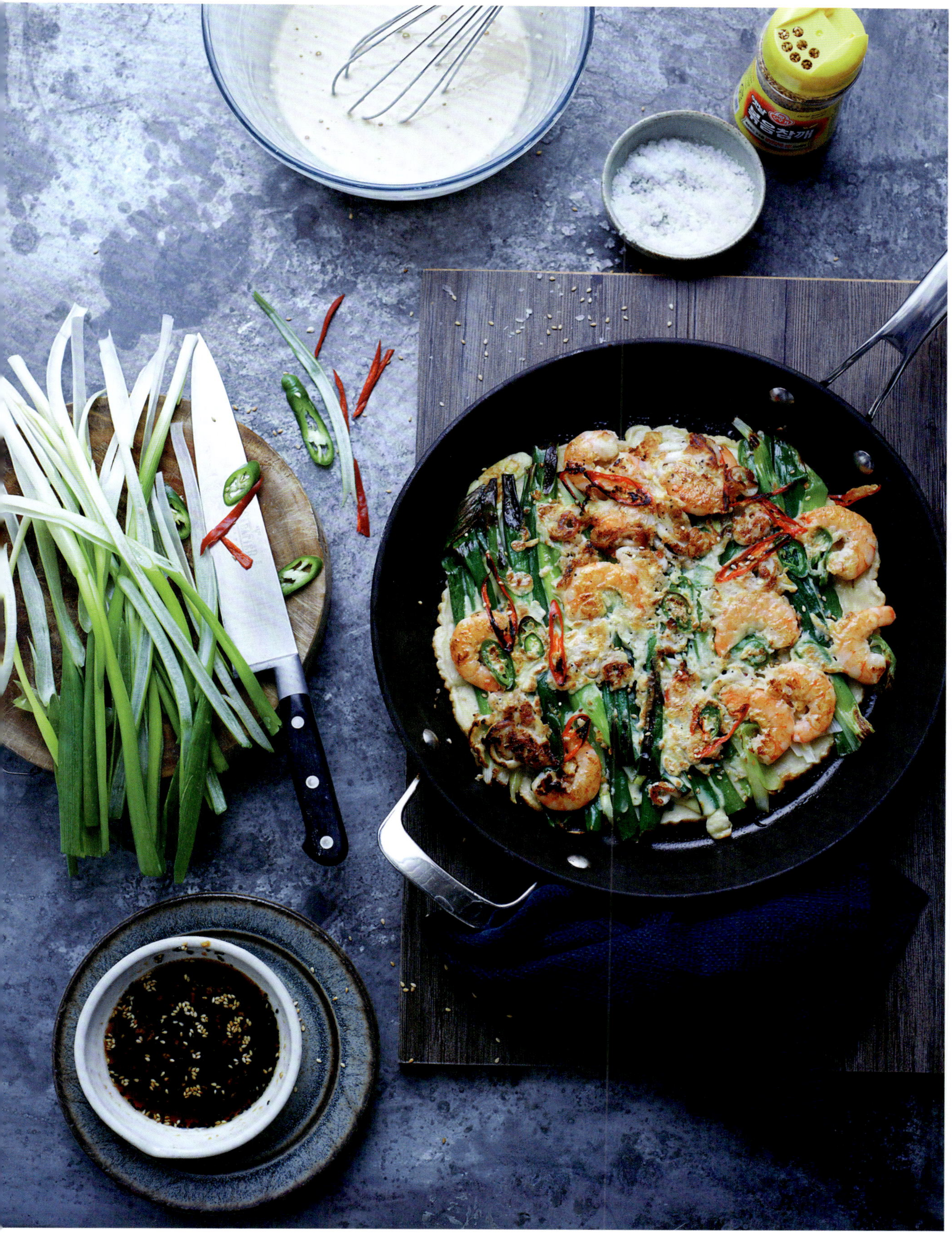

Serves 2

Kimchi Pancake
kimchi jeon

김치전

Batter
150g kimchi
100g plain flour
40g glutinous rice flour (or plain flour)
3 tbsp kimchi liquid
good pinch of sea salt
2 tbsp vegetable oil, plus 1 tsp to drizzle

Dipping sauce
1 tbsp soy sauce
1 tsp rice wine vinegar
pinch of toasted sesame seeds
pinch of gochugaru red pepper powder (optional) (page 14)

The contrast of the slightly sour, crunchy kimchi with the chewy batter, makes these pancakes unique. They can be whipped up in no time, and are great made with slightly older, mature kimchi. I find a little glutinous rice flour gives the pancake an added crispiness (corn or potato flour also work well). However it is also fine to use plain flour only – just use 140g in total.

Slice the kimchi into bite-size pieces. Place the pieces in a large bowl, together with 130ml of water and the remaining batter ingredients (apart from the vegetable oil). Mix until just combined and the consistency of thick batter.

In a small bowl, combine the dipping sauce ingredients.

Heat 2 tablespoons of oil in a large non-stick pan over a high heat. When hot, pour in the batter and use the back of a spoon to smooth the batter out to the edge of the pan – this will take a little effort, as the batter is thick. Fry for 3 minutes until golden and crispy, then flip over and drizzle the remaining teaspoon of vegetable oil around the side of the pancake. Fry for another 2–3 minutes until golden and crispy, then slide onto a plate or board, cut into pieces and serve immediately with the dipping sauce.

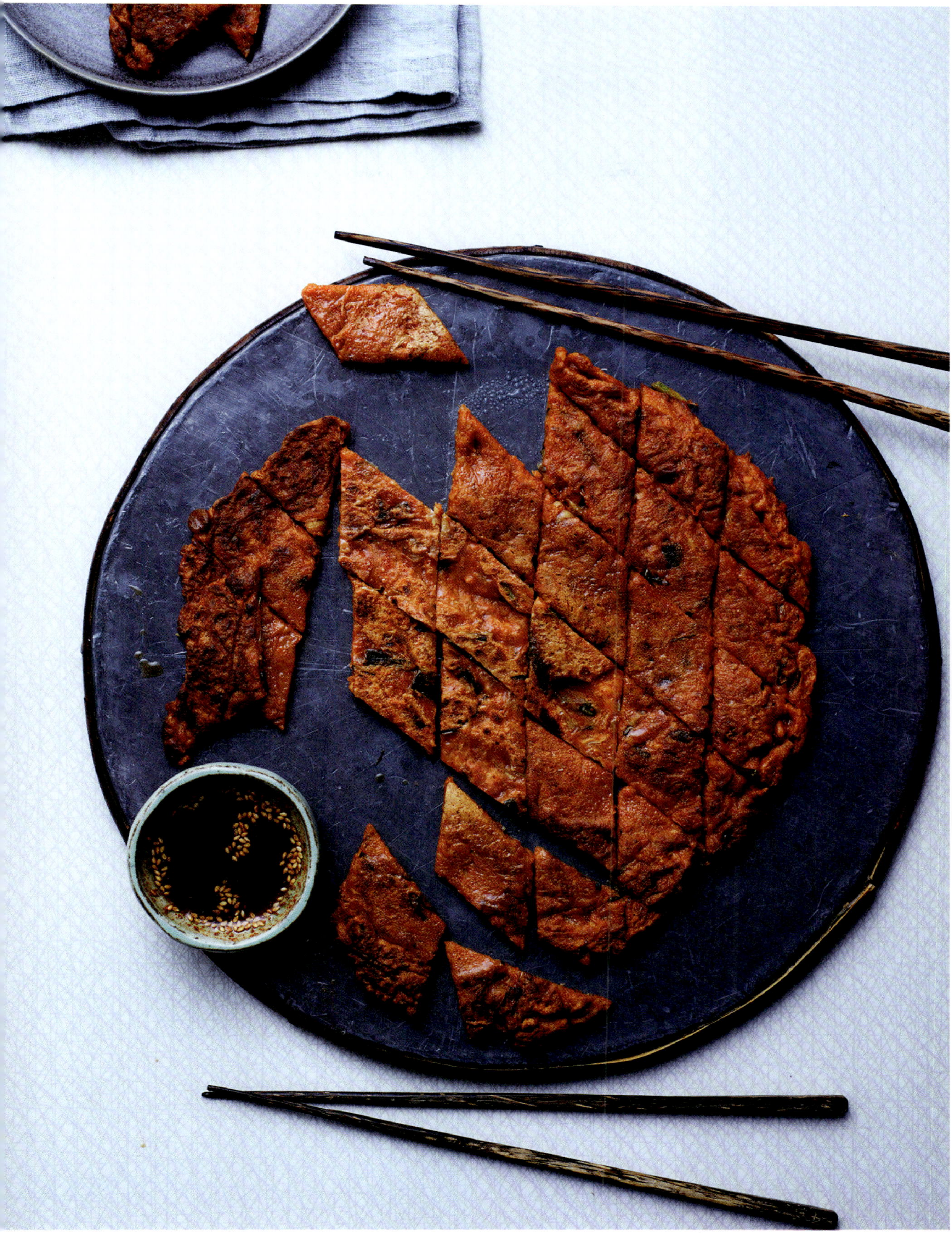

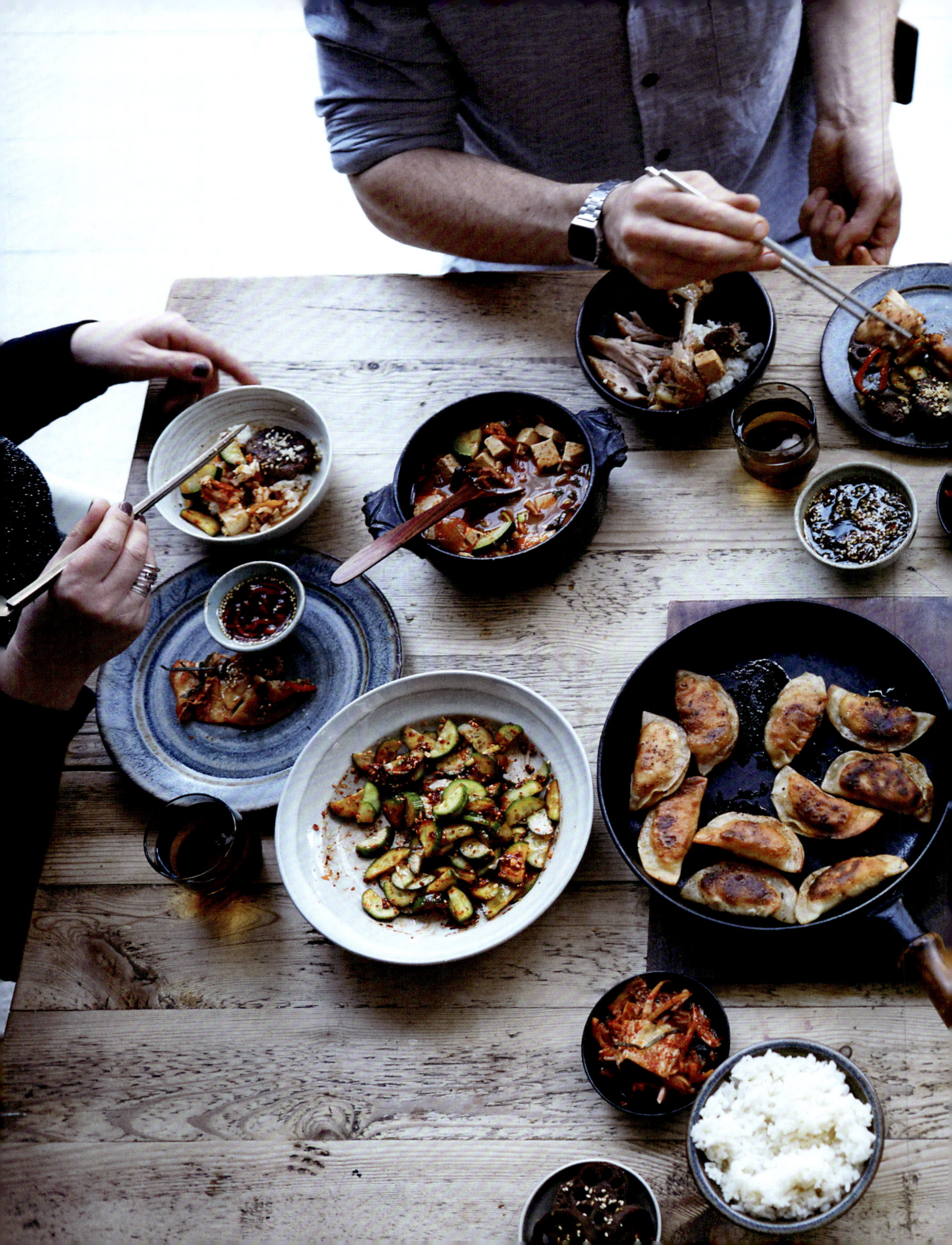

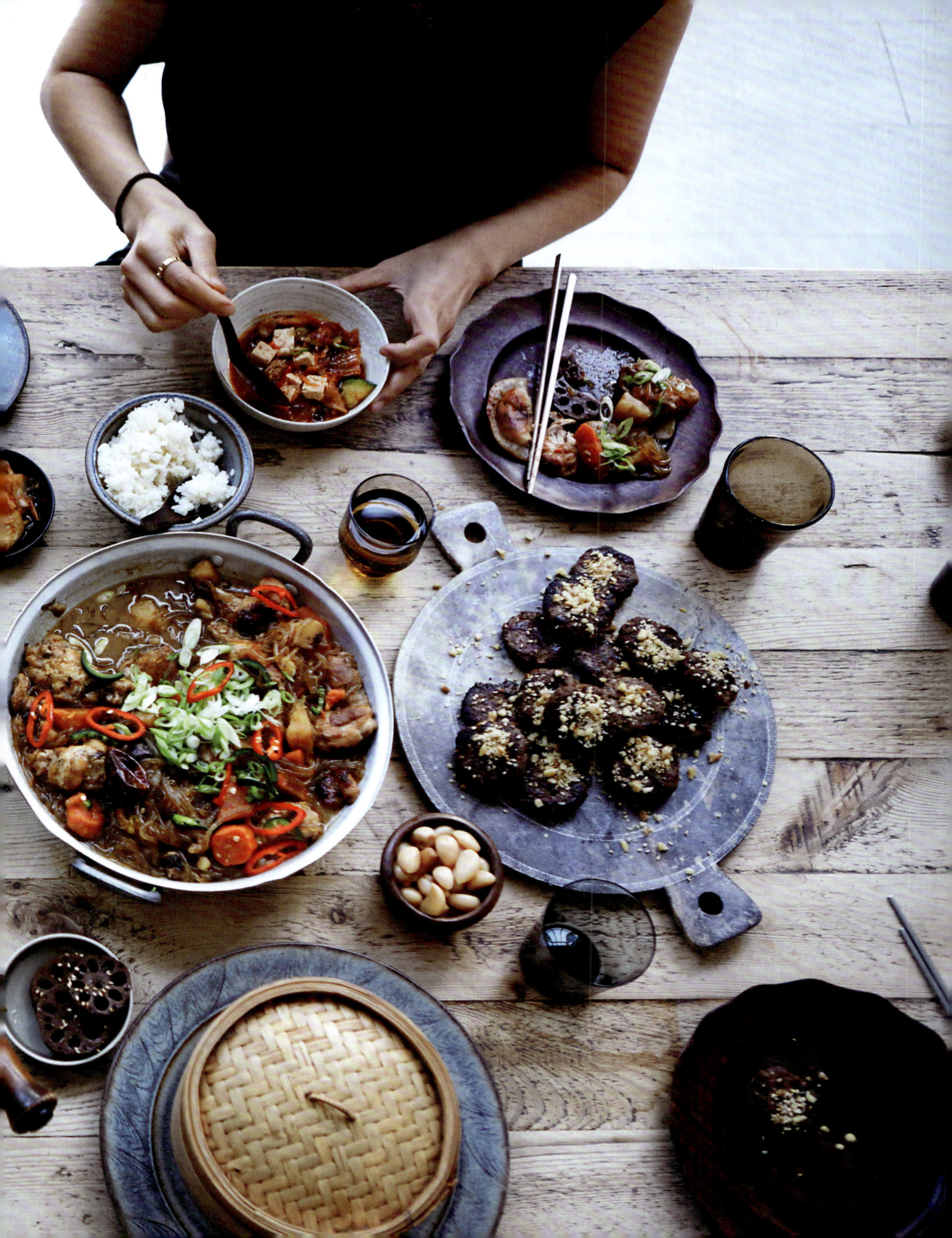

Serves 4

Mung Bean Pancakes
bindae-ddeok

300g mung beans, soaked overnight in plenty of cold water
3 tbsp kimchi juice
200g kimchi, chopped
30g glutinous rice flour (or plain flour)
6 spring onions, finely chopped
100g beef mince
4 tsp soy sauce
½ tsp sea salt
3 garlic cloves, crushed
2½ cm piece of ginger, finely grated
1½ tbsp roasted sesame seed oil
sunflower oil, for frying

<u>Dipping sauce</u>
2 tbsp soy sauce
1½ tsp rice wine vinegar
½ tsp toasted sesame seeds

These savoury and dense mung bean pancakes are a little more involved than the average pancake recipe, but they are absolutely worth the effort. In Korea, they peel off the skins from the beans after soaking them, by rubbing the beans between their hands. However, it is a laborious process and the end result is not much improved, so we always leave the skins on. You can also leave out the beef mince if you prefer.

Drain the soaked mung beans and add them to a food processor or blender with the kimchi juice and 150ml of water. Blitz on high, scraping down the sides at intervals, until you have the consistency of thick batter. The mixture will look a little coarse, but when pressed between your fingers it should be soft. Transfer the batter to a bowl and mix together with the rest of the ingredients (apart from the sunflower oil), until well combined.

Heat 2 teaspoons of sunflower oil in a non-stick frying pan over a medium heat. When hot, add in a heaped ladleful of the mixture and use the back of the ladle to shape it into a 15cm diameter circle, about 2cm thick. Reduce the heat to medium-low and fry for 3–4 minutes until golden brown and crispy. Carefully flip the pancake over, add in another teaspoon of oil and fry for a further 3–4 minutes until the pancake is cooked through and feels slightly firm to the touch. Remove and keep warm while you make the remaining pancakes.

Combine the dipping sauce ingredients in a bowl and serve with the pancakes.

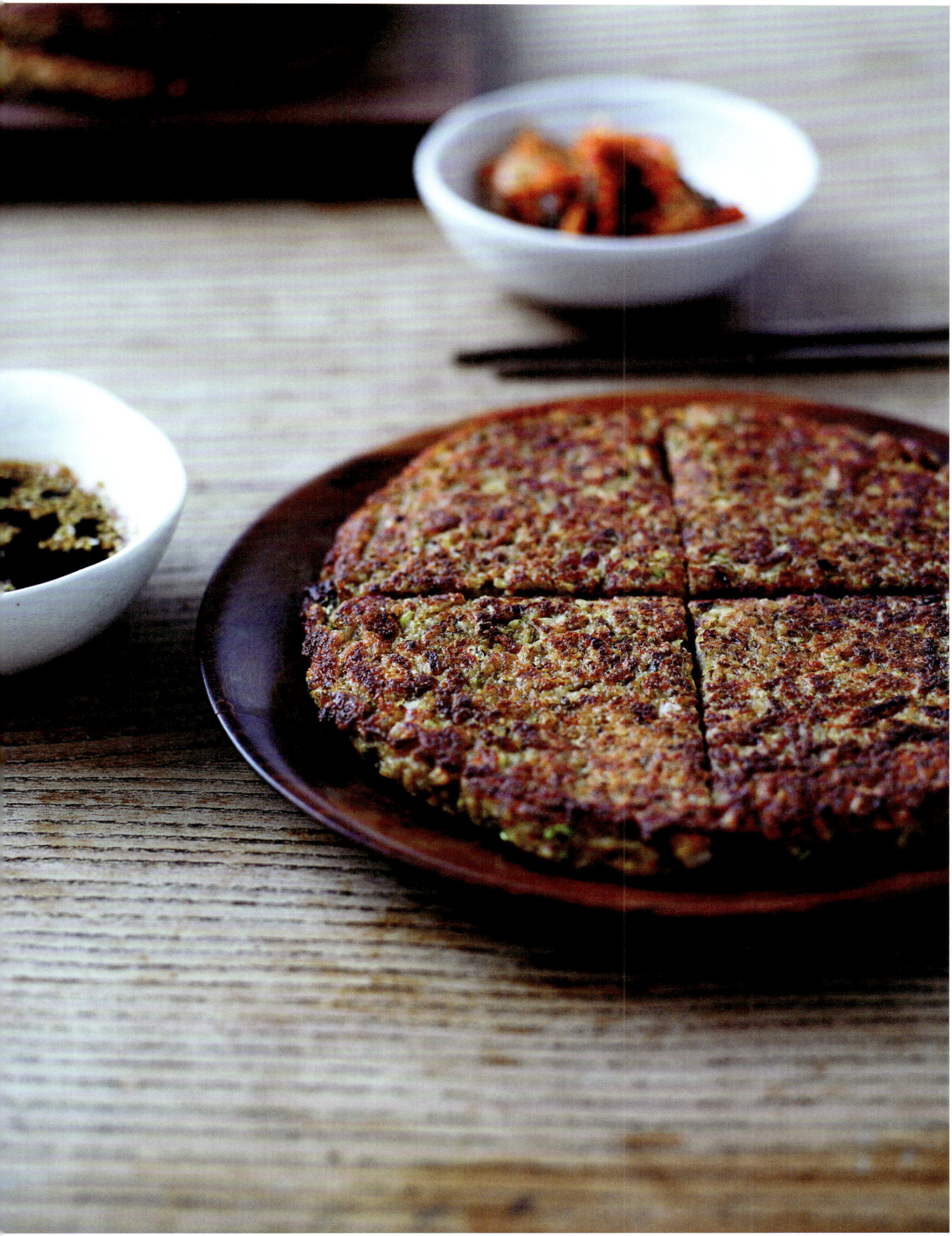

*Serves 4–6
as a side dish*

Stuffed Chilli Fritters
gochu jeon

16 large jalapeño chillies (or other mild chillies of your choice), halved and de-seeded
250g firm tofu, drained
250g beef or pork mince
3 spring onions, very finely chopped
2 garlic cloves, crushed
1½ cm piece of ginger, finely grated
2½ tsp soy sauce
2 tsp roasted sesame seed oil
1 tsp honey
1 tsp salt
½ tsp freshly ground black pepper
100g plain flour, plus 1 tbsp
2 eggs, beaten
2 tbsp vegetable oil

Dipping sauce
2 tbsp soy sauce
1½ tsp rice wine vinegar
½ tsp toasted sesame seeds

Stuffed chillies always seem to appear at any kind of Korean get-together or party, usually with some kind of pancake alongside. They are really handy as you can prepare them in advance and then just fry them on the day. A mild chilli, such as jalapeño, is best.

Rinse the chillies in cold water, pat them dry and set aside. (If you are worried the chillies will be too spicy you can soak them overnight, then pat them dry.)

Tightly wrap a clean tea towel around the tofu. Over a sink, squeeze the tofu very firmly, tightening the tea towel as you go to extract as much water as you can. Take a few minutes to do this – the tofu should be as dry as possible. Put the tofu in a bowl and combine with the beef mince, spring onions, garlic, ginger, soy sauce, sesame seed oil and honey. Season with the salt and pepper and mix well. Test to see if the mixture holds together when squeezed between your fingers, if not, add in the 1 tablespoon of flour and try again.

Sprinkle the remaining 100g of flour onto a plate and create an assembly line with the meat filling and beaten egg lined up alongside the flour. Coat each chilli half in the flour, then stuff with the filling, tightly compacting it into place. Gently coat in the flour again, shaking off any excess. Finally dip the chillies into the beaten egg mixture and shake off any excess. If you have any leftover filling, use it to make small bite-size patties.

Heat the oil in a large frying pan over a medium-low heat. When hot, fry the chillies in batches, for about 2 minutes on each side, until golden brown and cooked through. Combine the dipping sauce ingredients together in a bowl and serve with stuffed chillies.

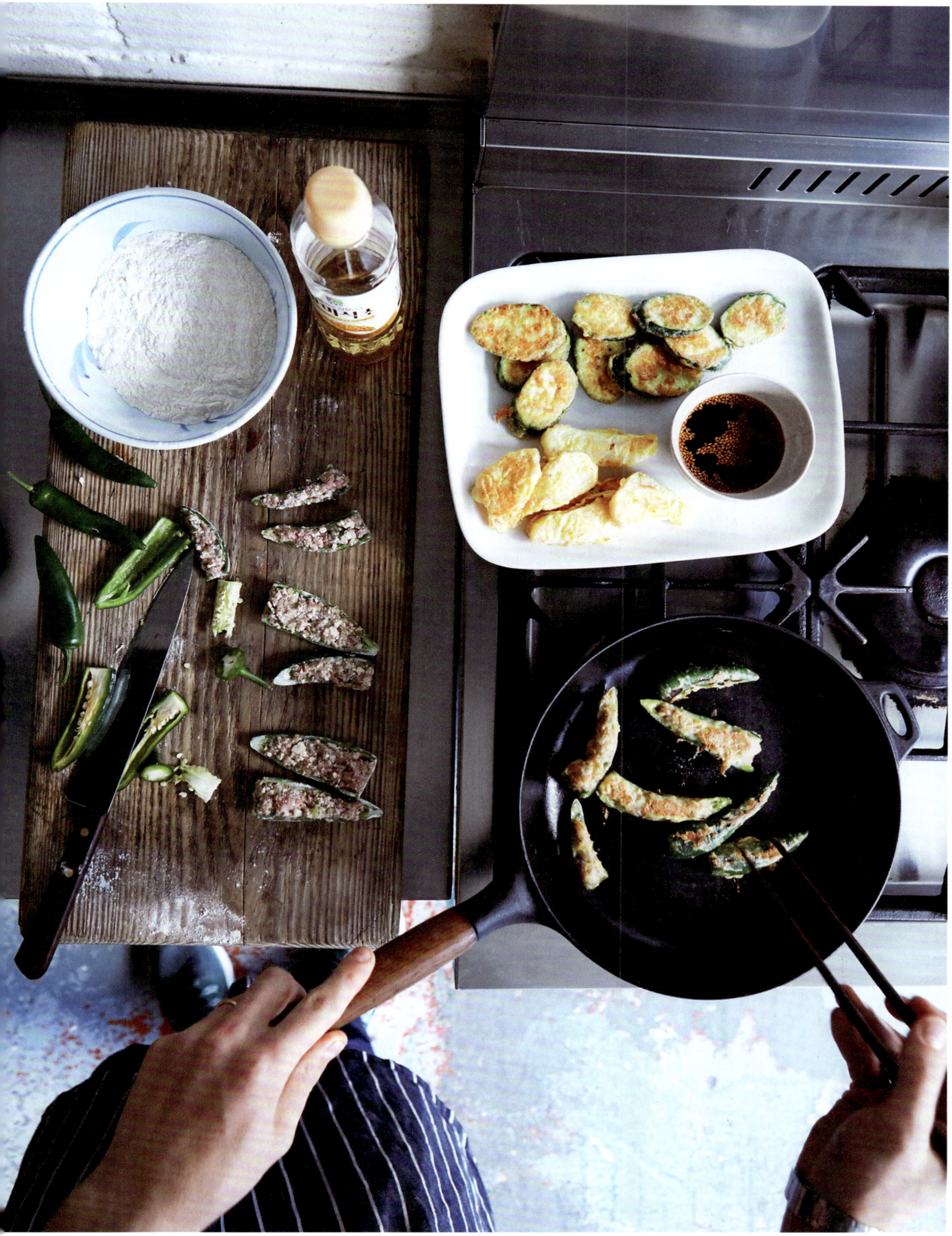

Battered Cod & Courgette
sengson jeon & hobak jeon

Serves 8–10 as a side dish

300g firm white fish fillets (cod, snapper, sole), skinned and deboned
300g courgettes, cut into thick slices
200g plain or white spelt flour
3 eggs, lightly beaten
vegetable oil, to fry
sea salt and ground white pepper

Dipping sauce
2 tbsp soy sauce
1½ tsp rice wine vinegar
½ tsp toasted sesame seeds

Pictured on page 145

This is a very simple dish. Slices of fish and courgette are dusted with flour and then dipped in egg before frying until golden. In Korea, it is cooked at the last moment when family and friends call in, together with a selection of little dishes to pick at, but here in London we often make this as a simple yet really satisfying lunch.

Slice the fish into ½ cm thick slices, about 6cm long. Spread them out onto a plate and season with salt and pepper. On a separate plate, do the same with the sliced courgette.

Put the flour and beaten egg into 2 separate bowls and position the bowls beside your stovetop.

Add 1 tablespoon of vegetable oil to a large pan and set it over a medium heat. In batches, coat the fish and courgette in flour, then dip them into the egg mixture to coat, and transfer them straight into the hot pan. Fry for 2 minutes on each side until golden, adding in a little more oil as you go as necessary. Remove and place in a heatproof dish and keep warm while you fry the rest. (Keep the heat at medium – if it is too high it will burn the outside before the inside is cooked and if the heat is too low you will end up with soggy fritters.)

In a bowl, combine the ingredients for the dipping sauce and serve immediately with the fish and courgette.

Serves 4 as a starter or side dish

Tofu with Soy Dressing
yangnyeom dubu

1 x 400g block of firm tofu (organic if possible)

<u>Sauce</u>
10 chives (8 very finely sliced and 2 sliced in half)
2½ tbsp soy sauce
1 tbsp mirin
1 tbsp roasted sesame seed oil
1 tsp honey
1½ tsp toasted sesame seeds
1½ tsp gochugaru red pepper powder (page 14)
1 garlic clove, very finely grated

The best way to prepare truly great ingredients is with absolute simplicity – and this is very much the case with this elegant tofu dish. One of our biggest food related gripes is the general derision with which tofu is treated by pretty much anyone in the Western hemisphere. It isn't packed full of flavour in its raw state, but then nor is pasta, or chicken breast or many other ingredients. It is what you put with it that brings it to life. This beautiful Korean dish pairs it with a few simple ingredients, but their quality is also important, especially the roasted sesame seed oil, so we would strongly recommend you buy a Korean brand in an Asian supermarket.

Drain the water out of the packet of tofu, then carefully and gently wrap the tofu block in a clean tea towel. Place it on a chopping board and balance another board or plate on top. It should be just heavy enough to exert a little pressure on the tofu to help press out the water, but not so heavy that the shape of the tofu distorts under its weight. Set aside for 30 minutes, turning it over halfway through.

Place the finely sliced chives in a bowl with the remaining sauce ingredients and combine.

Once the tofu has fully drained, carefully unwrap and place it on the chopping board. With a very sharp knife, cut the block into 4 squares of equal size. To serve, place each tofu square on a plate, spoon some of the sauce on top and finish with the remaining chives on top.

Serve at room temperature as a starter or side dish.

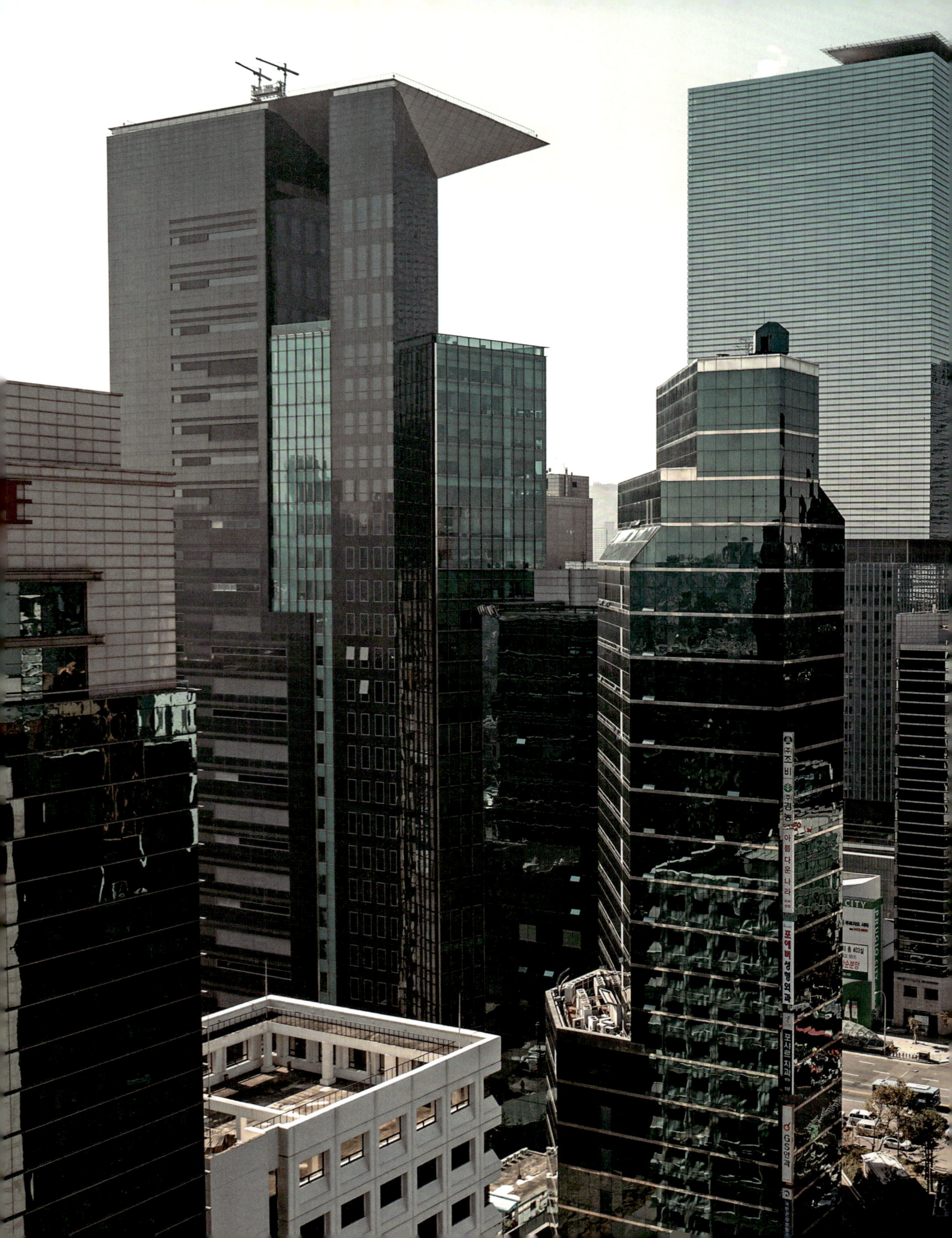

㈜조비
㈜경농
아름다운나라
포에버성형외과
포샤르치과
GS안과
CITY

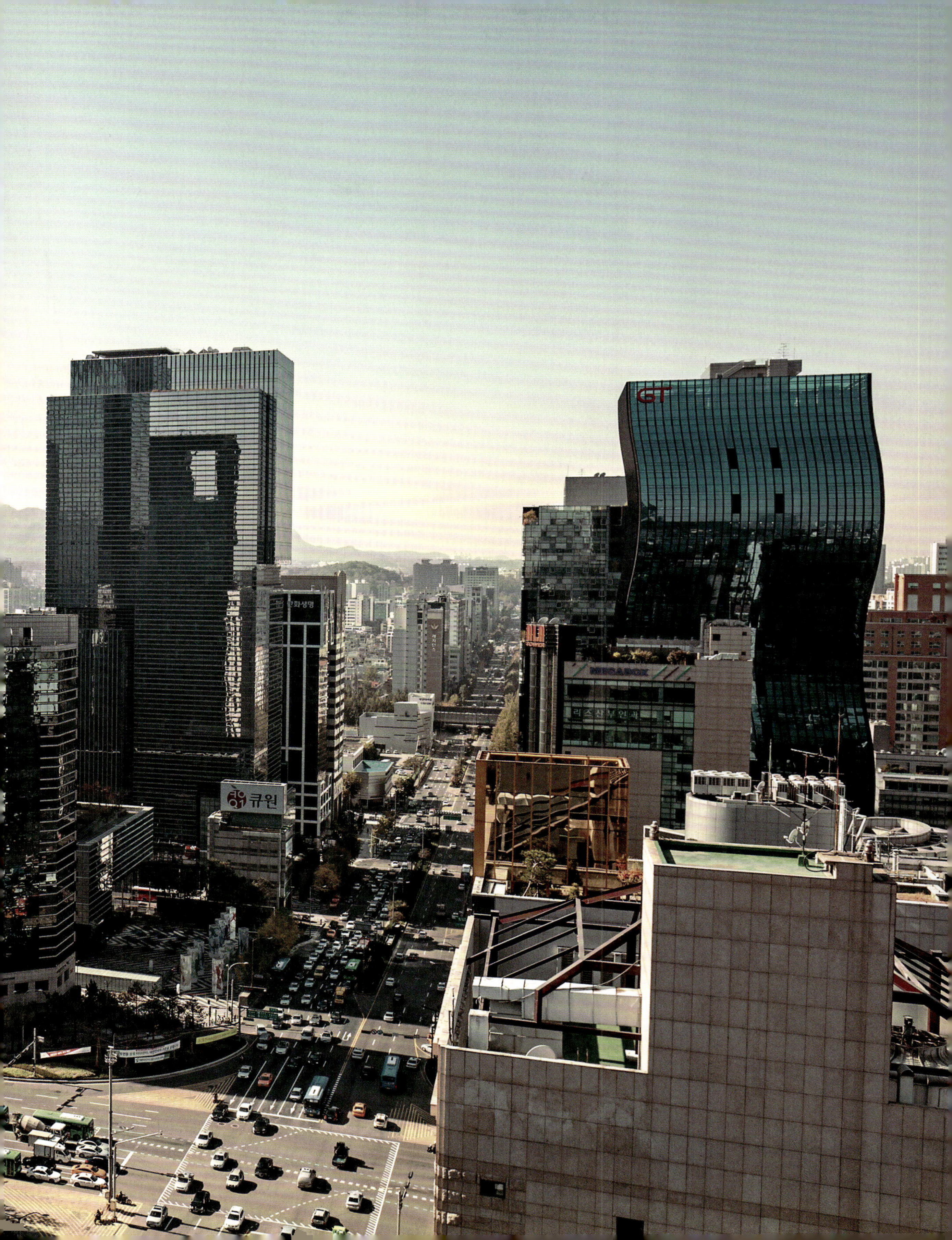
GT
큐원

Serves 4

Prawn & Sweet Potato Tempura
twigim

110g flour, plus a little extra to coat
90g glutinous rice flour
¼ tsp baking powder
¾ tsp sea salt
¾ tsp freshly ground black pepper
325ml ice-cold sparkling water
2 sweet potatoes, scrubbed and cut into ½ cm thick slices (no need to peel them)
8 king prawns, shelled and deveined, tails left on
600ml sunflower oil, for deep-frying

Dipping sauce
2 tbsp soy sauce
1 tsp mirin
1 tsp rice wine vinegar
½ tsp toasted sesame seeds

Eaten predominantly among strangers at street-side food carts throughout Korea, twigim is as much about the experience around eating it, as the food itself. The Braised Rice Cakes with Cabbage & Fishcakes (page 48) is commonly served alongside, with plenty of sauce to dip into.

Combine all the dipping sauce ingredients in a bowl. Set aside

If you have a deep-fat fryer, heat the oil to 175°C/350°F. If not, add the oil to a pan and place over a medium heat. Test the temperature by dropping a breadcrumb into the oil. It should turn golden in about 50 seconds. Any faster than this and the tempura will burn before the inside is cooked through. A cooking or jam thermometer is really useful for this.

While the oil is heating, combine the flours, baking powder, salt and pepper. Quickly stir in the cold sparkling water until you have a milky consistency. Don't over-whisk. It doesn't matter if the batter is lumpy, in fact, this improves the texture.

Lightly coat the sweet potato and prawns in the extra flour, then dip them into the batter and shake off any excess so you have a light coating. Carefully place them into the hot oil. Don't overcrowd the pan, as it will bring down the temperature of the oil, which you want to maintain at 170–175°C/340–350°F. Fry the sweet potato for about 4–5 minutes and the prawns for about 2–3 minutes, until lightly golden and cooked through. In Korea, they prefer tempura to be quite pale in colour.

Remove with a slotted spoon or a pair of tongs and drain on kitchen paper. Keep warm while you cook the rest, then serve immediately with the dipping sauce.

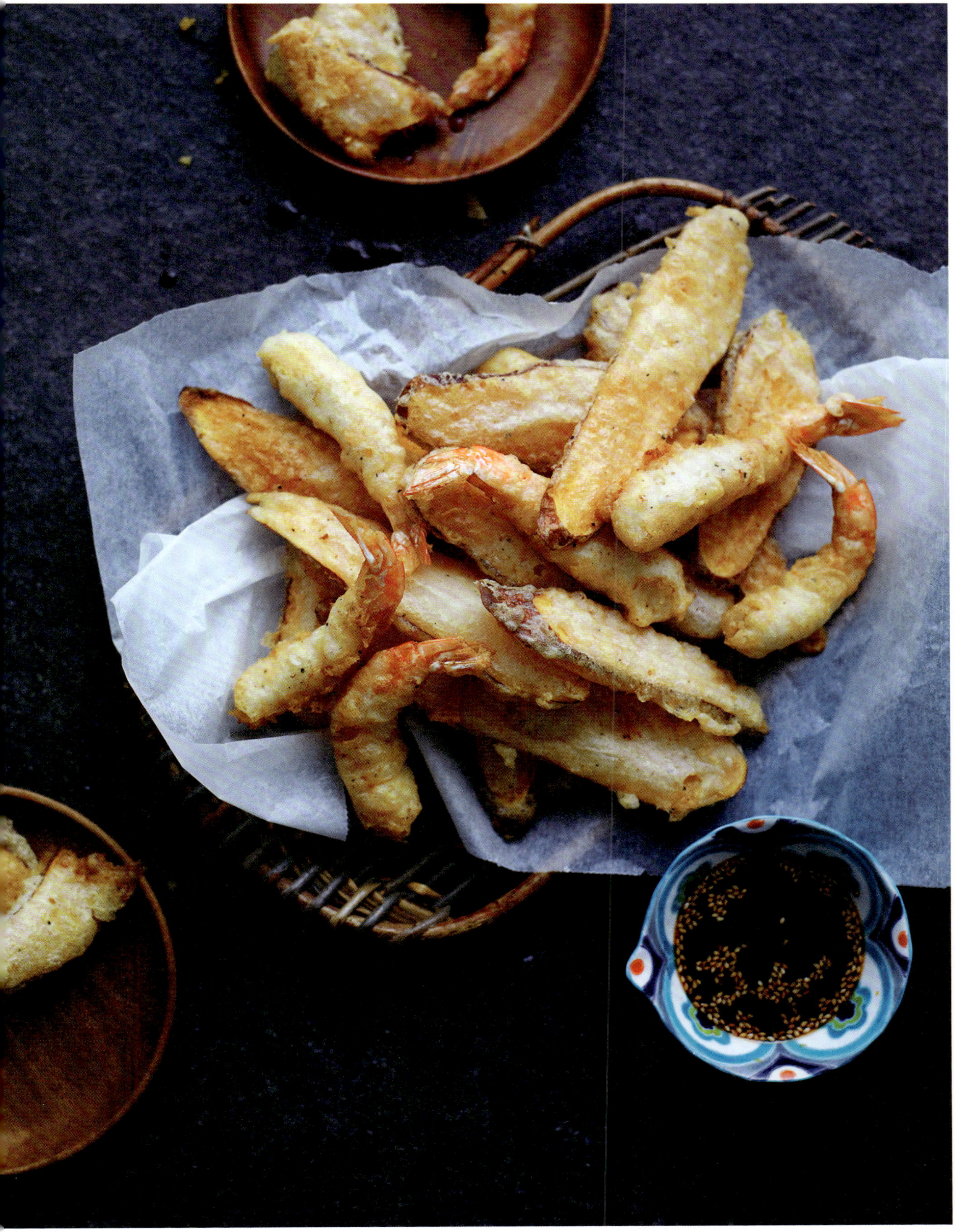

Serves 4

Tofu & Fried Kimchi
dubu kimchi

1 x 400g block of firm tofu
300g pork belly, very thinly sliced into bite-size pieces
1½ tbsp gochujang chilli paste (page 14)
2 tsp gochugaru red pepper powder (page 14)
1 tbsp soy sauce
3 garlic cloves, crushed
pinch of black pepper
2 tbsp honey
1 tbsp vegetable oil
350g kimchi, cut into bite-size pieces (mature, sour kimchi works best)
1 tbsp roasted sesame seed oil
2 spring onions, finely sliced
1 tsp toasted sesame seeds

In Korea, this is the ultimate 'an-joo' – or food to have while you are drinking – but getting trashed isn't obligatory if you decide to have this for your dinner. The subtle tofu is the perfect pairing for the deep, punchy flavours of the stir-fried pork and kimchi, and you can also serve the tofu uncooked, simply drained and cut into slices, without frying. Try it out both ways and see which you prefer.

Drain the water out of the packet of tofu, then gently wrap it in a clean tea towel. Place it onto a chopping board and balance another wooden chopping board or heavy plate on top. It should be just heavy enough to exert a little pressure on the tofu to help press out the water, but not so heavy that the shape of the tofu distorts under its weight. Set aside for 30 minutes.

Put the pork in a bowl with the gochujang paste, gochugaru powder, soy sauce, garlic, pepper and 1 tablespoon of the honey. Combine together and leave to marinate for 10 minutes, or longer.

Cut the tofu block in half and then each half into 1cm-thick slices. Heat the vegetable oil in a large non-stick pan over a high heat. Add in the tofu slices and fry for about 3 minutes, on each side, until just golden. Remove from the pan and keep to one side.

Add the pork mixture to the pan and fry for 4 minutes until cooked through. Add in the kimchi with the remaining honey and sesame seed oil and fry on a high heat for a further 3–4 minutes, stirring frequently to prevent it from catching.

Plate up the tofu and kimchi pork mixture, side-by-side, on a large serving dish, and sprinkle over the spring onions and sesame seeds. To eat, top a piece of fried tofu with the kimchi and pork and demolish.

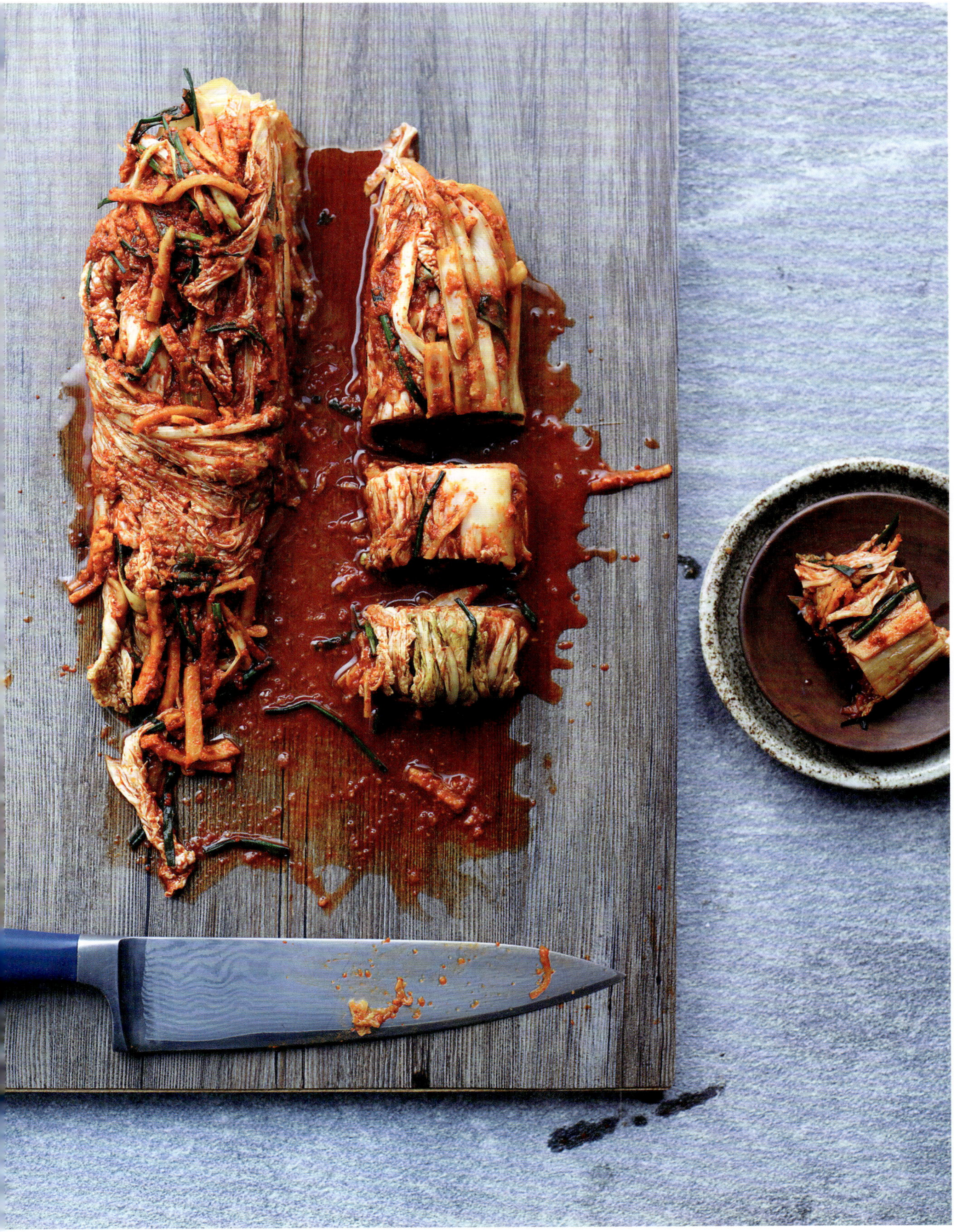

Noodles

면, 국수

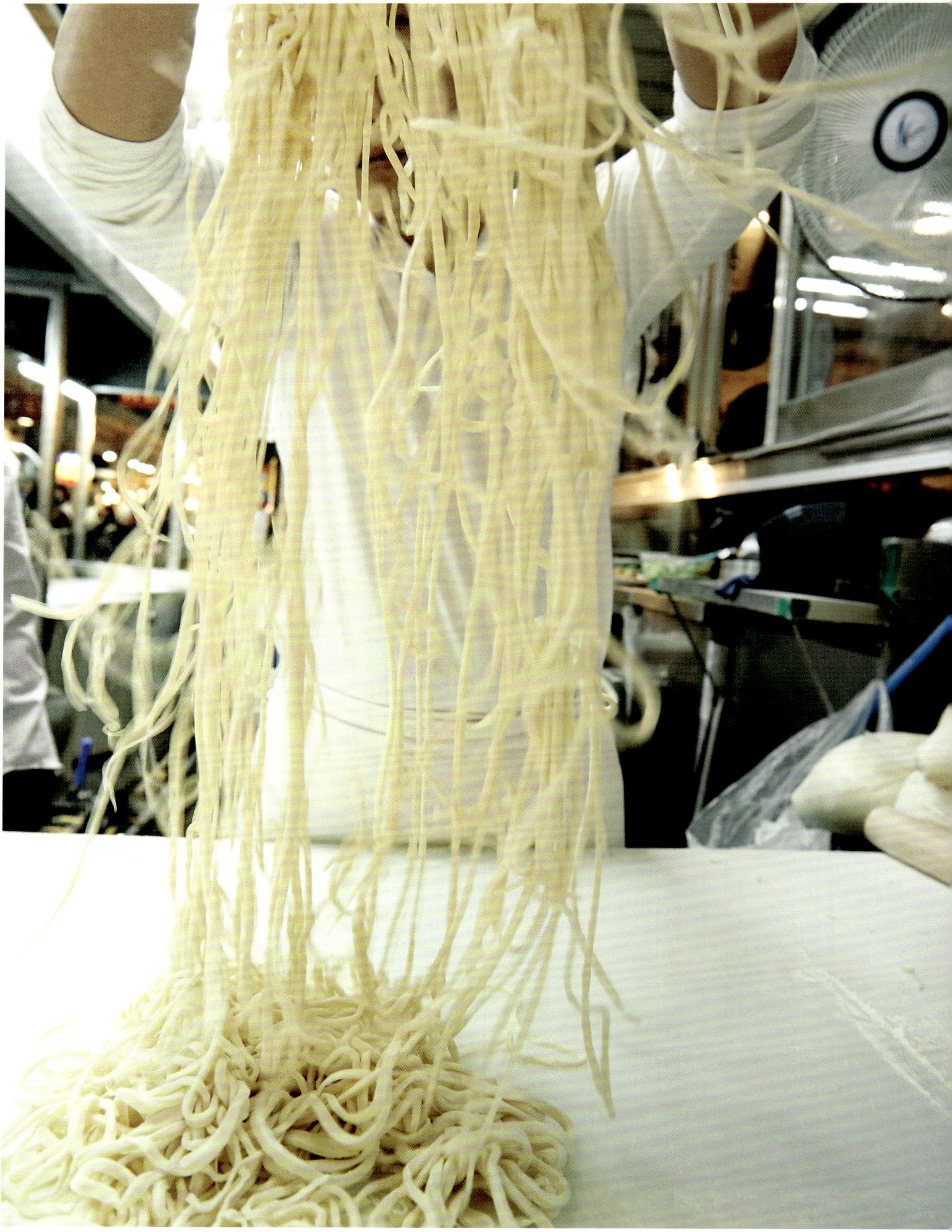

05

158. Chilled Kimchi Spiced Noodles
비빔국수

160. Buckwheat Noodles in Chilled Broth
물냉면

162. Noodles in Chilled Soybean Soup
콩국수

166. Beef & Vegetables with Sesame Glass Noodles
잡채

170. Knife-cut Noodles in Seafood Broth
해물 칼국수

172. Spicy Chilled Buckwheat Noodle Salad
비빔 냉면

173. Instant Chicken Ramen
라면

176. Black Bean Noodles
짜장면

178. Spicy Seafood Noodle Soup
짬뽕

Chilled Kimchi Spiced Noodles
bibim guksu

Serves 2

180g wheat noodles
1 tsp vegetable oil
1 hard-boiled egg, halved
100g cucumber, halved lengthways, deseeded and thinly sliced into half-moons
40g lettuce, chopped into bite-size pieces
2 sheets of roasted crispy seaweed, shredded
2 tsp toasted sesame seeds

<u>Sauce</u>
125g kimchi, cut into small bite-size pieces
5 tbsp kimchi juice
1 tbsp roasted sesame oil
1½–2 tbsp gochugaru red pepper powder (page 14), to taste
2 tsp rice vinegar
1 garlic clove, crushed
1½ tbsp honey

At first glance, this dish appears very similar to the Spicy Chilled Buckwheat Noodle Salad (page 172), especially topped with cucumber and egg, one of the most popular accompaniments for this dish in Korea. However the taste is altogether quite different, as no gochujang chilli paste is used, instead, the main ingredient besides the noodles, is kimchi, which cuts through the heavier sauce ingredients.

In a bowl, combine all the sauce ingredients and mix thoroughly. Cover and refrigerate. If you are using shop-bought kimchi, you may not be able to squeeze out 5 tablespoons of kimchi juice. In which case, make up the amount with a little extra finely chopped kimchi mixed with water.

Bring a large pan of water to the boil, add the noodles and cook according to the packet instructions. Drain and immediately plunge into cold water, repeat until the noodles are completely cold. Drain again fully and toss with vegetable oil to prevent the noodles from sticking together. Cover and refrigerate until very well chilled.

Divide the chilled noodles between 2 bowls, top with the sauce, hard-boiled egg, cucumber, lettuce and scatter over the seaweed and sesame seeds. Remember to mix everything together very well before eating – it is not called mixed (bibim) noodles (guksu) for nothing!

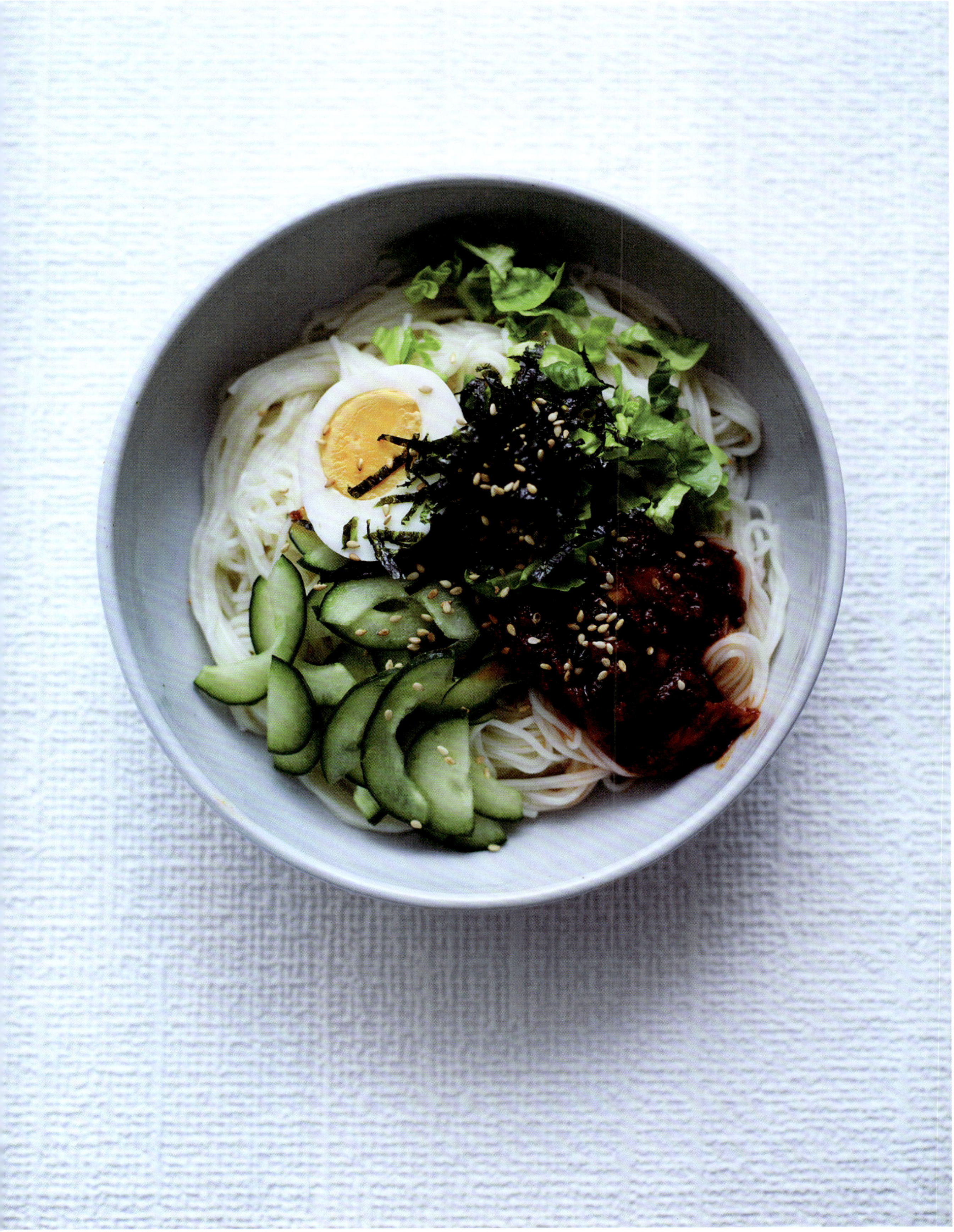

Serves 2

Buckwheat Noodles in Chilled Broth
mul naeng-myeon

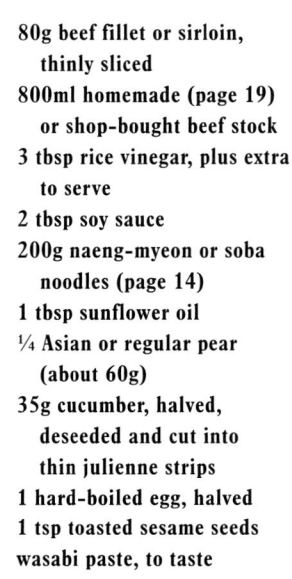

80g beef fillet or sirloin, thinly sliced
800ml homemade (page 19) or shop-bought beef stock
3 tbsp rice vinegar, plus extra to serve
2 tbsp soy sauce
200g naeng-myeon or soba noodles (page 14)
1 tbsp sunflower oil
¼ Asian or regular pear (about 60g)
35g cucumber, halved, deseeded and cut into thin julienne strips
1 hard-boiled egg, halved
1 tsp toasted sesame seeds
wasabi paste, to taste

This dish has so often been our saving grace on blisteringly hot summer days in Seoul. Mounds of noodles served ice cold in a beef broth seasoned at the table with wasabi and rice wine vinegar, it is so refreshing. Naeng-myeon noodles can be found in Asian markets, or soba noodles can be used if you can't find them.

Place the beef slices in a large, deep pan with just enough of the beef stock to cover. Bring to the boil, reduce the heat to medium and simmer for 3 minutes until the beef is cooked through. Remove the beef slices and keep to one side. In a bowl, combine the hot beef stock with the cold stock and leave to cool completely. Season with the rice vinegar and soy sauce, then cover and refrigerate until very well chilled.

Bring a large pan of water to the boil, add the noodles and cook for 4 minutes, or until just cooked through, but still a little chewy. Drain and refresh with cold water until the noodles are cold. Drain again and toss with the sunflower oil to prevent them from sticking together. Refrigerate until well chilled.

When you are ready to serve, peel and core the pear (if you haven't already done so) and cut into thin julienne strips (don't cut too far ahead of time as the pear will discolour). Divide the noodles between 2 bowls, place the slices of beef, pear, cucumber and hard-boiled egg on top and scatter over the sesame seeds. Divide the chilled broth between the bowls and serve with the wasabi and some more rice vinegar. At the table, add in a little of each to taste, it should have a distinct flavour of wasabi. Stir everything together and enjoy.

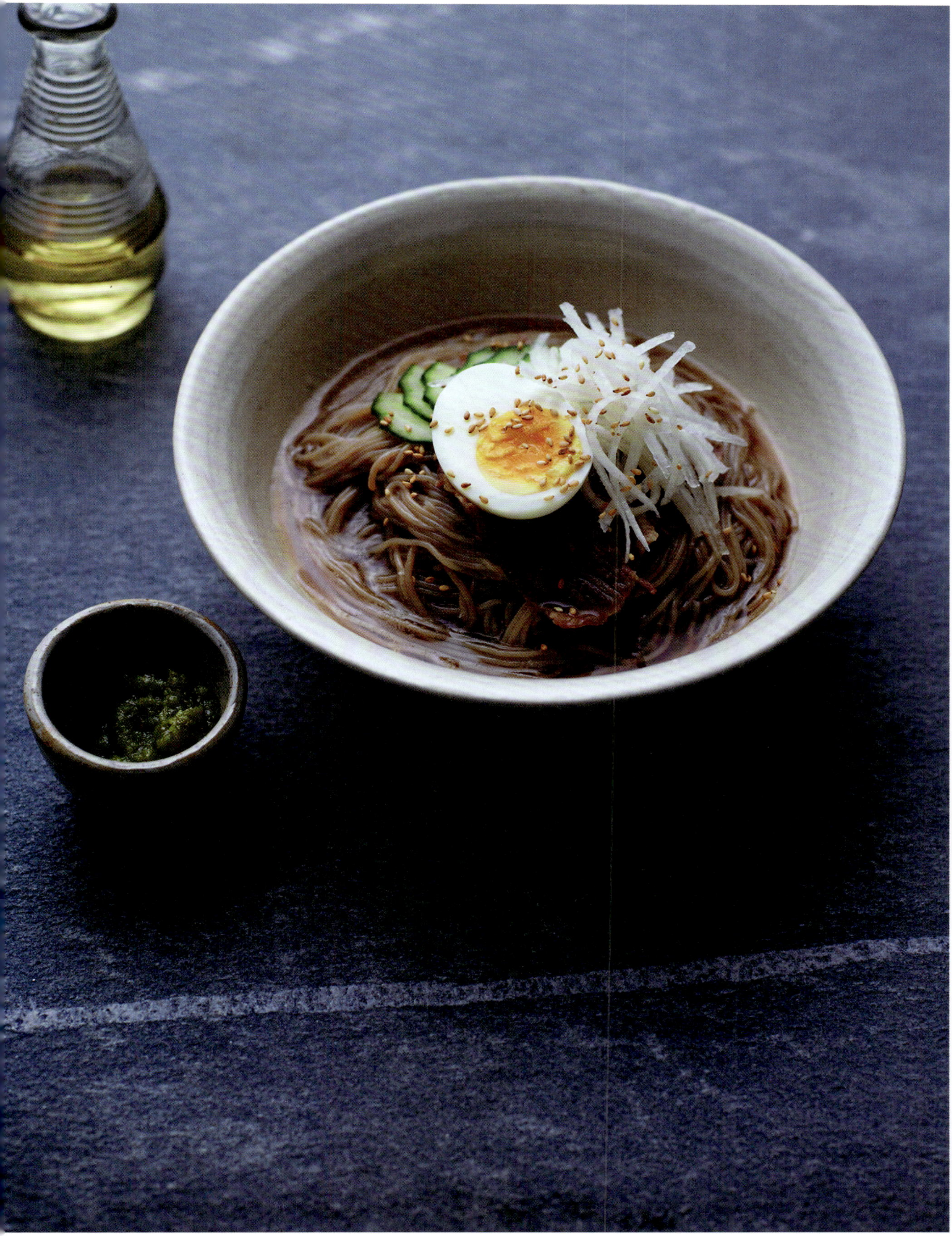

Serves 4

Noodles in Chilled Soybean Soup
kong-guksu

50g blanched almonds
200g soybeans, soaked overnight in double their quantity of water
40g toasted sesame seeds
1½ tsp sea salt, plus extra, to serve
300g wheat noodles
100g cucumber, halved, deseeded and sliced into thin julienne strips
1 very ripe beef tomato
1 tsp black sesame seeds, to garnish
radish kimchi, to serve (optional)

This delightful chilled noodle dish is made with soybeans that have been ground up into a milk. It was taught to us by Jina's father, who makes a particularly good version. It is a very subtle tasting dish, but the addition of the roasted almonds adds a little extra depth of flavour. This is best consumed within 24 hours and is commonly served with Radish Kimchi (page 102).

Preheat the oven to 180°C/fan160°C/350°F/gas mark 4. Spread the almonds out on a tray and roast for 5 minutes until they are a shade darker and aromatic. Remove and leave to cool completely.

Drain the beans and rinse under water. Add them to a pan and cover them with a few inches of cold water. Bring to the boil for 5 minutes. Drain and refresh with cold water until chilled. Drain the beans and add them to a food processor with the sesame seeds, almonds and salt. Blitz for a minute or 2 until everything is ground down to a fine powder, then gradually pour in 850ml water, a little at a time, until you have a smooth milk. (Don't add all the water at once as it prevents the machine from grinding the beans and nuts finely.) Strain the milk through a fine sieve lined with muslin or cheesecloth. Squeeze out as much liquid as possible and discard the pulp. Refrigerate the milk until very well chilled.

Bring a pan of water to the boil, add the noodles and cook according to the packet instructions. Immediately drain and plunge into ice-cold water until completely chilled.

Divide the noodles in mounds between 4 large bowls. Sit the cucumber and tomato on top and scatter over the black sesame seeds. Pour on the chilled soy milk. Serve with sea salt, to taste.

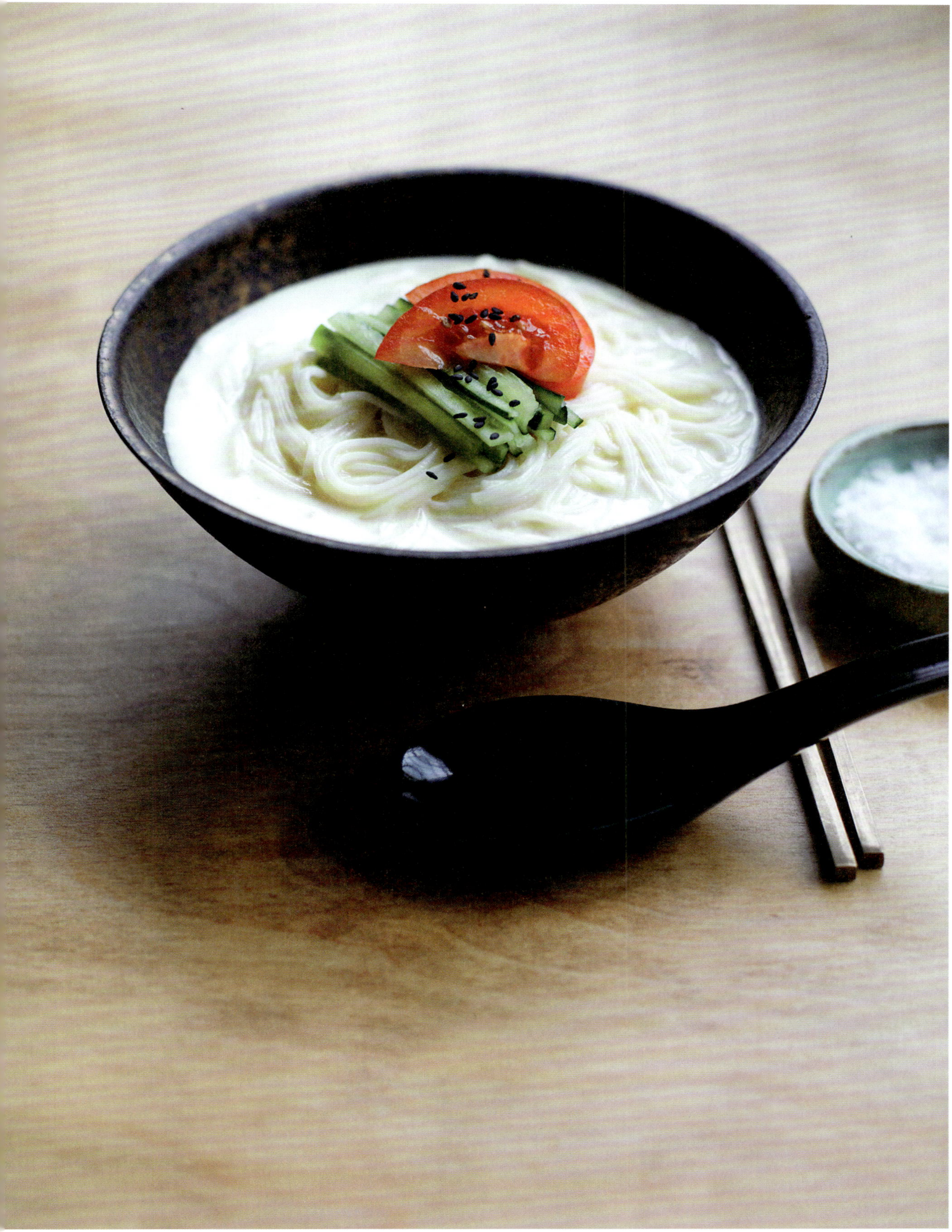

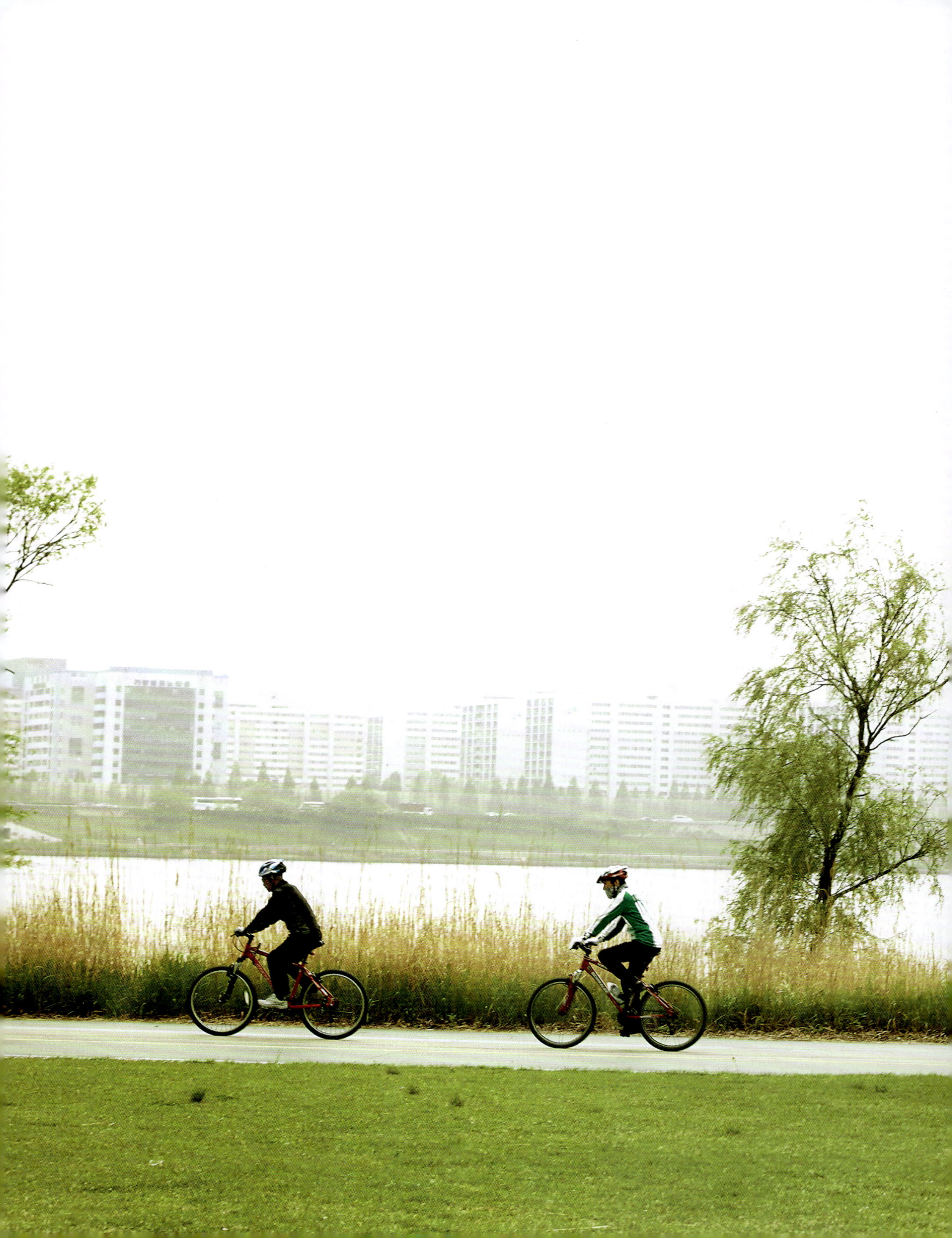

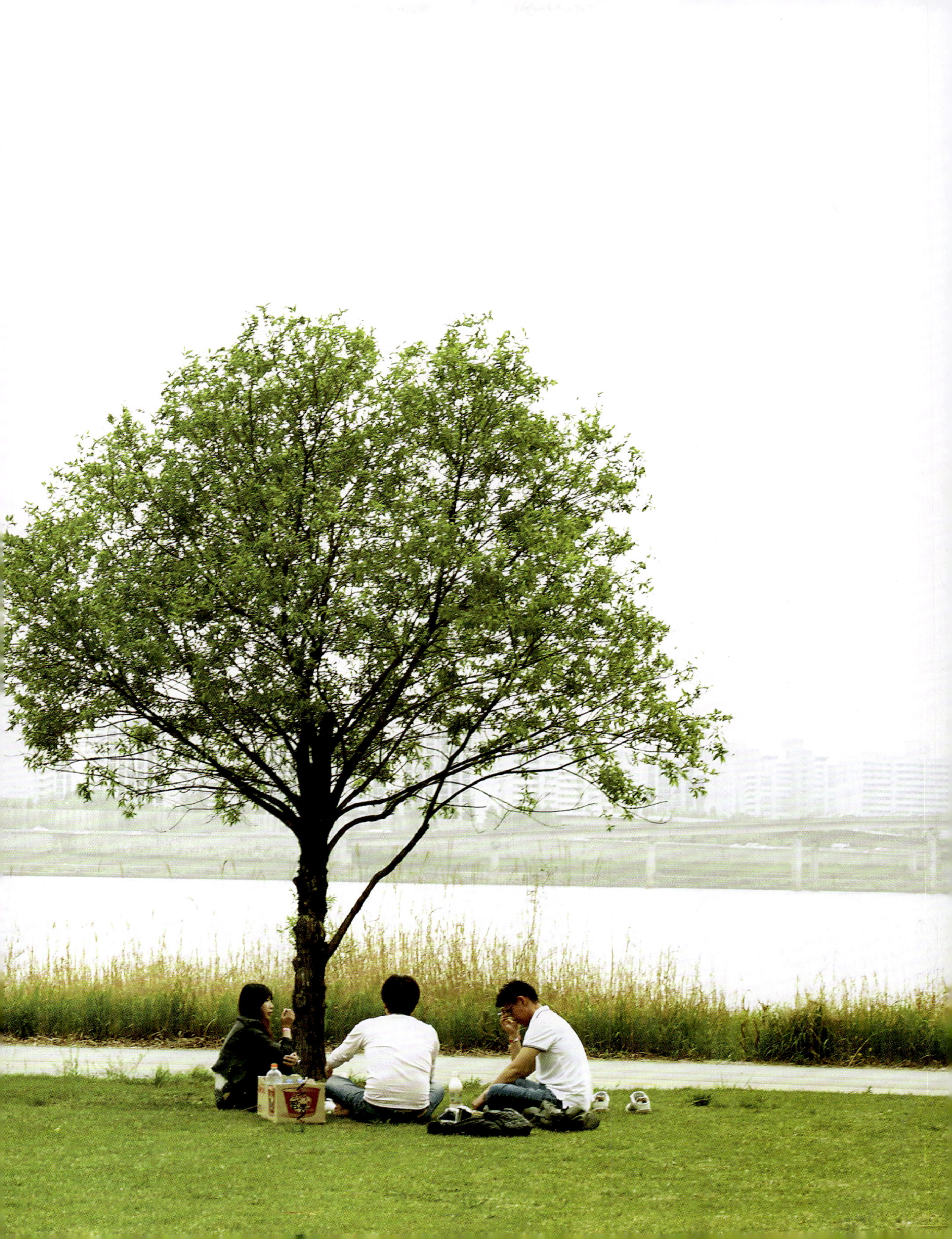

Serves 4–6

Beef & Vegetables with Sesame Glass Noodles
japchae

4 tbsp soy sauce, plus extra to season
1 tbsp roasted sesame seed oil, plus extra to season
1 tbsp honey or maple syrup
large pinch of black pepper
3 garlic cloves, crushed
150g beef, very thinly sliced
1 egg, beaten and seasoned with a pinch of sea salt
200g spinach
10 shiitake mushrooms, thinly sliced
200g carrots, sliced into thin julienne strips
½ onion, sliced thinly
240g sweet potato glass noodles (page 13) or glass noodles
1 tsp black or toasted white sesame seeds
1 red chilli, thinly sliced, to garnish (optional)
sunflower oil, for frying

Easily one of the most popular noodle dishes in Korea, it is easy to make, healthy and packed full of flavour from the soy sauce and sesame soaked noodles. Traditionally, this is eaten on holidays and special occasions, but you will find it in practically every Korean restaurant these days. The Korean glass noodles used here are made from sweet potato starch, and have a delicious chewiness to them. While they are undoubtedly the best choice, you could also use any glass noodle available in your local supermarket.

In a bowl mix together the soy sauce, sesame seed oil, honey, pepper and garlic. In a separate bowl, place 2 tablespoons of the mixture with the sliced beef, combine and leave to marinate for at least 15 minutes. Set aside the remaining mixed sauce.

In the meantime, add a drizzle of sunflower oil to a frying pan and place over a medium heat. Add the beaten egg and fry gently for a couple of minutes on each side, until set, taking care not to colour it too much. Remove from the pan and cool, then slice into 3 equal lengths, lay each piece on top of the other and cut them into julienne strips. Set aside.

Rinse the spinach, then put it straight into a large empty pan on a high heat. Turn the spinach as it wilts down, this will only take a couple of minutes. Transfer the spinach to a sieve and gently press the remaining water out of it, then place it on a plate while still warm and season with ½ a teaspoon each of sesame seed oil and soy sauce. Set aside.

In the same pan, add in 1 tablespoon of sunflower oil and stir-fry the mushrooms, carrots and onion over a high heat for 3–4 minutes, until slightly softened but not coloured. Remove from the heat and season with 1 teaspoon each of soy sauce and sesame seed oil. Finally add in the beef and fry over a high heat for 2–3 minutes until cooked.

Bring a large pan of water to the boil. Add the noodles and cook for 7–8 minutes until tender. Drain the noodles fully and then return them to the pan with the remaining mixed sauce from earlier. Stir-fry for 2 minutes until the noodles have soaked up all the sauce. Turn off the heat and add all of the cooked vegetables and the beef, and half of the sliced egg. Gently combine everything together then place into bowls with the remaining sliced egg on top. Sprinkle over some sesame seeds and, if using, chilli. Serve immediately.

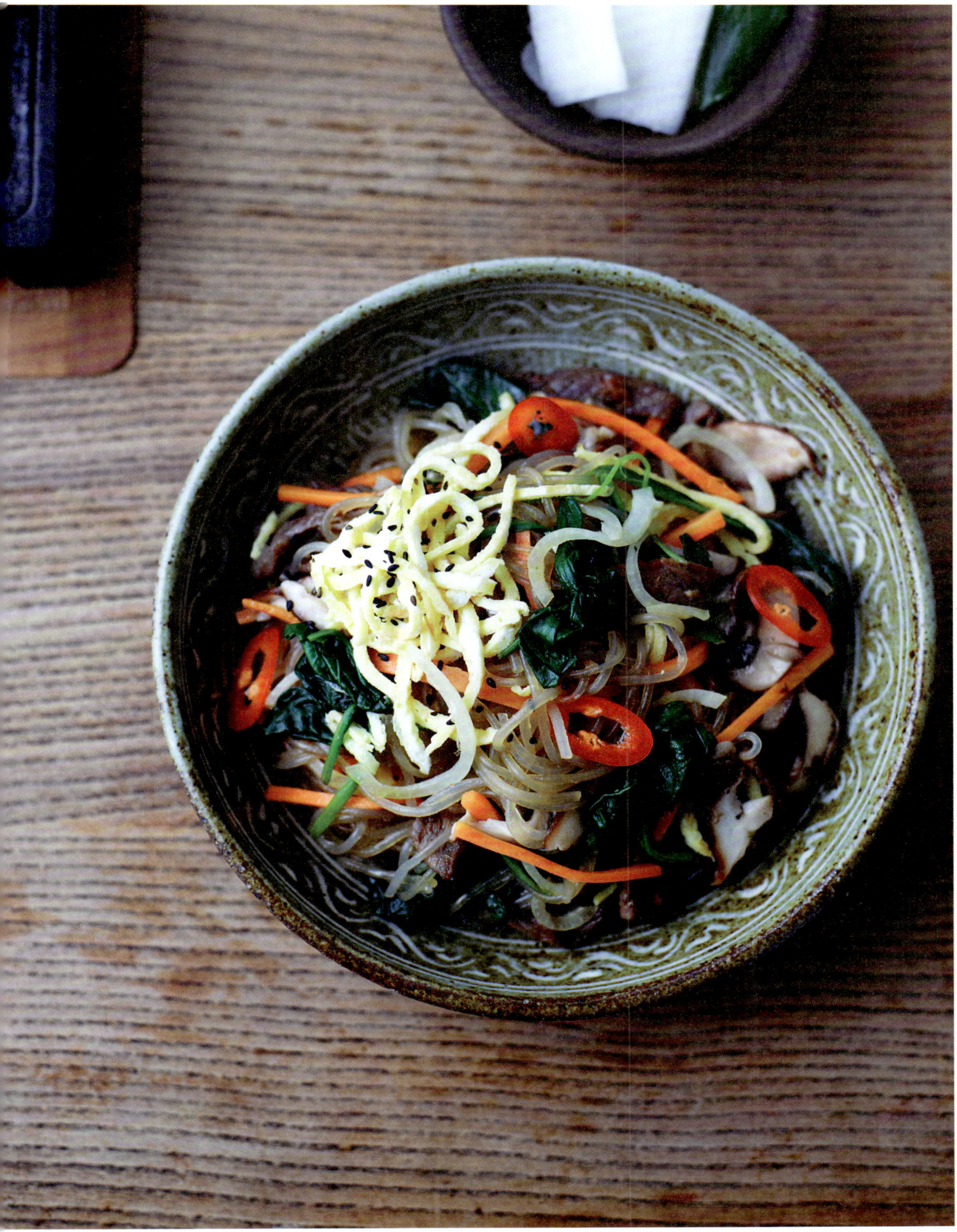

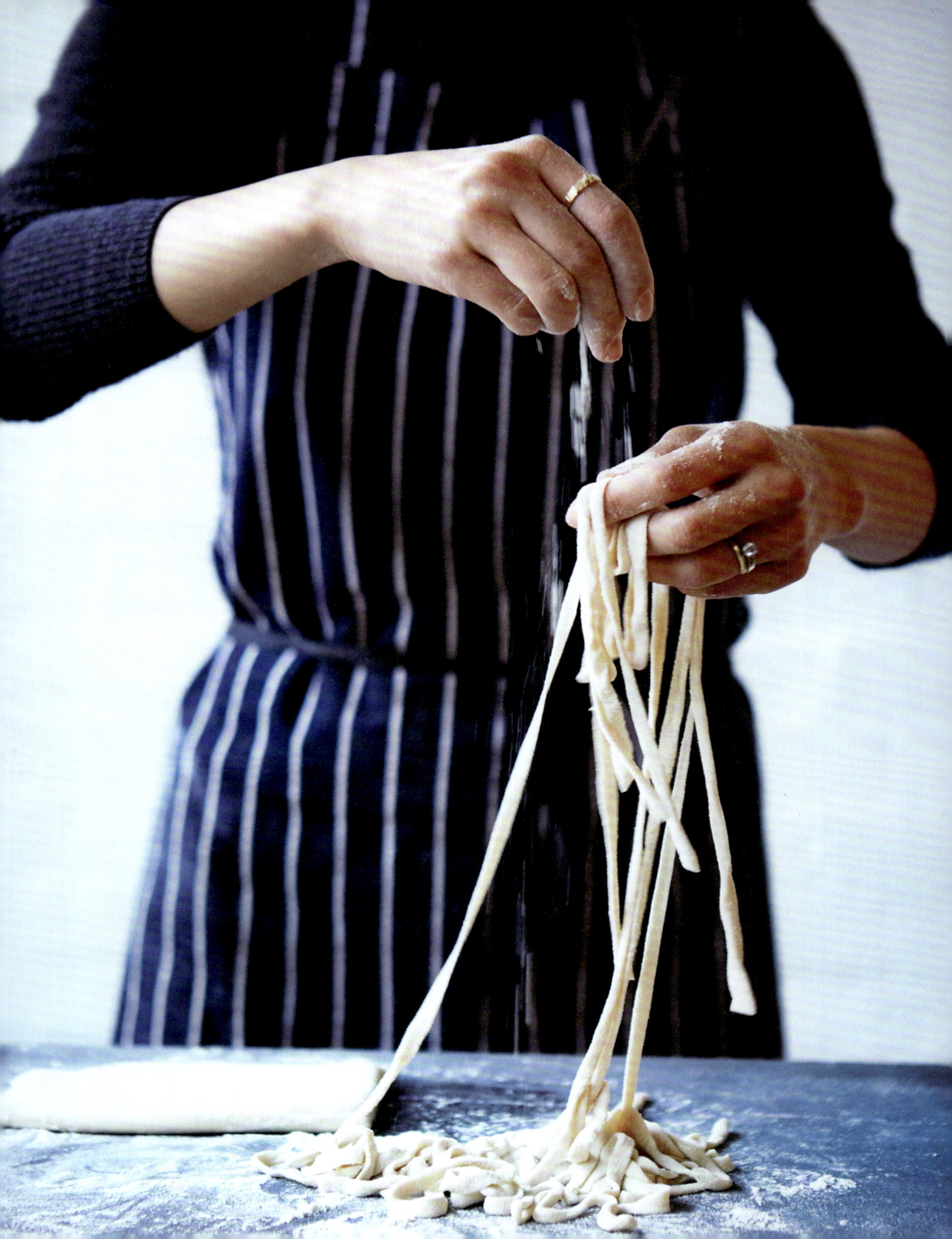

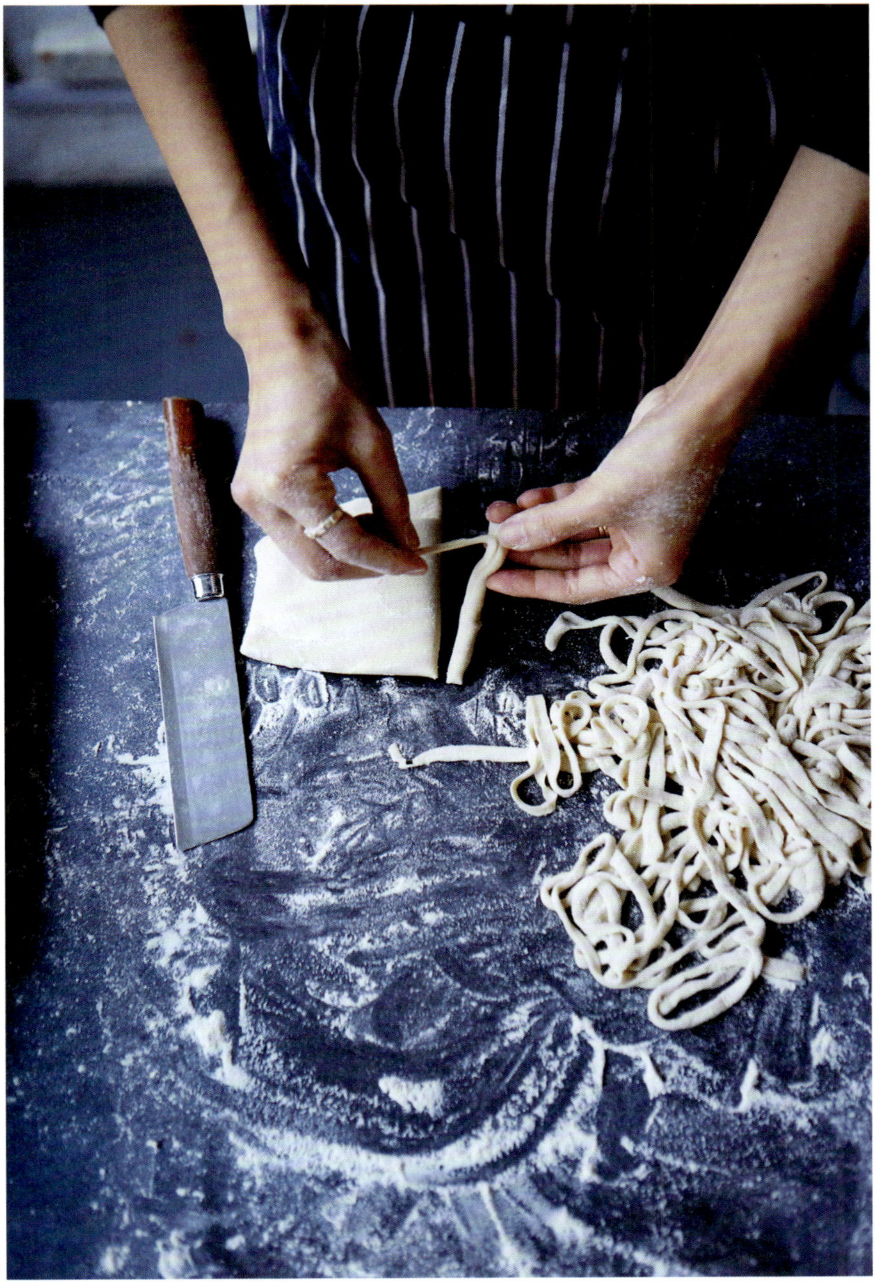

Serves 2

Knife-cut Noodles in Seafood Broth
haemul kalguksu

<u>Noodles</u>
190g flour, plus 75g for dusting
½ tsp salt
2 tsp roasted sesame seed oil

<u>Broth</u>
800ml homemade (page 19) or shop-bought fish stock
150g courgettes, halved lengthways and cut into half-moon shapes
½ onion, sliced
12 prawns, shells removed
2 spring onions, cut into 5cm lengths
2 garlic cloves, crushed
1½ tbsp soy sauce
2 tsp roasted sesame seed oil
1 sheet roasted crispy seaweed, cut into thin strips
1 tsp toasted sesame seeds
kimchi, to serve

As a child, Jina used to help her father make the noodles for this dish. They do require a bit of elbow grease when kneading, but apart from that they are really quite simple to make. We usually make the noodles in advance, then simply throw it together at the last moment. If you can't be bothered to roll and cut the dough into noodles, you can also tear it directly into the broth in small pieces. It is then known as 'haemul soojebi'!

First, make the noodles. Sift the flour and salt into a large bowl and combine with the sesame oil. Measure out 90–95ml of warm water in a jug and gradually pour it into the flour, mixing everything together to form a rough dough. It may appear a little dry and flaky at first, but use your hands to gently knead it and it will come together after a while. Place the dough in a resealable plastic bag, squeeze out the air, and leave at room temperature for 10 minutes. Then remove the dough from the bag and knead vigorously for about 10 minutes (depending on your strength) until the dough is elastic and completely smooth. Place the dough back in the bag and leave to rest at room temperature for 45 minutes.

Place the dough on a well-floured work surface and divide it in 2. Take 1 portion and roll it out into a rectangle shape of about 3mm in thickness, dusting regularly with flour to prevent sticking. Fold the dough in 3, like an A4 letter, folding up the bottom third and then folding the top third down over it, dusting with flour as you go. With a sharp knife, cut the folded dough into thin noodles, no more then 5mm thick. Repeat with the second portion of dough. Shake out the noodles so they are no longer folded in thirds and set to one side.

Now make the broth. In a large pan, bring the stock to the boil and add the courgettes, onion and prawns. Reduce the heat to medium and simmer for 1 minute, then add the noodles, spring onions, garlic, soy sauce and sesame seed oil. Simmer for 3–4 minutes, until the noodles are cooked, then remove from the heat and serve immediately in large bowls with the seaweed and sesame seeds scattered over the top and the kimchi on the side. Don't leave it sitting around for too long as the noodles will keep on cooking and loose their texture.

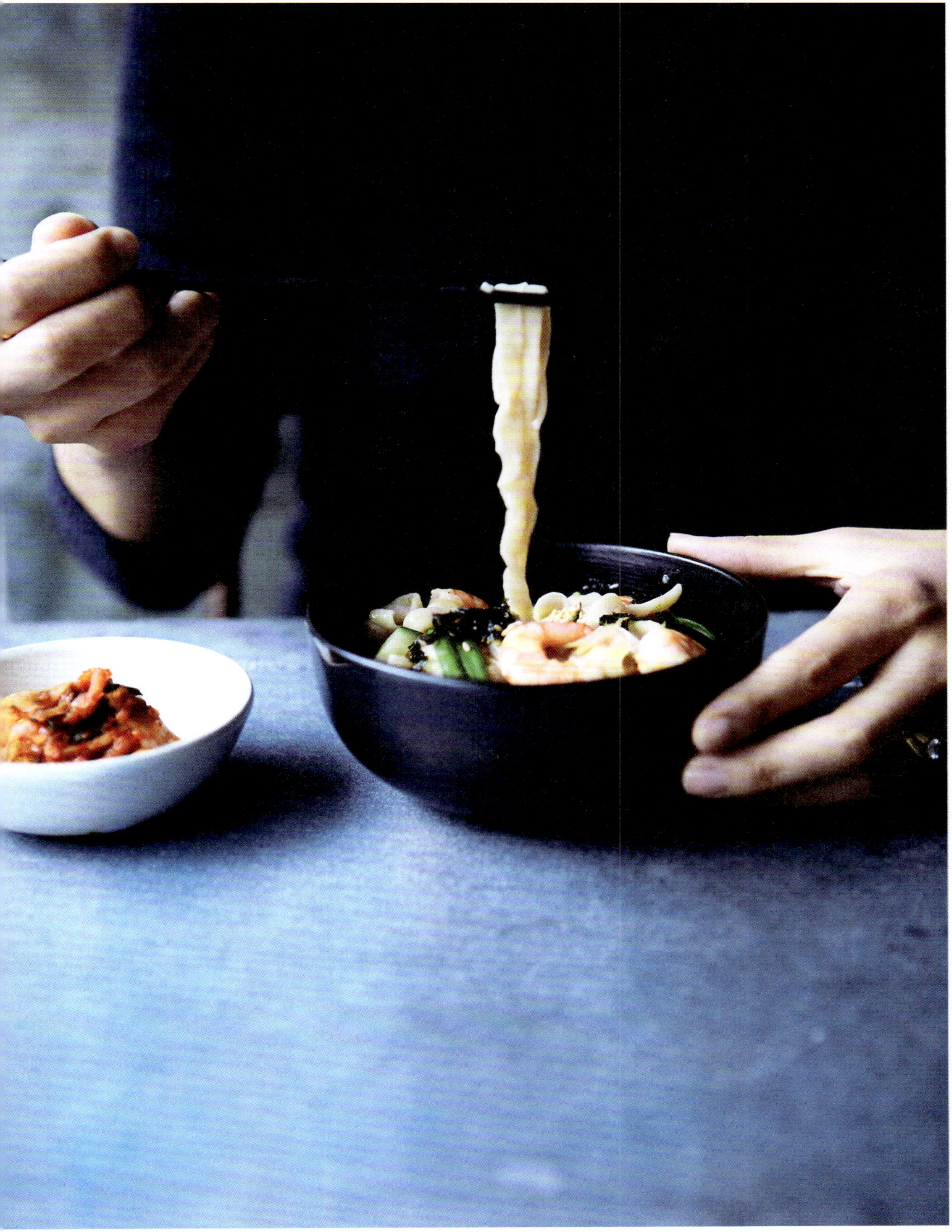

Spicy Chilled Buckwheat Noodle Salad

bibim naeng-myeon

Serves 2

200g naeng-myeon or soba noodles (page 14) or other noodles of your choice
1 tsp vegetable oil
½ large Asian pear or 1 regular pear
1 hard-boiled egg, shell removed and halved
100g cucumber, halved lengthways, deseeded and cut into thin julienne strips
1 tsp toasted sesame seeds

Sauce
2 tbsp gochujang chilli paste (page 14)
2 tsp gochugaru red pepper powder (page 14)
1½ cm piece of ginger, finely grated
1 garlic clove, peeled and finely grated
1½ tbsp honey
1 tbsp roasted sesame seed oil
1 tsp soy sauce
1 spring onion, very finely sliced

In contrast to many subtle and refreshing chilled Korean noodle dishes, bibim naeng-myeon is loud and proud, in both appearance and in taste. This is not one of those dishes where you can reduce the chilli element if you are of a gentle disposition, as it throws all the proportions out of whack, so you need to just go with it.

Bring a large pan of water to the boil. Add the noodles and cook according to the packet instructions, stirring frequently to prevent sticking. Drain and immediately plunge into cold water, repeat until the noodles are completely cold. Drain fully and toss with the vegetable oil to prevent clumping. Cover and refrigerate until very well chilled.

Peel, core and halve the pear. Slice 1 half into thin julienne strips and set aside. Very finely grate the other half, so that it is almost a purée, place in a bowl and combine with all the sauce ingredients, mixing very well.

Divide the noodles into 2 bowls, and top with half the sauce, the egg, cucumber and reserved strips of pear. Sprinkle over some sesame seeds and serve immediately, mixing everything together before eating.

Serves 2

Instant Chicken Ramen
ra-myeon

1 small chicken breast, cut into bite-size pieces
2 packets of instant Korean ramen noodles (each pack should contain about 120g of dried noodles)
2 spring onions, roughly chopped
2 eggs
toasted sesame seeds, to serve
kimchi, to serve

This is not a recipe in the true sense of the word. But in our defence, instant ramen is as authentically Korean as a jar of fermenting kimchi – so we had to include it. From young to old, whether hungover, time poor, or not in the mood to cook, the ubiquitous packets of Korean instant ramen (pronounced 'ra-myeon') are loved by one and all. In Korea, it is very common to jazz up an instant pack of noodles with a few fresh ingredients that give it a real lift. We use the spicy flavour ramen as our base, but feel free to choose whatever flavour you like best.

Fill a pan with 1.1 litres of water and bring to the boil. Add the chicken, dried ramen noodles and the seasoning sachets supplied with the packets. Bring back to the boil and simmer for 4 minutes until the chicken is cooked through. Add the spring onions and crack in the eggs, stirring quickly to break up the egg. Cook for another 1–2 minutes until the noodles are done.

Remove from the heat and serve straight from the pan with the sesame seeds sprinkled over the top and the kimchi on the side. Or if Korean communal style is a bit too much for you to handle, divide it between 2 bowls – but to be honest, trying to make instant noodles into a civilised affair somewhat defeats the purpose.

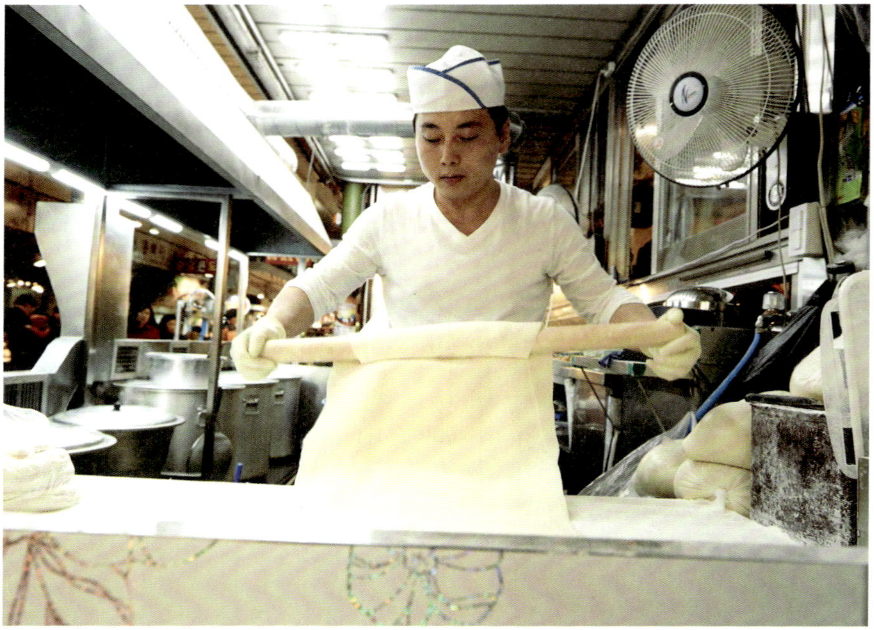

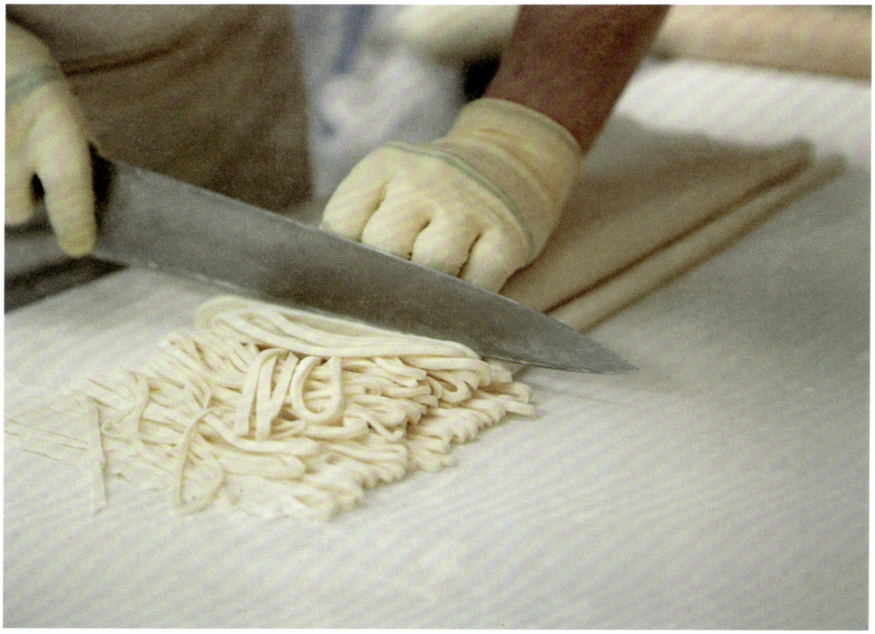

국수 2,500
제비 3,000

잔치국수

Serves 4

Black Bean Noodles
jajang-myeon

1 tbsp vegetable oil, plus a little extra
300g lean pork belly, cut into cubes
150g potato, cut into cubes
1 carrot, cut into cubes
1 large onion, roughly chopped
1 medium courgette (150g), cut into cubes
3 garlic cloves, crushed
1½ tbsp roasted sesame seed oil
7 tbsp black bean paste (we like Korean chunjang paste)
450g udon noodles
2 tbsp cornflour
1½ tbsp honey
75g cucumber, halved, de-seeded and cut into thin julienne strips
1 tsp toasted sesame seeds

Strictly speaking, this is not a traditional Korean dish – but a re-imagining of the famous Chinese original. However, it is so phenomenally popular in Korea, and indeed in our house, that we had to include it. Feel free to use whatever vegetables you like, or tofu instead of the meat. Korean black bean paste (chunjang) is available in Asian supermarkets, but you could also use regular black bean paste available in good supermarkets. In Korea it is served with 'dan-muji', a yellow Korean pickled radish (page 17), but it is also delicious with a side of kimchi, or indeed just on its own.

Add the vegetable oil to a large frying pan and place over a high heat. Add the pork and stir-fry for 4–5 minutes until it begins to colour. Pour off all but 2 teaspoons of the oil and fat. Add the potato, carrot and onion, to the pan, and fry over a medium-high heat for 3 minutes. Add the courgette and garlic and fry for a further 2 minutes, taking care not to burn the garlic. Transfer to a bowl.

Add the sesame seed oil to the pan together with the black bean paste and stir-fry over a high heat for 1–2 minutes. Put the semi-cooked vegetables and pork back in, pour over 650ml of water, bring to the boil, then reduce the heat to medium and simmer for 10 minutes, until the vegetables are cooked through.

Meanwhile, bring a large pan of water to the boil. Add the noodles and cook according to the packet instructions (usually 3–4 minutes). Drain, refresh in cold water and toss with a little vegetable oil to prevent the noodles from sticking.

Put the cornflour in a small bowl and slowly whisk in 2 tablespoons water, then stir in the honey. Gradually pour this mixture into the pan of simmering pork and vegetables, stirring for a minute or 2 over medium-high heat until the sauce thickens to a viscous, glossy consistency.

Plate up the noodles with the black bean mixture and top with a little mound of the sliced cucumber. Sprinkle over some sesame seeds and serve immediately.

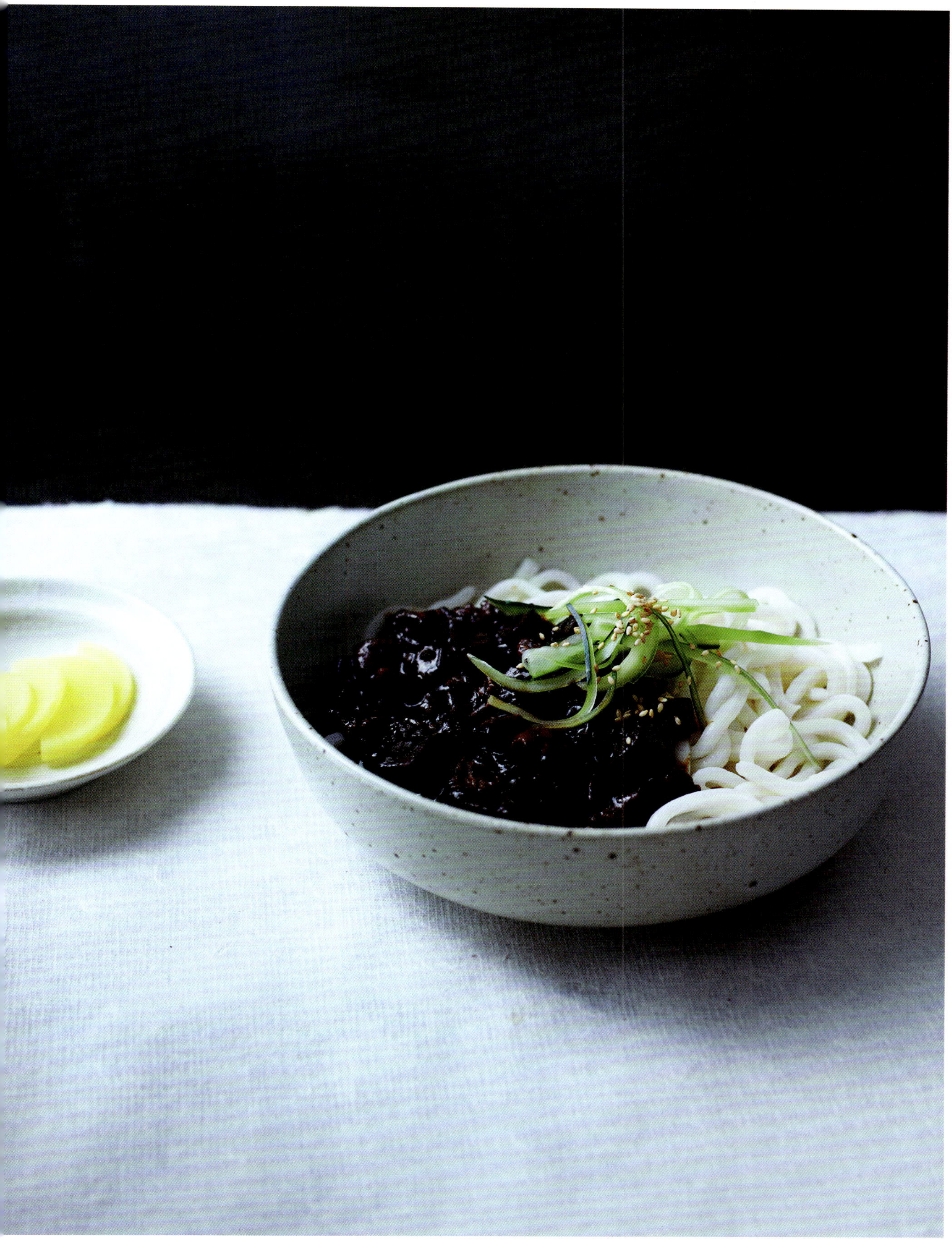

Serves 4

Spicy Seafood Noodle Soup
jjampong

2 tbsp vegetable oil
2½ tbsp gochugaru red pepper powder (page 14)
50g pork loin, cut into thin bite-size pieces
1 small carrot, peeled, halved lengthways and cut into half-moon slices
200g white cabbage, chopped
1 onion, halved and sliced
100g shiitake mushrooms, sliced
6 garlic cloves, crushed
2cm piece of ginger, very finely grated
2 tsp soy sauce
1 tsp roasted sesame seed oil
12 king prawns, shells removed and deveined
16 mussels, cleaned and debearded
150g squid, ask your fishmonger to clean it for you, then cut into bite-size pieces
1 litre homemade (page 19) or shop-bought fish stock
1 tsp sea salt
650g udon noodles
2 spring onions, finely sliced
freshly ground black pepper

As with the Black Bean Noodles (page 176), this is another dish that travelled over to Korea with early Chinese immigrants, before being re-imagined by the locals. However, they are now as much a part of Korean food culture as any of their most loved native dishes. This is quite a spicy dish, so if you prefer it a little milder, reduce the quantity of gochugaru powder used.

Bring a large pan of water to the boil, ready to cook the noodles.

While that is heating up, in a large, heavy-based pan with a lid, add the vegetable oil and the gochugaru powder and place over a medium heat. Stir-fry for 1 minute until aromatic. Add the pork, carrot and cabbage and stir-fry for 2 minutes, then add the onion, mushrooms, garlic and ginger and stir-fry for 3 minutes until the vegetables have slightly softened. Season with the soy sauce and sesame oil and fry for 1 minute, then add the prawns, mussels and squid to the pan, followed by the stock and bring to the boil over a high heat. Cover, reduce the heat a little and simmer for 4 minutes until the vegetables are cooked through but still have a bite and the mussels have opened up (discard any mussels that don't open up). Season with the salt and a few grinds of pepper, to taste.

Meanwhile, add the noodles to the pan of boiling water and cook according to the packet instructions (usually 3–4 minutes). Drain and divide the noodles between 4 large bowls, ladle over the spicy seafood and vegetable soup and scatter over the spring onions. Serve immediately.

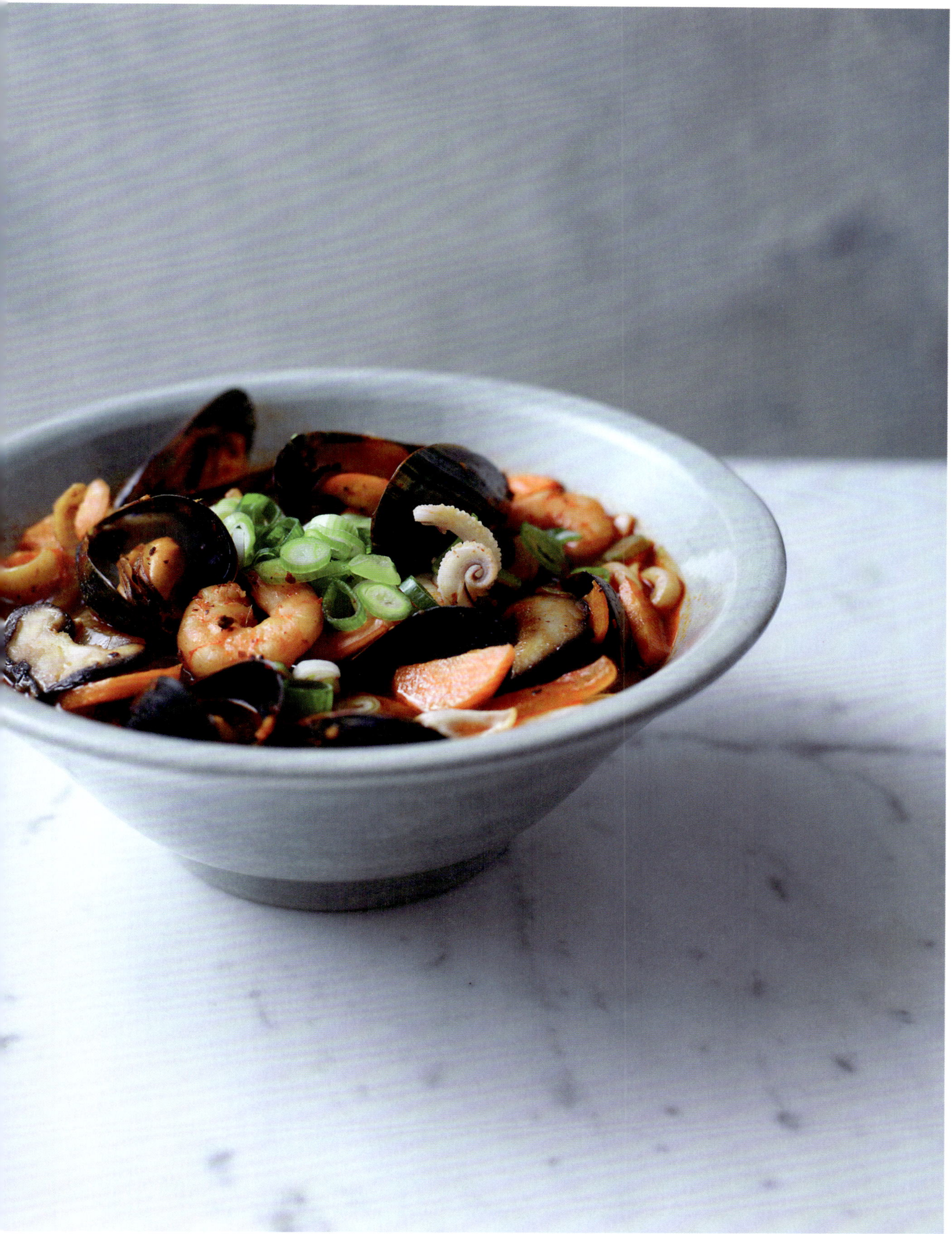

Fish

생선

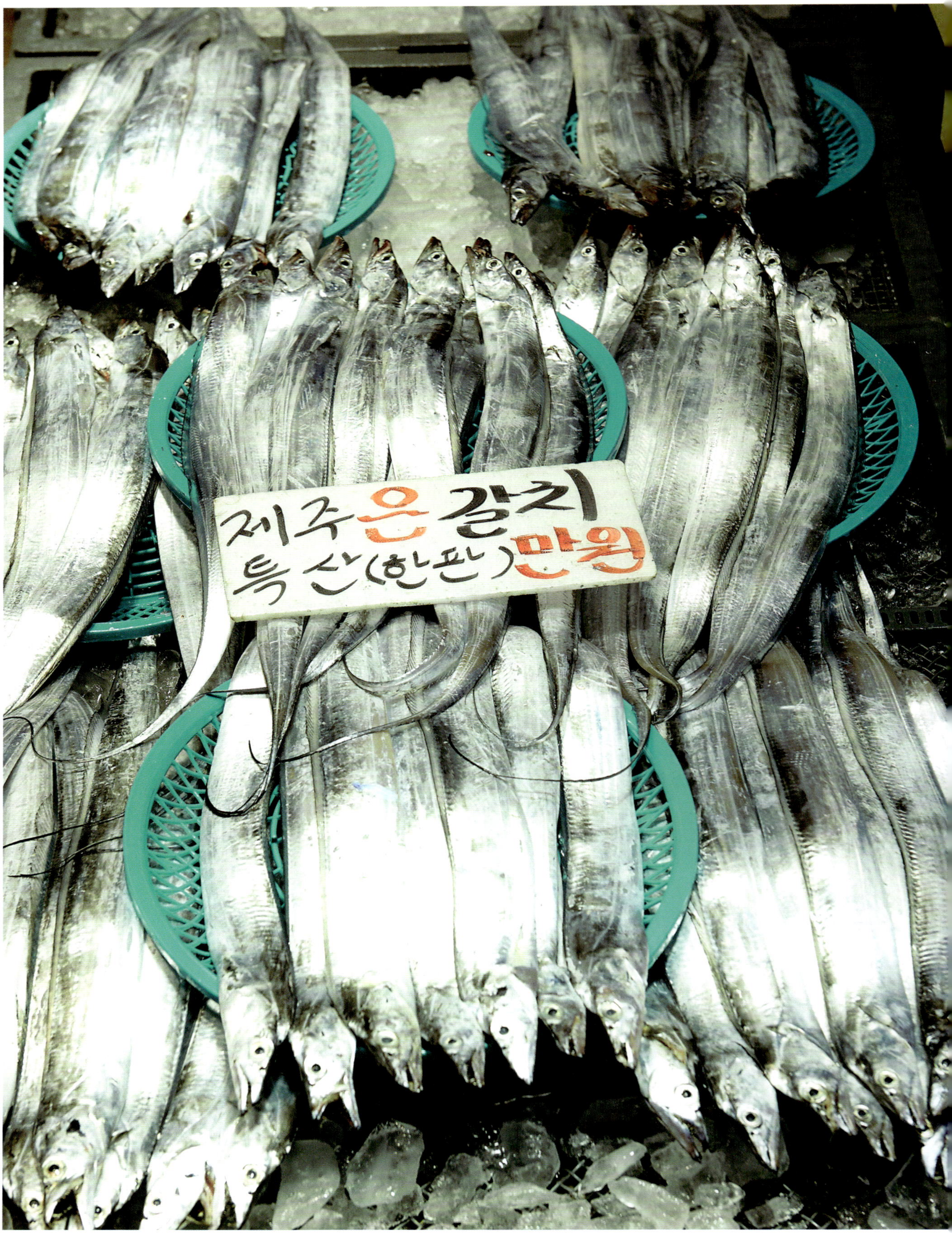
제주은갈치
특산(한판)만원

06

184. **Scallops with Salted Sesame Oil**
패주 구이

186. **Raw Tuna with Chilli Sauce**
참치회

188. *Food for All Seasons*

192. **Stir-fried Spicy Squid**
오징어 볶음

194. **Pan-fried Mackerel**
고등어구이

196. **Pan-fried King Prawns**
대하찜

197. **Braised Halibut in Seasoned Soy**
생선찜

198. **Scallops & Prawns with Pine Nut & Pear Soup**
잣해물냉국

200. **Soy-marinated Crab**
간장게장

204. **Seafood Salad with Wasabi Dressing**
해물 냉채

Serves 6

Scallops with Salted Sesame Oil
paeju gui

12 scallops
1½ tbsp vegetable oil
1 garlic clove, crushed
squeeze of lemon juice
1 tsp toasted sesame seeds
1 tsp chopped chives
sea salt and freshly ground black pepper

<u>Salted sesame oil</u>
1 tbsp roasted sesame seed oil
½ tsp sea salt

One of the chefs I've worked with used to make this as a snack – it's such a simple dish, and so quick, so we often make it when having guests over. The scallops work really well as a canapé or as a light starter, where you can serve them on or off the skewers. The sesame salt is unadorned here, so make sure to use good-quality roasted sesame seed oil.

Soak 6 wooden skewers in water for 15 minutes.

In a small serving dish, mix together the sesame seed oil and salt.

Rinse the scallops and cut off the tough white muscle tissue on the side. If preferred, you can also remove the orange-coloured roe, but we think they taste great and have a brilliant colour.

Heat the oil in a pan over a high heat. Thread 2 scallops onto each skewer. Lightly season both sides with salt and pepper. When the pan is very hot, place the skewers flat onto the pan (cook in batches if there is not enough space) and fry, undisturbed, over a high heat for 1 minute until golden. Flip over and fry for 40 seconds. Then add the garlic and a squeeze of lemon juice. Fry for another 10 seconds, just to allow all the flavours to come together, making sure the garlic does not burn. Then remove from the heat.

Serve immediately with the sesame seeds and chives scattered over the top and the salted sesame oil on the side to dip into.

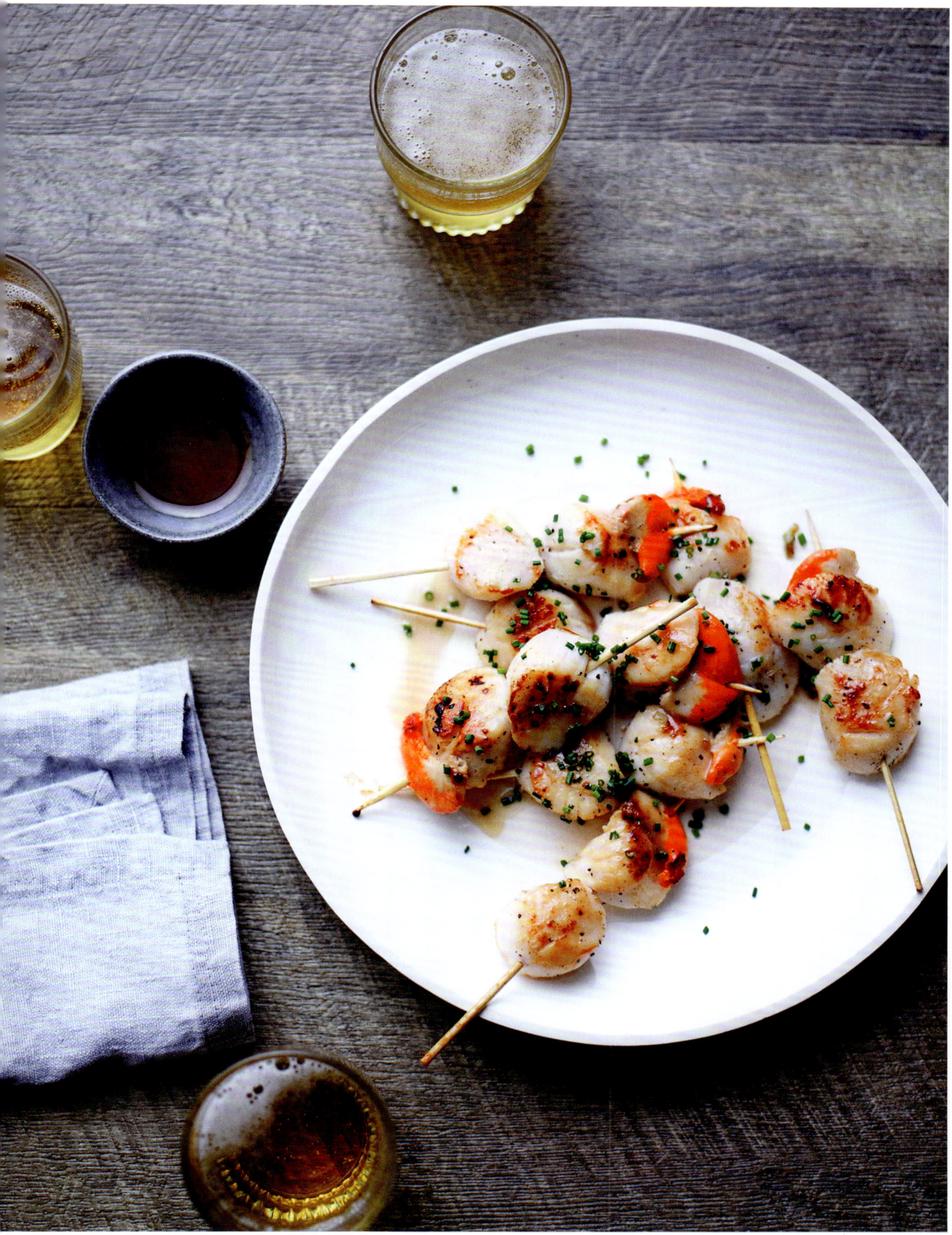

Serves 2

Raw Tuna with Chilli Sauce
chamchi whe

250g fresh tuna (ask your fishmonger for the freshest fish possible)
1 spring onion, halved lengthways, sliced into very thin 5cm lengths and covered in ice-cold water until curled up
1 tsp toasted sesame seeds

<u>Sauce</u>
2 tbsp gochujang chilli paste (page 14)
½ tsp gochugaru red pepper powder (page 14)
1 tbsp rice wine vinegar
2 tsp honey
2 tsp roasted sesame seed oil
½ tsp soy sauce
1 garlic clove, crushed

As with the Sesame, Soy & Chilli Beef Tartare (page 210), this tuna dish depends on the quality of the ingredients used, so be sure to use really fresh fish and good-quality Asian sesame seed oil (page 16). Apart from that, this could not be simpler to make and it is always incredibly popular at dinner parties or as a light lunch with salad or mixed with rice.

Place all the sauce ingredients in a bowl and mix together until thoroughly combined. Refrigerate for at least 45 minutes until well chilled.

When ready to serve, chop the tuna into bite-size cubes. Add them to the sauce and gently stir to combine. Serve ice-cold in little mounds with the drained spring onion and sesame seeds scattered over the top.

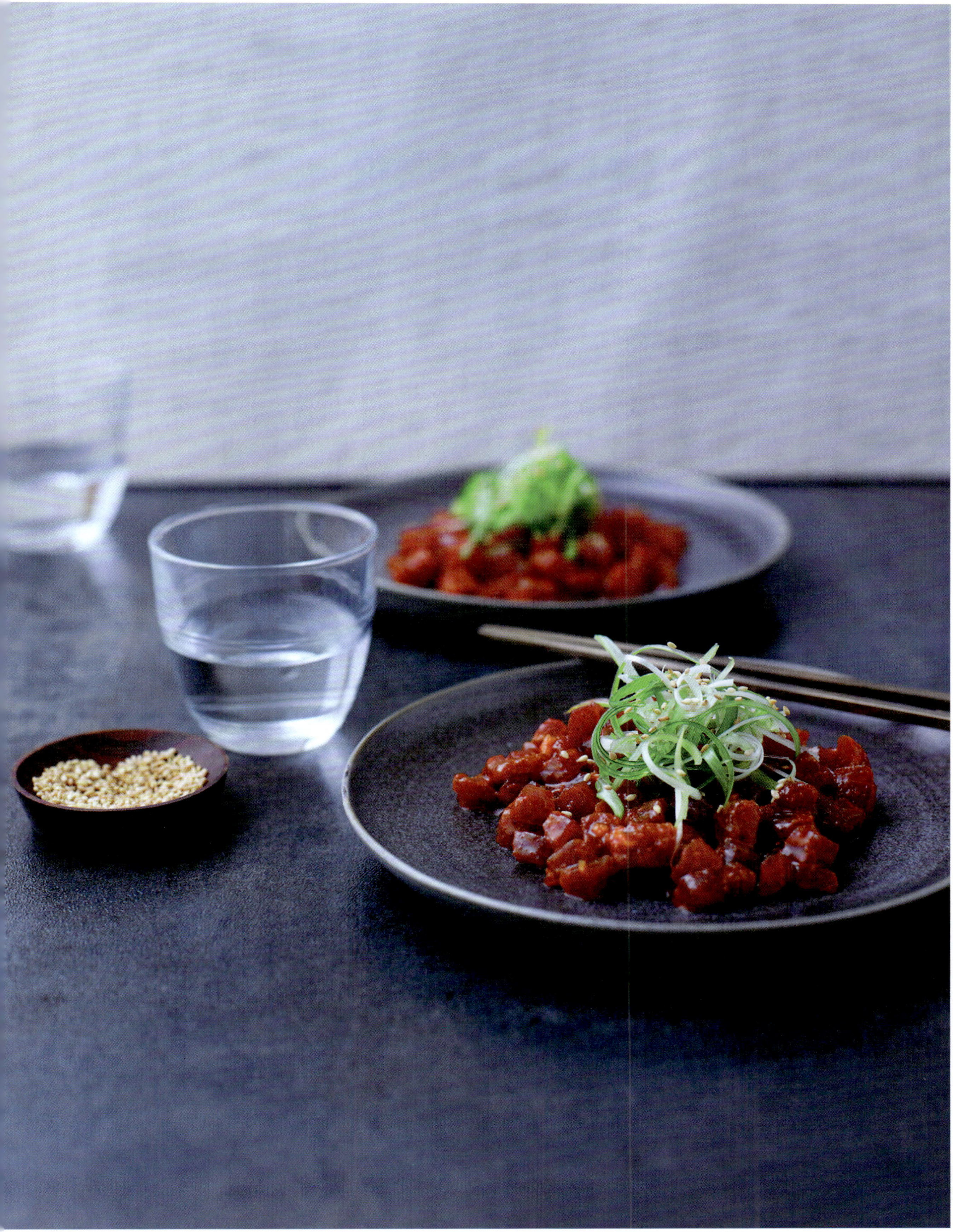

Food for All Seasons

Whatever the season there will always be an appropriately delicious Korean recipe to suit the weather. This is because the seasons in Korea are very pronounced, ranging from bitterly cold, harsh winters to swelteringly hot summers, with a mild spring and autumn in between. As a result many of their favourite national dishes are geared towards particular times of the year – from subtle, chilled soups, salads and light fish dishes perfect for spring and summer, to hearty, warming and fiery stews and meat dishes, ideal for chilly autumn and winter days.

This fish chapter is a perfect example of the kind of dishes we are referring to. On a hot and balmy day the light and fresh Scallops & Prawns with Pine Nut & Pear Soup (page 198) or the Seafood Salad with Wasabi Dressing (page 204) is the perfect antidote to the heat. While those freezing and windswept winter days are just calling out for something like the Braised Halibut in Seasoned Soy (page 197) or the Stir-fried Spicy Squid (page 192) that are sure to warm you up on even the coldest of days.

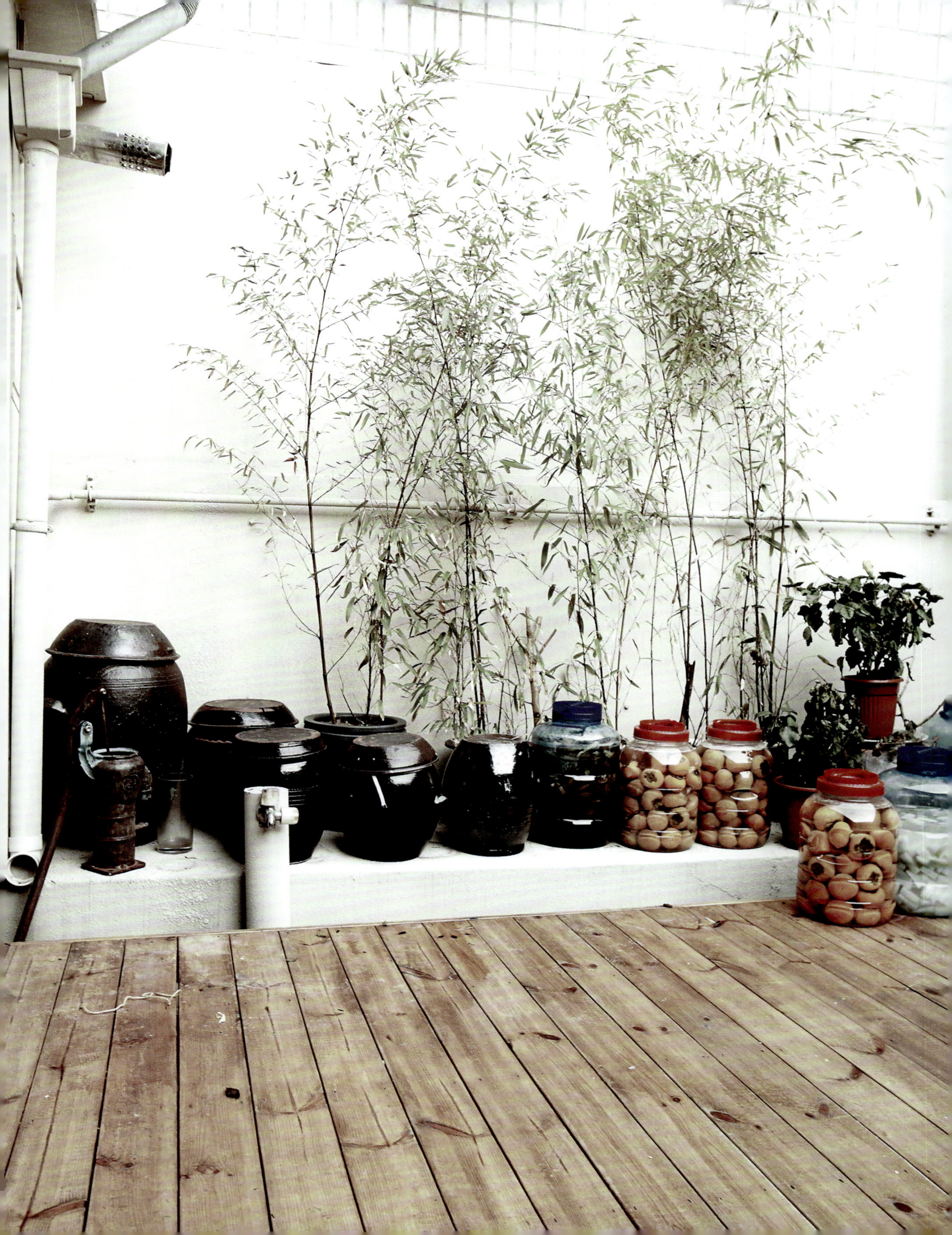

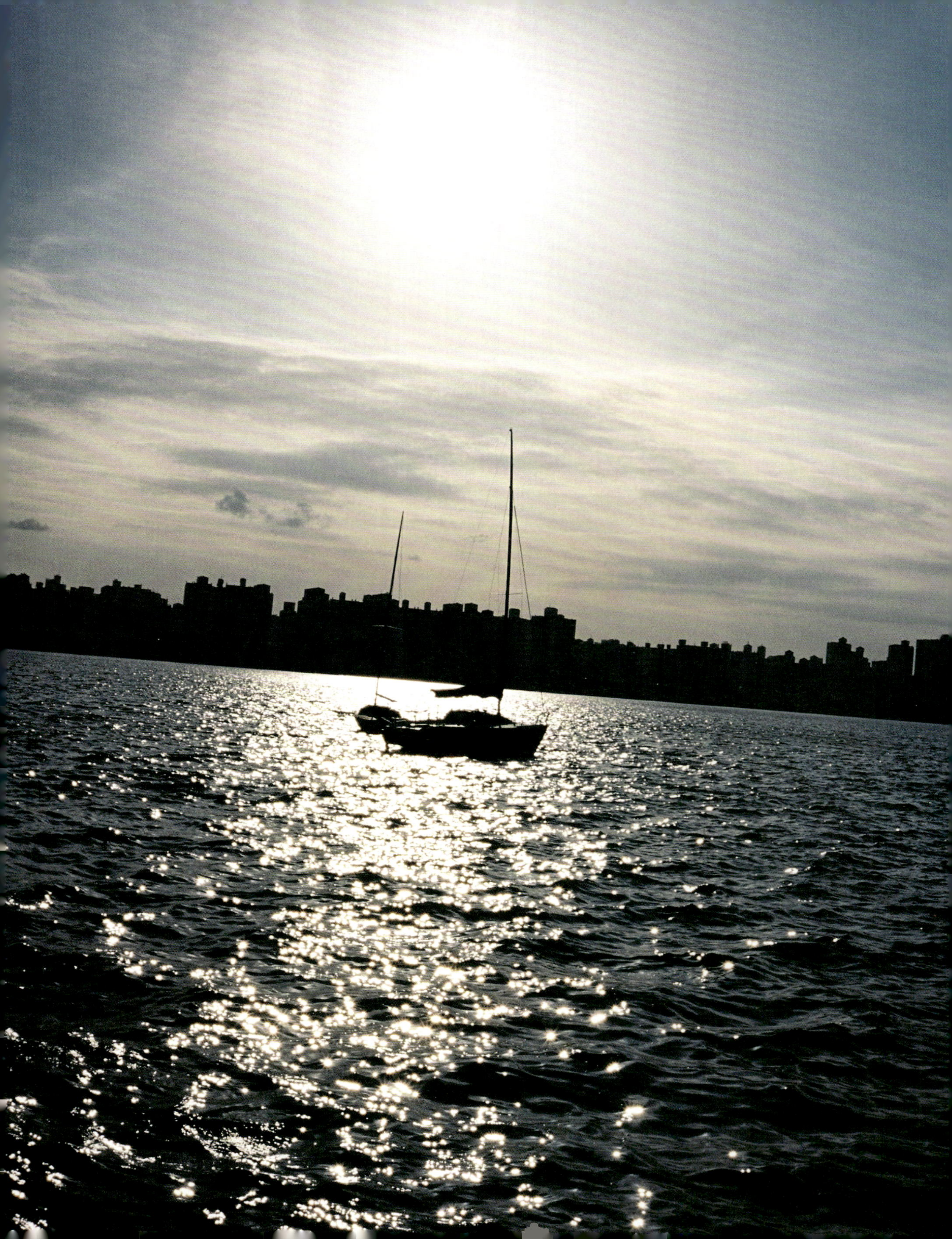

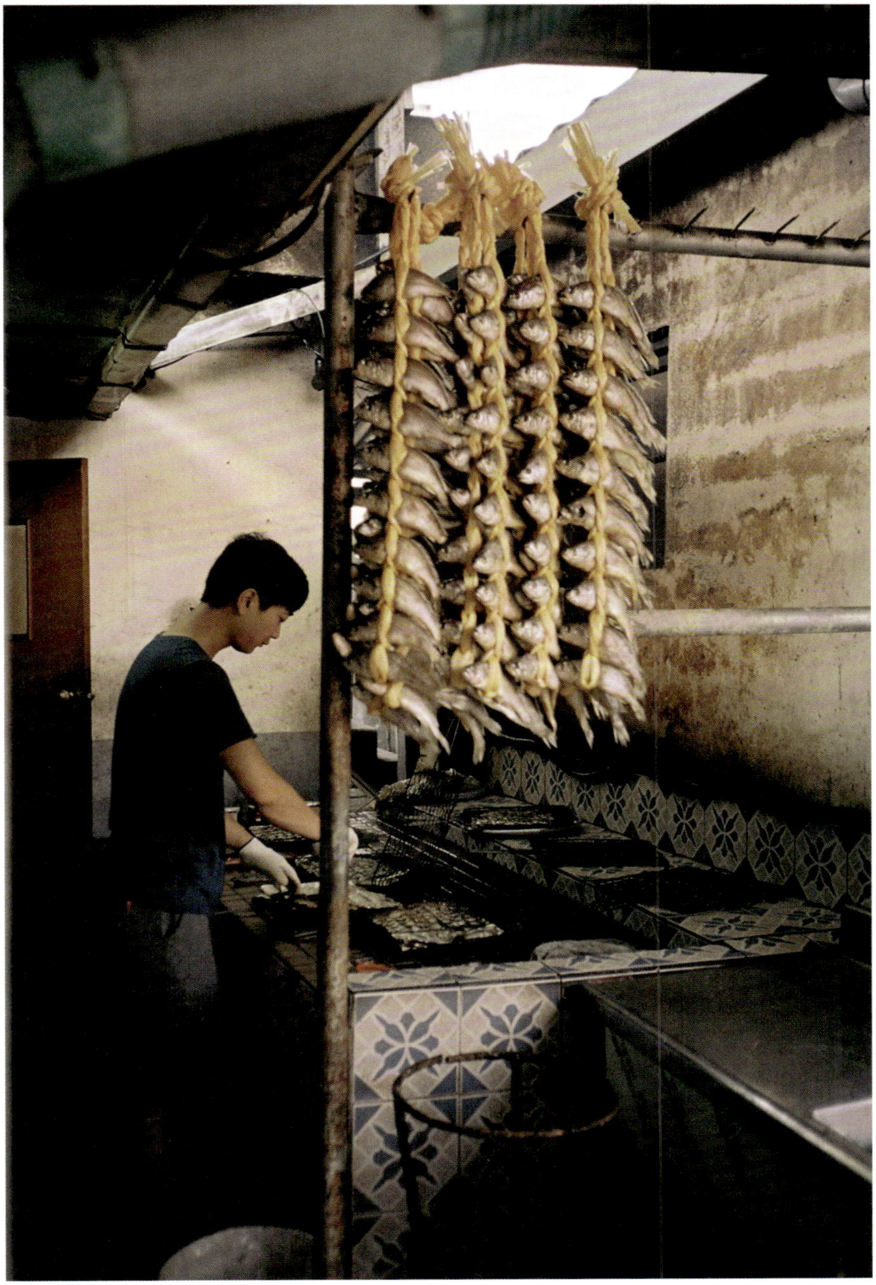

Serves 2–3

Stir-fried Spicy Squid
ojingeo bokkeum

500g squid, cleaned
2 tbsp vegetable oil
1 large carrot, halved lengthways and sliced
1 onion, halved and cut into thin half-moon slices
1 green chilli (optional), sliced thinly
3 spring onions (2 cut into 3cm lengths, 1 thinly sliced)
2 tsp roasted sesame seed oil
1 tsp toasted sesame seeds
cooked rice or noodles, to serve

Sauce
2 tbsp gochujang chilli paste (page 14)
1 tbsp gochugaru red pepper powder (optional) (page 14)
1 tbsp mirin
2 tsp soy sauce
1 tbsp honey
4 garlic cloves, crushed
2½ cm piece of ginger, finely grated

In Korea, this is often served as a side dish, but at home it is perfect for a quick midweek meal, either with rice or any kind of noodles, all tossed together. It is spicy, but you can reduce the quantity of the gochujang chilli paste and gochugaru powder if you prefer it less so. You can also add in any other vegetables you have lying about – it is quite adaptable.

In a bowl, combine all the sauce ingredients and set aside.

Slice the squid body open and lay out flat. With a sharp knife, gently score a criss-cross pattern on the inside flesh, taking care not to cut the whole way through. Then cut it into roughly 5cm odd shapes. Cut the tentacles into similar lengths.

Add the vegetable oil to a large pan and place over a high heat. When hot, add the carrot and onion and stir-fry for 3 minutes, keeping everything moving the whole time, until just beginning to soften.

Add the squid, chilli, if using, spring onion lengths and all the sauce. Maintain the highest heat, and stir-fry for about 2–3 minutes, just until the squid is opaque and cooked through. Remove from the heat, stir in the sesame seed oil. Plate up with the sesame seeds and sliced spring onion scattered over the top and serve the rice on the side.

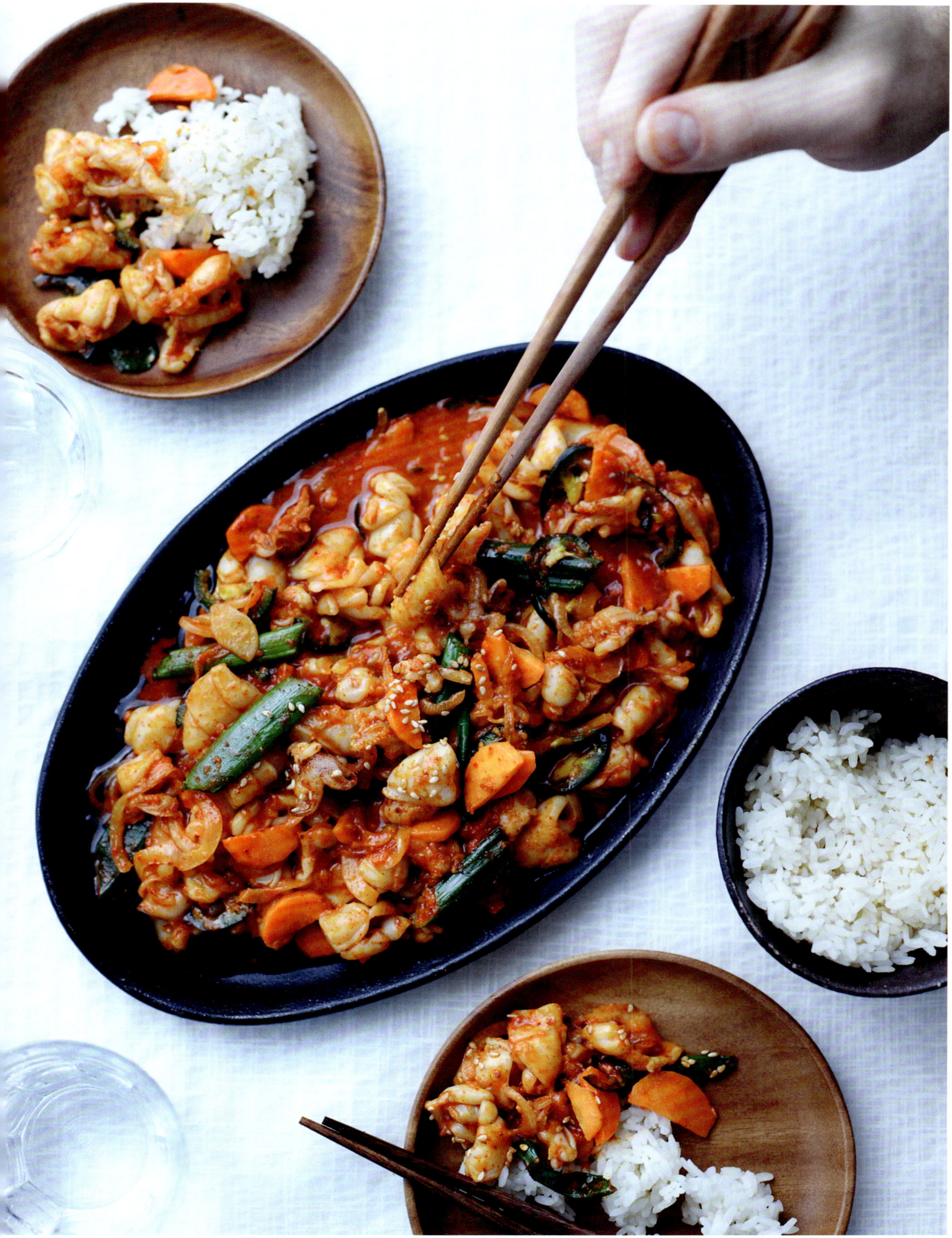

Serves 2

Pan-fried Mackerel
godeungeo gui

2 tsp vegetable oil
2 mackerel fillets or 1 whole mackerel
sea salt and freshly ground black pepper
1 tsp roasted sesame seed oil
2 spring onions, sliced into very thin 5cm lengths and covered in ice-cold water until curled up
2 tsp dried chilli threads (page 14) or 1 red chilli finely sliced (optional)
cooked rice, to serve
kimchi, to serve

In Korea, there is a kind of salted yellow corvina fish that is adored by all, lightly grilled and eaten in small mouthfuls with rice and other side dishes as it is highly salted. It is really excellent, but alas, you can't get that kind of fish here. This mackerel recipe is a very good alternative however – it is not pre-salted in the same way but you can achieve something similar when seasoning. We love eating this with rice, kimchi and the Seasoned Lotus Root (page 112).

Heat the vegetable oil in a pan over a medium-high heat. Season the fish generously on both sides with a good pinch of salt and pepper. When hot, add the whole mackerel or fillets skin-side down. Fry for 2–3 minutes on one side, using your fish slice to press down on the flesh to prevent it from curling up, then flip over and fry for another 2–3 minutes, depending on the thickness of the fish, until just cooked. Remove from the heat and drizzle over a little sesame seed oil.

Serve straight out of the pan with the drained spring onions and chilli threads tangled on top and bowls of rice and kimchi alongside.

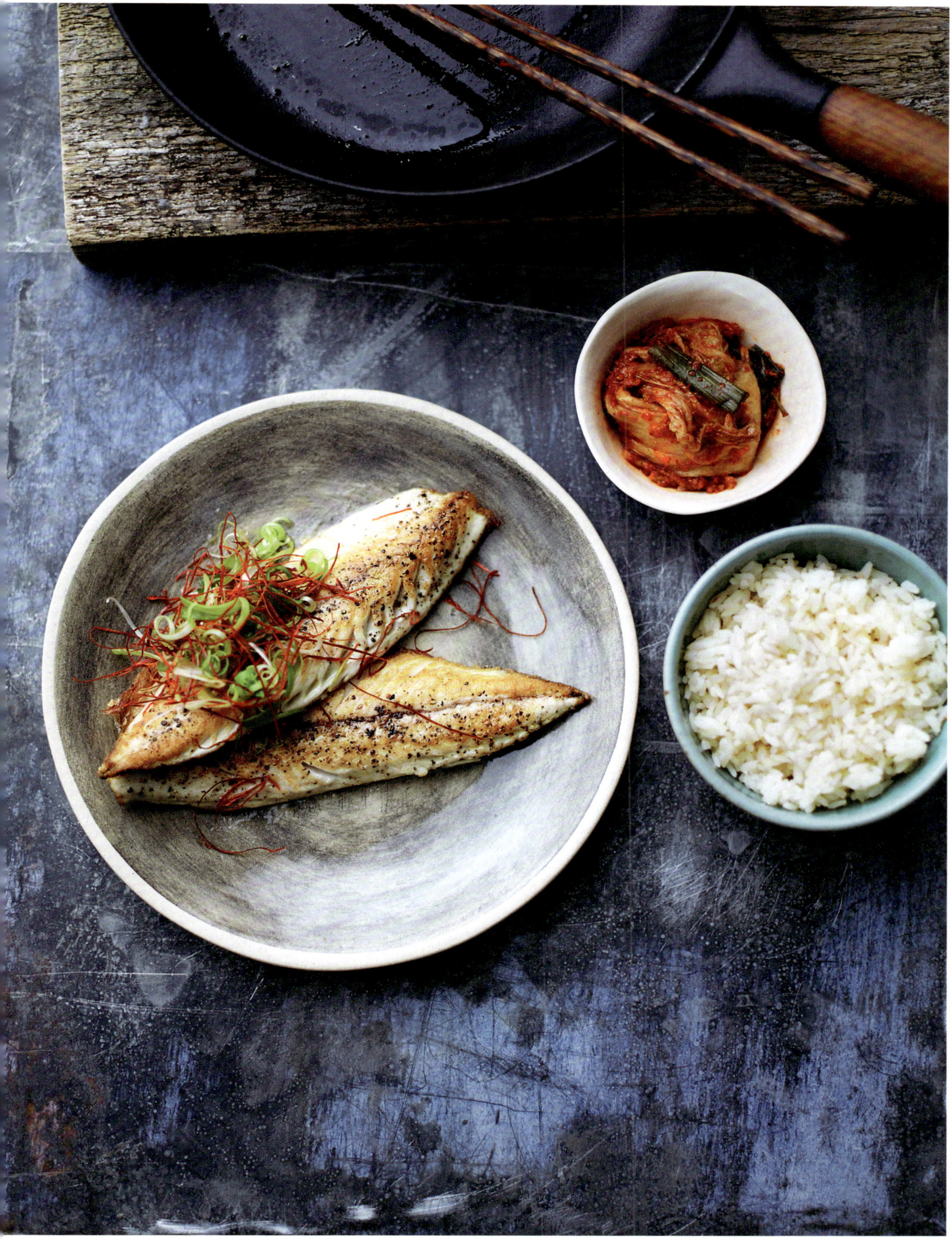

Serves 2

Pan-fried King Prawns
daeha jjim

대
하
찜

1 garlic clove, crushed
½ cm piece of ginger, peeled and finely grated
2 tsp soy sauce
2 tsp roasted sesame seed oil
1 tsp honey
1 tsp vegetable oil
150g king prawns, shelled
1 spring onion, thinly sliced
2 tsp roasted pine nuts, roughly chopped

You can fling this together in minutes, and it can be served on its own as a starter, or as a side dish. We have used shelled prawns here for speed, but you could also cook them with the shell on if you prefer to serve them whole. Tiger prawns and langoustines also work well and make for a more elegant affair.

To make the sauce, combine the garlic, ginger, soy sauce, sesame seed oil and honey in a bowl.

Heat the vegetable oil in a pan over a high heat. When very hot, add in the prawns and cook for 1 minute, then turn them over. Add in the sauce and fry for another minute until cooked through.

Remove and place on a plate, sprinkle over the sliced spring onion and pine nuts. Serve immediately.

Serves 2

Braised Halibut in Seasoned Soy
sengson jjim

생선찜

50ml soy sauce
3 tbsp soju (you can also use sake or mix 1½ tbsp vodka and 1½ tbsp water)
1 tbsp mirin
1 tbsp honey
2 garlic cloves, crushed
1 tbsp gochugaru red pepper powder (page 14)
250g baby new potatoes, halved
400g halibut, cut into large bite-size chunks
100g shiitake mushrooms
1 red chilli, sliced
cooked rice, to serve

Braising fish in this way creates a beautifully moist and fragrant dish, with the potatoes and mushrooms soaking up the delicious sauce in the process. Most other white fish will work very well in this recipe, so feel free to substitute with cod or seabass if you wish.

To make the sauce, mix together the soy sauce, soju, mirin, honey, garlic, gochugaru powder and 220ml of water in a bowl.

Place the potatoes in a medium saucepan and pour over the sauce. Cover and bring to the boil over a high heat, then reduce the temperature and simmer for 10 minutes until the potatoes are almost cooked through. Add in the fish and mushrooms and continue to simmer for 5–7 minutes until the fish, potatoes and mushrooms are just cooked.

Plate up and scatter over the sliced chilli. Serve with a bowl of rice alongside and any other side dish you like.

Serves 2

Scallops & Prawns with Pine Nut & Pear soup
jat haemul naengook

250g fresh pine nuts, plus a few extra to garnish
550g Asian or regular pear, peeled and cored
½ tsp sea salt, plus extra to season
1½ tsp lemon juice
2 tsp vegetable oil
4 king prawns, shelled and deveined
2 scallops, hard white muscle on the side removed
1 tsp roasted sesame seed oil
1 tsp finely chopped chives
finely ground black pepper

A great chef we know introduced us to this dish – it is so subtle, but an absolute delight on a warm day or as an elegant starter – the nuts and gentle sweetness of the pear are perfect with the fish. Fresh, preferably organic pine nuts are absolutely essential – as they have nothing to hide behind – so that year-old bag at the back of your cupboard is not going to cut it.

Preheat the oven to 180°C/fan 160°C/350°F/gas mark 4.

Lightly roast the 250g of pine nuts for 6–8 minutes or until very lightly golden, taking care not to burn them. Leave to cool completely.

Add the cooled pine nuts and pear to a food processor and blitz until completely smooth. Pass the mixture through a fine sieve, into a bowl, pressing as much liquid through as possible and discarding the pulp. Season with ½ a teaspoon of salt and add the lemon juice. It should be served at room temperature, so unless you live in a very hot climate there is no need to refrigerate it.

Heat the vegetable oil in a pan over a high heat. Season the prawns and scallops on both sides with a pinch of salt and pepper. Place them in the hot pan and cook for 1–1½ minutes on each side, until just cooked through. Remove from the heat and drizzle over the sesame seed oil.

Divide the pine nut and pear soup between 2 small bowls and gently top with 2 prawns and 1 scallop. Scatter over a few pine nuts and the chives and serve immediately.

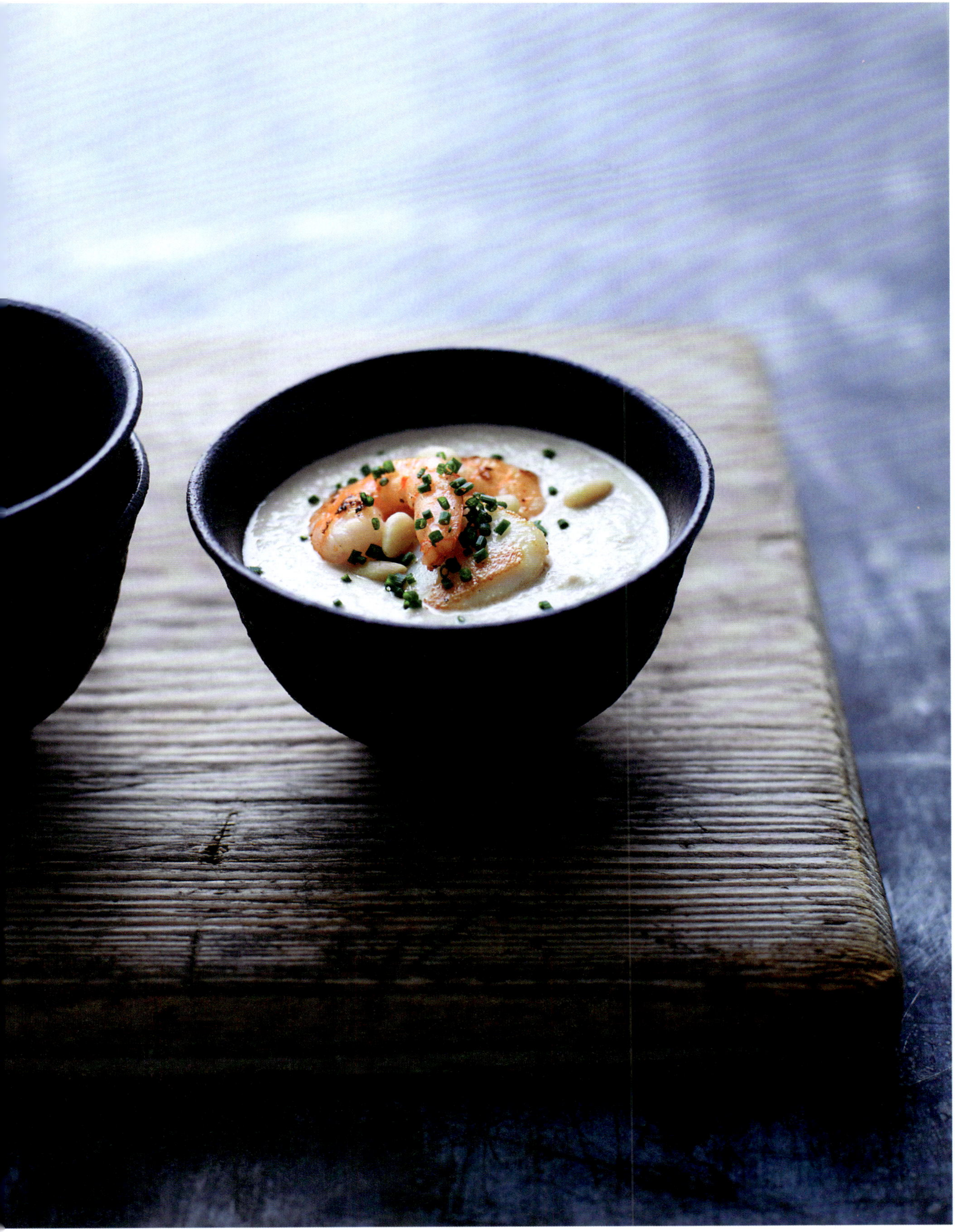

Serves 3–4

Soy-marinated Crab
ganjang ke jang

간장게장

1 live or very fresh brown crab (800g–1kg) or 3 blue crabs (you can ask your fishmonger to kill it for you – just make sure to use it as soon as possible)
2 spring onions, finely chopped
cooked rice, to serve

<u>Marinade</u>
350ml soy sauce
125ml mirin
3 tbsp roasted sesame seed oil
4 tbsp honey
½ onion, peeled and chopped
5 garlic cloves, peeled
5cm piece of ginger, finely chopped
1 Asian or 2 regular pears, cored and chopped
3 tsp dried chilli flakes

We first had this dish together in Jeju-do, an island off the south coast of Korea, known for its superb fish. Raw crabs are marinated in a soy sauce based stock, infusing the soft meat with the most wonderful flavours. As it is salty, it is mainly served as a side dish with rice, in fact this dish is commonly referred to as 'the rice thief'. In Korea, they use blue crabs, which are small and ideal for this dish. However, in the UK, we make them with brown crab as it is difficult to find fresh blue crabs. Because they have a thicker shell, less of the soy sauce penetrates into the flesh, so we cook them to make sure the flesh is safe to eat. If you manage to find fresh small blue crabs you can eat them raw once properly marinated, as they do in Korea.

If using a live crab, place it in the freezer for 2 hours. If your fishmonger has already killed it for you, simply keep it refrigerated.

Meanwhile, place the marinade ingredients along with 800ml of water into a saucepan, put the lid on and bring it to the boil. Reduce the heat and simmer for 10 minutes. Leave to cool, then strain the sauce into a bowl, through a fine sieve. Discard the flavouring ingredients. Set aside.

If your fishmonger killed the crab, skip the following step. Remove the crab from the freezer. Rinse and scrub under cold running water. Place it belly-up on a board and lift up the 'apron', the pointed flap in the centre of the belly. Beneath the apron, you will see a small hole. Using a clean screwdriver or strong chopstick, quickly and in one firm movement, pierce down into the opening right through to the other side of the shell. This will kill the crab instantly. Twist off the apron.

Flip the crab over so that the belly is facing down. Hold the legs firmly with one hand, then pull the main back shell up and away from the legs, leaving the body flesh exposed. Scrape away the grey-brown gills at the sides and discard. Break off the thin ends of the legs and the antennae. Rinse, then put the main back shell back onto the body, as you originally found it.

Place the cleaned crab belly-up in a bowl or resealable container and pour over the cold strained marinade liquid, ensuring the crab is submerged. Cover and refrigerate for 24 hours.

The next day, half-fill a large pan with water and bring it to the boil. Add the crab and pour in all of the marinade liquid. Bring it back to the boil and cook for 20 minutes for a crab weighing 1 kilogram, adding on an extra 5 minutes for every kilogram thereafter. Carefully remove the crab and leave to cool completely.

Once cool, serve immediately. Place the crab on a board and remove the back shell. Sprinkle over the spring onions and serve with rice and any other side dishes of your choice. We like Garlic & Sesame Bean Sprouts (page 123), or Honey and Soy-glazed Potatoes (page 127). Use your chopsticks or a teaspoon to scoop out the flesh from the belly. For the claws and legs, break them open with a pestle or a rolling pin and scoop out the flesh in the same way.

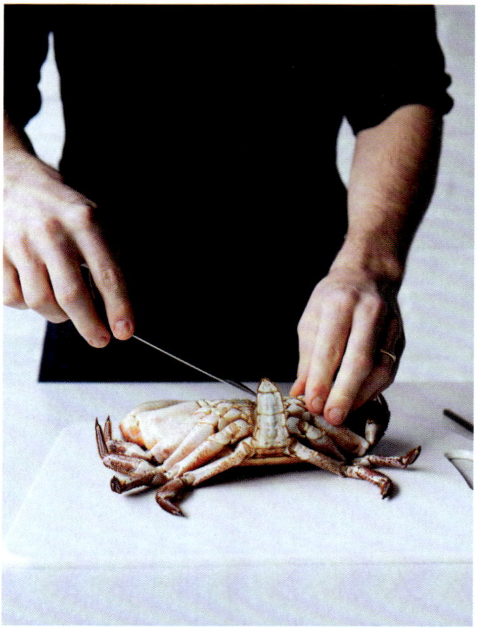
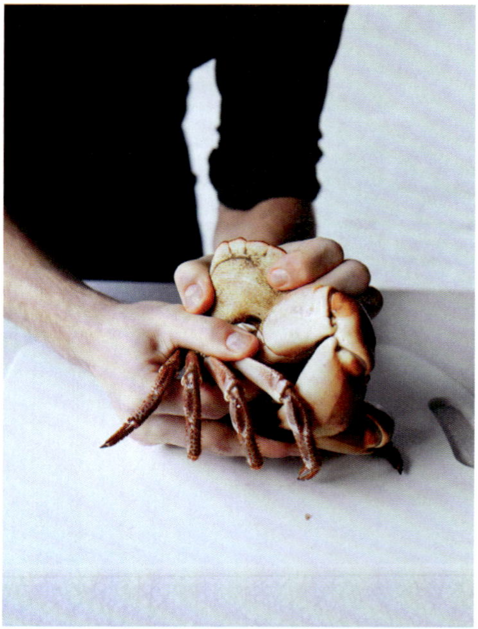
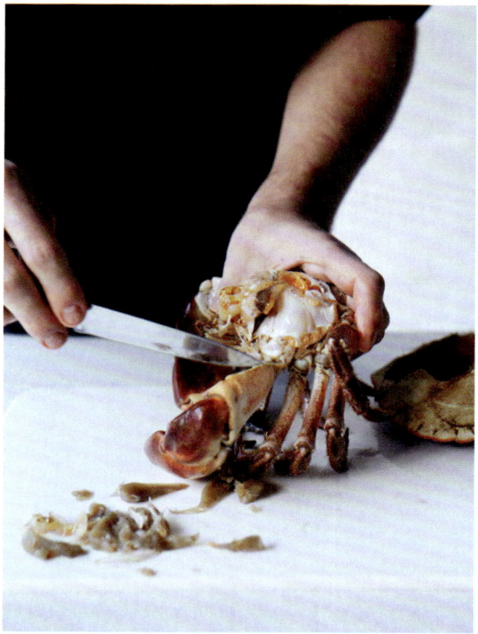
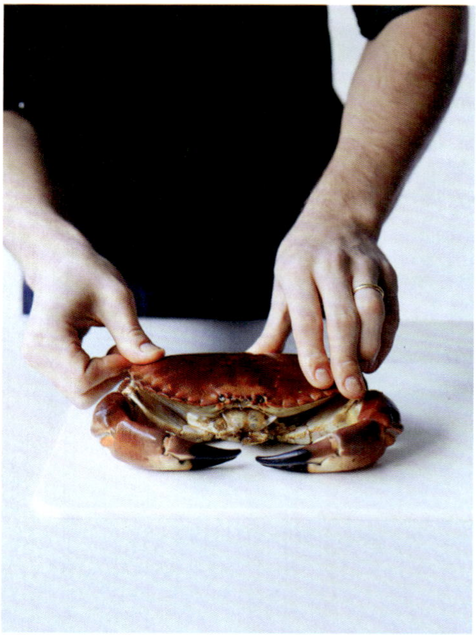

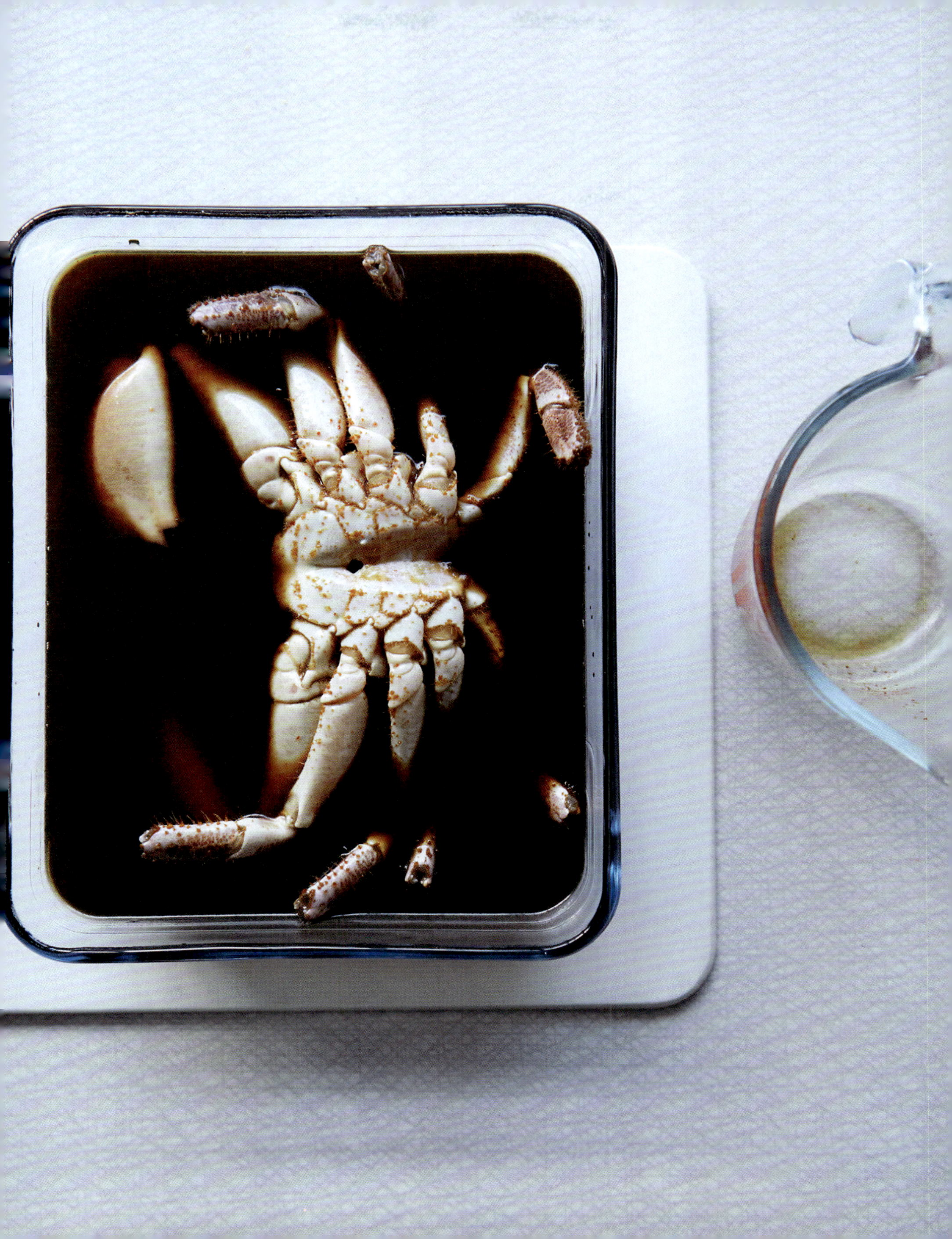

Serves 2

Seafood Salad with Wasabi Dressing
haemul naengche

8 king prawns, shelled and deveined
100g squid, cleaned, flesh and tentacles cut into 5cm pieces
60g crabmeat
½ Asian or 1 regular pear
2 spring onions, sliced into very thin 5cm lengths and covered in ice-cold water until they curl up
80g cucumber, halved and sliced into thin julienne strips
80g carrot, halved and sliced into thin julienne strips
1 baby gem lettuce, base cut off, leaves washed and roughly chopped

<u>Wasabi dressing</u>
1½ tsp wasabi paste (add more to taste)
1 garlic clove, crushed
3 tbsp rice wine vinegar
2½ tbsp honey
1 tsp sea salt

This light and fresh seafood salad is brought to life by the wasabi dressing, without being at all overpowering. It is very quick to make and is perfect as a starter or side dish. Jina's mum refers to it as the dish to reignite the appetite when you don't feel like eating.

In a bowl, combine all the wasabi dressing ingredients with 2 teaspoons water. Set aside.

Bring a saucepan of lightly salted water to the boil, add the prawns and squid and simmer for 2–3 minutes until cooked through. Remove with a slotted spoon and set aside on a plate. Pick over the crabmeat to ensure no shell is present.

Peel and core the pear, then slice it into thin julienne strips. Drain the spring onions.

In a bowl, combine the pear, cucumber, carrot, baby gem lettuce and most of the spring onions. Arrange in 2 bowls with the prawns, crabmeat and squid and top with the remaining spring onions. Pour over the dressing and mix together at the table. If you like, you can add more wasabi.

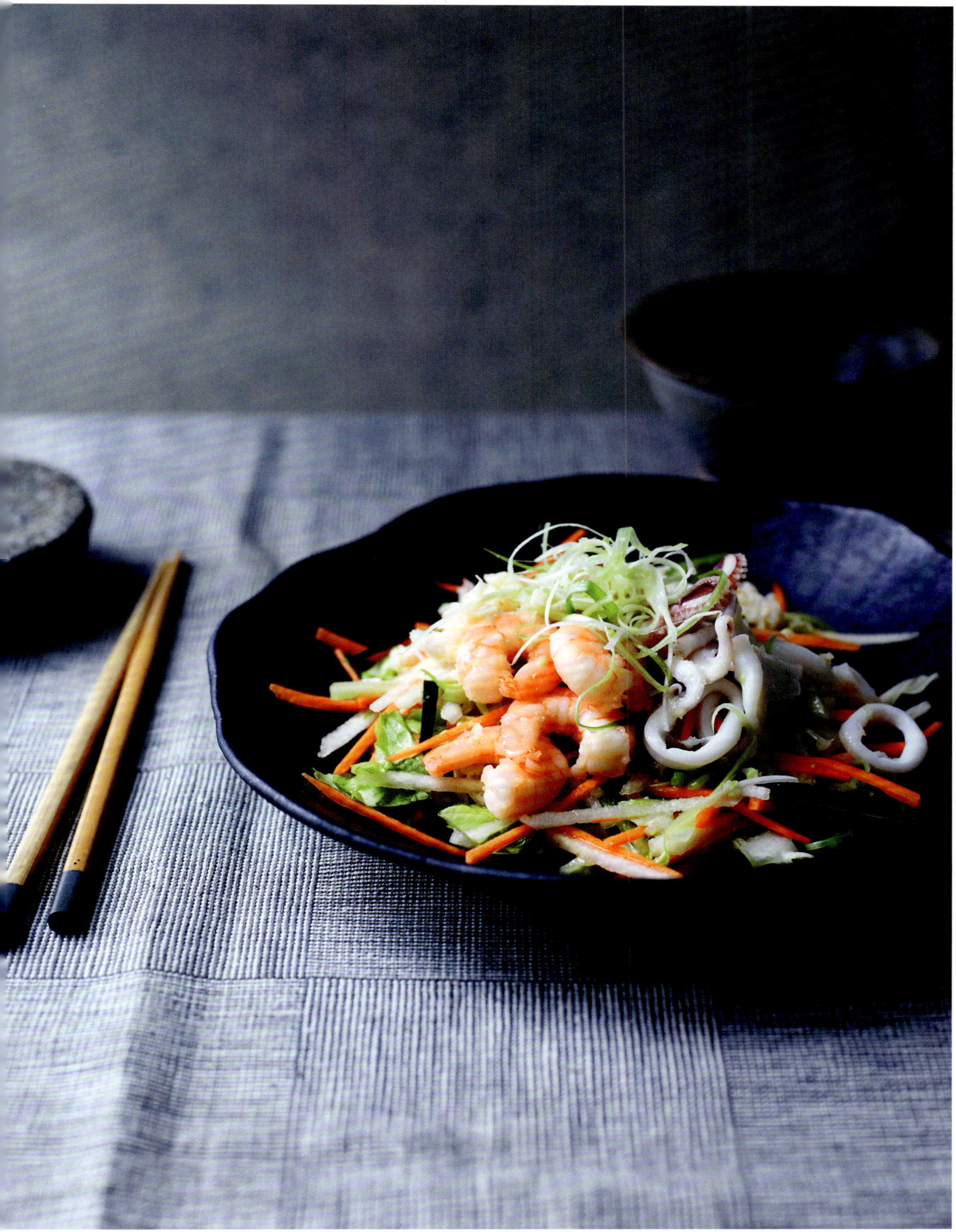

Meat

고기

| 왕족발 국내산 中 18,000 | 뼈 없는 족발 국내산 小 13,000 | 우리가게는 정직하게 판 |

07

210. **Sesame, Soy & Chilli Beef Tartare**
육회

212. **Sesame & Soy-marinated Beef**
불고기

214. **Soy-braised Beef Short Ribs with Vegetables**
갈비찜

218. **Grilled Pork Belly with Sesame Dip**
삼겹살

223. **Succulent Pork & Kimchi Wrapped in Leaves**
보쌈

224. **Grilled Beef Short Ribs**
갈비구이

226. **Deep-fried Sweet & Spicy Chicken Wings**
양념치킨

229. *Festivals & Feast Days*

230. **Chicken, Rice Cakes & Vegetable Hotpot**
닭갈비

232. **Pork & Tofu Dumplings**
돼지고기 만두

236. **Dumpling Wrappers**
만두피

237. **Fried Minced Meat Patties with Sesame Seeds**
떡갈비

240. **Chicken, Vegetable & Noodle Hotpot**
닭찜

Serves 2

Sesame, Soy & Chilli Beef Tartare
yukhoe

200g beef fillet, well chilled
½ Asian or 1 regular pear
3 tsp gochujang chilli paste (page 14)
4 tsp roasted sesame seed oil
1½ tsp soy sauce
2½ tsp honey
3 garlic cloves, crushed
1cm piece of ginger, finely grated
2 quail eggs, yolks only (optional)
1 tsp pine nuts
½ tsp black sesame seeds
a few cress leaves or pea shoots

The beef, sesame oil, garlic, chilli paste and Asian pear are in perfect harmony here, making for a truly memorable dish. Please don't be put off by the notion of raw beef and egg yolk, this is nothing short of sublime. The key to its success, however, is the ingredients. Seek out very fresh, good-quality beef and Korean chilli paste. It is excellent as a starter for a dinner party.

With a sharp knife, cut the beef into very thin slices. Line a small tray with cling film and place the slices flat on top, with a sheet of cling film in between each layer. Place in the freezer for 1–2 hours until the slices are almost fully frozen and stiff. (Or freeze completely to use at a later date.) Freezing improves the texture of the beef and makes it easier to cut into fine strips. If you wish, you can skip this step and make the dish straight away without freezing the beef, just make sure that it is well chilled.

Peel and core the pear, then slice into thin julienne strips. When ready to serve, take the beef out of the freezer, layer the slices 1 on top of another, and slice into very thin strips. It will still be slightly stiff and frozen, but it will defrost rapidly as you prepare and season it, leaving it perfectly chilled when served. Place the beef strips in a bowl with the gochujang paste, sesame seed oil, soy sauce, honey, garlic and ginger and mix together until very well combined.

To serve, divide the pear strips between 2 plates, place the beef on top in a little mound, and, if using, gently place the egg yolks on top of the beef. Sprinkle over some pine nuts and black sesame seeds and finish with a few leaves of cress or pea shoots. Serve immediately.

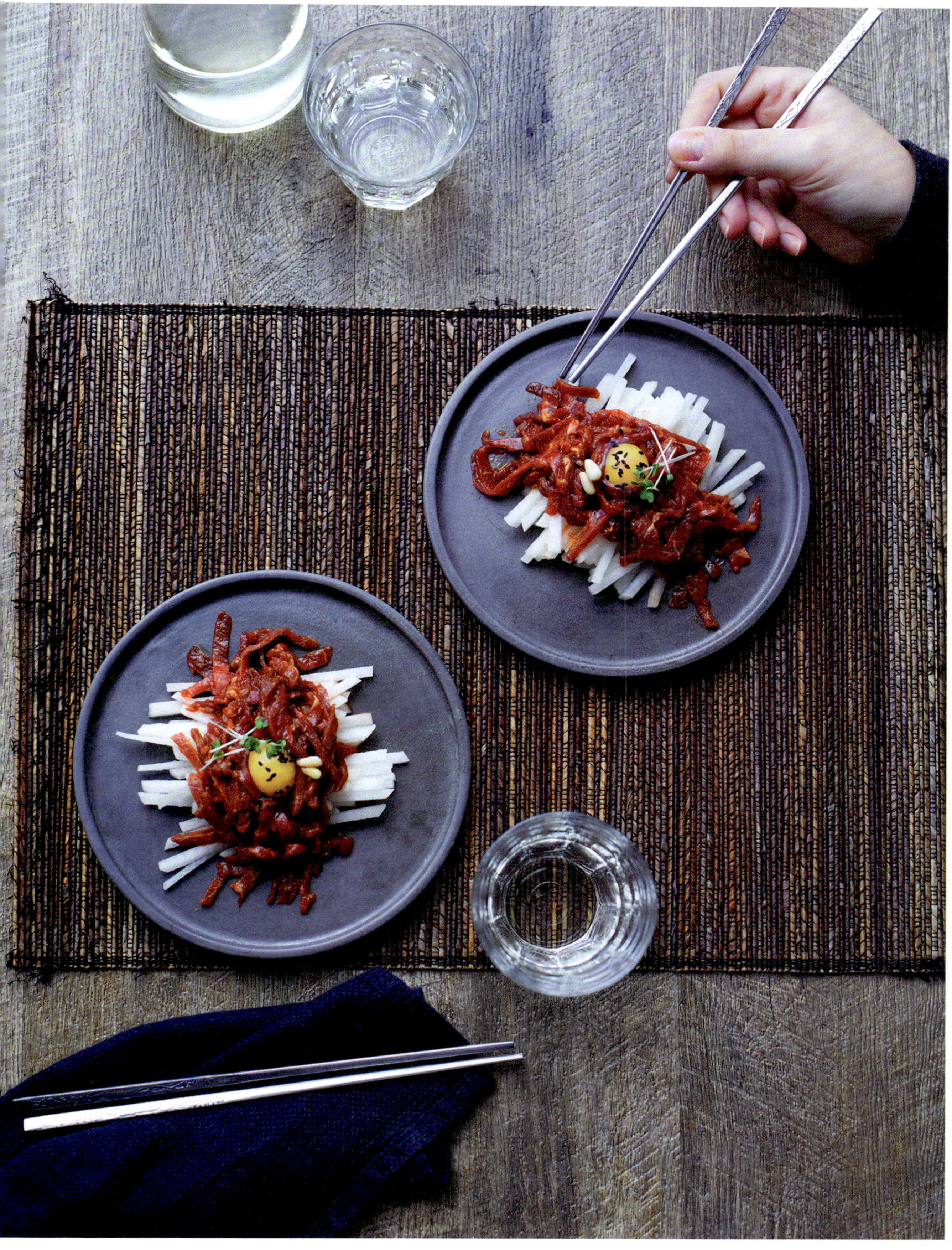

Serves 4–6

Sesame & Soy-marinated Beef
bulgogi

450g beef sirloin, cut into very thin bite-size pieces
½ onion, sliced
1 spring onion, thinly sliced, or cut into very thin 5cm lengths and covered in ice cold water until they curl up
cooked rice, to serve

Beef marinade
1 Asian or 2 regular pears, peeled, cored and finely grated
¼ onion, finely grated
1cm piece of ginger, finely grated
4 garlic cloves, crushed
2½ tbsp soy sauce
1½ tbsp honey
1½ tbsp roasted sesame seed oil
½ tsp freshly ground black pepper

Perhaps one of the most famous and well-known Korean meat dishes, 'bulgogi' literally means 'fire' (bul) 'meat' (gogi), as slices of soy and sesame-marinated beef were originally barbecued on a grill over an open flame. Of course you can still cook it this way if you like, but you can also achieve near perfection with a decent grill pan. The key is not to let the beef poach in the liquid it was marinating in – it is important to char the meat a little on the edges, to give it a lovely, slightly caramelised flavour.

Put all the marinade ingredients in a food processor and blitz until smooth. Alternatively, finely grate the pear, onion, ginger and garlic and combine with the other ingredients. Add the sliced beef to the marinade, mixing thoroughly to coat each piece. Cover and refrigerate for at least 30 minutes.

Heat a large griddle pan over a high heat. When very hot, add the sliced onion and the marinated beef to the pan, leaving as much of the marinade sauce behind as possible. Leave to sizzle over a high heat undisturbed for 2–3 minutes, then stir and cook for another 1–2 minutes, until the meat is caramelised and slightly charred. You do not want to burn the meat though, so keep an eye on it. Pour the reserved marinade sauce into the pan and allow it to sizzle for 30 seconds.

Remove the beef and place it on a plate. If using the curled spring onion, drain fully and pat dry, then position it on top of the beef. Serve immediately with rice on the side.

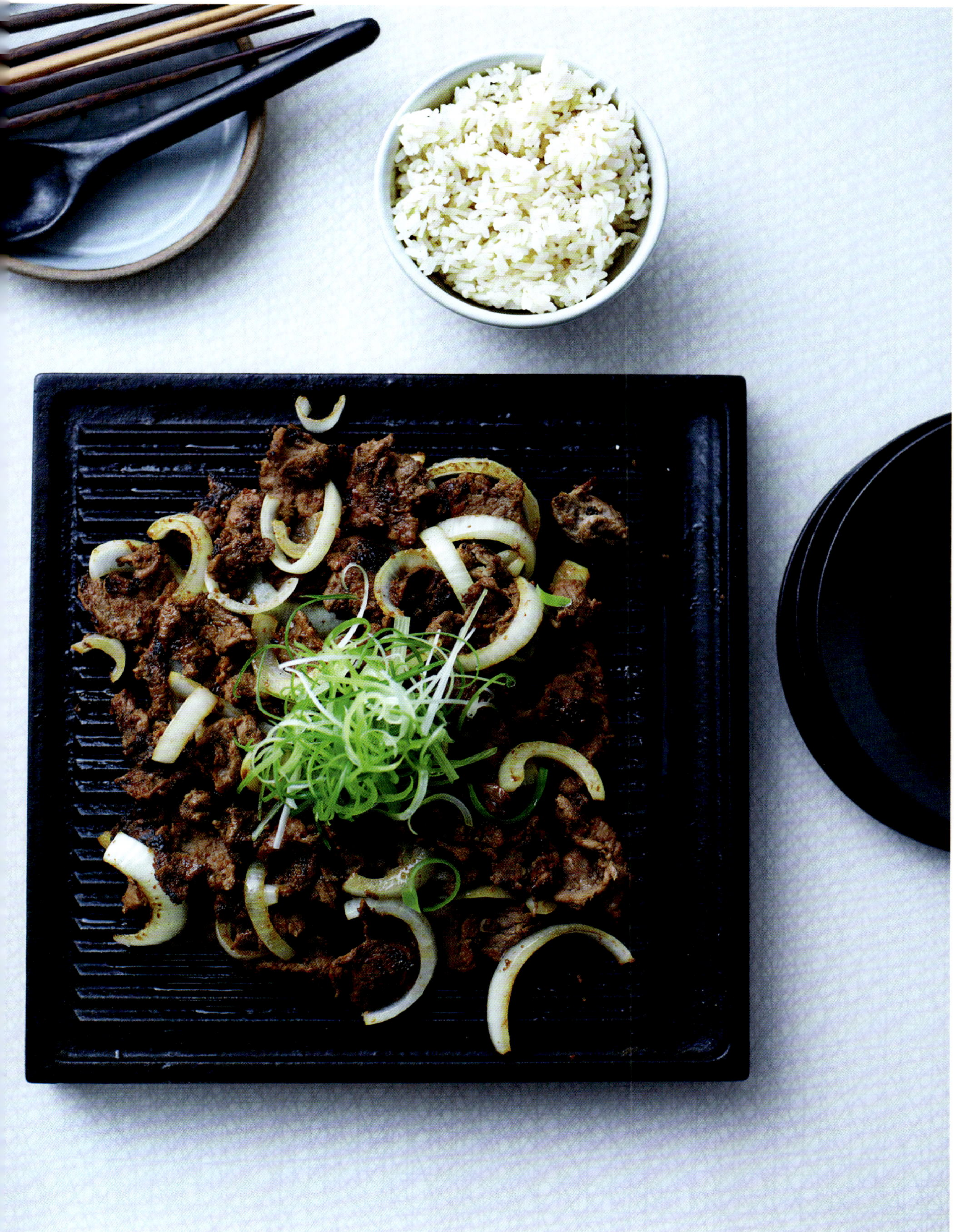

Soy-braised Beef Short Ribs with Vegetables
galbi jjim

Serves 4–6

800g beef short ribs, fat trimmed off, or braising beef
150g daikon radish, peeled, halved lengthways and cut into thick slices
100g carrots, cut into thick slices
5 shiitake mushrooms, stems removed and quartered
1 tsp toasted sesame seeds
1 spring onion, thinly sliced
cooked rice, to serve

Marinade
½ Asian or 1 regular pear, peeled and cored
½ onion, chopped
½ tsp freshly ground black pepper
2 tbsp mirin
2 tbsp honey
1 tbsp roasted sesame seed oil
4 tbsp soy sauce
3cm piece of ginger, finely grated
6 garlic cloves, peeled

This dish takes a couple of hours to make, but it is worth it for the end result – beautifully succulent and deeply flavoured short ribs. In Korea, jujube, a kind of date, and gingko nuts, are also added. They can be found in some Asian stores if you want to go the whole hog. Ask your butcher to cut the ribs across the bone into 4cm pieces or buy them pre-cut in a Korean supermarket. You could also use braising beef as an alternative.

Soak the ribs in cold water for 30–60 minutes to draw out any blood, change the water at intervals, then drain. In the meantime, place all the marinade ingredients along with 450ml of water into a food processor and blend until smooth.

Add the soaked meat to a large pan of fresh water. Bring to the boil and simmer for 1 hour, removing any scum as you cook and replenishing the water now and again so the meat is always submerged. Drain the water and rinse out the pan. Place the beef back in and pour over the marinade. Bring to the boil, then reduce the heat a little and simmer for 30 minutes. Add the radish and carrots and gently simmer for a further 40 minutes. Add the mushrooms and simmer for a further 10 minutes, until the liquid has reduced to a thick sauce and the meat is tender. Simmer for a little longer if need be.

Serve in bowls with the sesame seeds and spring onion scattered over the top and some rice on the side.

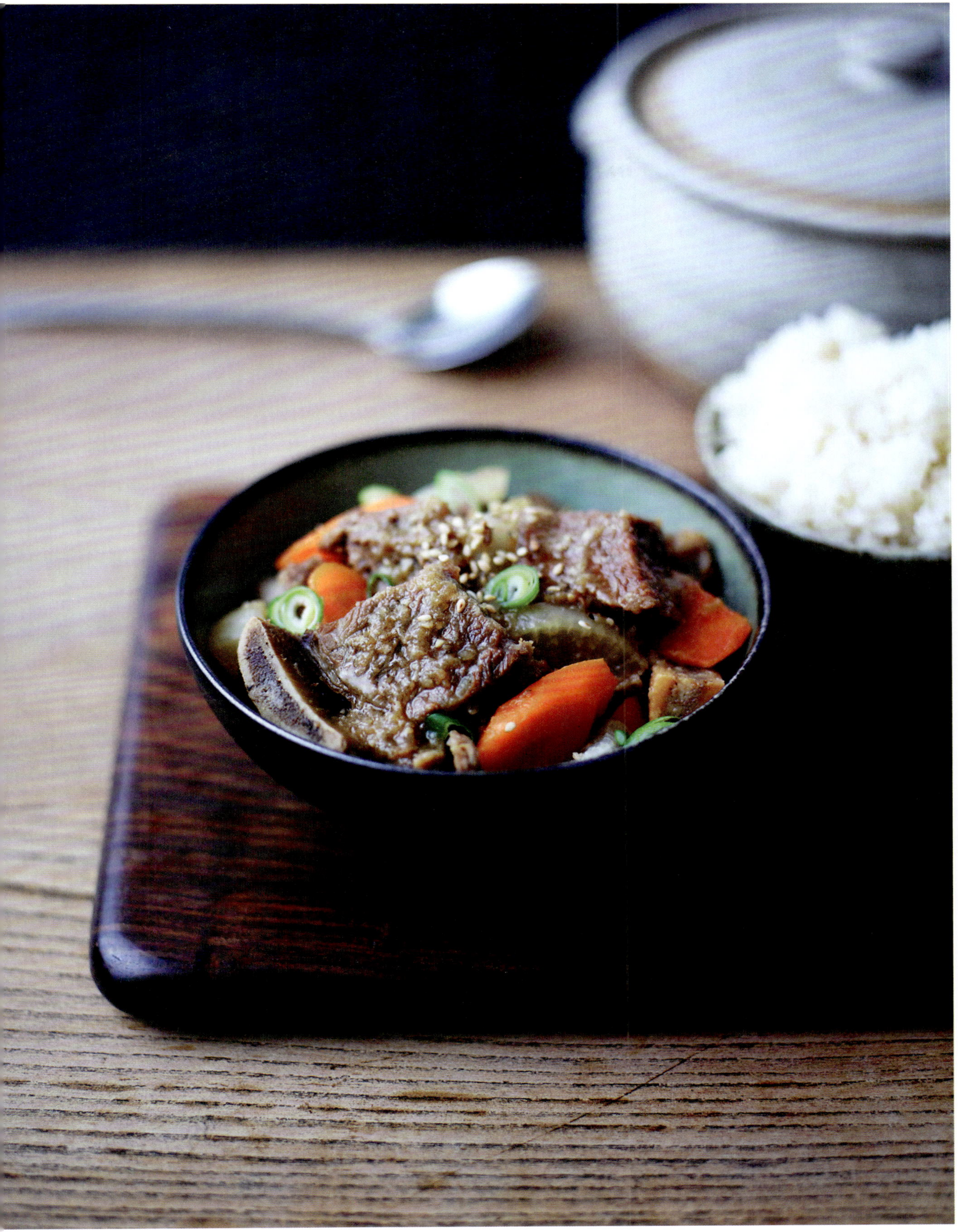

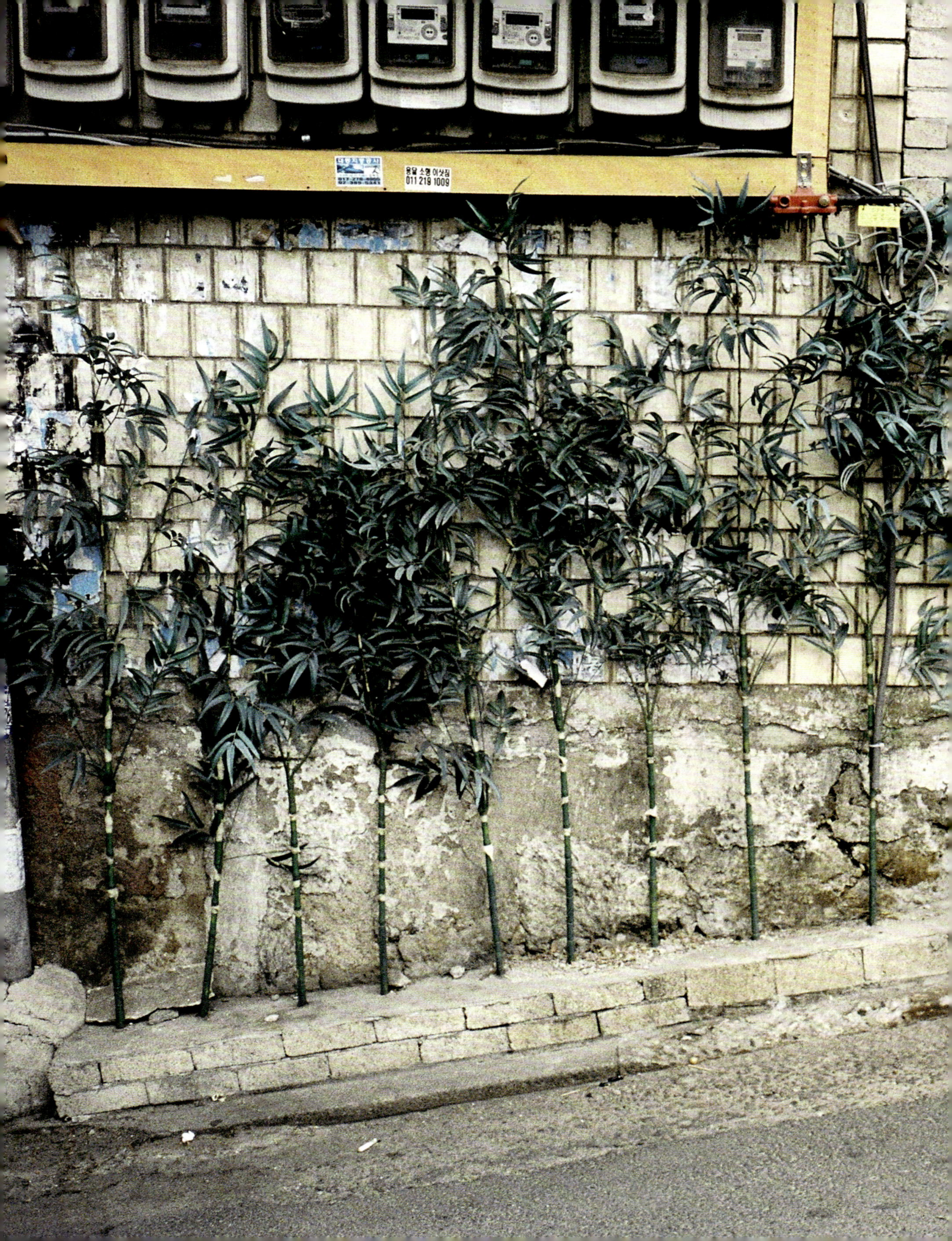
용달 소형 이삿짐
011 219 1009

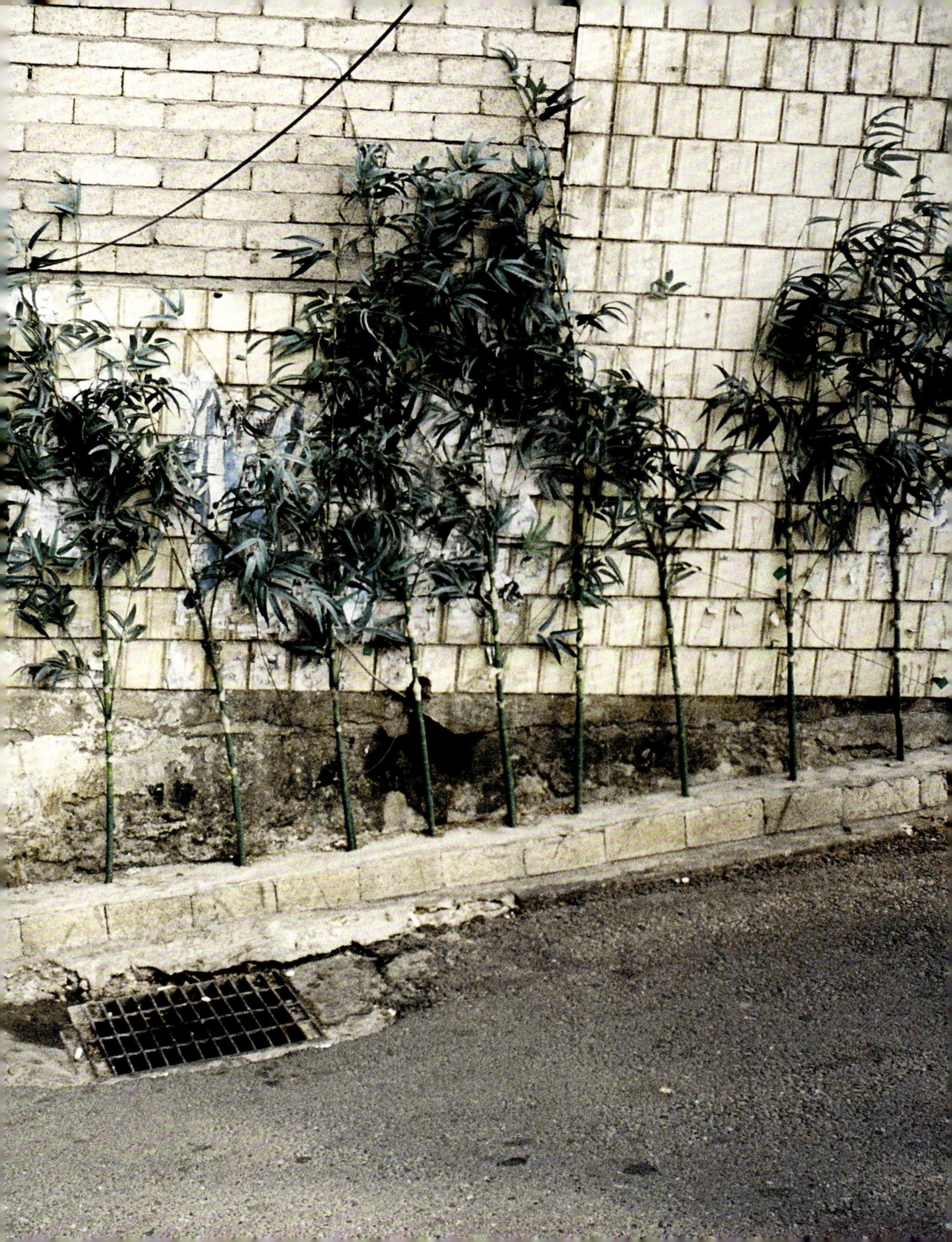

Serves 4–6

Grilled Pork Belly with Sesame Dip
samgyeopsal

3 tbsp roasted sesame seed oil
1½ tsp sea salt
½ tsp freshly ground black pepper
650g pork belly, skin removed (ask your butcher to cut it into very thin ½ cm slices. Or freeze it for 45 minutes to firm up, then with a sharp knife cut it into thin slices)
1 onion, thinly sliced
6 garlic cloves, thinly sliced lengthways
1 head of iceberg lettuce, to serve
kimchi, to serve
cooked rice, to serve

Ssamjang sauce
4 tbsp doen-jang soybean paste (page 14)
3 tbsp gochujang chilli paste (page 14)
2 tbsp rice wine vinegar
1 tbsp roasted sesame seed oil
1 tbsp honey or maple syrup
3 garlic cloves, crushed

Easily one of the most-loved dishes in Korea, thin slices of pork belly grilled at the centre of the table, dipped in seasoned sesame oil and then wrapped up in little lettuce leaf parcels with onion and garlic. Such a simple dish, but a fantastic way to get everyone involved at a barbecue, or if indoors, a portable gas ring can be used or a good grill pan. Samgyeopsal literally means three layers of flesh, and Koreans treasure the fatty layers, as when cooked it adds flavour and provides a melt-in-the-mouth texture, not to mention a good source of gelatin which they believe is good for the skin. If you are vegetarian, you can use large slices of mushroom. The ssamjang sauce is like the coming together of Korea's two most famous stars of the sauce world: gochujang, Korean chilli paste, and doen-jang, Korea's version of Japanese miso paste. The result is ridiculously good.

In a small bowl, combine the sesame seed oil, salt and pepper and set aside. In another bowl, mix together all of the ssamjang sauce ingredients and keep to one side.

Heat a heavy grill pan over a medium-high heat. When hot, add the pork belly, onion and garlic in batches. Grill the pork for about 6 minutes, turning once and the onions and garlic for a couple of minutes on each side. Use a pair of scissors to cut up the pork into smaller bite-size pieces. If you have a portable stove, this can be done at the table, and is a really nice way of eating it with friends.

To eat, dip a piece of pork belly into the seasoned sesame seed oil, then place on a lettuce leaf with some rice, a slice of garlic, onion and a little of the ssamjang sauce. Wrap the lettuce up into a parcel and demolish.

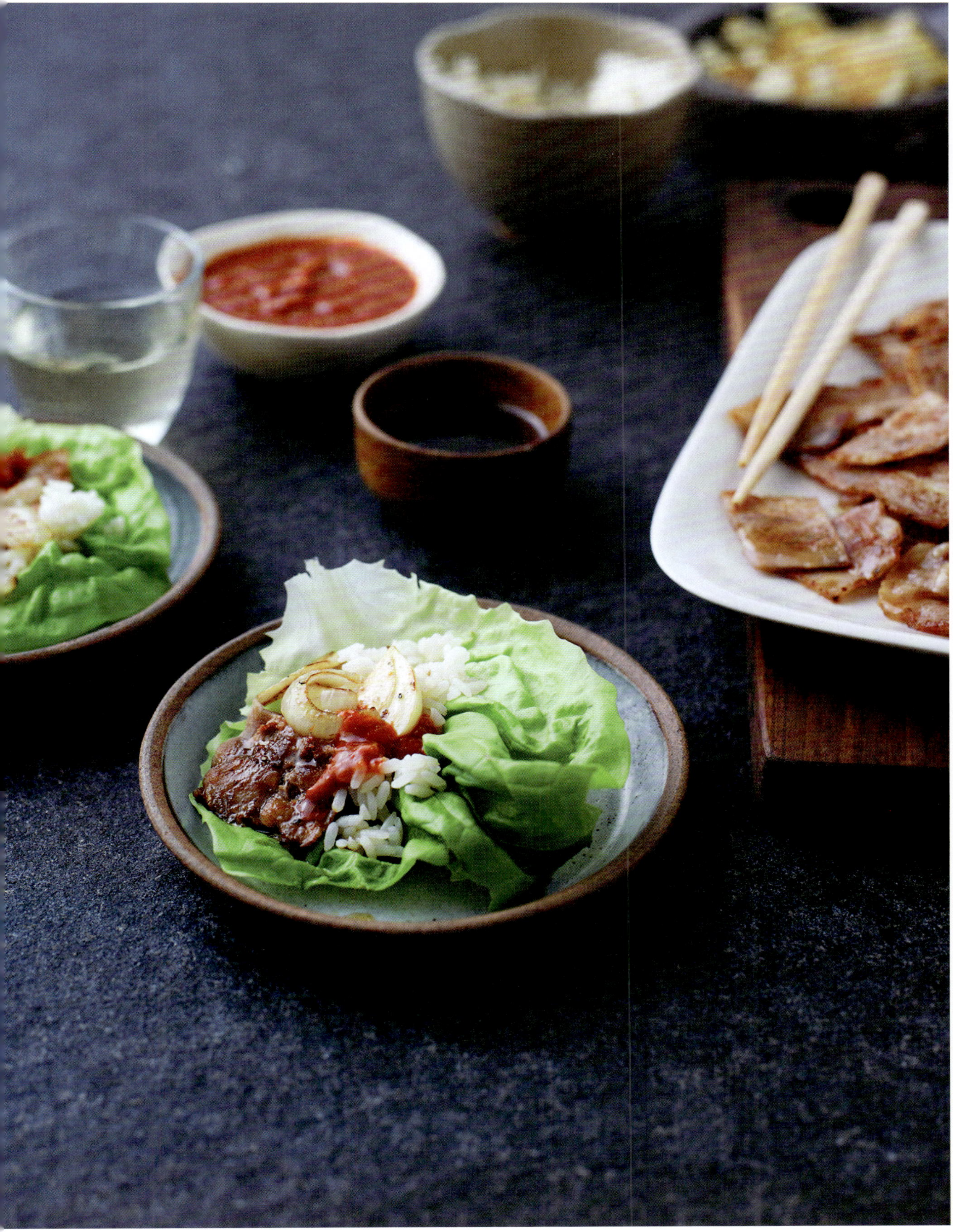

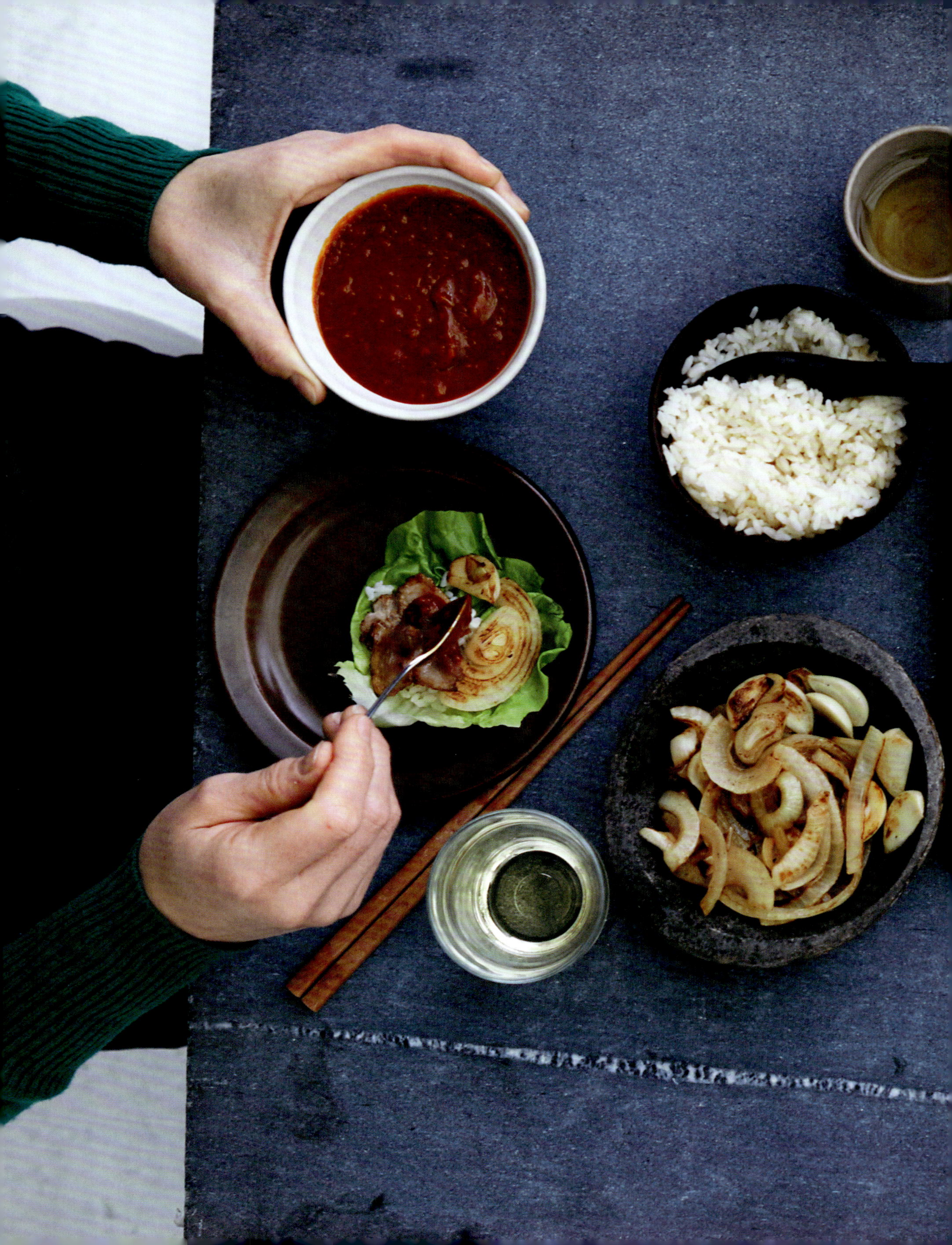

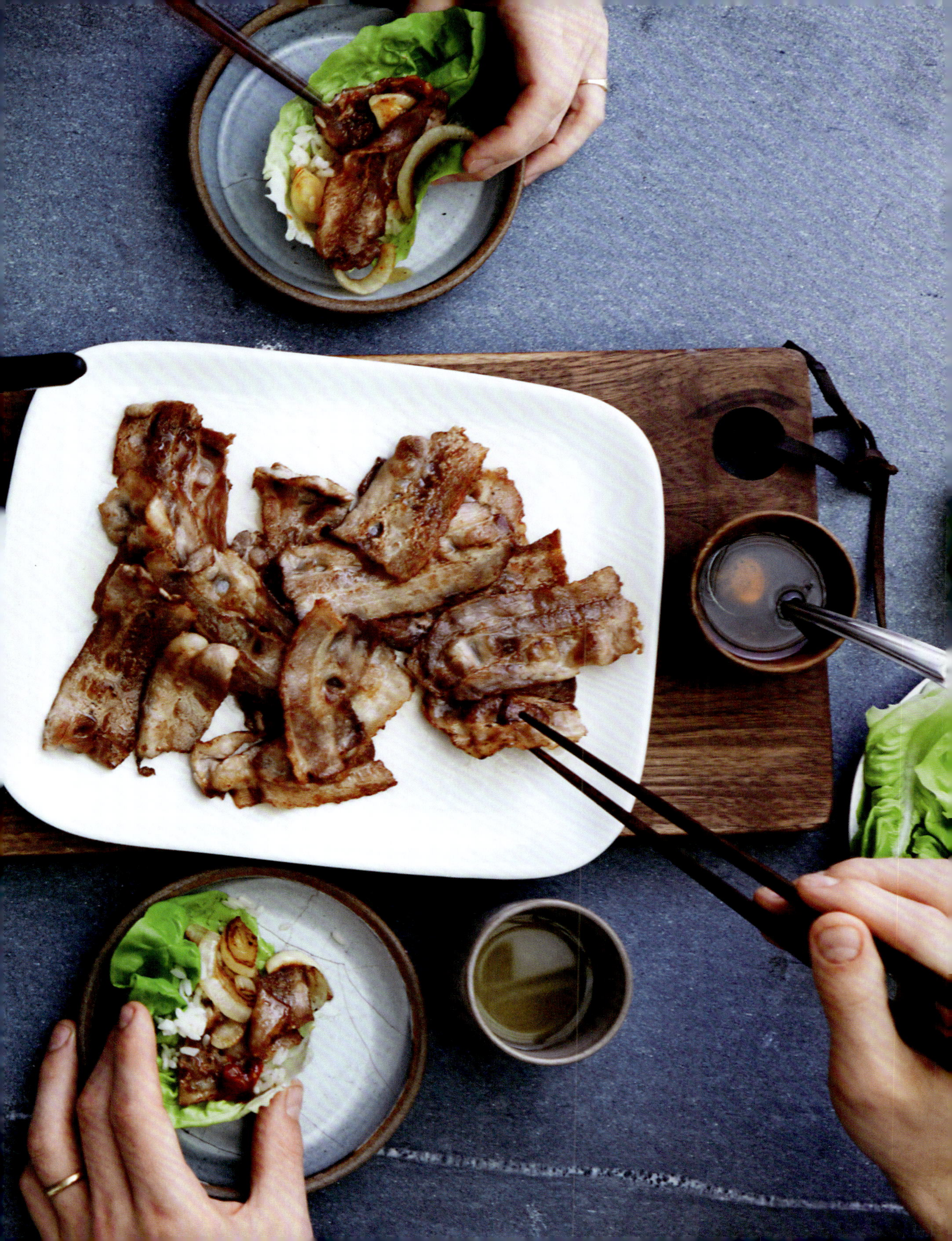

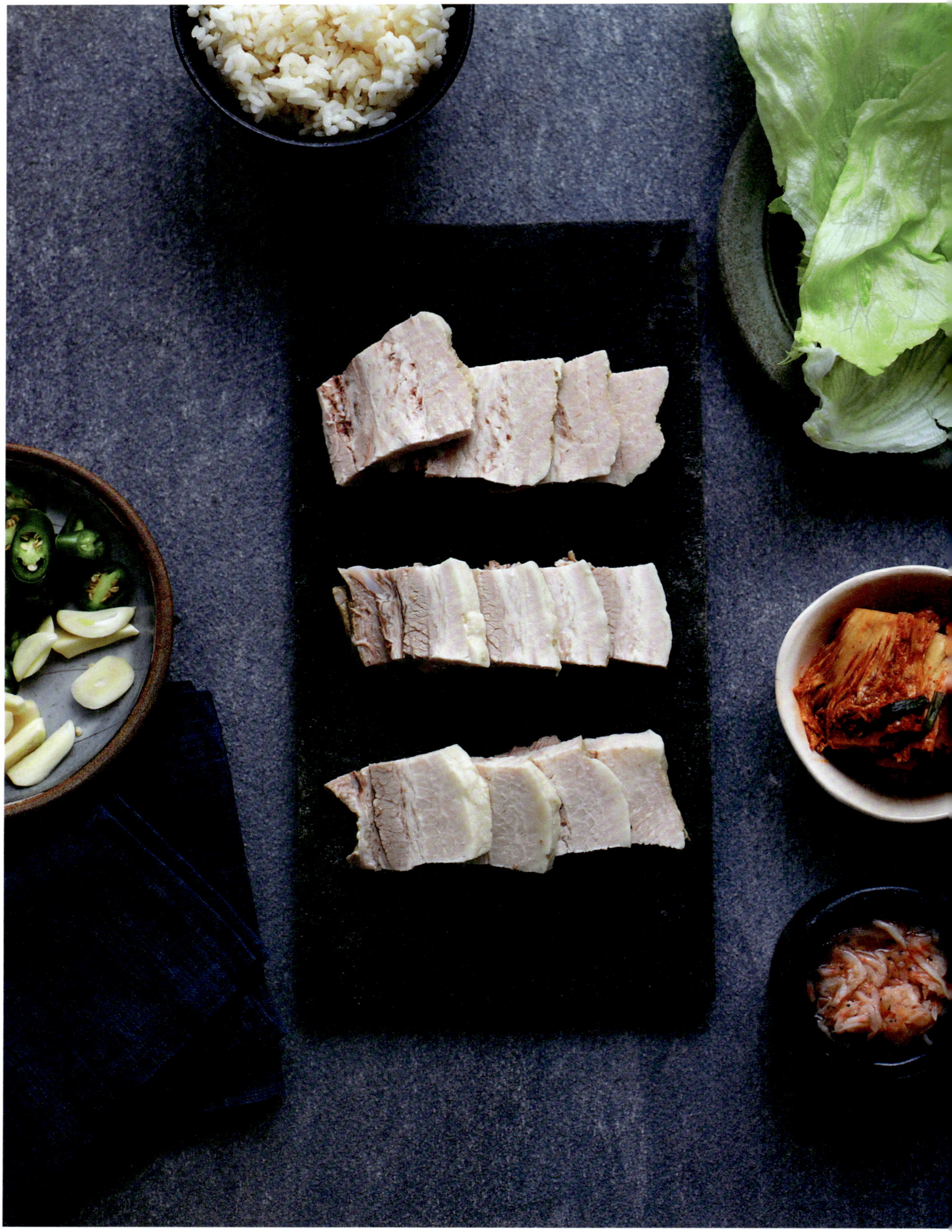

Serves 8–10

Succulent Pork & Kimchi Wrapped in Leaves
bo ssam

Poaching ingredients
1 x 1½ kg pork belly (ask your butcher to remove the skin)
4cm piece of fresh ginger, halved
6 garlic cloves, roughly chopped
1 onion, cut into chunks
1 tsp whole black peppercorns
1 tbsp sea salt

To serve
400g cooked short-grain rice (page 26)
kimchi (page 98) or shop-bought, young kimchi is best
1–2 heads of iceburg lettuce
5 garlic cloves, thinly sliced
1 green chilli, thinly sliced
2 tsp salted baby shrimp or sea salt or ssamjang sauce (page 218)

This is a great weekend sharing dish, as you assemble these delicious parcels of succulent pork, garlic, kimchi and rice at the table, so everyone is involved. It does take a few hours to pull this dish together, but you are not really doing anything for about half of that time while the pork is cooking, so it's perfect for a lazy Sunday, culminating in a big lunch or dinner feast with all your family and friends. The traditional Korean way of cooking the pork is to poach it, which is so delicious and moist. Pork belly is the traditional cut of choice, but pork shoulder could also be used. In Korea, salted baby shrimp are used to dip the pork into for a salty, fishy kick but you could use sea salt instead if you prefer, or the ssamjang sauce (page 218).

Place all the poaching ingredients in a large pan and pour in enough water to cover the meat. Cover with a lid and bring to the boil for 5 minutes. Reduce the heat, remove the lid and simmer for 1½–2 hours (topping up the water as needed to keep the meat submerged), or until the meat is tender. A skewer or chopstick should be able to glide into the pork without too much resistance. Turn off the heat and 15 minutes before serving, remove the pork from the pot and cut it into small ½ cm-thick slices.

Serve the pork with the rice, kimchi, lettuce, garlic, chilli and salted baby shrimp dotted around it in little bowls. To eat, dip a piece of pork belly into the salted shrimp, then place it on a lettuce leaf together with some rice and any of the other fillings. Wrap up the lettuce into a parcel and devour. The kimchi can be included in the parcel, or eaten on its own.

Serves 4–6

Grilled Beef Short Ribs
galbi gui

800g beef short ribs, LA cut

<u>Marinade</u>
5 tbsp soy sauce
2 tbsp roasted sesame seed oil
3 tbsp honey
2 tbsp mirin
½ Asian or 1 regular pear, peeled, cored and roughly chopped
½ onion, peeled
6 garlic cloves, crushed
4cm piece of ginger, very finely grated
½ tsp freshly ground black pepper

<u>To serve</u>
iceberg lettuce leaves
cooked rice
radish kimchi (page 102) or shop-bought
quick pickled onions (page 123)

For Koreans, galbi is the ultimate grilled beef dish, beautifully tender and absolutely packed with flavour. Marinating the ribs overnight makes a big difference, so it's worth getting everything together the night before you want to cook it. In Korea, two different cuts of short ribs are used for this dish, but the easiest cut to find outside Korea, is the LA galbi cut, where a rack is cut in very thin slices across the bone. You can buy it ready-cut in the freezer section of Korean stores or ask your local butchers for the LA cut. Galbi is at its best when barbecued, but you can also cook them on a grill pan.

Rinse the ribs, then cover them in water and soak for 30–45 minutes, changing the water once or twice. Drain.

Meanwhile, place all the ingredients for the marinade in a food processor and blitz until smooth. Place the soaked ribs and marinade in a baking tray or wide, flat bowl, and, using your hands, massage the sauce into the meat. Cover and refrigerate overnight.

If barbecuing, place the grill 12–15cm above the flame. Turn every now and again to cook the ribs evenly until they are a caramel brown colour, and slightly charred in places. Alternatively, place a heavy grill pan over a medium-high heat and when hot, add the ribs to the pan in batches, cooking for about 6 minutes on each side. Once cooked, use a pair of scissors to cut off the strip of bones and discard, then snip the meat into bite-size pieces.

Serve it immediately with the salad leaves, rice, kimchi and pickled onions, using the leaves to make little parcels containing a little of everything.

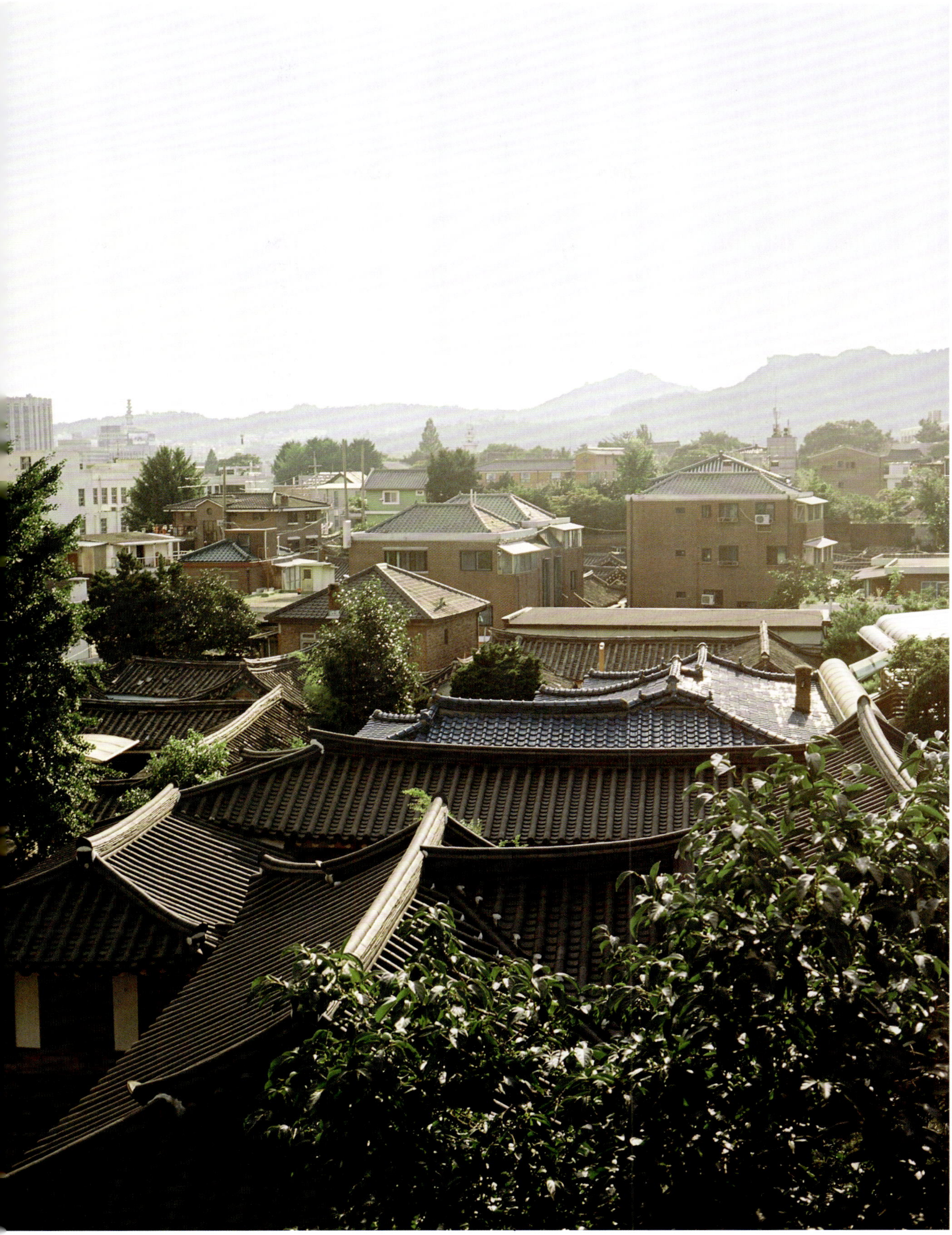

Serves 4–6

Deep-fried Sweet & Spicy Chicken Wings
yang-nyeom chicken

800ml vegetable oil, for frying
10 chicken wings (about 1½ kg), wing tips removed and cut in 2 through the joint
1 tsp toasted black sesame seeds
1 tsp toasted white sesame seeds
2 spring onions, halved lengthways and sliced into very thin 5cm lengths and soaked in cold water until they curl up

Sweet & Spicy Sauce (see variation below)
5 garlic cloves, crushed
4cm piece of ginger, very finely grated
4 tbsp gochujang chilli paste (page 14)
1 tbsp gochugaru red pepper powder (optional) (page 14)
4 tbsp maple syrup
1 tbsp roasted sesame seed oil
4 tbsp rice wine vinegar
2 tbsp brown sugar or coconut palm sugar
1 tbsp mirin

Flour mix
40g potato flour
40g plain flour
30g glutinous rice flour
1 tsp baking powder
2 tsp sea salt
1 tsp freshly ground pepper

While there is no doubt that this recipe is neither the most authentic or traditional of Korean dishes, its enormous popularity over the past few years at street food stalls around the world has been incredibly helpful in raising the overall profile of Korean food – and that can only be a good thing. In Korea, this dish is also very popular, largely because its sweet, spicy and addictive coating would make even an old leather boot irresistible. A chef I worked with in Seoul showed me the key to the perfect crunch – the double-frying method, which we have employed here.

Place all the sauce ingredients into a saucepan over a medium-high heat until it begins to bubble. Turn the heat down a little and cook, stirring frequently for about 6–8 minutes until the sauce thickens and becomes syrupy. Take care not to burn it. Remove the pan from the heat and set aside.

Pour the vegetable oil into a medium-size, deep pan, with at least 5cm between the surface of the oil and the rim of the pot. Place over a medium-high heat and, using a cooking or jam thermometer to guide you, bring the oil to 150°C/300°F. Alternatively, use a deep-fat fryer.

Meanwhile, place the ingredients for the flour mix in a bowl and mix thoroughly. Add the chicken to the flour mix, coating every part evenly. When the oil has reached 150°C/300°F, add the chicken in batches and cook for 12 minutes. Remove and drain on kitchen paper while you increase the temperature of the oil to 185°C/365°F. Return the chicken to the oil and fry for a further 6 minutes until golden brown and crispy. Remove and drain once again.

Gently reheat the sauce, then add it to the chicken in a bowl, and gently toss to completely coat it. Serve in a mound with the sesame seeds and drained spring onions scattered over the top.

Garlic & Soy Sauce Variation

If you're not keen on a spicy sauce, simply make a milder sauce using 6 crushed garlic cloves, a finely grated 4cm piece of ginger, 1½ tablespoons of rice wine vinegar, 5 tablespoons of soy sauce and 5 tablespoons of maple syrup and cook in the same way as above.

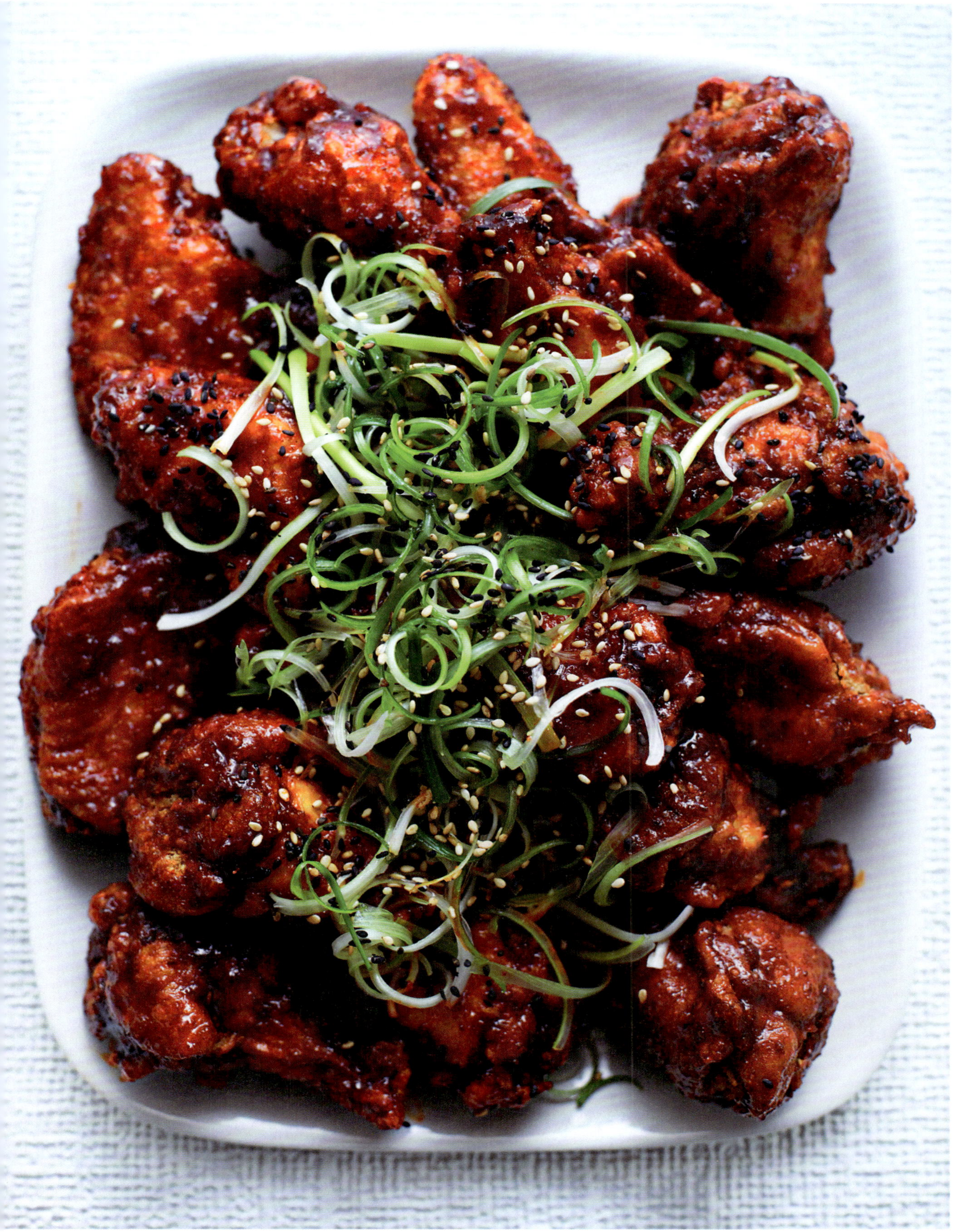

Meat

Festivals & Feast Days

Korea has numerous ancient feast days dotted throughout the year. The Pork and Tofu Dumplings (page 232) play a part in the lunar New Year celebration, which is one of the most significant traditional Korean family holidays and takes place each February, usually on the day of the second new moon after the winter solstice.

Much like Christmas or Thanksgiving, a three-day national holiday in Korea allows people to get together and celebrate with a feast. The traditional meal of the day is a rice cake soup called 'ddeokgok', which often contains dumplings (page 62). Because dumplings are reasonably time-consuming to make, Jina recalls the whole family getting together in a kind of production line to stuff each dumpling wrapper with a meat filling – sometimes this would even take on a competitive edge with her cousins to see who could make the largest amount of beautiful dumplings within a given time. The dumplings are then added to a deeply flavoured beef broth along with rice cake slices, egg and spring onion. It is said that you cannot become another year older if you do not eat this dish on New Year's day, but as it is so delicious we don't really see that being an issue at all!

Other Korean feast days include the first full moon day in spring. Traditionally, the Five-grain Rice (page 26) is served for breakfast, and a series of rituals are carried out to ward off bad luck for the coming year – most of them including food or drink of some kind. In the summertime heat, the festival of sambok is celebrated on the three hottest days of the year, known as chobok, jungbok and malbok, which represent the beginning, middle and end of the hottest period of the lunar calendar. The Baby Chicken Soup (page 64) is traditionally eaten on these days, the ginseng, Korean jujube red dates and nutritious chicken broth providing sustenance and stamina for the body during the unwavering heat.

Much like an American Thanksgiving, the Korean festival chuseok, gives thanks for the plentiful bounties of the autumn harvest, with all the family gathered around for a feast, including a half-moon shaped rice cake that is synonymous with this day. The final festival of the year comes in December on the day of the winter solstice when red bean porridge is eaten. The red colour of this dish is particularly significant to Koreans, who believe it will ward off evil spirits and bad luck over the coming winter months.

Serves 6

Chicken, Rice Cake & Vegetable Hotpot
dak galbi

닭갈비

500g boneless chicken thighs or drumsticks, cut into bite-size chunks
2 tbsp vegetable oil
300g rice cakes (page 14)
250g cabbage, chopped into bite-size chunks
1 small onion, peeled and sliced
200g sweet potato, cut into small chunks
8 perilla leaves (optional) (page 116) or 2 spring onions, sliced
1 tsp toasted sesame seeds

Sauce

3½ tbsp gochujang chilli paste (page 14)
2 tbsp gochugaru red pepper powder (page 14)
8 garlic cloves, crushed
2½ tbsp soy sauce
4cm piece of ginger, finely grated
3 tbsp mirin
1 tbsp honey
1½ tbsp roasted sesame seed oil
½ tsp freshly ground black pepper

In Korea, dak galbi is really popular as a fun dish to share with friends. We know Westerners are not as accustomed to sharing food in the same way, so it is hard to grasp the feeling that can be conveyed by the mere mention of this dish, but if you can picture yourself and your best group of friends all digging into a central platter, while chatting, drinking and laughing … you will have the idea. Do bear in mind that this is quite a spicy dish, so reduce or halve the quantity of gochujang chilli paste and gochugaru powder if you prefer a milder version.

In a bowl, combine all the sauce ingredients. In a separate bowl, combine the chicken along with half the sauce mixture. Set aside.

Pour the vegetable oil into a large heavy-based pan with a lid and set over a medium-high heat. Add the chicken, rice cakes, cabbage, onion and sweet potato, and cook for 4 minutes, stirring to prevent sticking. Pour in 120ml of water and the remaining sauce and bring to the boil. Reduce the heat to low, place the lid on and simmer gently for 20 minutes. Add the perilla leaves, if using, and continue to simmer for 5 minutes with the lid off, until the chicken and sweet potato are cooked through.

Serve in a communal pan to share, or in bowls with the sesame seeds scattered over the top.

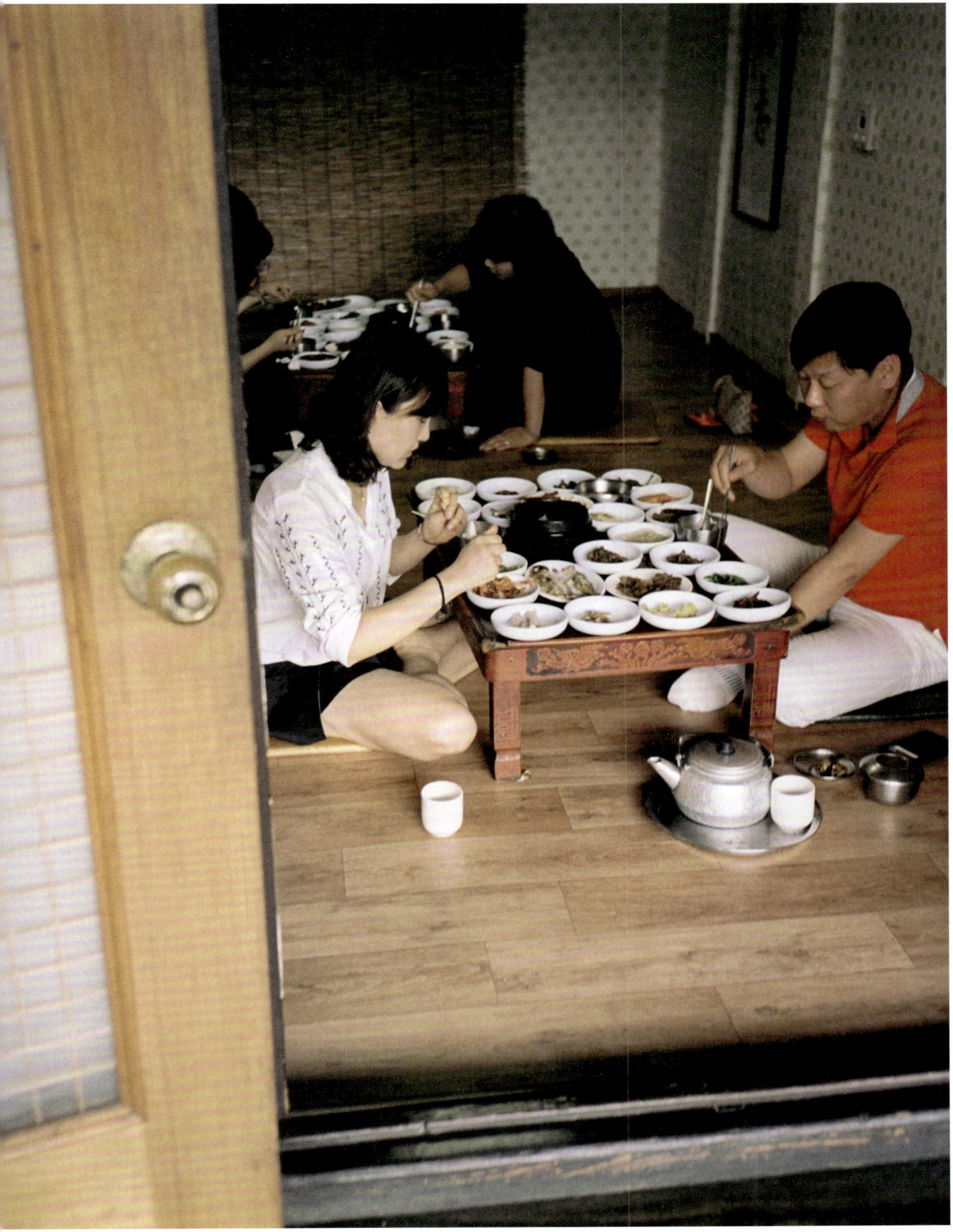

Pork & Tofu Dumplings
doegi-gogi mandoo

Makes 56–60 dumplings

260g firm tofu
200g napa cabbage, stalks removed, leaves roughly chopped
3 garlic cloves
6cm piece of ginger
½ onion
4 spring onions
700g pork mince
1 egg
2 tbsp soy sauce
2 tbsp roasted sesame seed oil
sea salt and freshly ground black pepper
flour, for dusting
approx. 60 homemade dumpling wrappers (page 236 or shop-bought)
vegetable oil, for pan-frying

<u>Dipping sauce</u>
2 tbsp soy sauce
4 tsp rice wine vinegar
1 tsp roasted sesame seed oil
½ red chilli, halved, deseeded and thinly sliced
1 spring onion, finely chopped
½ tsp toasted sesame seeds

Pictured overleaf

These are not as difficult to make as you would think and they keep for months in the freezer if wrapped up well. The dough is the same as the dough used for the knife-cut noodles (page 170) where the consistency is beautifully light and springy. Of course you can also use shop-bought dumpling wrappers – their flavour and texture is not quite as good, but they come a close second. If you do buy them, look for round skins.

Tightly wrap a clean tea towel around the tofu. Over a sink, squeeze the tofu very firmly, tightening the tea towel as you go to extract as much water as possible. Take a minute or 2 to do this, as you want the tofu as dry as possible.

In a bowl, combine all the ingredients for the dipping sauce together. Set aside.

Put the cabbage, garlic, ginger, onion and spring onions into the bowl of a food processor and blitz until everything is finely chopped. Add in the tofu, pork, egg, soy sauce, sesame seed oil and ¾ of a teaspoon of salt and 1 teaspoon of freshly ground black pepper. Pulse until the mixture is just blended together. Don't over-blitz.

Line 2 large flat baking sheets with floured greaseproof paper and have a pastry brush, a small bowl of water and a teaspoon close by. Place 1 dumpling wrapper in the palm of your hand and put about 2 teaspoons of the filling into the centre. Use a pastry brush or your fingertips to lightly moisten the edges of the wrapper with water. Fold the wrapper in half encasing the filling, firmly press the edges closed, eliminating any air pockets as you go, to create a half-moon shape.

You can leave the dumplings as they are if you are pan-frying them. If you are using them in the Chicken Dumpling Soup (page 62) or steaming them, go a step further and moisten the opposing corner ends of the half-moon and then join the corners together, pressing firmly to secure (see pictures on pages 234–235) – we call these dumplings 'nuns-hats'. Sit them on the tray and continue with the rest ensuring there is a little space in between each dumpling. If you are not cooking them immediately, dust them with a little more flour and cover with cling film. Freeze overnight on trays, then once completely frozen they can be placed in bags and stored in the freezer until required.

To pan-fry the dumplings, cover the base of a large non-stick pan with a thin layer of vegetable oil and place over a medium heat. Gently place a batch of the flat dumplings down on their side, making sure the dumplings do not touch. Fry for 2–3 minutes, on each side until golden brown and crispy, taking care not to burn them.

Alternatively, steam the dumplings. Place as many of the rounded 'nun hat' dumplings as will fit into your steamer basket, keeping a little space in between each one to prevent them from sticking. Place your steamer basket over boiling water and steam on high for 10–12 minutes until the dumpling skin becomes transparent.

Serve the dumplings piled onto a plate, with the dipping sauce on the side.

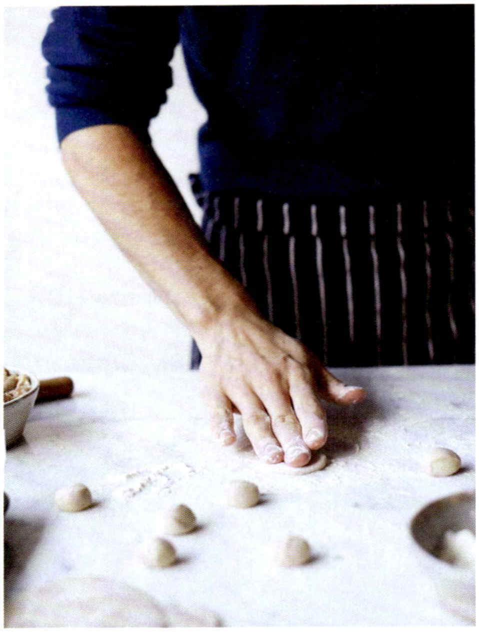
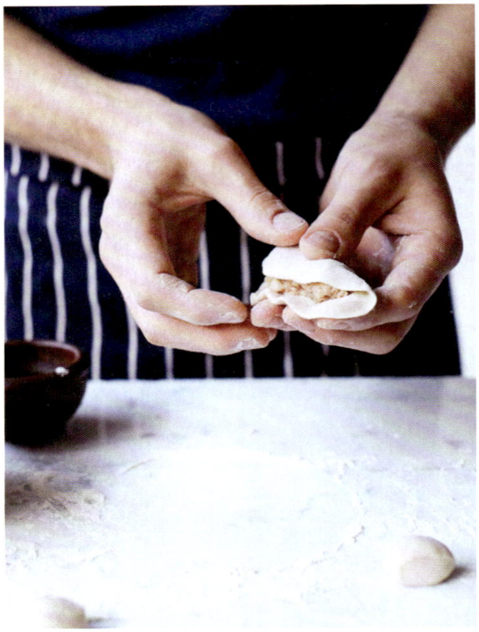
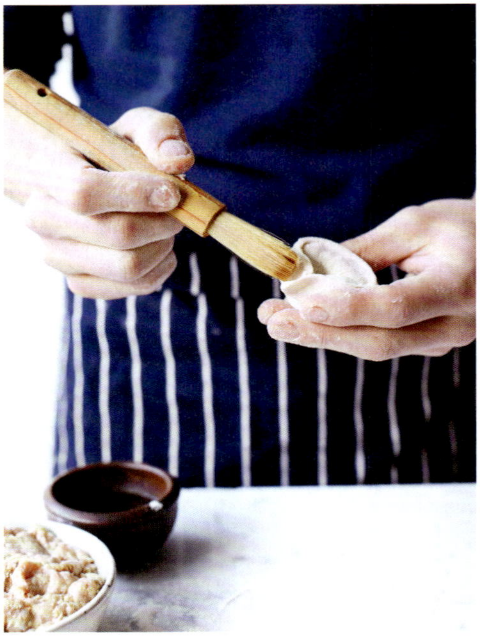
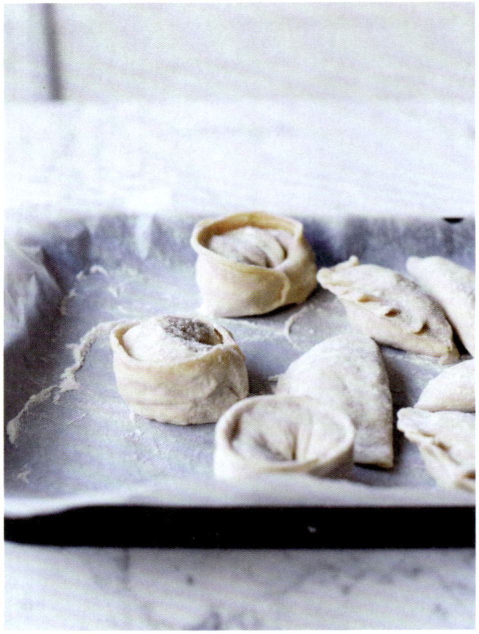

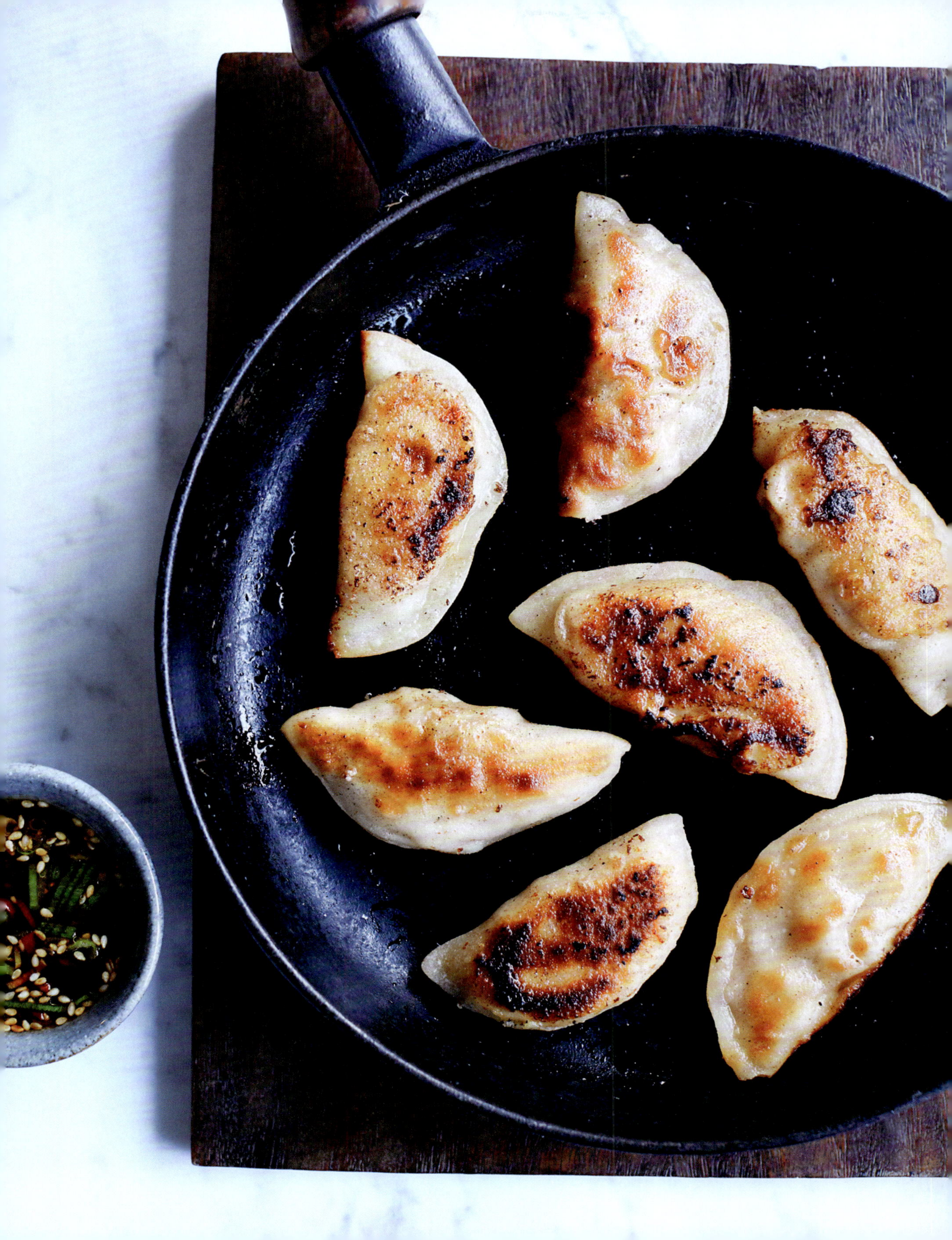

Makes about 56 wrappers

Dumpling Wrappers
mandu-pi

만두피

380g plain flour, plus 150g, for dusting
1 tsp sea salt
1 tbsp roasted sesame seed oil

This recipe makes about 56 wrappers. We always make at least this amount to make it worth our while. We've given options for two different sizes depending on how big you like your dumplings.

Sift the flour and salt into a large bowl and stir in the sesame seed oil. Gradually pour in 180–185ml of warm water, mixing everything together to form a rough dough. It may appear a little dry and flaky at first, but use your hands to gently knead it and it will come together after a short while. Place the dough in a resealable plastic bag, squeeze out the air, and leave it at room temperature for 10 minutes. Remove the dough from the bag and knead vigorously for about 10 minutes (depending on your strength and perseverance) until the dough is elastic and completely smooth. Place the dough back in the bag and leave to rest at room temperature for 45 minutes.

Place the dough on a well-floured work surface. With lightly floured hands, roll the dough into 1 long sausage shape. Cut this in half, and then each piece in half again, to get 4 even lengths of dough. Dust a sharp knife with flour and cut 2 of the 4 lengths of dough into 16 pieces of equal size, so that you have 32 pieces altogether, plus the 2 longer lengths. Group them together, without letting them touch, and cover them with a damp tea towel. Cut the remaining 2 lengths of dough into 12 pieces of equal size, so that you have 24 pieces, and cover them with a damp tea towel again.

Individually, roll each piece of dough into a ball, then flatten it with your hand and roll it into a smooth circular disk. The 32 smaller pieces of dough should measure about 7–8cm in diameter when rolled, while the 24 slightly larger pieces should measure about 10cm in diameter. Dust with plenty of flour as you work to prevent sticking, and dust again when finished. Store the wrappers with cling film in between each disk on a floured flat tray in small stacks. Refrigerate if using within a day or freeze for future use.

Serves 4–6

Fried Minced Meat Patties with Sesame Seeds
ddeok galbi

60g walnuts
45g pine nuts
500g beef sirloin (or 1kg short ribs, bones removed leaving 500g meat)
½ Asian or 1 regular pear, cored
¼ onion, roughly chopped
4 garlic cloves
3 tbsp soy sauce
1½ tbsp honey
1½ tbsp mirin
1 tbsp roasted sesame seed oil
½ tsp freshly ground black pepper
2 tsp vegetable oil
2 tsp toasted sesame seeds
cooked rice, to serve
kimchi, to serve (optional)
lettuce leaves, to serve (optional)

Pictured on page 241

While these mini patties may appear at first glance nothing more than small burgers, they are in fact quite different and perhaps even better. Traditionally the meat from short ribs is used, but beef sirloin works just as well, minced up with nuts, onion, pear, sesame oil, garlic and various other delicious ingredients. The result is a burger of sorts with the most delectable flavour and texture. You can eat them as they are or wrapped up in lettuce leaves with kimchi and rice to create little parcels.

Preheat the oven to 180°C/fan160°C/350°F/gas mark 4. Spread the walnuts and pine nuts onto a baking tray and lightly roast them in the oven for 3–5 minutes until they are a shade darker and aromatic. Leave to cool.

Place the nuts in a food processor and pulse on and off until finely chopped, being careful not to grind them to a powder. Transfer the nuts to a bowl, keeping 1 tablespoon aside for the final garnish. Put the beef into the food processor and pulse until the meat is minced. Transfer to the bowl with the nuts. Add the pear, onion and garlic into the processor and blitz into a purée. Add to the bowl with the beef, together with the soy sauce, honey, mirin, sesame seed oil and pepper.

Using your hands, very thoroughly mix everything together until well combined, then take a minute to massage the seasoning into the beef. Take a tablespoonful of the mixture at a time and shape into small flat and compact patties, about 5cm across. Cover and refrigerate for 1–2 hours to allow the meat and nuts to soak up the flavours and until the patties have firmed up a little.

Heat the vegetable oil in a pan and set over a medium heat. When hot, add a few patties at a time and fry for 2–3 minutes on each side until golden brown and cooked through, basting with any juices that collect in the pan. Remove and place in a serving dish, pour over any pan juices and garnish with some of the remaining chopped nuts and the sesame seeds. Serve with rice, kimchi and lettuce leaves if you wish.

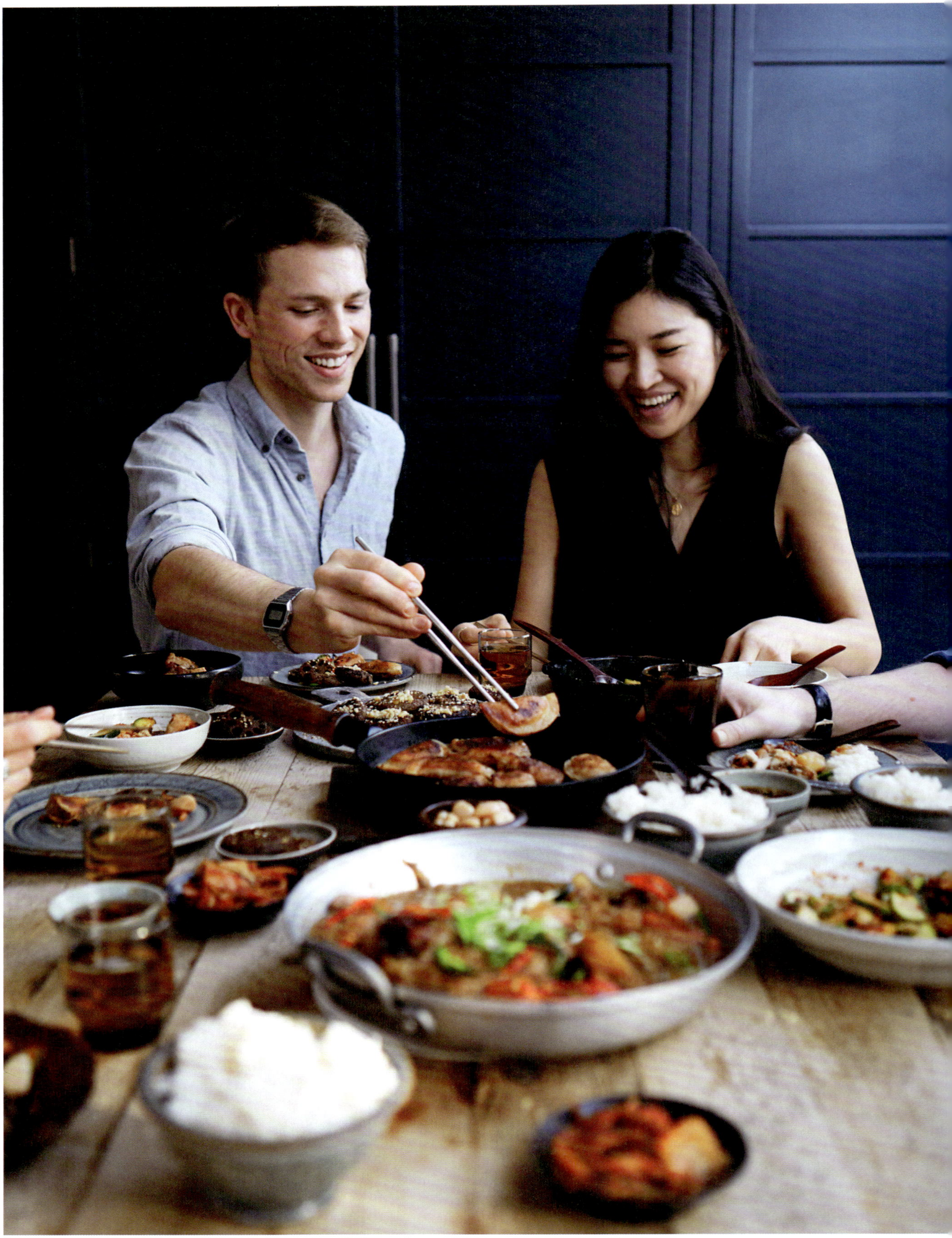

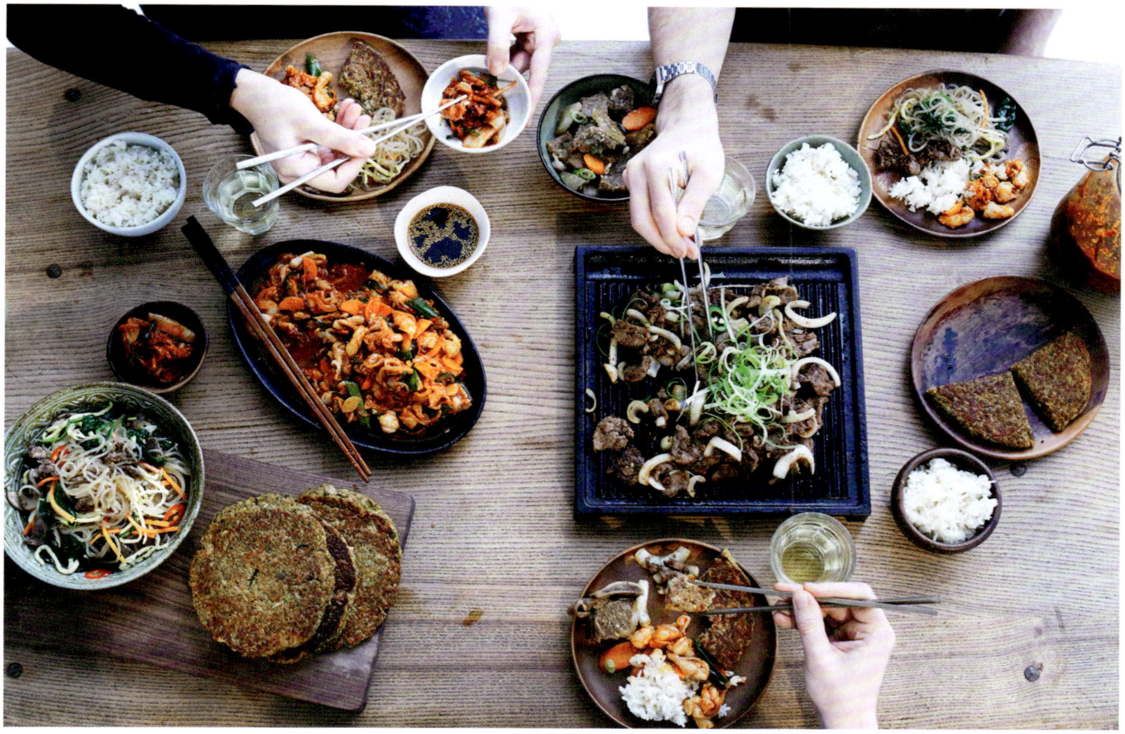

Serves 4–6

Chicken, Vegetable & Noodle Hotpot
dak jjim

120g sweet potato glass noodles (page 13)
2 tbsp vegetable oil
800g chicken, cut of your choice – thighs, wings, drumsticks
2 medium potatoes, cut into bite-size chunks
1 large carrot, cut into bite-size chunks
1 large onion, cut into bite-size chunks
2 whole dried chillies (optional)
6 garlic cloves, crushed
4cm piece of ginger, very finely grated
½ red chilli, deseeded and finely sliced
½ green chilli, deseeded and finely sliced
2 spring onions, thinly sliced or sliced into very thin 5cm lengths and soaked in cold water until they curl up

<u>Sauce</u>
5 tbsp soy sauce
2 tbsp mirin
1 tbsp honey
1½ tbsp roasted sesame seed oil
½ tsp freshly ground black pepper
700ml chicken stock or water

The Korean sweet potato glass noodles are the absolute making of this dish. They have a rather unique springy texture that soak up all the wonderful flavours in the hotpot, and so for this reason we wouldn't recommend substituting them for another kind of noodle. They are easy to find in Asian supermarkets or online, and they have a very long shelf life so you can buy a few packets to have on hand for when you need them.

Put the noodles in a bowl and cover with water. Leave to soak.

Meanwhile, heat the vegetable oil in a large heavy-based pan with a lid over a high heat. Add the chicken and fry for 3–4 minutes on all sides, or until golden brown. Remove from the pan, then add the potatoes, carrot, onion and, if using, dried chillies and cook for 4 minutes, stirring now and again. Add the garlic and ginger and fry for 1 minute. Return the chicken to the pan together with all of the sauce ingredients. Cover and bring to the boil, then reduce the temperature a little and simmer for 15 minutes.

Drain the noodles from their soaking water and add them to the pan. Put the lid on and simmer for another 5 minutes until the chicken, vegetables and noodles are cooked through.

Serve up in bowls with the sliced chillies and drained (if you soaked them) spring onions scattered over the top.

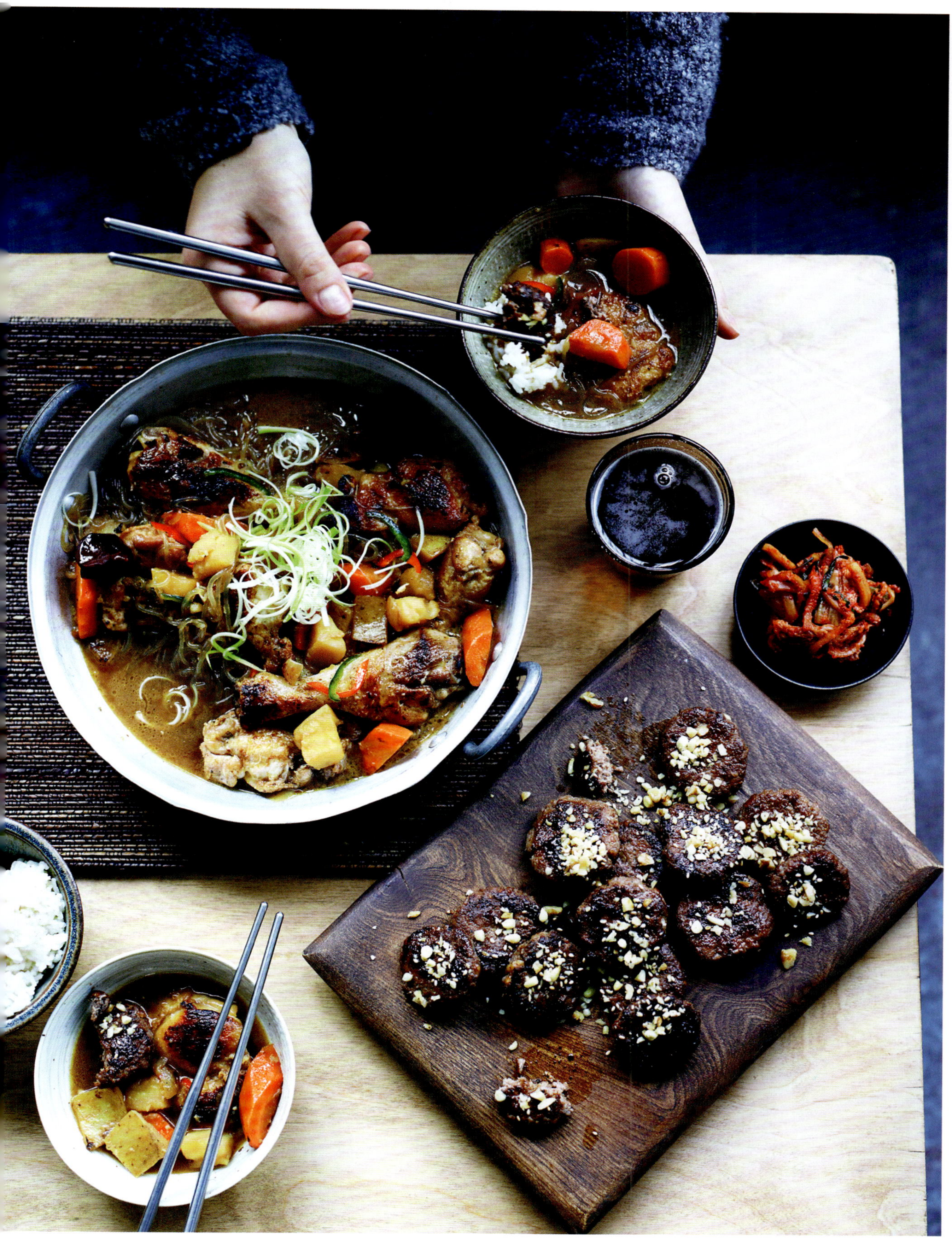

Dessert

디저트

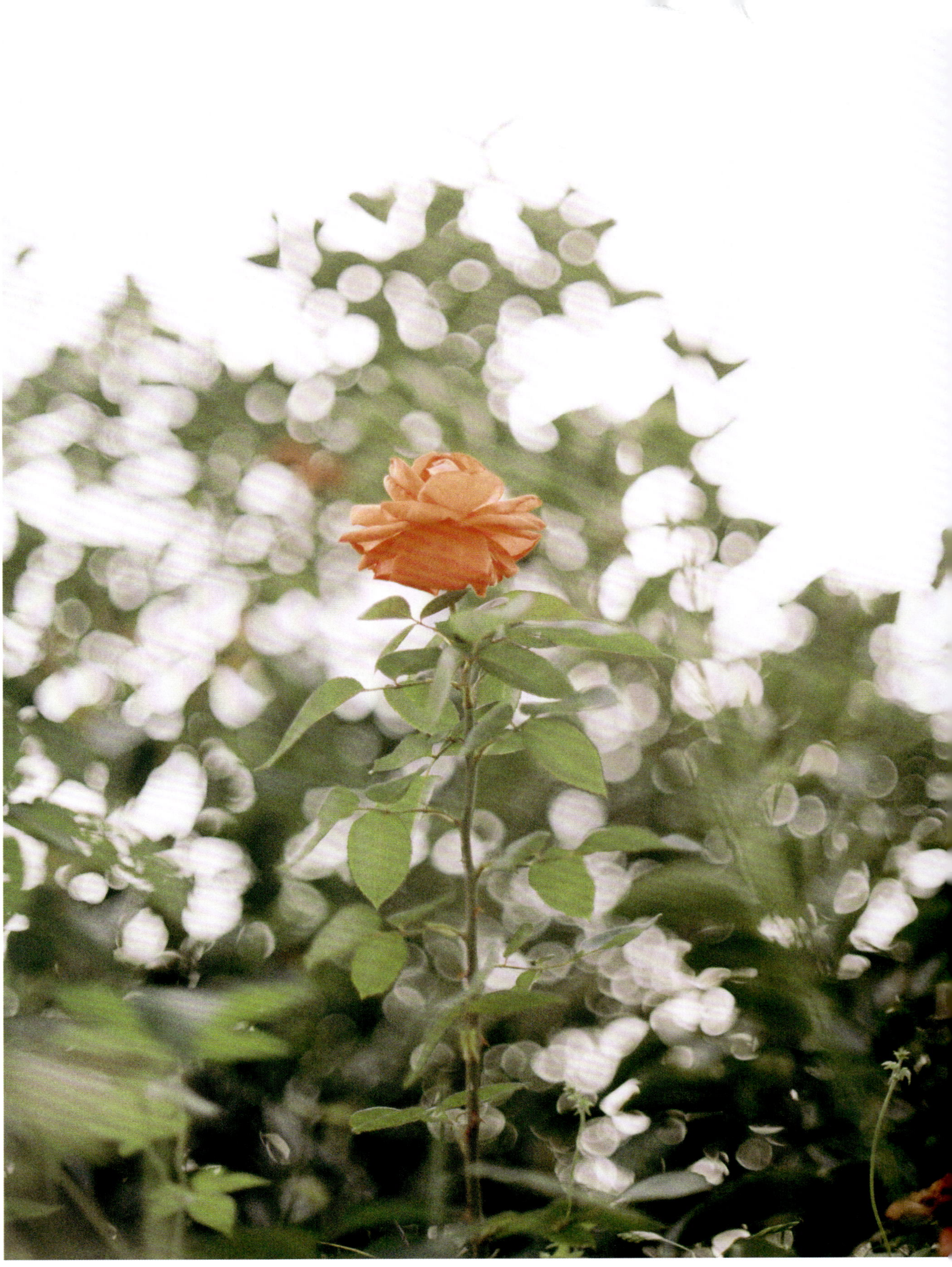

08

246. **Black Sesame Seed Ice Cream**
흑임자 아이스크림

248. **Shaved Ice with Sweet Red Beans, Ice Cream & Rice Cakes**
팥빙수

250. **Pine Nut Bars**
잣박산

252. **Deep-fried Honey Cookies**
약과

253. **Persimmon with Maple Syrup & Lime**
홍시

254. *Persimmons*

256. **Sweet Rice Cakes**
경단

260. **Pecan & Cinnamon-stuffed Pancakes**
호떡

Black Sesame Seed Ice Cream
hoogim-ja ice cream

Serves 8

50g black sesame seeds
60g agave syrup
2 x 400ml tins of coconut milk
100g unrefined sugar or coconut palm sugar
pinch of sea salt
3 tbsp cornflour

On a tiny street near Insadong-gil (the tourist mecca of Seoul) and up a flight of winding wooden stairs, we found ourselves, to our delight, in a paper-screened little oasis of calm away from the masses. We had come for iced tea but were unable to resist their black sesame seed ice cream. It was subtle and naturally flavoured, with an almost chewy creaminess, yet made without any dairy at all. It took ages to develop this recipe, but we got there in the end. You must use good-quality, fresh black sesame seeds, otherwise the taste won't be as perfect.

Put the black sesame seeds in a dry frying pan over a medium heat. The moment they begin to pop and release their aroma, remove them from the heat and cool. Blitz the seeds in a coffee grinder or food processor until finely ground, then place them in a bowl and combine them with the agave syrup to form a paste.

Heat 1 tin of the coconut milk, the sugar and the salt in a heavy-based saucepan over medium-low heat until the sugar has dissolved. In a bowl, slowly whisk the remaining tin of coconut milk into the cornflour, ensuring there are no lumps. Add this to the saucepan, mix everything together and cook for 4–6 minutes over a medium-high heat, stirring constantly, until the mixture becomes thick. Use a spatula to stir the mixture, making sure the bottom does not burn or become lumpy. When thickened, remove the pan from the heat and transfer the mixture to a large bowl. If there are any lumps pass the mixture through a sieve into a bowl.

Stir the sesame seed paste into the ice cream mixture until combined. Place parchment paper onto the surface to prevent a skin forming and leave to cool completely. Refrigerate for 1–2 hours until well chilled. You can speed this process up by placing the bowl into an ice bath.

Churn in an ice cream maker according to the instructions. Alternatively, pour the mixture into a wide, flat (preferably metal) tray and place in the freezer. After 40 minutes, use a fork to mix and break down the ice crystals. Repeat this process twice more, at 40-minute intervals. You can blitz it all in a food processor at the final stage to make it really smooth. Return to the tray and leave in the freezer to set fully. Remove 15 minutes before serving to give the ice cream a chance to soften.

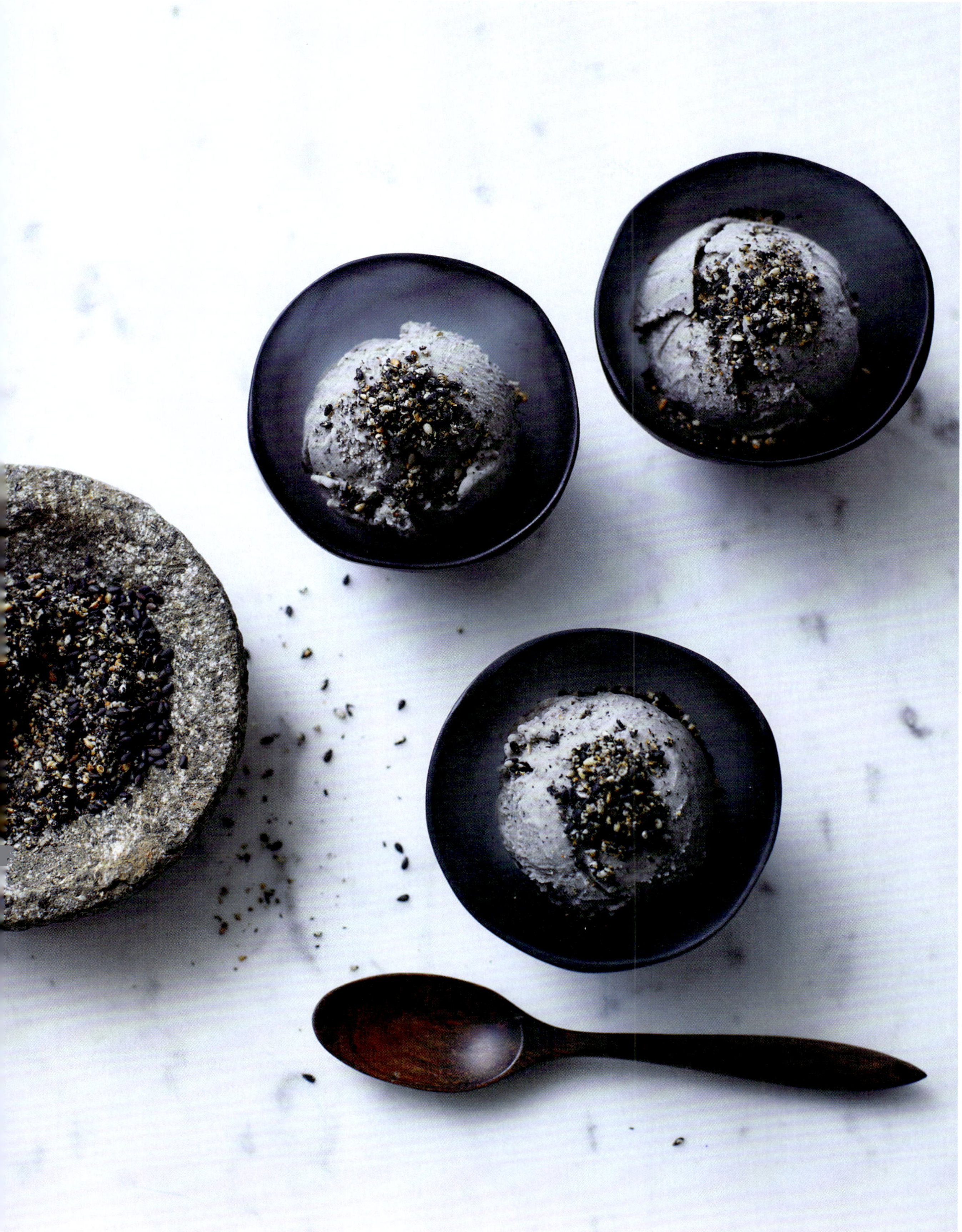

Serves 2, to share in 1 large bowl

Shaved Ice with Sweet Red Beans, Ice Cream & Rice Cakes
pat bingsu

팥빙수

100g red beans, soaked overnight or tinned sweetened red beans
100g unrefined sugar or coconut palm sugar
1 tsp vanilla extract
large pinch of sea salt
400ml dairy, rice or soy milk, poured into ice cube trays and frozen
1 large scoop of vanilla ice cream or dairy-free ice cream, if you prefer
3 soft Korean rice cakes or Japanese mocha, available in Asian supermarkets (optional)
2 tbsp agave syrup
2 tbsp toasted flaked almonds

Red beans? In a dessert? Yes, we know, it does sound somewhat horrifying, but we promise you this works. In fact it's so good we eat it daily when visiting Korea in the summertime! Ready cooked and sweetened red beans (or aduki beans) can be found in any Asian supermarket, or buy the dried beans and prepare them at home. You will also need a good food processor to grind down the ice to a powder. In Korea, this dish is always served as one large portion, so that two people can share. I have done this here, but you could always divide it into two smaller bowls if you prefer.

For homemade red beans, drain the soaking water, place the beans in a heavy-based pan and cover with plenty of water. Bring to the boil for 5 minutes, then reduce the heat and leave to simmer until the beans are completely soft, adding more water now and again to keep them submerged. (Depending on the age of the beans this can take anywhere from 1–2 hours.) Drain off the water and place the beans back into the dry pan with the sugar, vanilla and salt. Set over a low heat and gently stir the beans until the sugar and salt has dissolved. Don't worry if the beans go mushy, this only adds to the consistency. Leave to cool then refrigerate.

Place your serving bowl in the freezer to chill. When ready to serve, grind the milk ice cubes in batches in a food processor until they become powdery in consistency. Add the 'ice' to the bowl in the freezer as you go, so that it remains frozen, as it melts quickly otherwise. When you have ground up all the ice to a powder, top with the red beans and a large scoop of ice cream. Place the soft rice cakes around the ice cream, if using, and drizzle over the agave and then scatter over the flaked almonds. Serve immediately.

The most important part of eating pat bingsu is the bit before you actually eat it. You absolutely have to spend a good 5 minutes mashing everything together with your spoon until the shaved ice, red beans and ice cream are completely blended together. Koreans adore this part of the process, diving in with their spoons until the whole thing looks like it has been put through a washing machine. The more unsightly it looks, the better it will taste.

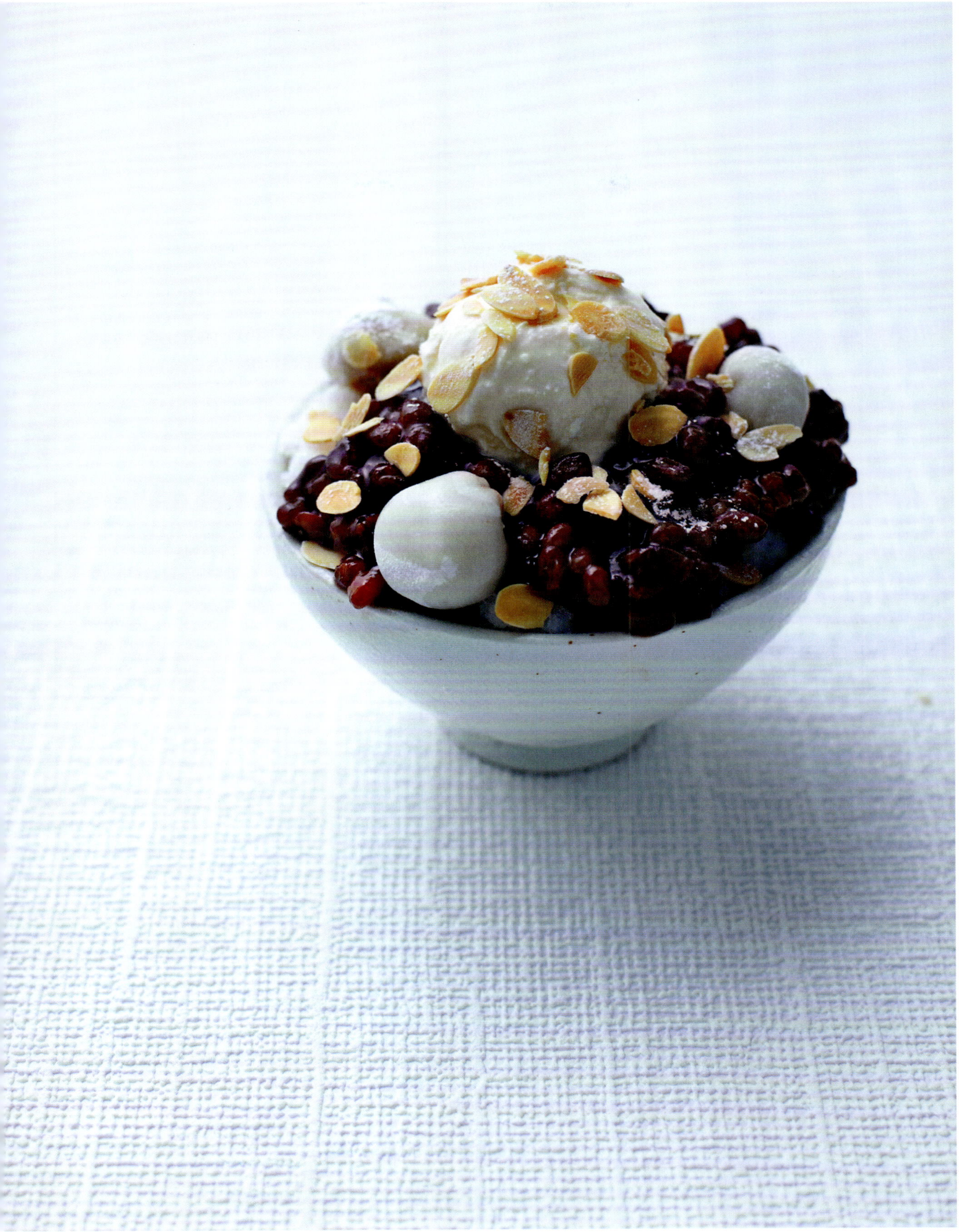

Makes about 12 bars

Pine Nut Bars
jatbaksan

잣박산

vegetable oil, for greasing
300g pine nuts
60g rice syrup (available in health food shops)
45g unrefined sugar or coconut palm sugar
good pinch of sea salt

These are really easy to make and look great too. They exemplify Korean desserts, which are invariably not too sweet and made up of just a few simple ingredients, like grains or nuts. The funny thing is when you eat a lot of Korean food you rarely crave heavy, Western-style desserts. So this kind of thing is ideal. It's really important that you use fresh pine nuts for this, as old nuts have a rancid taste that will ruin the end result. They are pictured here with the Deep-fried Honey Cookies (page 252).

Preheat the oven to 170°C/fan 150°C/340°F/gas mark 3. Lightly grease a 20 x 15cm baking tray with oil and line it with parchment paper.

Lightly roast the pine nuts in the preheated oven for 5 minutes or until they are a shade darker and aromatic. Remove and set aside to cool.

In a saucepan, heat the rice syrup, sugar and 1 teaspoon of water over a high heat. When bubbling, reduce the temperature and simmer gently for 8–9 minutes until the syrup has become thicker and more viscous. Remove from the heat, add the salt and the pine nuts, then stir well until thoroughly combined.

Spread the mixture into the prepared baking tray and use the back of a spoon to flatten the surface to get an even layer. Work quickly, otherwise the mixture will become stiff. Leave to cool completely then refrigerate for 1 hour.

Carefully turn the layer of pine nuts out onto a board, remove the parchment paper and cut it into bars.

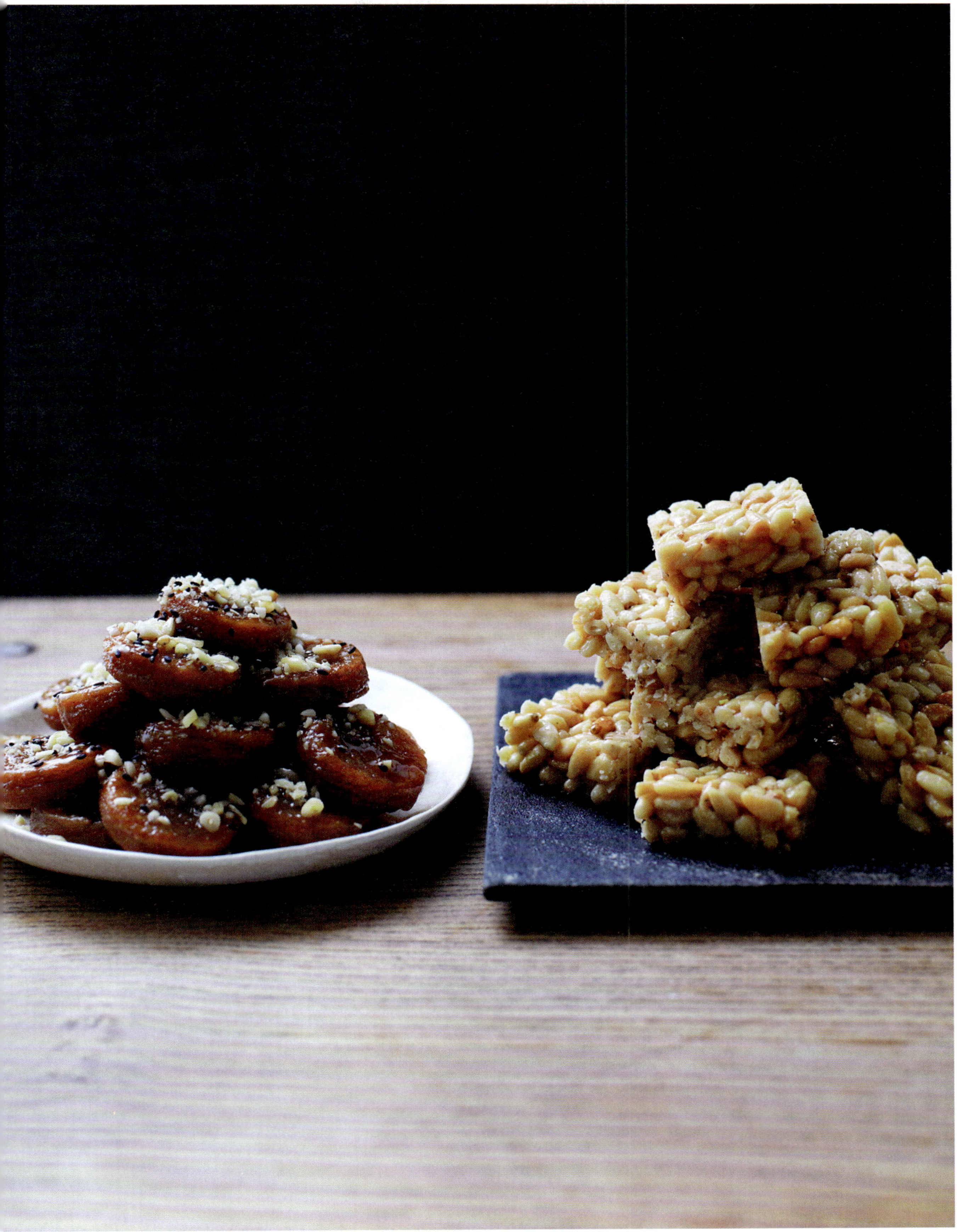

Makes 28–30 cookies

Deep-fried Honey Cookies
yakgwa

Dough
200g plain or white spelt flour, plus extra for dusting
1 tsp ground cinnamon
½ tsp ground ginger
10g fresh ginger, peeled and very finely grated
¼ tsp sea salt
1 tbsp roasted sesame seed oil
65g honey
3 tbsp soju, sake, vodka or water
1 litre sunflower oil, for frying
2 tbsp pine nuts, finely chopped
2 tsp black sesame seeds

Syrup
350g honey
5cm piece of ginger, sliced
1 tsp ground cinnamon

Pictured on page 251

These are one of the most traditional Korean sweet treats served on feast days and holidays. These sticky honey, ginger and cinnamon cookies are deep-fried and then marinated in a honey syrup, giving them a beautiful gloss. Jina is wild about them. It took us many trips to Korean bakeries, quizzing the owners, to get this recipe right. If you have tried the real thing in Korea, bear in mind that homemade yakgwa is crispier on the outside than the shop-bought versions. You will need a liquid or jam thermometer for this recipe.

First make the dough. In a large mixing bowl, sift the flour and mix in the cinnamon, gingers and salt. Stir in the sesame seed oil, honey and soju. It will appear a little dry and flaky at first, but continue to bring it together into a ball of dough using your hands. Knead it gently for 30 seconds, it will still appear a little rough, but this is fine. Wrap it tightly in cling film and set aside.

Meanwhile, place all the syrup ingredients along with 300ml of water into a saucepan and bring to the boil (with the lid off), reduce the heat a little and simmer for 8 minutes until it has reduced by about 100ml. Take off the heat, strain into a bowl and leave to cool.

Roll the dough out onto a lightly floured work surface to 5mm in thickness. This may seem rather thin but it is important for the consistency. Use a 4cm cookie cutter to cut out the dough, or cut the dough into small 4cm squares and diamond shapes of even size. Using a toothpick, pierce a hole in the centre of each cookie to allow them to cook evenly.

Pour the sunflower oil into a medium-size saucepan and set over a medium-high heat. When the temperature reaches 100°C/210°F on a thermometer, very carefully add the cookies. Fry for 10 minutes, making sure the temperature stays between 95°C/200°F–105°C/220°F, then increase the heat until the temperature rises to between 150°C/300°F–160°C/320°F, then reduce the heat to maintain the temperature. Fry the cookies for a further 5–6 minutes, until they are a deep golden brown. Remove the cookies, individually, from the hot oil with tongs and put them straight into the cooled honey syrup. Set aside to infuse for 2 hours then remove. (Keep the syrup to serve on other desserts.) To serve, arrange the cookies on a plate, with the chopped pine nuts and sesame seeds scattered over. These cookies will keep refrigerated in an airtight container for up to a week.

Serves 2

Persimmon with Maple Syrup & Lime
hongsi

홍시

2 fully ripe hachiya persimmons (page 254)
zest of ½ lime
1–2 tsp maple syrup, to taste

In Korea, persimmons are in season in autumn. They are highly regarded and the perfect fruit is sought after with the same zeal as Brits on the hunt for the perfect summer strawberry. They are spectacularly good when ripe, and spectacularly bad when unripe, so with this simple recipe, we have also given you some information on what to look out for when buying the fruit.

When the persimmons have reached a stage of ripeness where their skin can barely contain the heaving mass of soft flesh within, that is the moment you want to strike. When they get to this stage, place them in the fridge a few hours before you plan on eating them. Handle them with great delicacy or they will burst asunder.

Position the fruit on a plate. Tease off any leaves and gently prise the fruit apart into 2 halves. Combine the lime zest with the maple syrup and drizzle a little over the fruit. Of course they can also be eaten totally unadorned.

Serve at once with a spoon.

Frozen Persimmon

Jina's mother introduced us to another great way to enjoy persimmon at this stage of ripeness. Simply freeze it. Yes it is that simple. The flesh is so extraordinarily gelatinous that when frozen, it has a perfectly creamy smooth texture, without an ice crystal in sight. Just remove it from the freezer, leave it at room temperature for 40 minutes, then slowly delve into it with a fork as it begins to thaw.

Dessert

Persimmons

Persimmons (also known as Sharon fruit and cachi) are available in two varieties: hachiya and fuyu. These look quite similar but have completely different textures and uses. Confusingly, the hachiya and fuyu varieties will often be sold under one general name, either persimmon, Sharon fruit or cachi, but really it is their varietal name that is most important, so be sure to ask if you are unsure. The easiest way to know what you are buying is by their appearance.

Hachiya are larger then fuyu, and if you look at them from above, they are completely round with no edges, whereas fuyu have a slightly more square shape. Firm, unripe hachiya are astringent and extremely tart, so don't try to eat them. They must be fully ripe, so buy them ripe or let them ripen at home. They will go from orange to a very deep orange, almost red colour, and their flesh will be completely soft, almost exploding out from their skin, and gelatinous once opened.

Fuyu are smaller and squatter in shape, and are the most common variety sold in the UK, usually under the name Sharon fruit. They remain reasonably firm on the outside, with a slightly softer inside. The texture is a little crunchy and they have a mild sweetness. The fuyu variety is very nice though, and ideal for eating as you would an apple.

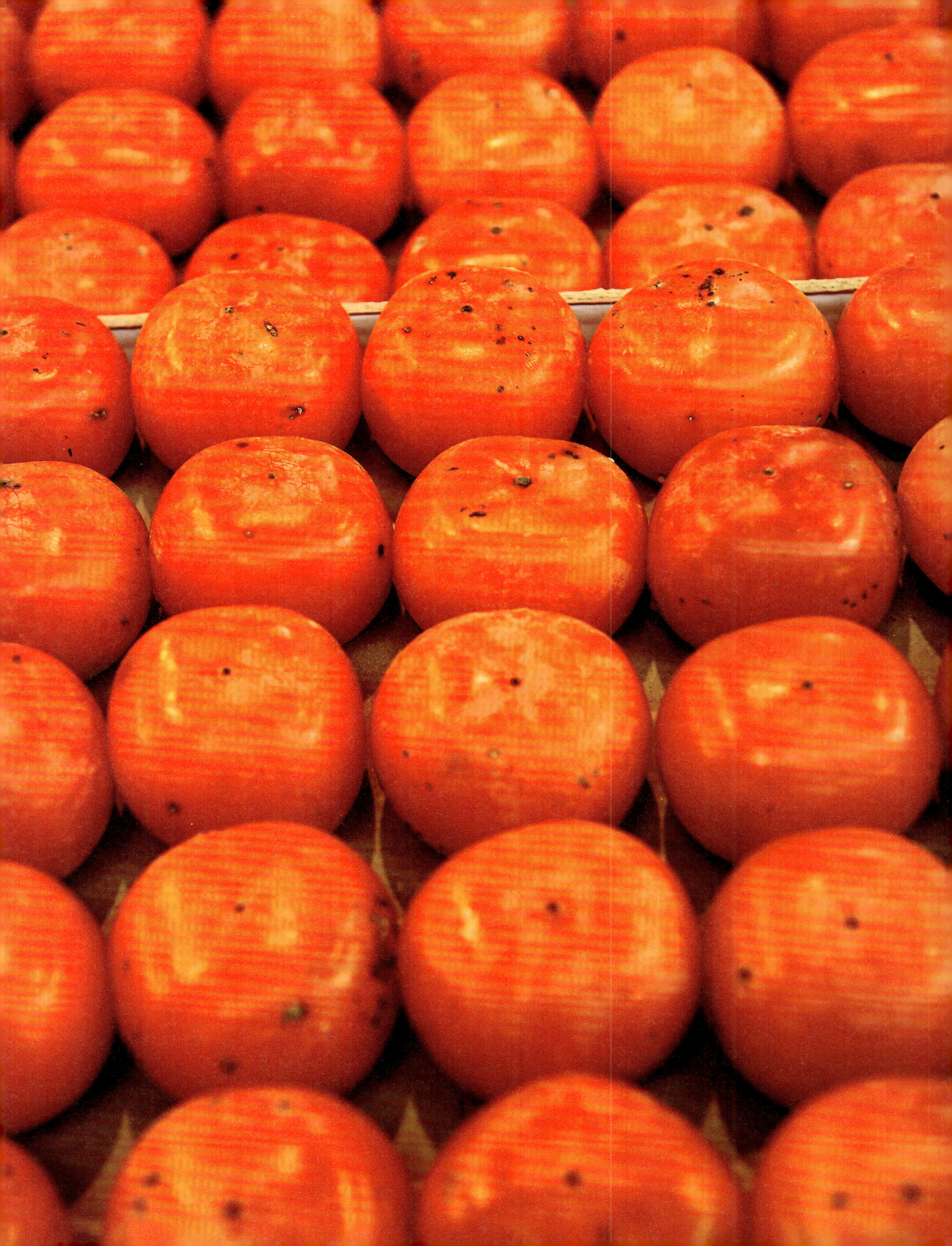

Makes 32

Sweet Rice Cakes
gyeongdan

200g glutinous rice flour, plus extra for dusting
¼ tsp sea salt
1 tbsp maple syrup
2 tbsp black sesame seeds
50–60g icing sugar
2 tbsp desiccated coconut
1 tbsp green tea powder

Pictured overleaf

All over Korea they make their own regional rice cakes. Some are stuffed, some are coated, others are just plain and gloriously squidgy in texture. Here they are rolled in three different coatings – black sesame, green tea powder and desiccated coconut, making for a beautiful and delicious little sweet treat. Roasted, chopped up nuts and dried dates are also commonly used, so feel free to use whatever coating you wish.

Place the flour in a large bowl with the salt and maple syrup. With a metal spoon, gradually stir in 125–130ml of boiling water, a little at a time, until the mixture starts to come together. It will seem a little dry and flaky at first, but after a minute or so of kneading, it will come together into a soft ball. If it is a little sticky, dust your hands with a little flour (not too much otherwise the dough will become dry) and handle it lightly. Cover tightly with cling film and set aside.

Place the black sesame seeds in a small frying pan and fry gently over a medium heat for a few minutes until the seeds are aromatic. Remove and leave to cool, then use a pestle and mortar or spice grinder to grind the seeds down to a rough powder. Transfer to a bowl and mix with 2 teaspoons of the icing sugar. Set aside.

In a second bowl, combine the coconut and another 2 teaspoons of icing sugar. In a third bowl, combine the green tea powder with the remaining 5–6 teaspoons of icing sugar. The bitterness of green tea powder will depend on the brand, so you may need to adjust the quantity of icing sugar to get the right balance of flavours.

Dust a clean surface very lightly with flour, place the dough on top and with lightly floured hands roll the dough out into a long even sausage shape. Cut it in half, then each piece in half again. Then evenly divide each of the 4 pieces of dough into 8 pieces of equal size. You should end up with 32 small pieces. One at a time, roll them into a ball shape then set aside covered with a damp, clean tea towel to prevent the dough from drying out.

Bring a large pan of water to the boil. Add the rice balls and bring the water back to a rolling boil for roughly 3 minutes until the balls rise to the surface. Remove the balls and refresh them in cold water until completely cold. Once cool, strain off as much water as possible, then lay out the balls onto 2 sheets of kitchen paper.

While still slightly damp, divide them between the bowls of sesame seeds, coconut and green tea powder. Toss the balls to coat them evenly, gently pressing the coating into the surface of the balls. Keep them in the bowls until you are ready to serve, as the coating will become a little wet from the moisture inside the balls. When ready to serve, gently mix them again so they are perfectly coated, then arrange on a plate or bowl. These are best eaten within a day of making them.

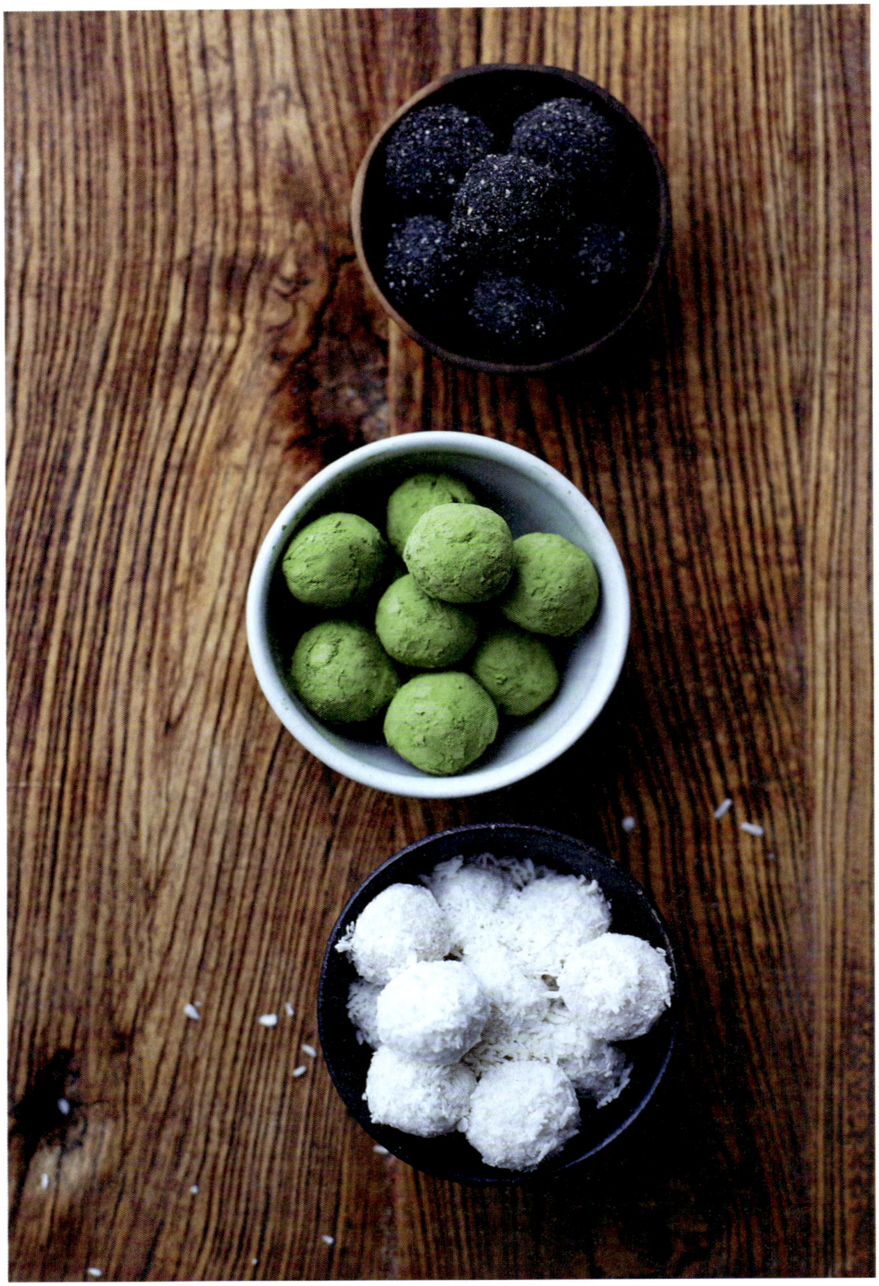

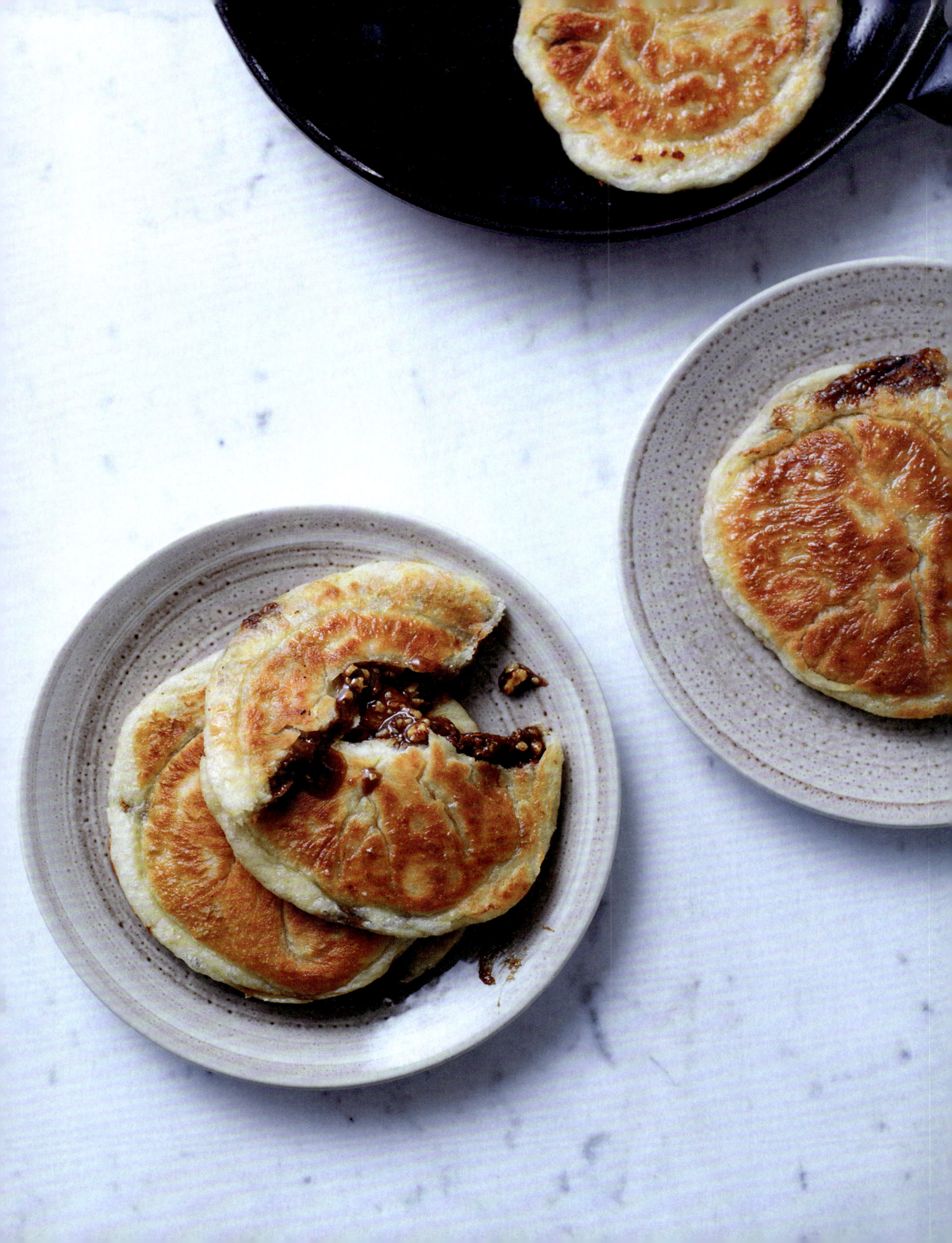

Makes 12 pancakes

Pecan & Cinnamon-stuffed Pancakes
hoddeok

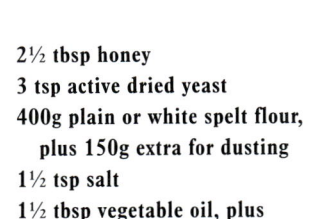

2½ tbsp honey
3 tsp active dried yeast
400g plain or white spelt flour, plus 150g extra for dusting
1½ tsp salt
1½ tbsp vegetable oil, plus extra for frying

Filling
80g brown or coconut palm sugar
1½ tsp ground cinnamon
30g toasted pecan nuts, finely chopped
¼ tsp of sea salt

Pictured on page 259

Koreans have the perfect street-side snack for all weather conditions, and this gloriously soft, pecan and cinnamon-stuffed pancake is the ultimate winter-time treat. In fact, it is so good we have been known to indulge in the height of summer too. It takes more time to make than the average pancake but it really is worth it – they are phenomenally good. Be sure to serve them hot, straight out of the pan, or if the mood takes you, adorned with a single ball of ice cream.

Place 270ml of warm water in a bowl with the honey and yeast. Stir well to combine and set to one side for 10 minutes until frothy.

Put the 400g of flour into a large mixing bowl with the salt. Slowly stir in the vegetable oil and water-yeast mixture, thoroughly mixing to form a sticky, quite wet dough. Cover with cling film and leave in a warm spot for an hour or until doubled in size. Once risen, knock the dough back with a spatula, then re-cover with cling film and leave to rise again for 25 minutes.

Meanwhile, combine all the filling ingredients in a bowl and set aside. Add the remaining flour to your work surface in a neat layer – it may seem like a lot but it will prevent sticking. Knock back the dough once again, then scrape it directly onto the flour. Flour your hands and roll the dough so that all sides are coated with the flour and it is no longer sticky. Shape the dough into a rough oblong shape, then, using a sharp knife dusted in flour, cut the dough in half, then cut each piece in half again, and finally cut each of the 4 pieces into 3 pieces of equal size. You should have 12 pieces in total. Clean off the knife after each cut. Roll the 12 pieces of dough in the flour to coat them and prevent them from sticking.

Take 1 ball of dough at a time and flatten it out in the palm of your hand, brushing off any excess flour. Add a tablespoon of the filling to the centre, then pull the edges of the dough up and around the filling, sealing it at the top by pressing together between your fingers, encasing the filling completely. Flour your fingers as you go to prevent sticking. Continue with the remaining dough and filling.

Add a little vegetable oil to a large non-stick pan and set over a medium heat. Add 2 or 3 dough balls to the pan, leaving plenty of room around them as they will be flattened out. After about 1 minute, or when the bottom is golden, flip over and gently but firmly flatten out the balls with a spatula. Fry for another 2 minutes or until golden brown then flip over again, reduce the heat to low and fry for another 2 minutes. Remove and serve immediately while you cook the rest. Wipe the pan as you go, with kitchen paper, adding more vegetable oil as needed.

채
납품전문
양상추
1통
1,500
매운
청양고추
봉지
1,000
청경채
한팩
2,000
경기도
진양
상추
봉지
1,000
경기도 이천
깻잎
봉지
1,000
새송이
콩알
한팩
2,000
담양
안매운
꽈리고추
한봉
2,000
진주
국산표고
1근
새송이
봉지 1,300

Suppliers
재료 구입처

It is becoming increasingly easy to get your hands on Korean ingredients these days. So much so that even some good supermarkets are getting in on the act. However, the easiest place to find the authentic Korean food stuffs used in this book will be in a Korean or Asian supermarket, which are dotted around all over the place. If you live in an area without access to a good Asian supermarket, fear not – as everything is also available online, ready to be delivered to your door.

Do remember that pretty much all of the ingredients listed on pages 13–17 have a very long shelf life, with the exception of one or two fresh ingredients. If you find yourself near an Asian supermarket, try to stock up on all the main ingredients as they will happily sit in your fridge or storecupboard for months, sometimes years on end.

The list here is by no means extensive. It covers some of the main Asian online stores, as well as a handful of physical shops in the UK, USA, Australia and Ireland – some of which ship worldwide. And don't forget Amazon, as many Korean ingredients can be found in their grocery section.

UK & IRELAND

www.skmart.co.uk
www.kmart-uk.com
www.souschef.co.uk
www.orientalmart.co.uk — best site
www.starryasianmarket.co.uk
www.waiyeehong.com
www.matthewsfoods.co.uk
www.koreafoods.co.uk
www.asiamarket.ie

USA

www.hmart.com
www.lotteplaza.com
www.koamart.com
www.hy1004.com

AUSTRALIA

www.asiangrocerystore.com.au
www.myasiangrocer.com.au

Index
목록

Page numbers in *italic* refer to the illustrations

A
acorn jelly: chilled tofu, cucumber & kimchi broth 90, *91*
aduki beans: five-grain rice 26, *27*
almost-instant cucumber kimchi 104, *105*
anchovies: dried anchovies 15, *17*
    dried seasoned anchovies 124, *125*
    fishcake soup 58, *59*
Asian aubergines: soy sauce & garlic-steamed aubergine 127
Asian pears 15, *16*
    fried minced meat patties with sesame seeds 237
    scallops & prawns with pine nut & pear soup 198, *199*
    sesame & soy-marinated beef 212, *213*
    sesame, soy & chilli beef tartare 210, *211*
    soy-marinated crab 200–1, *202–3*
aubergine: soy sauce & garlic-steamed aubergine 127
aw-muk guk 58, *59*

B
baby chicken soup 64, *65*
banchan 10
bap 26, *27*
bapsang 10
barbecues 21
battered cod & courgette 146
bean sprouts: bean sprout soup 70, *71*
    garlic & sesame bean sprouts 123
    mixed rice with vegetables & beef 28, *29*
baechu kimchi 98–9
beef: beef & vegetables with sesame glass noodles 166, *167*
    beef rib soup 69
    buckwheat noodles in chilled broth 160, *161*
    fried minced meat patties with sesame seeds 237
    grilled beef short ribs 224
    marinated beef & vegetable stew 78, *79*
    mixed rice with vegetables & beef 28, *29*
    mung bean pancakes 142, *143*
    rice & seaweed rolls 34–6, *35*, *37*
    seaweed & beef soup 68
    sesame & soy-marinated beef 212, *213*
    sesame, soy & chilli beef tartare 210, *211*
    soy-braised beef short ribs with vegetables 214, *215*
    spicy beef & vegetable stew 72, *73*
    stock 19
    stuffed chilli fritters 144, *145*
    tofu & soybean paste soup 82
bibim guksu 158, *159*
bibim naeng-myeon 172
bibimbap 28, *29*
bindae-ddeok 142, *143*
black bean paste: black bean noodles 176, *177*
black beans: five-grain rice 26, *27*
black sesame seed ice cream 246, *247*
black sesame seed porridge 43
bo-seot namool 118, *119*
bo ssam 222, 223
braised halibut in seasoned soy 197
broths: buckwheat noodles in chilled broth 160, *161*
    chilled tofu, cucumber & kimchi broth 90, *91*
    clear clam broth 60, *61*
    knife-cut noodles in seafood broth 170, *171*
buckwheat noodles 12, *14*
    buckwheat noodles in chilled broth 160, *161*
    spicy chilled buckwheat noodle salad 172
bulgogi 212, *213*
bulgogi jeongol 78, *79*
butternut squash: pumpkin rice porridge 44, *45*

C
cabbage: braised rice cakes with cabbage & fishcakes 48
    chicken, rice cake & vegetable hotpot 230
    pork & tofu dumplings 232–3, *234–5*
    spicy seafood noodle soup 178, *179*
    see also Chinese cabbage; kimchi
cachi see persimmons
carrots: beef & vegetables with sesame glass noodles 166, *167*
    black bean noodles 176, *177*
    chicken, vegetable & noodle hotpot 240, *241*
    marinated beef & vegetable stew 78, *79*
    mixed rice with vegetables & beef 28, *29*
    soy-braised beef short ribs with vegetables 214, *215*
    stir-fried spicy squid 192, *193*
    warming chicken & potato stew 76, *77*
chamchi whe 186, *187*
chicken: baby chicken soup 64, *65*
    chicken & sesame oil porridge 42
    chicken dumpling soup 62, *63*
    chicken, rice cake & vegetable hotpot 230
    chicken, vegetable & noodle hotpot 240, *241*
    deep-fried sweet & spicy chicken wings 226, *227*
    instant chicken ramen 173
    warming chicken & potato stew 76, *77*
chilled cucumber soup 88, *89*
chilled kimchi spiced noodles 158, *159*
chilled tofu, cucumber & kimchi broth 90, *91*
chilli: chicken, vegetable & noodle hotpot 240, *241*
    chilli paste 14, *15*
    chilli powder 14, *15*
    clear clam broth 60, *61*
    crispy chilli rice cakes 50, *52*
    dried chilli threads 14, *15*
    fishcake soup 58, *59*
    gochujang sauce 29
    pickled perilla leaves 116, *117*
    radish water kimchi 106, *107*
    raw tuna with chilli sauce 186, *187*
    seafood & silken tofu stew 85
    seafood & spring onion pancake 136, *137*
    sesame, soy & chilli beef tartare 210, *211*
    steamed eggs with spring onion & chilli 128, *129*
    stir-fried spicy squid 192, *193*
    stuffed chilli fritters 144, *145*

tofu & soybean paste soup 82
warming chicken & potato stew 76, 77
Chinese cabbage 15, 16
   classic cabbage kimchi 98–9
   see also cabbage
chives: tofu with soy dressing 147
chopsticks 10–11
cinnamon: pecan & cinnamon-stuffed pancakes 260–1
clams: clear clam broth 60, 61
   seafood & silken tofu stew 85
classic cabbage kimchi 98–9
clear clam broth 60, 61
coconut: sweet rice cakes 256–7, 258–9
coconut milk: black sesame seed ice cream 246, 247
cod: battered cod & courgette 146
cookies, deep-fried honey 252
courgettes: battered cod & courgette 146
   black bean noodles 176, 177
   knife-cut noodles in seafood broth 170, 171
   marinated beef & vegetable stew 78, 79
   mixed rice with vegetables & beef 28, 29
   seasoned courgettes 120, 121
   tofu & soybean paste soup 82
crab: seafood salad with wasabi dressing 204, 205
   soy-marinated crab 200–1, 202–3
crispy chilli rice cakes 50, 52
crispy soy rice cakes 51, 53
cucumber: almost-instant cucumber kimchi 104, 105
   chilled cucumber soup 88, 89
   chilled kimchi spiced noodles 158, 159
   chilled tofu, cucumber & kimchi broth 90, 91
   mixed rice with vegetables & beef 28, 29
   noodles in chilled soy bean soup 162, 163
   Persian (pickling) cucumbers 15, 17
   whole pickled cucumbers 110, 111

D
daeha jjim 196
daikon radishes 15, 16
   beef rib soup 69
   classic cabbage kimchi 98–9
   fishcake soup 58, 59
   mixed rice with vegetables & beef 28, 29
   radish kimchi 102
   radish water kimchi 106, 107

soy-braised beef short ribs with vegetables 214, 215
dak doritang 76, 77
dak galbi 230
dak jjim 240, 241
dakjuk 42
dashima 16
   bean sprout soup 70, 71
dates, Korean jujube red 15, 16
ddeok galbi 237
ddeok mandu guk 62, 63
ddeokbokki 48
ddukbaegi 11
deep-fried honey cookies 252
deep-fried sweet & spicy chicken wings 226, 227
dinner parties 21
doegi-gogi mandoo 232–3, 234–5
doen-jang jjigae 82
dongchimi 106, 107
dubu kimchi 152, 153
dumplings: chicken dumpling soup 62, 63
   dumpling wrappers 236
   pork & tofu dumplings 232–3, 234–5

E
eggs: instant chicken ramen 173
   kimchi fried rice 31
   mixed rice with vegetables & beef 28, 29
   seafood & silken tofu stew 85
   steamed eggs with spring onion & chilli 128, 129
enoki mushrooms: marinated beef & vegetable stew 78, 79
   soy-seasoned mushrooms 118, 119
   tofu & soybean paste soup 82

F
feast days 229
feasts 21
festivals 229
fish: battered cod & courgette 146
   pan-fried mackerel 194, 195
   raw fish, vegetable & rice salad 32, 33
   raw tuna with chilli sauce 186, 187
   stock 19
fishcakes: braised rice cakes with cabbage & fishcakes 48
   fishcake soup 58, 59
five-grain rice 26, 27
fried minced meat patties with sesame seeds 237
fritters: battered cod & courgette 146
   deep-fried sweet & spicy chicken wings 226, 227

prawn & sweet potato tempura 150, 151
stuffed chilli fritters 144, 145
frozen persimmon 253
fuyu persimmons 254

G
galbi gui 224
galbi jjim 214, 215
ganjang ke jang 200–1, 202–3
garlic: garlic & sesame bean sprouts 123
   garlic & soy sauce 226
   pickled garlic 108, 109
   soy sauce & garlic-steamed aubergine 127
geran jjim 128, 129
glass noodles: beef & vegetables with sesame glass noodles 166, 167
   chicken, vegetable & noodle hotpot 240, 241
glutinous rice 12, 13
   baby chicken soup 64, 65
   chicken & sesame oil porridge 42
   five-grain rice 26, 27
gochu jeon 144, 145
gochujang sauce 29
godeungeo gui 194, 195
green tea powder: sweet rice cakes 256–7, 258–9
grilled beef short ribs 224
grilled pork belly with sesame dip 218, 219
gyeongdan 256–7, 258–9

H
hachiya persimmons 254
haemul kalguksu 170, 171
haemul naengche 204, 205
haemul pa-jeon 136, 137
halibut: braised halibut in seasoned soy 197
hobakjuk 44, 45
hobak namool 120, 121
hoedeopbap 32, 33
honey: deep-fried honey cookies 252
   honey & soy-glazed potatoes 127
   whole pickled cucumbers 110, 111
hongsi 253
hoogim-ja ice cream 246, 247
heukimjajuk 43
hotteok 260–1

I
ice cream: black sesame seed ice cream 246, 247
   shaved ice with sweet red beans, ice cream & rice cakes 248, 249
ingredients 13–17
instant chicken ramen 173

J

jajang-myeon 176, *177*
jamppong 178, *179*
japchae 166, *167*
jat haemul naengook 198, *199*
jatjuk 40, *41*
jatbaksan 250, *251*
Jeonju bibimbap 30–1
jogae-tang 60, 61

K

ka-jee namool 127
kaenip jorim 116, *117*
kalbi tang 69
kamja jorim 127
kelp, dried *15*, 16
   bean sprout soup 70, *71*
   fishcake soup 58, *59*
   seaweed & beef soup 68
ki-rum ddeokbokki 50, *52*
ki-rum ganjang ddeokbokki 51, *53*
Kim Yeon Im 30, 130
kim-bap 34–6, *35*, *37*
kimchi 96, *97*
   almost-instant cucumber kimchi 104, *105*
   chilled kimchi spiced noodles 158, *159*
   chilled tofu, cucumber & kimchi broth 90, *91*
   classic cabbage kimchi 98–9
   kimchi fried rice 31
   kimchi pancake 138, *139*
   kimchi stew 86, *87*
   mung bean pancakes 142, *143*
   radish kimchi 102
   radish water kimchi 106, *107*
   succulent pork & kimchi wrapped in leaves *222*, 223
   tofu & fried kimchi 152, *153*
kimchi bokum-bap 31
kimchi jeon 138, *139*
kimchi jjigae 86, *87*
king prawns: pan-fried king prawns 196
   prawn & sweet potato tempura 150, *151*
   scallops & prawns with pine nut & pear soup 198, *199*
   seafood salad with wasabi dressing 204, *205*
   spicy seafood noodle soup 178, *179*
   knife-cut noodles in seafood broth 170, *171*
kong-guksu 162, *163*
kongnamul guk 70, *71*
Korean meals 10–11
Korean pears *see* Asian pears

L

leeks: spicy beef & vegetable stew 72, *73*
lettuce: grilled pork belly with sesame dip *218*, 219
   seafood salad with wasabi dressing 204, *205*
   succulent pork & kimchi wrapped in leaves *222*, 223
lime: persimmon with maple syrup & lime 253
lotus root, seasoned 112, *113*
lunches 20

M

mackerel, pan-fried 194, *195*
mandu-pi 236
maneul chang-achi 108, *109*
maple syrup: dried seasoned anchovies 124, *125*
   persimmon with maple syrup & lime 253
   sweet rice cakes 256–7, *258–9*
marinated beef & vegetable stew 78, *79*
menu ideas 20–1
mixed rice with vegetables & beef 28, *29*
miyok-guk 68
moo kimchi 102
muk sabal 90, *91*
mul naeng-myeon 160, *161*
Mum's spicy dried squid 124, *125*
mung bean pancakes 142, *143*
mushrooms: beef & vegetables with sesame glass noodles 166, *167*
   braised halibut in seasoned soy 197
   marinated beef & vegetable stew 78, *79*
   mixed rice with vegetables & beef 28, *29*
   soy-braised beef short ribs with vegetables 214, *215*
   soy-seasoned mushrooms 118, *119*
   spicy beef & vegetable stew 72, *73*
   spicy seafood noodle soup 178, *179*
   tofu & soybean paste soup 82
mussels: spicy seafood noodle soup 178, *179*
myeol chi bokkeum 124, *125*
myeonsang 10

N

naeng-myeon noodles *12*, 14
napa cabbage *15*, 16
   pork & tofu dumplings 232–3, *234–5*
   see also cabbage
New Year 229
noodles 10, *12*, 13–14, *168–9*

beef & vegetables with sesame glass noodles 166, *167*
beef rib soup 69
black bean noodles 176, *177*
buckwheat noodles in chilled broth 160, *161*
chicken, vegetable & noodle hotpot 240, *241*
chilled kimchi spiced noodles 158, *159*
instant chicken ramen 173
knife-cut noodles in seafood broth 170, *171*
marinated beef & vegetable stew 78, *79*
noodles in chilled soy bean soup 162, *163*
spicy chilled buckwheat noodle salad 172
spicy seafood noodle soup 178, *179*

O

ogokbap 26, *27*
oh-ee ji 110, *111*
oh-ee kimchi 104, *105*
oh-ee neng-guk 88, *89*
ojingeo che 124, *125*
ojingeo bokkeum 192, *193*
onion squash: pumpkin rice porridge 44, *45*
onions: chicken, rice cake & vegetable hotpot 230
   chicken, vegetable & noodle hotpot 240, *241*
   quick pickled onions 123
   stir-fried spicy squid 192, *193*
   warming chicken & potato stew 76, *77*

P

pan-fried king prawns 196
pan-fried mackerel 194, *195*
pancakes: kimchi pancake 138, *139*
   mung bean pancakes 142, *143*
   pecan & cinnamon-stuffed pancakes 260–1
   seafood & spring onion pancake 136, *137*
pastes 14, *15*
pat bingsu 248, *249*
patties: fried minced meat patties with sesame seeds 237
pears *15*, 16
   fried minced meat patties with sesame seeds 237
   scallops & prawns with pine nut & pear soup 198, *199*
   sesame & soy-marinated beef 212, *213*

sesame, soy & chilli beef tartare
   210, 211
soy-marinated crab *200–1*, 202–3
pecan & cinnamon-stuffed
   pancakes 260–1
paeju gui 184, *185*
peppers: marinated beef
   & vegetable stew 78, *79*
perilla leaves: chicken, rice cake
   & vegetable hotpot 230
   pickled perilla leaves 116, *117*
Persian cucumbers: almost-instant
   cucumber kimchi 104, *105*
   whole pickled cucumbers 110, *111*
persimmons 254
   frozen persimmon 253
   persimmon with maple syrup
      & lime 253
pickles: pickled garlic 108, *109*
   pickled perilla leaves 116, *117*
   quick pickled onions 123
   whole pickled cucumbers 110, *111*
   see also kimchi
pine nuts: deep-fried honey
   cookies 252
   fried minced meat patties with
      sesame seeds 237
   pine nut & rice porridge 40, *41*
   pine nut bars 250, *251*
   scallops & prawns with pine nut
      & pear soup 198, *199*
pork: black bean noodles 176, *177*
   grilled pork belly with sesame
      dip 218, *219*
   kimchi stew 86, *87*
   pork & tofu dumplings 232–3,
      234–5
   spicy seafood noodle soup 178, *179*
   stuffed chilli fritters 144, *145*
   succulent pork & kimchi wrapped
      in leaves *222*, 223
   tofu & fried kimchi 152, *153*
porridge: black sesame seed
   porridge 43
   chicken & sesame oil porridge 42
   pine nut & rice porridge 40, *41*
   pumpkin rice porridge 44, *45*
potatoes: black bean noodles 176, *177*
   braised halibut in seasoned soy 197
   chicken, vegetable & noodle
      hotpot 240, *241*
   honey & soy-glazed potatoes 127
   warming chicken & potato stew
      76, *77*
prawns: knife-cut noodles in seafood
   broth 170, *171*
   pan-fried king prawns 196
   prawn & sweet potato tempura
      150, *151*
   scallops & prawns with pine nut

      & pear soup 198, *199*
   seafood & silken tofu stew 85
   seafood & spring onion
      pancake 136, *137*
   seafood salad with wasabi
      dressing 204, *205*
   spicy seafood noodle soup 178, *179*
pumpkin rice porridge 44, *45*

Q
quick pickled onions 123

R
ra-myeon 173
radishes *see* daikon radishes;
   yellow radishes
ramen, instant chicken 173
raw tuna with chilli sauce 186, *187*
red beans: shaved ice with sweet
   red beans, ice cream & rice
   cakes 248, *249*
red pepper (chilli) powder 14, *15*
rice 10, *12*, *13*, 39
   baby chicken soup 64, *65*
   black sesame seed porridge 43
   chicken & sesame oil porridge 42
   five-grain rice 26, *27*
   Jeonju bibimbap 30–1
   kimchi fried rice 31
   mixed rice with vegetables
      & beef 28, *29*
   pine nut & rice porridge 40, *41*
   pumpkin rice porridge 44, *45*
   raw fish, vegetable & rice salad
      32, *33*
   rice & seaweed rolls 34–6, *35*, *37*
   short-grain rice 26, *27*
   succulent pork & kimchi wrapped
      in leaves *222*, 223
rice cakes *12*, 14
   braised rice cakes with cabbage
      & fishcakes 48
   chicken dumpling soup 62, *63*
   chicken, rice cake & vegetable
      hotpot 230
   crispy chilli rice cakes 50, *52*
   crispy soy rice cakes 51, *53*
   shaved ice with sweet red beans,
      ice cream & rice cakes 248, *249*
   sweet rice cakes 256–7, *258–9*
rice cookers 11
rice milk: shaved ice with sweet
   red beans, ice cream & rice
   cakes 248, *249*
rice wine vinegar: pickled garlic
   108, *109*
   whole pickled cucumbers 110, *111*

S
salads: raw fish, vegetable & rice

   salad 32, *33*
   seafood salad with wasabi
      dressing 204, *205*
   spicy chilled buckwheat noodle
      salad 172
salted baby shrimp *15*, 17
samgyetang 64, *65*
samgyeopsal 218, *219*
scallops: scallops & prawns with
   pine nut & pear soup 198, *199*
   scallops with salted sesame oil
      184, *185*
seafood: seafood & silken tofu
   stew 85
   seafood & spring onion
      pancake 136, *137*
   seafood salad with wasabi
      dressing 204, *205*
   spicy seafood noodle soup 178, *179*
   see also crab, prawns etc
seasonal food 188
seasoned courgettes 120, *121*
seasoned lotus root 112, *113*
seaweed: chilled tofu, cucumber
   & kimchi broth 90, *91*
   rice & seaweed rolls 34–6, *35*, *37*
   roasted crispy seaweed *15*, 16
   seaweed & beef soup 68
sengson jjim 197
sengson jeon & hobak jeon 146
sesame seed oil *15*, 16
   chicken & sesame oil porridge 42
   garlic & sesame bean sprouts 123
   grilled pork belly with sesame
      dip 218, *219*
   scallops with salted sesame oil
      184, *185*
   sesame & soy-marinated beef
      212, *213*
   sesame, soy & chilli beef tartare 210,
      211
sesame seeds: black sesame seed
   ice cream 246, *247*
   black sesame seed porridge 43
   deep-fried honey cookies 252
   deep-fried sweet & spicy chicken
      wings 226, *227*
   dried seasoned anchovies 124, *125*
   fried minced meat patties
      with sesame seeds 237
   garlic & sesame bean sprouts 123
   honey & soy-glazed potatoes 127
   soy sauce & garlic-steamed
      aubergine 127
   sweet rice cakes 256–7, *258–9*
   tofu with soy dressing 147
   warming chicken & potato stew,
      76, *77*
Sharon fruit *see* persimmons
shaved ice with sweet red beans,

Index **269**

ice cream & rice cakes 248, *249*
shitake mushrooms: beef & vegetables with sesame glass noodles 166, *167*
 braised halibut in seasoned soy 197
 marinated beef & vegetable stew 78, *79*
 mixed rice with vegetables & beef 28, *29*
 soy-braised beef short ribs with vegetables 214, *215*
 soy-seasoned mushrooms 118, *119*
 spicy beef & vegetable stew 72, *73*
 spicy seafood noodle soup 178, *179*
short-grain rice *12*, *13*, 26, *27*
shrimp: salted baby shrimp *15*, *17*
 see also prawns
side dishes 10
silken tofu: seafood & silken tofu stew 85
soba noodles *see* buckwheat noodles
sook-ju namool 123
soups: baby chicken soup 64, *65*
 bean sprout soup 70, *71*
 beef rib soup 69
 chicken dumpling soup 62, *63*
 chilled tofu, cucumber & kimchi broth 90, *91*
 clear clam broth *60*, 61
 fishcake soup 58, *59*
 noodles in chilled soy bean soup 162, *163*
 scallops & prawns with pine nut & pear soup 198, *199*
 seaweed & beef soup 68
 spicy seafood noodle soup 178, *179*
 tofu & soybean paste soup 82
soy beans: noodles in chilled soy bean soup 162, *163*
soy milk: shaved ice with sweet red beans, ice cream & rice cakes 248, *249*
soy sauce 17
 braised halibut in seasoned soy 197
 crispy soy rice cakes 51, *53*
 dried seasoned anchovies 124, *125*
 garlic & soy sauce 226
 grilled beef short ribs 224
 honey & soy-glazed potatoes 127
 pickled garlic 108, *109*
 pickled perilla leaves 116, *117*
 seasoned lotus root 112, *113*
 sesame & soy-marinated beef 212, *213*
 sesame, soy & chilli beef tartare 210, *211*
 soy-braised beef short ribs with vegetables 214, *215*
 soy-marinated crab *200–1*, 202–3
 soy sauce & garlic-steamed aubergine 127

soy-seasoned mushrooms 118, *119*
tofu with soy dressing 147
soybean curd *see* tofu
soybean paste 14, *15*
 grilled pork belly with sesame dip 218, *219*
spices 11, 14, *15*
spicy beef & vegetable stew 72, *73*
spicy chilled buckwheat noodle salad 172
spicy seafood noodle soup 178, *179*
spinach: beef & vegetables with sesame glass noodles 166, *167*
 mixed rice with vegetables & beef 28, *29*
 rice & seaweed rolls 34–6, *35*, *37*
spoons 10
spring onions: seafood & spring onion pancake 136, *137*
 spicy beef & vegetable stew 72, *73*
 steamed eggs with spring onion & chilli 128, *129*
squash: pumpkin rice porridge 44, *45*
squid: seafood & spring onion pancake 136, *137*
 seafood salad with wasabi dressing 204, *205*
 spicy seafood noodle soup 178, *179*
 stir-fried spicy squid 192, *193*
squid, dried *15*, 16
 Mum's spicy dried squid 124, *125*
ssamjang sauce 218
steamed eggs with spring onion & chilli 128, *129*
stews: kimchi stew 86, *87*
 marinated beef & vegetable stew 78, *79*
 seafood & silken tofu stew 85
 spicy beef & vegetable stew 72, *73*
 warming chicken & potato stew 76, *77*
stir-fried spicy squid 192, *193*
stock 19
stuffed chilli fritters 144, *145*
succulent pork & kimchi wrapped in leaves 222, *223*
sundubu jjigae 85
surasang 10
sweet potato glass noodles *12*, 13
 beef & vegetables with sesame glass noodles 166, *167*
 chicken, vegetable & noodle hotpot 240, *241*
 marinated beef & vegetable stew 78, *79*
sweet potatoes: chicken, rice cake & vegetable hotpot 230
 prawn & sweet potato tempura 150, *151*
sweet rice cakes 256–7, *258–9*

T
tempura, prawn & sweet potato 150, *151*
tofu 81
 chilled tofu, cucumber & kimchi broth 90, *91*
 kimchi stew 86, *87*
 pork & tofu dumplings 232–3, *234–5*
 seafood & silken tofu stew 85
 stuffed chilli fritters 144, *145*
 tofu & fried kimchi 152, *153*
 tofu & soybean paste soup 82
 tofu with soy dressing 147
tomatoes: noodles in chilled soy bean soup 162, *163*
tuna: raw tuna with chilli sauce 186, *187*
twigim 150, *151*

U
udon noodles *12*, 13
 black bean noodles 176, *177*
 spicy seafood noodle soup 178, *179*

V
vinegar: pickled garlic 108, *109*
 whole pickled cucumbers 110, *111*

W
wakame 16
 seaweed & beef soup 68
walnuts: fried minced meat patties with sesame seeds 237
warming chicken & potato stew 76, *77*
wasabi dressing, seafood salad with 204, *205*
wheat noodles *12*, 14
 chilled kimchi spiced noodles 158, *159*
 noodles in chilled soy bean soup 162, *163*
whole pickled cucumbers 110, *111*
wrappers, dumpling 236

Y
yakgwa 252
yang-nyeom 226, *227*
yangpa jorim 123
yangnyeom dubu 147
yellow radishes: pickled yellow radish *15*, *17*
 rice & seaweed rolls 34–6, *35*, *37*
yeongeun jorim 112, *113*
yuk gaejang 72, *73*
yukhoe 210, *211*

Acknowledgements
감사의 글

This book is the culmination of many years of cooking and learning from a range of people all over South Korea and in the UK, all of whom have in some way informed our love of Korean food. However, our greatest thanks must go to Jina's parents, In Seok (인석) and Sung Sook (성숙), who have shown us the true beauty of Korean home cooking and the sumptuous feasts that can be created with simple seasonal produce, handled with respect and consideration – we dedicate this book to you.

To our agent Claudia Young, and our publisher Amanda Harris and editors Kate Wanwimolruk and Tamsin English at Orion, all of whom believed in *Our Korean Kitchen* in the first place and went above and beyond the call of duty to make it all happen – it has been an immense pleasure working with you. Also to Sara Griffin and Lucie Stericker and everyone at Orion, we feel privileged to have had such fiercely talented, visionary and kind people working on our book.

To our creative collaborators, Tara Fisher, her assistant Sue Prescott, Wei Tang, Sarah Sanghee Woo, Kisik Pyo, Roly Grant, Jonathan Jarvis and Philip Koh at Buro Creative, who between them photographed, prop styled and designed the hell out of this book, both in London and all around Korea. You realised our vision in the most stunningly beautiful way, bringing Korea and Korean food to life on these pages.

Thank you to our incredibly organised food styling assistants Livia Brockhaus and Fiona Giles. Also to Katie Marshall and Elisa Crestani who helped us with all the recipe testing – your support and indeed your excellent taste buds and cooking skills were very much appreciated.

We would also like to express our sincere thanks to the many people in the UK and Korea who assisted us with the research stage of this book over the past few years, in particular the Korean Foreign Ministry, his Excellency Sungnam Lim (임성남) the South Korean Ambassador to the UK, his Culture and Information Attaché Yoon Seog Song (송윤석), and in Seoul Soo Yeong Shin (신수영), Eunsol Lee (이은솔) and Hanee Lee (이한이) and also Korean Air.

To the many great chefs, writers and artisan food producers with whom we have had the great pleasure of working and learning from. Your wisdom and generosity have been invaluable to us. In particular we would like to thank Han Chul Bae (배한철) executive chef and director of kitchens at the Intercontinental Seoul Parnas, and the many talented chefs with whom Jordan has cooked alongside – Eun sun Na (나은선), Namhyeon Hwang (황남현), Byeongu Nam (남병우), Chohui Kim (김초희), Jihwan Park (박지환), Junyeong Song (송준영), Minjae Kim (김민제) and to Carrie Yoon (윤소윤).

Also to Chris Kwon (권헌준), Vivian Han (한윤주), Han Lee (이환), and Fiona Bae (배지영) at Kongdu restaurant, Young hee Roh (노영희) at Poom restaurant, Axel Chung (정덕영) and Jungsuk Park (박정석) at Oneul restaurant, Yeong han Kim (김영환), Won seok Yoon (윤원석) and Sang ah Ho (허상아) at Byeokjae Galbi restaurant, Jia Choi (최지아) and Daniel Gray at O'ngo Food and Jung Gunyoung (정건영) at the Korean Tea Culture Association.

A special thank you to executive chef R. Bruce Lee (이병우) and Yunjeong Lee (이윤정) at Lotte Hotel, Professor Sook-Ja Yoon (윤숙자) and Mija Lim (임미자) at the Institute of Traditional Korean Food and the master of Korean food Nyeon Im Kim (김년임) and her daughter Yang Mi (양미) at Kajok Hwe-gwan. Finally our thanks to Hyeonee Lee (이현희) and Myeong-so Gu (구명서).

First published in Great Britain in 2015
by Weidenfeld & Nicolson
Carmelite House, 50 Victoria Embankment
London EC4Y 0DZ
An Hachette UK Company

10 9 8 7 6 5 4 3 2 1

Text © Jordan Bourke and Rejina Pyo 2015
Design and layout © Weidenfeld & Nicolson 2015

All rights reserved. No part of this publication may be reproduced, stored in a retrieval system, or transmitted, in any form or by any means, electronic, mechanical, photocopying, recording or otherwise, without the prior permission of both the copyright owner and the above publisher.

The right of Jordan Bourke and Rejina Pyo to be identified as the authors of this work has been asserted in accordance with the Copyright, Designs and Patents Act 1988.

A CIP catalogue record for this book is available from the British Library.

ISBN: 978 0 297 60971 1

Photography © Tara Fisher
with the exception of
Pages 24, 38, 49, 56, 66–67, 74–75, 80, 84, 103, 114, 115, 130–131, 134, 156, 164–165, 174, 175, 182, 189, 190, 208, 216–217, 225, 228, 244, 255, 262–263, 264 © Sarah Sanghee Woo and Kisik Pyo
Endpapers © Sarah Sanghee Woo
Pages 4, 9, 18, 94, 122, 191, 231 © Rejina Pyo
Page 148–149 © Gavin Hellier/Alamy
Design by BuroCreative
Food styling by Jordan Bourke
Props by Wei Tang
Edited by Kate Wanwimolruk
Proofread by Elise See Tai
Indexed by Hilary Bird

Printed and bound in China

The Orion Publishing Group's policy is to use papers that are natural, renewable and recyclable products and made from wood grown in sustainable forests. The logging and manufacturing processes are expected to conform to the environmental regulations of the country of origin.

by BOOK or by COOK
COOKING
EATING
SHARING

Follow us
@bybookorcook

Find us
facebook.com/bybookorbycook

For lots more delicious recipes plus articles, interviews and videos from the best chefs cooking today visit our blog **bybookorbycook.co.uk**

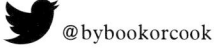

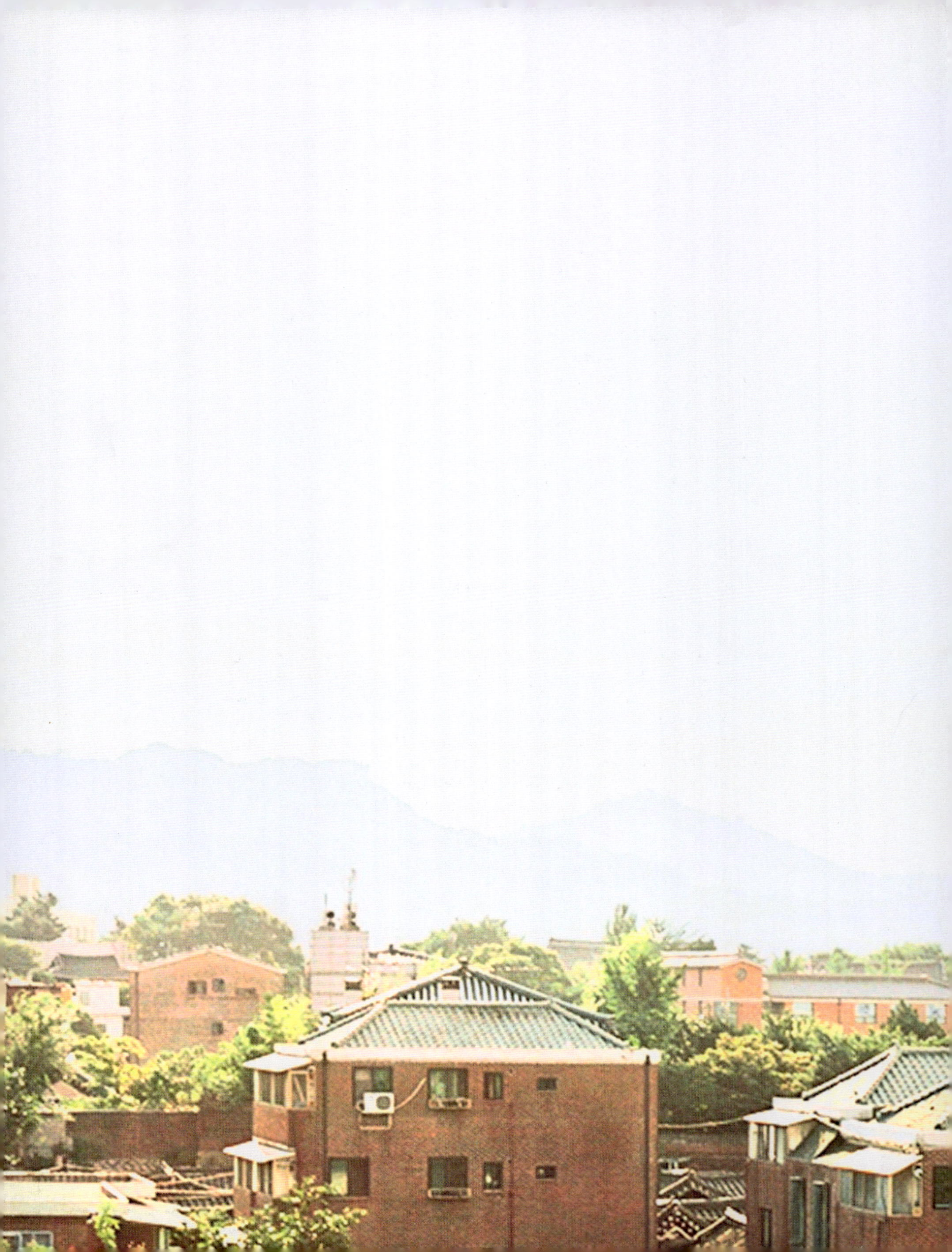